Henry Dunster And His Descendants...

Samuel Dunster

HENRY DUNSTER

AND

HIS DESCENDANTS.

BY

SAMUEL DUNSTER,

ATTLEBOROUGH, MASS.

See page 8. note III

CENTRAL FALLS, R. I.:
E. L. FREEMAN & Co., STEAM BOOK AND JOB PRINTERS.
1876.

KD 54195

INTRODUCTION.

When the life of Henry Dunster was published in 1872, a genealogy of the male branches of his descendants, as far as known, was added in an appendix. Some of the female descendants were grieved that they and their children could not be noticed. This just appeal could only be met by urging the want of space allotted, and the difficulty of identifying many of them after having parted with their patronymic.

It is our purpose, as far as we are able, to amend this acknowledged wrong and add more information, not then accessible, of those who retain the name, as well as those who by marriage have dropped it.

The name Dunster signifies a dweller upon a dun, or down, and is of Saxon origin. There is a market town in Somersetshire, England, and a castle there by that name. Hence, we suppose, the origin of the crest— (Book of Family Crests, Vol. I., page 155, and Vol. II., plate 85, No. 25,)—"Dunster, out of the top of a tower, ar. an arm emboss, vested gri., cuffed of the first, holding a tilting spear, sa." But no knowledge or intimation has ever reached the writer that that or other crest was ever used or referred to by the American head of the family. He was quite too democratic for that, as his whole life shows.

There are several families in this country by the name besides those descended from President Dunster, the earliest of which appears to be Charles Dunster, who, as Mr. Oliver Dunster, his great grandson, of Barnardsville, New Jersey, states "was one of the twelve proprietors of all South Jersey, and owned a great deal of land in West

Jersey," on some of which he now resides. The Dunsters in Leesville, Ohio, appear to be descended from him. But the Dunsters of western New York, are of a more recent immigration. They came from the County of Kent. There is also in Grass Valley, California, an Isaac Dunster, who came only a few years ago. There was a Thomas Dunster in Newark, New Jersey, not related to Oliver, who had a son Henry, who was a Methodist minister. He had a son—an eminent bank note engraver—now in the employ of the Russian government.

In the Army Hospital at Memphis, Tenn., in 1863, there was the death of a "Dunster," but we have not been able to identify his parentage. The account is from a correspondent of the St. Louis Republican, which we copy:

"A HOSPITAL SCENE AT MEMPHIS.—We came to the body of a non-commissioned officer, a fine, large man, who during the last few hours had become insane. The bone of his thigh was shattered by a ball, so high up that amputation could not be performed, so nothing was offered him but to lay there and die. Watching the terrible hues of mortification come upon his limb, feeling the horrible poison steal up toward his vitals, grasping and deadening new tissues each hour, it proved too fearful for even the strong man, who to his physicians had uttered no cry or complaint, and his mind fled for relief to insanity.

"As we approached he fixed a pair of cold, despairing eyes upon us and exclaimed, pointing back over his shoulder, 'Do you see him, old Death there, sitting on the headboard and laughing? A grim army joker in truth. The other night I felt a cold touch, and it woke me. The moon flung in a bar of light, and I saw old Death feeling of my wound. The icy touch numbed it, and the next time I woke his hand was closer to my body. So it goes; and he will soon be pulling on my heart chords.' The maniac then stopped as if for the purpose of reflecting, and during our stay would part of the time be musing, part laughing, occasionally breaking out with the exclamation: 'I plead to him that they would be lonely at the old home; a wife and child are pleasanter than a tomb.'

"And so we left him, the utter corruption, the rottenness of the tomb, and the vitality of a great man joined in one being, grappling upon the hospital bed. Life, with the full, strong pulse of thirty years, had marshalled its forces, been defeated, and was retreating upon its citadel, pursued by the decay growth of a few days. The arteries would soon, stung by the poison tide, stagnate, and block up the gates of the heart. His name was C. P. Dunster, from Illinois, I believe, but the regiment he belonged to I have forgotten."

The name appears to have been originally written Dunstone. In an old letter in our possession, on the back of which is the most extended sermon extant in President Dunster's hand, it is so written, as it also is in a record in Henry VIII. time. Could it, in the formation of surnames, have had any reference to the expression, "A great rock in a *weary* land ?" This letter having never been printed, we insert entire:

"1655, the 20 Augt

Cousin Dunstone my kind love remember.d unto you my wife yor Cozen mary Baldis Coy [Kay] tho growing od is in good health I heard from her the last April I heard yor wife is dead I desire you to remember my love to my sonn in Law Benjamin Phillipps and ye rest of o.r ffreinds Crave here leave to rest.
Yor Loving Kinsman

This day we saled   Tho. Greene
from y° Barbadoes
to England. I came
from Ginny to Barbadoes"

The name is an ancient one in England, especially in Lancashire. As early as Henry VIII., there are records in the parish of Middleton of the burials of Hugo, Katherine, Johannes, and Georgius Dunster, all within the year 1543; and in Edward VI. reign, George, Jannet, Elizabeth ux Johannes Dunster and Johannis Dunster. In Mary's reign, (1553), Anna, and before 1600 seven others.

Among the nine weddings of "Dunsters" recorded in the parish of Middleton between 1544 and 1594, is Henry Dunster and Anne Strctc, 25th July, 3 Edw. VI., 1550; Edmund Dunster and Jane Hopwood, July 29, 4 Edw. VI., 1551; also Henry Dunster and Katherine Kaye, 15th May, 6 Edw. VI., 1553.

There are seven births recorded there before 1600, among which are Martha *filia Jac.* Dunster, 27th Jan., 1593, and Mary *filia Jac.* Dunster, 4th May, 1595, and other children of *Edmund* and *Richard* Dunster.

There were several Dunsters of some note. John, who was Bachelor of Divinity, a *canon regular* in 22 Henry VIII., 1530 ; Roger Dunster, a London merchant ; John Dunster, A. B., Magdalen College, 1600, A. M., 1604, Proctor of the College, 1611 ; Thomas Dunster, Proctor

1*

of Wadham College, 1688, D. D., 1690; Henry Dunster, Esq., married Mary, daughter and heir of Henry Gardner, Esq., M. P. for Ilchester, 1660; Samuel Dunster published Anglia Rediviva, 1699, (Willard Memorial). There is also Horace's Satires, Epistles, and Art of Poetry, done into English, with notes, by S. Dunster, D. D., Prebendary of Sarum. London, 1729. 4 Ed.

In the life of Henry Dunster, page 254, is a record of one marriage and ten baptisms, furnished by Charles Deane, Esq., of Cambridge, who procured it in 1854 from the Parish Clerk of Bury, in Lancashire. This record did not give any baptisms between 1595 and 1618. Although it appeared identical with some facts in the "Balehoult" Letter, it failed to give satisfaction as to the birth of President D., or reconcile statements made by him. These discrepancies are fully stated by Mr. Chaplin. We sent to Bury and had the record of the old church there examined from 1594 to 1650. An attested copy is printed below:

"Extracts from the Register of the Parish Church, Bury, Lancashire.

Anno. Dom. 1594, June, Robt., son of Henry Dunster.
1595, August, Henry, son of William Dunster.
1597, April, Elizabeth, daughter of Henry Dunster.
1600, August, Daniel, son of Henry Dunster.
1602, March, James, son of Henry Dunster.
1605, August, Robert, son of Henry Dunster.
1606, August, John, son of Henry Dunster.
1609, Nov., Henry, son of Thos. Dunster.
1611, Nov., Thos., son of Henry Dunster.
1618, June, Mary, daugh. of Henry Dunster (minor).
1620, Nov., Henry, son of Henry Dunster,
1622, Mar., Daniel, son of Robert Dunster, of Elton.
1622, May, John, son of Henry Dunster.
1625, Aug., Daniel, son of Henry Dunster, of Elton.
1627, Dec., Alice, daughter of Henry Dunster, of Elton.
1628, March, Margaret, daughter of Robert Dunster, of Tottington.
1632, July, Elizabeth, daughter of Henry Dunster, of Elton.
1635, April, James, son of Henry Dunster, of Elton.
1638, Dec., Bitiah, daughter of Robert Dunster.
1640, March, Faith, daughter of Robert Dunster.
1649, Aug., Henry, son of John Dunster, of Elton.

The above are all the entries of the name of Dunster from 1590 to the end of 1650, as examined by me. S. BAILEY.
Parish Clerk, Bury, Lancashire."

This record agrees substantially after 1617—at which time, October 10, Henry Dunster was married to Isabell Kay—with the one in the life of H. D.; but the entry "1619, April xxii, baptised Elisabeth, daughter of Henry Dunster," is entirely wanting in Mr. Bailey's copy.

In the parish records at Elton, a short distance from Bury, is the registration of *John* Dunster's family of four children,—"Henry, son of John Dunster, of Elton, born Aug. 21, baptised Sept. 9, 1649." There can hardly be a doubt that *this* Henry is the same mentioned in the Bury records as having been baptised there. The other children are Daniel, baptised July 27, 1652; "Henry, son of John Dunster, of Elton, born Aug. 24, baptised 26, 1655." [The first Henry probably died in infancy]. Also, Mary, daughter of John D. This John Dunster was church warden there in 1677, and appears to have been related to the Bury Dunsters—possibly might have been the "John, son of Henry, baptised 1606." There is also the record,—"John, son of Henry Dunster, buried Sept. 14, 1687,"—perhaps the same.

It is remarkable that there is a connected list of the children of HENRY DUNSTER from 1597 to 1611, inclusive, with the single exception of 1609, where *Henry* is named as the son of *Thomas*. There is not in the whole list of fifty-six years another child of Thomas named; and their births came at such regular intervals as to raise a doubt whether *this* Henry was not also the son of Henry. If so, it would reconcile all the disagreements to which Mr. Chaplin refers, and make HENRY DUNSTER to have been baptised in November, 1609, and thirty or thirty-one years old at the time of being elected President of Harvard College.

This doubt appeared of so much consequence that, learning the records by age were in some places hard to make out, Mr. Bailey was requested by us to re-examine them, which he did, and wrote us as follows:

"11 Parson's Lane, Bury, Lancashire, England,
Feb'y 18, 1876.
Dear Sir:—I have carefully read over your letters to Mr. Kay

and Mr. Nabb respecting the entries in the register of the Parish Church here. I have gone over the list I sent you, and compared the names and dates with the register. The one in 1609 is plain and distinct,—'Henry, s. of Thos. Dunster.' * * *

SAMUEL BAILEY."

This letter removes all doubt of the correctness of the copy, and shows that if there be any mistake it must have been in the original entry in the register. It would be very easy for the Parish Clerk to mistake the Rector's memorandum, and write Th. for H., and the long ∫ [s] of that day for the y, and thus Henry would become Thomas, with hardly a change in the chirography of the other letters. We hope that some one who has the opportunity to do so will further investigate the record of that family, from whom we verily believe President Dunster to have sprung, by examining the wills, conveyances, court records, and tax books of that day; also the births, baptisms, burials, which might leave the record clear. It would be a grateful tribute of Harvard College to the memory of her first President, whom she used so roughly.

The Mr. Nabb referred to in Mr. Bailey's letter, whose name is Thomas Dunster Nabb, is the son of Sarah Dunster, who married John Nabb, and lives at 27 Back Garden street, Bury. They trace their relationship back to John Dunster, whose ancestors owned the "Bolholt" (as now written) estate. He lived at Higher Wood Hill, in Bury. This John Dunster had seven children.

I. Richard Dunster. He came to Southampton, Long Island, about 1830; was a wheelwright; had four daughters; no sons. The oldest, Emma Dunster, married Mr. Schroeder, and lives at Southampton. They have had four sons, one of whom she named Samuel Dunster Schroeder. He is 15 years old.

II. William Dunster, son of John, came to America with his brother Richard, and was last heard of in Philadelphia. He had a son Richard.

III. James Dunster.

IV. John Dunster.

V. Betsey Dunster.

VI. Sarah Dunster, who married John Nabb.

Sarah (Dunster) Nabb   9 Dec 12 1875

VII. Jane Dunster, who married Edwin Twigg, of Bury, had four children. Isabella, the oldest, married Jeremiah Smith, of Bury. About a year ago we had a visit from him, and learned many facts of the Dunster family. The name does not exist in Bury now. Were the Newark Dunsters of this family? If so, the George H. Dunster, of St. Petersburg, Russia, who graduated at the New York College of Dentistry, Feb. 23, 1875, and received the "Faculty prize for the best examination in all the studies of the course," was, as we think, descended from the same stock as Rev. Henry Dunster.

In Rev. Dr. Quint's oration, at Dover, N. H., the name Thos. Dun*star* appears, page 18, as a signer of "The Combination for Government by y* people at Pascataq, 1640." This is the earliest document in the history of Dover, and was dated 22d day of October, 1640. As the earliest settlers of Dover and Portsmouth came from the west of England, it is probable that this Thos. Dunster was from Somersetshire. He could possibly have been President D.'s brother *Thomas*. He was in England, March 20, 1640, having buried both wife and children recently. The name appears signed last on the "Combination." Nothing further is known of him.

In Worcester, Mass., is a William Dunster, who came in 1854 from Waterford, Ireland, with a brother, who is in Canada. They were expelled for not paying the rents. They are traditionally from Lancashire, Eng., but have no written record.

The plan of the genealogy is made as simple as possible. Following the head of a family are the children, arranged according to age, and numbered i, ii, &c., and over the baptismal name a small figure to denote the *generation*. This is followed by the surname, and when deemed necessary that is followed by the parentage of that child, in parenthesis, numbered as in the baptismal name, so that any one can easily be traced back to the earliest known record. The history of each child is then taken up, and *their* children numbered 1, 2, &c.; then follow the grand-children, numbered (i) (ii) in parenthesis; then the great grand-children, numbered (1) (2), also in parenthesis—each following its own parentage.

Isabella (Twigg) dived July. 25 - 1876

When the history of any one is long, or the children so numerous as to lead to confusion, *that* one is simply named, and against the name is placed a full face figure, **1,** with the sign §, and in a subsequent page, at the same figure, more of their history will be found.

The manuscript unexpectedly became more extended than it was judged prudent to print. It is therefore abridged in many places, and matter which we should have gladly put in is omitted. Where the record of any family terminates abruptly, it is for want of information which could not be obtained. It is hoped that the MS. letters and notes will be preserved in the family. To avoid numerous foot notes, references are often made in the text.

ABBREVIATIONS.—b. born; bap. baptised; bur. buried; chn. children; d. died; dau. daughter; m. married; unm. unmarried; r. or res. reside.

SAMUEL DUNSTER.

ATTLEBORO, MASS., Nov. 1, 1876.

HENRY DUNSTER

AND

HIS DESCENDANTS.

EMIGRANT ANCESTOR—HENRY DUNSTER.

Henry Dunster, the first of the name in this country, and the first President of Harvard College, was born in England, and came over in the year 1640. The only known reference to the place of his birth is found in a letter* of his own, dated Feb., 1648, and addressed to Ch. Ravius, Professor of Oriental languages in London. In that letter he says : *"Ego enim Lancastrensis sum"* (for I am from Lancashire). Another letter to President Dunster, from his father, is still extant,** and is dated "from Balehoult, this 20th of March, 1640." Balehoult (sometimes called Billyholt) is supposed to have been the name of a private gentleman's residence in

* Life of Henry Dunster, First President of Harvard College. By Rev. Jeremiah Chaplin, D. D. Boston, 1872. pp. 87, 271.

** Rev. Mr. Hunter (Willard Memorial, p. 345), says : "The Dunsters of America are fortunate in possessing such a piece of family evidence as this letter. It is one of the few cases which have come under my knowledge in which New England families can be traced by evidence that is indisputable to their English home when they had abandoned it at so early a period."

Bury, Lancashire. These letters, with others to friends in Bury, indicate the place of his residence, and in all probability of his birth, the date of which cannot be exactly ascertained, but was about 1610–12. His father, Henrye, had four sons (see Balehoult Letter), Henry, Richard, Thomas and Robert, and two or three daughters, only one of whom is mentioned by name in the letter. Richard came to this country, as appears both from the letter and from the college memoranda, in 1640, but nothing further is definitely known of him.

This letter, which is referred to in a manuscript sketch of the Dunster family prepared by the Rev. John Marrett, [Harv., 1763,] was long supposed to be lost. It was found in the year 1853 by my son, Edward S. Dunster, at that time a student in Harvard College, in the house of Miss Hannah Dunster, of Pembroke, Mass., and was by her presented to him, with other papers and books which had been the property of President D. She was great grand-daughter of President D., and was then eighty-four years of age, the sole living descendant of her branch of the family. The letter, herewith appended, was published, together with the other papers, under the editorship of the Rev. Samuel Sewell, of Burlington, Mass., in the Mass. Hist. Coll., IV Series, Vol. II., p. 190.

THE BALEHOULT LETTER.

Grace mercy and peace bee multiplyed in Christ Jesus vppon you Amen Kind and Louinge Sonns I am very glad of your wellfare and good psperity I haue receiued 4 letters from you since you Ariued in new England the first dated the 17th of August by Robte Haworth of Boulton the second dated the 21th of August both wch came to my hands in scauen weekes after you sent them the Redd wheat I receiued but ye Indian wampenpegs* weare lost out of your letter the third was dated ye 29th of 8ber wch I receiued on christms eue wth a letter of Richards inclosed in the same the last dated the 12th of 8ber wch I receiued of one Millns that had beene wth

* The wampenpeg was the Indian money, each piece being of the value of about the sixth of a penny.

you in new England who lodged with me about mid
January but it seemes it should haue come by Colier your
Sisters remember theire loues vnto you both but you
must not expect them so longe as your mother and I do
liue your brother Thomas remembers his loue and hath
sent you 2 dozen of Almanacks but now he is a widdow-
er for both wyffe and chyln are deade since michaellms I
pray god he take good wayes I do not know of any that
you sent for that entend to come as yett Touchinge
Richard I would aduise him not to come over againe as
yett for what soeuer is his due shall bee left in the hands
of his sisters for I haue taken a generall aquitance of
Robte so that Richard and his sisters may haue what wee
two ould folke leaue and wee shall make no willfull wast
now concerninge our England since you went ouer wee
have beene sore troubled for the Scotts came into England a month afore michaellms and came to Tyne watter
where some of our Troupers laye the Scotts proffered to
come over and our men wthstood them for a while but
ours beinge but 500 weare not able to wthstand 30 Thousand but fledd amaine insomuch as one Constable a gentleman of a company cryed to his band Ryde theeues Ryde
for your lyues and he himselfe for his pte Ridd so fast yt
he lost his capp and mist it not of rydinge two myles
Then the Scotts came pedentim towards newcastle in
some 203 [2 or 3 ?] dayes where ye yealded the towne
immediatly Then was England in a fright for the did
not knowe what to doe but att last all the freehoulders
and trayned bande weare caled togather every Hundred
by itselfe and trayned for a fortnight togather also all
betwixt 16 and 60 weare caled togather so that vpon the
8th of 7ber beinge Bury fayre there was at Burye 40
Thousand wth such weapons as ye could gett and those
that had no better tooke euery one a great clubb and it
was caled Club fayre att Burye and all the prouision for
the fayre was eaten vpp that daye So that ye 800 which
trayned there weare scanted for a fortnight after of vit-
uals the Buchers and Allewyues made a gayne of them
Then great troups of Souldiers weare sent into yorkeshire
and it was thought that there would haue beene some
Batayle speedely Butt the Lord turned all to peace and

a Parliment [The long Parliament.] was caled which
began the third of 9ber and the goe on very Joyffully
god bee praysed for the same And the Scotts are to re-
moue from newcastle before the 25th of march and the
must receiue 300 Thousand pounds to bringe them
whome againe Now for our great men of England the
most of them are proued traytors first lord deputy [Straf-
ford.] of Ireland and the Archbishopp of canterbury
[Laud—Both were subsequently executed.] and the great
Judges the rest of the Bishops are found in a premunire
except the bishopp of Lincolne who is suffered to bee in
the parliment house all the rest are Excluded finch ye
lord keeper is fledd wyndebancke the kings cheeffe secretary is fledd the Bishopp wrenn [Chaplain to Charles I.]
had thought to haue flowen but his wings weare to short
All non conformists are suffred to preach and our Altars
are some of them puld vpp Surplusses and communion
books some torne the communion tabls brought downe
into the bodye of the church: Burton and Preen are
brought into the Parliment house wth great respect and
weare mett out of the citye with 200 couches in triumphe
so that ye kinge did take it somwhat harshly and said so
many did not meete him when he came from Yorke from
quietinge the Scotts many peticions are prfered into the
Parliment against Idle dronken ministers and against
double beneficed parson [s] and suite made that all Chap-
pells shall be reliued out of church Liuings your sister
Elizabeth is turned scribe and can do very well of 3
weeks tyme I pray you giue Richard good counssell and
bee the meanes to trayne him vpp in goodness and make
much of each other for it repenteth mee very sore of my
lyffe heretofore spent in Idle company and I thanke god
hartelye that plonged my lyffe to see my erors and foly
The ould Lady Ashton and Mr. Rawsthorns heire dyed
wthin 2 howers togather vpon wednessday afore candlms
and weare buried att burye both in one graue vpon the
monday followinge The papists had conspired wth ye
deputye of Ireland to sett fightinge in the north pts that
ye might haue begun in the south where the should haue
had ayde out of Ireland and the spaniard laye watchinge
vppon the seas likewise to haue Ayded them but the

Holanders meetinge wth them gaue them a great shake
and scattered them sore so that wee may well say that
man purposseth but god disposseth my lord saye and my
lord Brooke are sworne of the kings priuy Counssell
whose lyves ye byshops had ment to haue taken away not
long since your ould friend doctor Cossins for his honesty is put in the cage to see if he can singe well or no
All the monepolies for lycencesses are disanulled so that
euery man may buye and sell att theire pleasure wthout
controule we haue gotten ould Mr Horocks to bee lecturer att Burye euery thursday he begun afore christmas
and hath promised for a tweueluemonth if god spare him
health and abilitie Mr Ashton of Midleton is one of our
knights for the Parliment who hath wth him for aduise
and counssell your friend ould Mr. Rathband who hath
beene wth him since it began The Scotts assone as the
came to new castle sange the 74th psalme: why art thou
lord so longe from vs &c [Sternhold and Hopkins's
version.] many great men are thought to bee faulty as
I writt afore Thus committinge you bothe to the ptection
of the Allmighty I rest
Your louing father
HENRYE DUNSTER

from Balehoult * this
20th of March 1640
This letter comes
by London."

Henry was educated at Magdalen College, Cambridge,
Eng., whence he was graduated A. B. in 1630, and A.
M. in 1634. The University here had, from an early

* Mr. Ellison, of Dover, N. H., who was born and reared in
Bury, and who is an engraver to calico printers, and therefore
accustomed to exact drawing, gave me a sketch of the vicinity,
on which he has marked a place still called Dunstar's. It is on
the Ramsbottom road, about a mile and a half from the Bury
bridge, over the river Irwell, and near the East Lancashire railroad. He has also located the place called Billyholt and the Bolholt print works on a cross-road running between the Tottington
road and Walshaw lane, about a mile from Bury bridge.
Rev. Mr. Sewall, the transcriber of the letter, had also obtained
from England independent and conclusive testimony to same
purport. [S. D.]

period, a reputation for liberality of opinion far beyond
that of her ancient rival, Oxford, and it is not at all sur-
prising that so many of her graduates, who were driven
from home by the then existing intolerance toward non-
conformists, were found among the early settlers of New
England.   Among his contemporaries at Cambridge,
were Jeremy Taylor and John Milton, Ralph Cudworth,
and John Pearson, John Harvard and others, who subsequently became more or less distinguished.   He was
trained for the ministry, but it is questionable whether
he ever took orders in the church; and after a few years
spent in teaching, he emigrated to this country, apparently, so far as we now know, with no settled purpose.
He was a man of retiring disposition, and although holding to the most positive conviction of duty, he was by
nature opposed to controversy and strife; and so we may
with propriety assume that he was influenced in his
movements by a desire to avoid taking part in the angry
scenes just then commencing in England, which culminated in the establishment of the protectorate under
Cromwell and the execution of King Charles and some
of his ministers.

He arrived in Boston "toward the latter end of this
Summer," [1640]* and for a short time resided "on his
own estate at the North East Corner of Court Street and
Washington Street."**   His reputation as a ripe scholar
had evidently preceded him, for "immediately upon his
arrival he was waited on by the Governor, magistrates,
elders and ministers" and asked "by a sort of acclama-
tion and general consent" to remove to Cambridge and
assume the Presidency of the College—a work which
proved to be his great life-occupation.   As to his fitness
for this work, there is abundant contemporaneous testimony.   Johnson, in his "Wonder-Working Providence,"
says he was "fitted from the Lord for the work, and by
those that have skill in that way, reported to be an
able proficient in Hebrew, Greek and Latin languages."

* Johnson.   Wonder-Working Providence of Sions Saviour in
New England, p. 162.

** Whitman.   Hist. Ancient and Honorable Artillery.   Quoted
by Chaplin.

Prince speaks of him as "one of the greatest masters of the Oriental languages that hath been known in these ends of the earth." Shepard, the pastor at Cambridge, calls him "a man, pious, painful, and fit to teach, and very fit to lay the foundations of the domestical affairs of the College; whom God hath much honored and blessed." Quincy, Pierce, and Eliot—the modern historians of Harvard College—have also recorded their testimony as to the purity and nobility of his character, and his great success in both the executive and the teaching departments of the College.

Thus fitted by education as well as by an experience of several years in teaching, he entered upon the work of organizing and conducting the College affairs. The College had been already established, but it was little else than an advanced school. The first allusion in colonial history to it, is in an order of the General Court, Oct. 28, 1636, making a grant of £400 "towards a schoale or colledge, whearof 200*l*. to bee paid the next yeare, and 200*l*. when the worke is finished." There is, however, great doubt whether any of this grant was ever paid. The Rev. John Harvard, from whom the College takes its name, died in 1638, and by his will left the half of his property, about £700, and his library, numbering 300 volumes, in aid of the College. This was its actual beginning, for it is certain nothing had hitherto been done in the way of starting the enterprise. A class of pupils at once began study under Nathaniel Eaton, the master, though little was accomplished in the direction of securing any plan of organization. Cotton Mather speaks of Eaton as "a blade, who marvellously deceived the expectations of good men concerning him; for he was one fitter to be the master of a Bridewell than a Colledge." He is remembered to-day only for his cruelty and his avarice, qualities not especially desirable in laying the foundation of an institution whose purpose was to "advance learning and perpetuate it to posterity." The task before the incoming President was, in view of this state of affairs, no ordinary one, but it is conceded on all sides that he was fully competent for it.

Soon after removing to Cambridge, he united with the

*2

church there on confession of faith.*   This would seem
to imply either that he had hitherto declined to participate in any church organization, or if, as stated by Cotton Mather, he had taken orders in the English church,
he must now have renounced all such connection, for
he was styled "an orthodox preacher of the truths of
Christ."   There are many references to his supplying
the pulpit in Cambridge and the vicinity during his
Presidency, and he took a prominent part in founding
the church at Woburn.   He manifested great interest in
the education and conversion of the Indians, and joined
heartily with John Eliot and the Mayhews in this work.
Lechford, the Boston lawyer, says of him in this connection: "He will, without doubt, prove an instrument
of much good in this country, being a good scholar and
having skill in the tongues.   He will make it good that
the way to instruct the Indians must be in their own
language, not English."   The second charter of the College, obtained in 1650 on his express petition, declares
its object is to include "the education of the English
and *Indian* youth of this country in knowledge and
godliness."

.Besides the business of instruction and discipline**
which largely devolved on him, he was charged with the
adminstration of the College matters, even down to such
particulars as the direction of the Commons, the keeping of the students' accounts *** (their bills being mostly

* His religious experiences are given at length in a manuscript
volume by the Rev. Thomas Shepard, entitled, "The Confessions
of Diverse propounded to be received, and were entertained as
members."   This volume is now in the library of the Historic
Genealogical Society of Boston.   Vide Chaplin *loc. cit.*, p. 257.

** Corporal punishment, which had been introduced from the
English Universities, flourished at Harvard in its earlier days,
and the President personally attended to this duty.

*** In the College Library there is still preserved an account
book, in President D.'s handwriting, wherein each student is
charged with the different articles which he consumed.   In the
same book, also in his writing, is the original sketch of the first
seal of Harvard College, with its simple motto, " VERITAS,"
and a record of the vote which authorized its adoption:
"C   At ye meeting of ye Governors of Harvard Colledge in

see little page for seal.

paid in commodities), the construction of the College edifice and the President's house, the collection of his own salary, &c. The requisites for admission into College, the details of the course of study, and the rules and precepts for the government of the students, were prepared by him; and Quincy says that the principles of education established by him were not materially changed during the whole of the seventeenth century. In College discipline he appears to have availed himself of the common belief of the age in the active agency of malevolent yet invisible beings, and there is a tradition in the family of his having formally exorcised the Evil One,* whom the students on one occasion had raised, but were

Colledge Hall, this 27 of 10th 1643 * * * It is ordered y.at yere shall be a Colledge seal in form following." A fac-simile of which is on the title page.

Mr. Benjamin Homer Hall, in his Chapter on the "Commons," Harvard Book, Vol. II., p. 83, says: "The great wisdom of President Dunster appears nowhere more clearly then in the capacity which he exhibited in dealing with the details of the business to which he gave the strength of his manhood and wealth that he could ill afford to spare." After further complimentary notice, he quotes in full the "orders" prepared by Presi-D., "by the scholars and officers of the College, to be observed, written 28th March, 1650."

* Raising the devil was understood in a very different sense in the middle of the 17th century from that which now obtains among College boys. There was a seriousness, not to say solemnity, about the business which ill-accords with the frivolity of modern College pranks. On whatever the tradition may have been based, it certainly dates far back in the history of the family, being found, in almost identical terms, in branches which were separated as early as 1741 and have had little or no association since. For the tradition in full, see response by Samuel Dunster in Proceedings Centennial Celebration, Town of Mason, N. H. By John B. Hill. Boston, 1870. p. 80.

This story, perhaps, might have had its origin from the famous interview between the President of the College and the Cambridge pastor on the question of infant baptism. Mather Magnalia, Vol. II., p. 96, and Life H. D., p. 106. Having failed to answer the President's logic, the "Matchless Mitchel" wrote in his diary, Dec. 24, 1653, "After I came from him (Mr. D.) I had a strange experience. I found hurrying and pressing suggestions against Paedobaptism. * * * Yet, methought, it was not hard to descern that they were from the Evil One." In that day this was the tribunal of last resort in knotty questions of orthodoxy.

unable to allay. Under Dunster, the College prospered,
and he was found equal in all respects to the expectations which had been formed of him. "That which was
before "—says the historian Hubbard—" but at best a
schola illustra grew to the stature and perfection of a
College " and "soon acquired so high a reputation that
in several instances youth of opulent families were sent
over to receive their education in New England." In
addition to the College work of so diversified a character,
he found time to correspond with learned men abroad,
and to devote his personal attention to the supervision,
through the press, of several publications. The first
printing press in North America, was set up in Cambridge, in 1639, " as an appendage of Harvard College;"
for it was considered too powerful an engine for good or
evil to be entrusted in private hands, and accordingly
for more than a hundred years it was kept under the
supervision of the General Court. In 1641 it was put
under President D.'s management, and it was transferred
to the President's house, where it remained until 1655.
Among its earlier issues, was "The whole Booke of
Psalmes Faithfully Translated into English Metre."
This book, now known as the "Bay Psalm Book," appeared in two editions—1640 and 1647. The translation
was made by three well known ministers of the day—
Mather, of Dorchester, and Eliot and Weld, of Roxbury—and it was intended to take the place of the Sternhold and Hopkins' version, in which, as is well known,
the translation was often very inaccurate, while the ver-
sification, as Mr. Chaplin says, " was too rugged even
for our not very fastidious fathers." The new version
" did not, however," says Neal, " satisfy the expectations
of judicious men," and accordingly for a further improvement it was committed to the President. Associated with him in the work of "revising and polishing,"
was Mr. Richard Lyon, and the result of their combined
labors seems to have been, on the whole, very satisfac-
tory, for in its new form the book passed through more
than fifty editions. The poetry * was, it is true, a little

* Mr. Chaplin, in his life of President D., says: "The Oriental learning necessary for the work of revision, was probably sup-

rough and shaky, though a great improvement on the
prior editions. The authors themselves seem to have
had mild doubts as to the smoothness of the metre, for
in their preface they say, "If the verses are not always
as elegant as some desire or expect, let them consider that
God's altar needs not our polishing; we have respected

plied in the main by the President, and this, we judge, was
worked up into something like poetry by the junior partner in
the enterprise; for Mr. Lyon, we are told, added to the original
work a number of songs and rhymes of his own composition. It
is due to Mr. Dunster's memory to relieve him, if possible, of the
charge of furnishing the poetry." It gives us pleasure to be able
to exonerate the partnership from at least one poetic error, which
we fear Mr. C. himself, or his printer, is justly chargeable with.
In printing as a specimen of the work the first psalm, he gives
the third verse, viz.:

> He shall be like a planted tree
>   by water brooks which shall
> In his due season yield his fruit,
>   whose leaf shall never fail.

Fail in the last line should read *fall*. The word shall in those
days was generally pronounced with a broad Scotch accent so as
to rhyme with fall. Scott—Lady of the Lake, Canto 4, XVII.,
l. 24—makes *shall* rhyme with *all*. The modern change in pronunciation has made many other of those old rhymes uncouth.
In Sternhold and Hopkins' version, the first verse of this psalm
reads:

> The man is blest that hath not lent to wicked men his ear:
> Nor led his life as sinners do, nor sat in scorner's chair.

I can remember well the very common pronunciation of the
word *chair* as if it were spelled *cheer*. For the following amusing
illustration of this I am indebted to Mr. A. A. Tufts, of Dover,
N. H. The Rev. Hugh Adams, minister in Durham, N. H.,
1718—1750, was a graduate of Harvard College, in the class of
1697. His classmate, Southmayd, cut the legs nearly off a chair,
and then sent Read, another classmate, to ask Adams to visit him.
On entering the room, he was politely invited to be seated. The
chair gave way, and Adams found himself sprawling on the floor.
Collins, a fourth classmate, being present to see the fun. On getting up, Adams immediately made this parody on the verse:

> Blest is the man who hath not lent
>   To wicked Read his ear,
> Nor hath his life like Collins spent,
>   Nor sat in Southmayd's chair.

rather a plain translation than to smooth our verses with the sweetness of any paraphrase. We have attended conscience rather than elegance, fidelity rather than ingenuity," &c. The quaint Cotton Mather bears his testimony as follows: "Now, though I heartily join with those gentlemen who wish that the *poetry* hereof were mended; yet must I confess that the Psalms have never yet seen a *translation,* that I know of, nearer to the Hebrew *original.*"

For some twelve or thirteen years Mr. D. remained President of the College, and administered its affairs with eminent success. Indeed it is doubtful if in the early history of Harvard any one person ever had so large an influence in perpetuating her existence and shaping her policy as her first President. But at this time the public avowal on his part of sentiments of opposition to infant baptism created an intense excitement in the colony, and roused a violent spirit of opposition toward him. Says Eliot,* one of the historians of Harvard, "the orthodox spirit of the whole colony was instantly roused; and the strongest because involuntary testimony is borne to the intellectual power and moral influence of Dunster, by the alarm his defection excited, and the harsh measures dictated by that feeling, while his conscientiousness is attested by the meekness of his submission to the rebukes which were sternly administered."

The first public and official movement taken against him was by the magistrates who sent a letter to the ministers in the early part of the year 1653, directing them to make an examination of the whole matter as a basis for their future action. Upon this a conference was held at Boston, Feb. 2d and 3d, 1653–4, at which were present nine leading ministers of Boston and vicinity, besides Mr. D. and two ruling elders, twelve in all, and before them Mr. D. publicly defended his views. The conference labored with the "erroneous gentleman" and endeavored to convince him of his mistake. But having failed, as Cotton Mather quaintly puts it, "to expedite

* Sketch of the History of Harvard College, and of its present state. Boston, 1848. p. 15.

the entangled out of the briars," the General Court, in May following, passed a vote commending it "to the serious consideration and special care of the overseers of the College * * * not to admit or suffer any such to be continued in the office or place of teaching that have manifested themselves *unsound in the faith*," etc. Mr. D. understood the significance of this action, and the next month, June 10, 1654, he forwarded through the overseers a letter of resignation. This was "ungraciously" accepted by the Court on the 25th of the same month and referred back to the overseers, with an order to secure "some meet person to carry on the work of the College" in case he (D.) should persist in his resolution more than a month. Here was an avenue of escape opened to him, for he could now retain his position at the cost of silence only. Hubbard says he might have remained "in the place where he had spent the choise part of his studies and his life * * * if he had been endowed with that wisdom, which many others have wanted besides himself, to have kept his singular opinion to himself, when there was little occasion of venting thereof." But he was thoroughly and conscientiously an honest man—not as too many are honest only from motives of policy—and there was for him but one course to pursue. It is no surprise, therefore, to learn that in the following month, July, he made another public avowal of his sentiments, on the Sabbath day, in the church at Cambridge. The overseers then being no longer in doubt, and feeling that he was past recovery from the "briars" aforesaid, proceeded "to inform him that the interests of the College and the colony required his removal." Thereupon a second time, October 24, 1654, he sent his resignation, the final one to the overseers. It is interesting here to note that his successor, Mr. Chauncey, who was appointed a few days subsequently, was notified in the tender to him of the position that "it was expected and desired that he forbear to disseminate or publish any tenets concerning the necessity of immersion in baptism, and celebration of the Lord's supper at evening, or to oppose the received doctrines therein." What a difference between the two men

—the one sacrificing his position rather than stultify his conscience, the other purchasing a place on the condition of silence as to doctrines which it was well known he entertained.

For his offence in July, Mr. D. was indicted some months subsequently by the grand jury, the presentment being "for disturbance of the ordinances of Christ uppon the Lord's daye." He was tried, convicted and sentenced according to the ecclesiastical law, "to be publiquely admonished and give bond for his *good behavior*." A second time, also some two years later—a child having meantime been born to him—he was indicted by the grand jury and tried by the County Court, for practically the same offence, the presentment being now "for not bringing his child to the Holy Ordinance of Baptisme." He was again convicted, solemnly admonished of his dangerous error, and ordered to give bonds for his appearance at the next court of assistants at Boston. The bond was executed, but there is no record of any further proceedings in the case.

Eleven days after his forced resignation, Mr. D. sent to the General Court a petition,* wherein, without receding in the slightest particular from his avowed position, he invoked their merciful consideration of his circumstances. After expressing his hope that it might not be thought nor reported that he "cast off his place out of any froward morosity, foolish levity, or ingrateful despising, either of the Court's forbearance or the overseers' amicable conferences," he makes three special requests. First, for an allowance in salary which had been commended to the Court by a committee thereof ; second, to be permitted to remain in the President's house during the settlement of his accounts with the corporation, and third, to be allowed to continue in the colony in the work of teaching or preaching, "or in any other laudable or liberall caling as God shall chalk out my [his] way." This appeal, says Quincy, was treated in a heartless way, and in the reply to the third request was equivalent to warning him out of the colony.

* The original of this petition is now in the library of Harvard College.

Notwithstanding this contemptuous treatment, six days later—Nov. 10, 1654—he sent to the Court a brief paper of "Considerations," intended as a rejoinder to the reply of the Court to his second request, which had been dismissed "as most unreasonable." These considerations had reference to the material circumstances of himself and his family, and to the necessity of his remaining at Cambridge in order to acquaint the incoming President with the administration of the College duties. This paper, which shows not only a most positive conviction of the correctness of his position, but a most commendable spirit of submission, closes in these words: "The whole transaction of this business is such, which in the process of time, when all things come to mature consideration, may very probably create grief on all sides; yours subsequent, as mine antecedent. I am not the man you take me to be. Neither if you knew what I hold and why, can I persuade myself that you would act, as I am at least tempted to think you do. But our times are in God's hands, with whom all sides hope, by grace in Christ, to find favor, which shall be my prayer for you, as for myself." The "simple, touching pathos" of this appeal was not without effect, and he was allowed to remain until the following March—some three months —in the President's house.*

Shortly afterward he removed to Scituate, in the adjoining colony of Plymouth, which was much more tolerant in religious matters than her sister of Massachusetts Bay. Mr. Deane, in his history of the place, says, "we find notices of him the same autumn (1655) employed in the ministry, in which he continued nearly five years." His persecutions had already attracted the attention of the Baptists of the mother country, and on the 10th of July, 1656, he received from Mr. Edward

* The history in detail of this treatment of Dunster—which was a notable specimen of the intolerance of the early settlers of New England—is well told by Mr. Chaplin in his life of President D. The original documents bearing upon the case are quoted in full by him. The reader who may desire further information regarding the matter is referred to this book, it being impossible here to give more than this brief summary of the transaction.

3

Roberts, a leading member of that denomination in Dublin, a letter,* dated Dublin, 3d, 1655, urging him to make that place his home, and informing him that £50 had been granted by the Lord Deputy (Henry Cromwell, younger son of the Protector) for the transportation thither of himself and his family. The invitation Mr. D. saw fit to decline, and he remained in the place which had given him so kindly a welcome, and which, says Mr. Chaplin, deserves honorable mention for its friendly treatment of dissenters.

President D. died at Scituate, Feb. 27, 1659-60. In his will,** which was dated Feb. 8, 1658, he directed that his body should be transported "to Cambridge there to be enterred by my [his] lovinge wife [babes] and other relaccons:" and it is a striking evidence of the character of the man that he made special legacies to persons who during his life had been his most unrelenting persecutors. Also to a number of relatives and friends, among whom he mentions "my cousin Bowers,"[1] "my cousin fayth Dunster,"[2] "my sister Willard"[3] and "sister Hills[4] and all her children borne in this country."

* The original of this letter, which is a remarkable specimen of chirography for that day, is now in my possession. It is endorsed in President D.'s handwriting—"Received 10th of July, 1656, from ye hand of Goodwife Price. ye order of ye consel inclosed." Unfortunately the order has been lost.

** The original of President D.'s will was stolen from the Probate office in East Cambridge about the year 1850. It is difficult, therefore, to reconcile the discrepancy in different copies between the words "wife" and "babes." Mr. Pulsifer's copy in the Probate office is clear and distinct, and reads "wife." Mr. Harris, Librarian of Harvard College, 1831—1856, and who, with his son, prepared an unpublished memoir of President D., a copy of which I was kindly allowed to make, insisted that the word in the original was "babes" A copy of the will, in the handwriting of Wm. G. Means, in the library of Harvard College, has it "babes." It seems probable, from internal and collateral evidence, that the word must have been "babes." For copy of the will, see Chaplin, loc. cit., p. 303. [E. S. D.]

[1] Bowers Bennaniel and Dunster Elizabeth, married at Cambridge, 9th day 10th month, 1653. "He was a Baptist, and arrived at the distinction of being more frequently fined by the

[handwritten note:] Wm. J Potts says in an article in Penn. Mag. vol. III no. 1 that "...ood Bowes was a Quaker. ... died in Philadelphia

The place of burial was in the old cemetery opposite the College grounds, a few rods northwest of the church now standing therein.   Over the grave was placed a horizontal slab of stone with an inlaid tablet of lead,

County Court for not attending public worship than any other man." Willard Memorial, p. 341.

[2] Faith married John Page, of Groton, Mass., May 12, 1664. She had children by this marriage in 1669, 1672 and 1674.   See Butler's Hist. Groton.

[3] It has been a question of considerable debate, whether Major Simon Willard's third wife was "sister" or "cousin" of President D.   Dr. Samuel Willard says Mary D. was the third wife of Major Willard and that she was "cousin."   The question is discussed at some length in the Willard Memorial without being authoritatively settled, but a final reference is made to the fact that President D., in his will, calls Major W.'s third wife his "sister;" and adds, "if this expression is to be taken literally it ends the question."

[4] "My sister Hills." Joseph Hills, of Malden, was married four times: 1. Probably in England.   "Rose Dunster, sister of Rev. Henry Dunster, first President of Harvard College.   She died at Malden, March 1, 1650-1. 2. Hannah, widow of Edward Mellows, married June 24, 1651. 3. Helen Atkinson, daughter of Hugh Atkinson, of Kendall County, of Westmoreland, Eng. Ceremony performed Jan., 1655–6, by himself, for which he was admonished by the Court, and fined £5. 4. Ann, widow of Henry Lunt, March 8, 1664–5." (Gen. Sketch of Descendants of Thos. Greene. App. p. 71.) His third wife was living at the date of President D.'s will, and had probably two children by Mr. H.   She was not a blood relation of H. D., neither was Mr. Hills.   Still he calls her "sister Hills."   Heretofore it has been understood that she was his natural sister.   This record precludes that relationship, and makes her sister only as she was the wife of his brother-in-law by a former marriage.   The language of the will in this connection is peculiar: "Concerning my daughter Elizabeth my mind and will is that she shall be at the disposing of her mother during her life in her minority and in case of my wive's death then to live with my sister Mrs. Hills of Mauldon during her minority and faithfully and carefully serve her as if shee were her own child, and in case there also the Lord by death should make such uncomfortable breaches in the family that shee could not live comfortably there then she shall live with my sister Willard of Concord." Did not the phrase "In case there also the Lord by death" allude to the possible death of Mr. Hills, a firm friend and the executor of his will? In that contingency, Elizabeth would be left with a step-aunt, whose own children might receive her best affections.

upon which was an inscription. This tablet has disappeared long since, and is supposed to have "done service for the country in the shape of revolutionary bullets." By reason of this loss, as well as by many years' neglect of the grounds, even the place of burial became at length doubtful. A most interesting account of its re-discovery and identification is given by Mr. Chaplin in his life of President D. This account was written by the late Mrs. H. C. Conant, a sister of Mr. Chaplin, who derived it from a personal narrative of Mr. Sibley, then assistant librarian of the College. Mr. T. W. Harris, the librarian, and his son, W. T. Harris, [Harvard, 1846] who were well known for their genealogical and antiquarian researches, were specially prominent in the matter of the identification of the grave. The grave was restored by the order of the College authorities in 1845, and the stone slab which now replaces the missing tablet contains the following epitaph from the classic pen of Mr. Charles Folsom:

HENRICUS . DUNSTER

PRIMUS . COLLEGII . HARVARDINI . PRÆSES

VIR . PIETATE . DOCTRINA . PRUDENTIA . INSIGNIS

OBIIT . SCITUATÆ . AN . $\overline{\text{M.DC.}}$LIX.

HUC . TRANSLATUM . EST . CORPUS

UT ΄QUOD . ILLE . IN . VOTIS . HABUERAT

PROPE . ACADEMIAM . A . SE . TUM . NUTRITAM . IN . CUNABULIS

EX . RE . FAMILIARI

TUM . RITIBUS . DISCIPLINIS . LEGIBUS . INSTRUCTAM

REQUIESCERET

MONUMENTUM . HOC . INJURIA . TEMPORIS . DIRUPTUM

SOCII . ÆTERNUM . ACADEMIÆ . DECUS . CURANTES

REFICIENDUM . JUSSERUNT . AN . $\overline{\text{M.DCCC.}}$XLV.

FAMILY SECTIONS.

THE NUMBERS OF WHICH ARE REPEATED AT THE TOP OF THE PAGES IN FULL FACE FIGURES.

3*

Fac-simile of Mr. Dunster's autograph writing taken from an interleaved copy of "A CONCENT OF THE SCRIPTVRE," a book which belonged to him, and is now in my possession.

1

HENRY DUNSTER.

Henry Dunster:

Fac-simile of autograph.

1. HENRY[1] DUNSTER, Rev., President of Harvard College, from Aug. 27, 1640, to Oct. 24, 1654, married June 21, 1641, Elizabeth, widow of the Rev. Jose, Josse or Joseph* Glover. She died Aug. 23, 1643. "She was buried in the ancient burying ground at Cambridge and has a stone much gone to decay." There were no children by this marriage. He married a second time, Elizabeth, (surname unknown.) The date of this marriage is also unknown. There is a tradition that she came from England when about eighteen years old, and was soon married. She appears to have been well educated and to have had a superior mind. She died Sept. 12, 1690. The Cambridge epitaphs state she was sixty years old. This is an evident error, or she would have been only fifteen years old when their eldest child was born, which is very improbable. His children, all by the second wife, were:

2§.   i.   DAVID[2] DUNSTER, born May 16, 1645.
      ii.   DOROTHY[2] DUNSTER, born Jan. 29, 1647–8, died young.
3§. iii.   HENRY[2] DUNSTER, born about 1650, died young.
4§. iv.   JONATHAN[2] DUNSTER, born Sept. 28 or Oct. 27, 1653; both dates appear on the town records.
5§. v.   ELIZABETH[2] DUNSTER, born Dec. 29, 1656.

* According to the Glover Memorial and Genealogies, the Christian name is Joseph on the church records at Sutton and wherever it occurs in English records and in the English County histories. Sibley's Harvard Graduates, p. 208.

2

2. DAVID[2] DUNSTER* (*Henry*[1]), born May 16, 1645, unfortunately fell under public censure. At the County Court, June 17, 1662, being only seventeen years old, he was adjudged guilty of a youthful indiscretion, for which he was sentenced "to pay a fine of £20 to the use of the county or to be whipt and also to give £50 bond with sufficient securities for defraying the charges," which might naturally be expected. (*Court Record.*) He soon after went to England, and probably never returned. In 1664 his mother, who was his guardian and who signed the £50 bond on his behalf, petitioned the Court for relief, alleging that she "hath been at great charge and expense for him since the death of your servant his father: 1. In learning here, in hopes of his progress therein, about £100. 2. His voyage to England in hope to settle him there about £50. 3. To Mr. Stedman** towards the court's sentence £30. 4. There is due to his sister out of his estate by will £50 so that it is indeed doubtful whether he have any clear estate of his own left beyond which your petitioner did not understand herself to be engaged." There is an old tradition (Rev. Isaiah Dunster's Bible,) that President Dunster's son *Henry* was a lawyer in England, and died there without issue. This tradition may be safely rejected as utterly false in regard to Henry, who undoubtedly died young, but it may be substantially true in regard to David. Their father says in his will: "I have given unto my son David liberal education in schools of learning from his childhood unto this very day;" and the mother says she expended about £100 during the next three years for his advancement in learning here, until he departed for England. A proper foundation was laid for subsequent legal studies, and it is possible, indeed not very improbable—and it is surely most devoutly to be wished—that he may have become a successful and eminent lawyer in England, but we have no certain knowledge of his history after he left Cambridge.

* Rev. L. R. Paige, Gen. Reg., Vol. XXVII., p. 307.

** The County Treasurer.

3-4

3. HENRY[2] DUNSTER (*Henry*[1]). "Among the births recorded in Cambridge in 1650 is that of Henry, son of Henry and Elizabeth Dunster, but neither the day nor month of birth is indicated, nor does the name subsequently appear. The tradition of his being a lawyer has been mentioned, and its lack of probability. There can be no reasonable doubt that he died before Feb. 8, 1658–9, the date of his father's will. Not only is his name omitted while other children are specially designated, but the testator's whole estate is bequeathed to others, no part being reserved for him or for any other person not named." There is strength in the conjecture that he and his sister Dorothy (ii) were the "babes" referred to in the will.

4. JONATHAN[2] DUNSTER (*Henry*[1]), born Sept. 28 or Oct. 27, 1653, was a farmer, and inherited lands lying on both sides of the division line between that part of Cambridge called Menotomy (now Arlington) and Charlestown (now Somerville). In the Charlestown Records, Dec. 30, 1706, there is an entry: "Ordered ———— ——— "Also to Warn A Negro Man and A Negro woman at Mr. Jona. Dunster's, to remove forthwith out of this Towne and also to Warn s'd Dunster that he Entertain them no Longer at the peril of the law." "Jona. Dunster Tything man for the year ensuing March y[e] 5th 1715–16." So that at this time he resided in Charlestown. In 1695, a difficulty arose between the town of Charlestown and Jonathan Dunster, of Cambridge, about a landing place on the south side of Mistick river, "and the said difference not yet ended." Charlestown appointed "Capt. John Cutter as their agent to prosecute the same to effect, and the said Cutter & Dunster not being able to compose the s'd difference," therefore "the above named Capt. John Cutter & Mr. Jonathan Dunston agree, Nominate & Choose, James Converse of Wooburn & Lieut. Peter Tufts * * * to hear & determine the said difference." They divided the landing place, and appear to have dissatisfied both parties. Another committee was appointed, who reported that they found the highway called the Bridgeway wch goeth through the field encroached on in sundry places and

ꝑ *Rev. L R Paige believes the word in the will was "wife" not babe* ploughed up & sown wth Indian corn by **Mr.** Dunster * * * but denied by him to bee any townway."

The day after his marriage contract with Ruth Eaton (Nov. 24, 1719), he gave a deed, the original of which is now in my possession, as follows:

"To all Christian People To whom This present writing shall come. Jonathan Dunster of Charlestowne in the county of Middlesex in the Province of the Macsachusett Bay in New-England Yeoman sends Greeting. Know ye That I the sd Jonathan Dunster (for and in consideration of the natural affection I have and bear unto my well beloved and only [by his first wife] son Henry Dunster of Cambridge * * * husbandman—and for other good considerations me thereunto moving) Have given and granted * * * unto the sd Henry Dunster his Heir and assigns forever the one full moiety or half of a certain piece of land containing by estimation thirteen acres * * * within the bounds of Cambridge aforesd (on part of which the house and Barn of sd Henry Dunster now stands —— —— being now in the actual possession of sd Henry) bounded Westerly by the Road leading to Concord—Northerly by land of William Russell and James Smith of Boston easterly on Woburn Road leading to Charlestown—Southerly by Walter Russels land—or however otherwise butted or bounded." To this deed, just above the signature, in his own hand, is written: "Memorandum. it is to be understood that I give this in part of my Sons portion"

"JONATHAN DUNSTER" [seal]

He died intestate in 1725, aged about 72 years. Henry Dunster, his son, was appointed administrator, his widow having refused to perform that duty. His estate was a long while unsettled. Henry, to whom as the oldest son a double portion was set off, was unwilling to accept the award of the committee, (Messrs. John Fillebrown, of Cambridge, Robert Converse and Josiah Johnson, of Woburn, Stephen Hall and William Willis, of Medford,) and complained that the part set off to him at 16s. per acre was no better than that set off to his brothers at 12s. Testimony as to the value of the land was given by

"Messrs. William Russell, Gershom Cutter and John Cutter, good friend to Henry D." The papers were recommitted by the judge to the committee, who reported that "In case we should proceed to make any alteration as we proposed it would no wise satisfie the uneasy party, but being willing To be resolved by the party him self we sent and desired his Company with us, who returned answer that he had run after us long enough already. Whereupon we wrote to the Gentleman and desired he would send us his minde in the same way. Whereupon he wrote a few lines Intimating that watt we proposed was yett in favor of the other party without even subscribing the same. Therefore we are humbly of Opinion there is not any Mesures that we Can Safely Take in Altering Either the Valluation or Distribution we have already perfected that will make that uneasy Gentleman any satisfaction" * * * The judge then offered the "same to Jonathan the 2d son who also refused, then to Thomas the third son who did the like, then to the dec'ds [deceased's] youngest son David who was willing to accept thereof at the Rate in the Inventory." "But afterwards it was mutually agreed among them all that each person should take their propotion in Land and they propose to make a distrobution among themselves and if they can't do it they are to come upon my citation to nominate Commr. to be appointed for that purpose." On the 10th of July, the heirs came together and chose a new commission of five, and "they are to divide the whole of the Real Estate of ye Dec'd equally among them (Eldest Son two parts) and what each has had in advance to be considered." "I the subscriber relict widow of the herein before named decea'd have perused the afore written accot and do hereby signify my satisfaction therewith.

her
RUTH R DUNSTER."
mark.

(*Court Records, Charlestown, Lib.* 18.)

JONATHAN² DUNSTER, married Dec 5, 1678, Abigail Eliot. She died, and he married April 5, 1692, Deborah Wade, daughter of Major Jonathan Wade, of Medford, and grand-daughter of Gov. Thomas Dudley. She died,

6-7

and he married (contract dated Nov. 23, 1719,) Ruth, widow of Joshua Eaton, of Reading. She survived him, and married Nov. 22, 1732, Lieut. Amos Marrett, of Cambridge, and was published Sept. 30, 1742, to Peter Hayes, of Stoneham.

His children by first wife were:

6 §. i. HENRY[3] DUNSTER, born July 17, 1680, m. Feb. 25, 1707-8, Martha Russel, daughter of Jason Russel, by whom he had eleven children, and died Jan. 28, 1753. His widow married March 15, 1759, Francis Locke. (*Book of Lockes.*)

ii. ELIZABETH[3] DUNSTER, born Feb. 22, 1681-2, died young.

His children by second wife, Deborah Wade, were:

iii. JONATHAN[3] DUNSTER, b. about 1695, at Charlestown, Mass., d. April 11, 1742, unm., aged 47 years and 5 months. He left by will his property to his brothers and sisters. The inscription on his grave stone at Arlington is: "Here lyes Buried ye Body of Mr. Jonathan Dunster, who departed this life April 11, Anno Dom[ni] 1742, aged 47 years & 5 mo."

7 §. iv. ELIZABETH[3] DUNSTER, b. about 1699, m. Capt. Philip Carteret, or DeCarteret, and died Jan. 25, 1787, aged 87 years.

v. THOMAS[3] DUNSTER, b. at Charlestown, and died between April 3, 1726, and April 1, 1728. He is mentioned in the agreement between the heirs of Jonathan[2] Dunster as having lately deceased at the latter date.

vi. DOROTHY[3] DUNSTER, b. about 1702, admitted to church in Medford—full communion—April 21, 1728. She was married April 13, 1732, the record in Charlestown being: "Mr. Solomon Page of Hampton in New Hampshire and Dorothy Dunster of this Town were joyned in marriage by the Rev'd Mr. Hull Abbot April 13, 1732." Mr. Page was the ninth child of Samuel Page by his second wife, Anne Marshall, whom he married Nov. 18, 1702, and was born March 16, 1710. He graduated at Harvard College, 1729, and was admitted to the church the same year. (*Hampton Records.*) Mr. Page was "schoolmaster of the Town" when a son named Lemuel was baptized Sept. 17, 1738. He supplied the pulpit in Hampton six months from March 15, 1733, at the request of the town, "the pastor being sick." He was dismissed by the church to the Second Church in Salsbury, Mass., Dec. 4, 1757, after which no trace of him could be found until the present month (Aug. 1875). A letter from Mr. A. G. Page, of Bath, Maine, states that in "the old grave yard at Bath, Maine, is a slate stone among the undergrowth with this inscription:"

"In Memory of
REV. MR. SOLOMON PAGE
who was educated at
Harvard College.
He departed this life
March 12, 1788.
Aged 78 years."

His wife (Dorothy) died at Hampton, Oct. 13, 1741, aged 39 years, leaving five children:

   i. —— — ——.
   ii. —— — ——.
   iii. HEPSEBETH⁴ PAGE, born about 1736, died at Capt. Carteret's, in Cambridge, Aug. 5, 1765, aged 29 years. Mrs. Carteret was her aunt. (See records of second parish Cambridge, now Arlington, by Rev. Samuel Cooke.)
   iv. LEMUEL⁴ PAGE, baptized at Hampton, N. H., Sept. 17, 1738.
   v. SIMON⁴ PAGE, baptized at North Hampton, N. H., May 11, 1740.

Mr. Page married again, and had Judith born in 1743, and Wilson in 1745. A further inquiry of Mr. A. G. Page, elicited the fact that he also had a son Edward H., who had descendants in Hartland, Maine. They could give no record of Edward, but referred to Mr. William H. Page, of Syracuse, Nebraska. From him was learned the fact that Edward H. Page, who kept the second public house in Bath, died there in 1822, and was 73 years old, therefore was not a son of Dorothy (D) Page. From William H. Page was also learned, that

5

Rev. S. Page preached the first sermon in the first Congregational Church at Bath. That church was torn down fifty years ago. It is hoped that the "Page Family" will fill up this deficient record.

5. ELIZABETH[2] DUNSTER (*Henry,*[1]) was born Dec. 29, 1656. Her birth, which has been supposed to have been in Scituate, is recorded in Middlesex County. She was the child whom her father refused to bring to the "Holy Ordinance of Baptisme," for which he was put under bonds for "Good Behavior." This transaction is fully recorded by Dr. Chaplin (*Life of Henry Dunster, pp.* 153—165). She lived with her mother, probably in Charlestown. It is doubtful if President D. took his family to Scituate, although the history of that town implies that he did. She married, about 1686, Major Jonathan Wade (his first wife died Nov. 1, 1683), of Medford. Major Wade died Nov. 24, 1689, leaving nine children, of whom four are mentioned (in the will of Dudley Wade, his only son, who never married) as "the four sisters of whole blood." Major Wade's children by Elizabeth[2] Dunster were (viii[th]* child) of Major Wade:

   i. ELIZABETH[3] WADE, born 1687. She died Aug. 19, 1721. Unmarried.

   ii. DOROTHY[3] WADE, b. Feb. 17, 1689, died young.

ELIZABETH[3] WADE (*Elizabeth,*[2] *Henry,*[1]) made a will, dated "Marshfield June 14 Annoq. Dom. 1715," proved Sept. 8, 1721. "I Elizabeth Wade daughter of Jonathan Wade late of Medford in the county of Middlesex, Esq., deceased —— give and bequeiath all my estate —— unto my dear and honor.d mother Elizabeth Thomas of Marshfield the wife of Nathaniel Thomas of Marshfield in the county of Plymouth, Esq." —— —— In a codicil, dated Aug. 4, 1721, she "further directs that if my honoured mother—doth not stand in need to sell my housing and lands nor will them away in her life-time, then I give them as follows to the three sons of Jonathan Dunster that were born of my sister—[half sister] Deborah Dunster: I give to Jonathan Dunster

* N. E. Hist. and Gen. Register, Vol. XXVII., p. 309.

5

and Thomas Dunster one half of my housing and lands to them and their heirs forever that are lawfully begotten of their body, and the other half of my housing & lands I give to David Dunster and the heirs of his body lawfully begotten forever." "And in case any of these sons should have any of these lands after my mother's decease to pay the income to my honoured uncle Jonathan Dunster during his life." Her mother was appointed sole executrix, and in her bond is styled "Madam Elizabeth Thomas widow of the late Honble Col. Nathl. Thomas Esq."

Major Wade died in 1689, and his widow, Elizabeth Wade, was administrator, with others, and the estate was divided March 23, 1697–8, to widow, Elizabeth, children, Dudley, Deborah Dunster, Prudence Swan, Katherine Wyer, Susanna Wade, and Elizabeth^3 (Dunster) Wade. In a subsequent division, June 11, 1744, a share was given to the heirs or assigns of the daughter Elizabeth [the children of Jonathan Dunster]. After the death of her husband (Major Wade), she remained a widow more than a quarter of a century. At length she became the wife (probably the third wife) of Col. Nathaniel Thomas, of Marshfield, about 1714 (his second wife died in 1713). Col. Thomas died Oct. 22, 1718, aged 74 years, and she returned to Medford, where, after a second widowhood of about eleven years, she died between May 31 and Nov. 8, 1729, and was probably buried at Medford. She made a will, which, as it exemplifies her character and disposition better than anything we can say, we give entire. It was copied for us from the Middlesex Records by Lorenzo Marrett, Esq., although the *substance* of it had been communicated before by Rev. L. R. Paige. All we knew of her, and all that had been published prior to 1872, was printed in Life H. D., p. 237, in these words: "Elizabeth is mentioned in her father's will." At that time she was only two years old.

ELIZABETH² (DUNSTER) THOMAS' WILL.

I, Elizabeth Thomas of Medford in the county of Middlesex, widow, do make this my last will and testament. I commit my soul to God and my Body decent

5

Burial. Imprs. My will is as follows: I give to my
Nephew Mr. Henry Dunster after my just debts and
funeral charges are paid, I give him all my stock of Cattle and horses only two cows and a horse I reserve Also
I give him all my utensils for husbandry Carts Plows
with all other of the like tools Also I give him one years
service of my Negro Boy named Daniel he using him
well and giving him two suits of Cloaths at the years end.

Item. I give to his son Henry Dunster my Silver
Porringer* marked $_H{}^D_E$ and I give him one third of my
Books.**

Item. I give to Jonathan Dunster and David Dunster and Elisabeth Cartrell and Dorothy Dunster all my
Housing and Land and meadows, marshes and pastures
woodlands and garden lands and all the lands from the
Brick House*** to the River that was their aunt Elizabeth
Wades I now give them with all the rights in the
thirds that would have fallen to Elizabeth Wade had she
lived, with all manner of Housing and land that belongs
to me I give to these four children that were born of

* This Porringer, which is now in my possession, being badly
worn in several places was repaired in 1854. The monogram was
not altered. There can be no doubt that it was the property of
President Dunster, who was the father of Mrs. Thomas. In the
inventory of his estate (Court Records, Charlestown, June 21,
1659) there is this entry: " In plate of divers sorts, a whistle and
corrall £38, 18s." The monogram will apply to no other family.
It has been in the family, as tradition has it, all the way down.

** Among the books from Rev. Isaiah Dunster's library now
in our possession, is one entitled, "English Liberties, or, The
Free-Born Subject's Inheritance, containing: I. Magna. Charta.
II. The Proceedings in Appeals of Murther. III. Laws Against
Conventicles, Protestant Dissenters, &c. London. Printed by
G. Larkin for John How, at the Seven Stars, at the south-west
corner of the Royal Exchange, in Cornhil." (No date.) It has
"Jonathan Wade 168¾" and "Jonathan Wade of Meadford"
written on the blank leaf, and in the same hand and ink, "have
allway God before you." In a later hand and different ink is
"husband's." Was this written by Elizabeth [2] (Dunster) Wade?

*** The third [brick] house was built by Major Jonathan Wade,
who died in 1689. It was sometimes called, like the other two, a
"fort," and is yet standing in good repair, and used as a comfortable residence. It is seen from the main street as we look up

5

Deborah Dunster and to the heirs of their Bodye lawfully begotten, forever, and if any of them die without heirs of their body then to the next Heir and so forever and I further add they shall let no lease for more than three years.

Item. I give to my two nieces Elizabeth Cartrell and Dorothy Dunster all my household goods—Plate Pewter & Brass fine Linnen and Bedding with all other things (only what I reserve for Peggy) equally divided. I give to my niece Dorothy my gold necklace and gold buttons and my case of silver Instruments. I give to Elizabeth Cartrell my great Bible and all my other two thirds of Books equal among the four Kinsfolk.

Item. I give to my Negro man named Toney his freedom, being a faithful servant for forty years. I also give him ten pounds in money and a cow and the liberty of one acre of my marsh for to mow for three years after my decease and also to pasture his cow three years and the liberty to live in that Chamber that is mine for three years and also to have half the Provision in the House at my Decease and also to improve one acre of land in my field for three years. I also give him the liberty of the Chamber for his life if he need it.

Item. I give to the Rev. Mr. James Gardener of Marshfield five pounds in money to be paid him by my executors in three months after my decease. I give to Jonathan * Dunster my great Copper that holds a barrel and a half. I give to him and to his Children if he have any and if not then to return to his sisters Cartrell and Dorothy Dunster.

Item. I give to Jack and Peggy one half of all the Provisions in the House at my decease and they have the liberty to pasture a cow and to get one load of Hay for their cow for three years after my decease.

the Governor's lane. Its walls are very thick, and it is ornamented with what has been called "port-holes." When first built it was only half its present size; the addition was made by Benjamin Hall, Esq., about seventy-five years ago. (*Hist. Medford,* p. 48.)

* Jonathan did not marry, and the "copper" kettle went to Henry [3] Dunster, who willed it to his son Henry [4].

4*

5

Item my will is that my heirs shall see that Toney
be relieved at all times as his need requires.   My will is
to my boy named Daniel, he shall be sold to Defray
charges while he is twenty one years of age and then I
free him and give him a cow or a horse which suits best
my executors.

Item my meaning is as to the Land I give to Jonathan Dunster & David Dunster and Elizabeth Cartrell
and Dorothy Dunster they shall be equally divided
amongst them for Quantity and Quality and to not any
ways Disagree.

Item.   I give to my two neices all my Silk Cloathes
the other I give to Margery my molatto woman.

Item.   My will is that my negro man named Jack
shall live with his wife and Children he paying to my
nephew Mr. Henry Dunster fifteen pounds in one year
after my decease.   I give to my mollato woman Margaret all her Children free from any claim of any body of
my heirs.   I also give her a small House Plott of Land
namely 30 feet one way and forty feet long lying next to
Nathaniel Halls House I give to her and her children,
and I give her a cow and a feather Bed and a Brass Kettle with some other small things.   I also give Jack the
liberty to improve one acre of Land for three years in
my field and also the liberty he and his wife to live in
the chamber that is mine for three years.   Also the Improvement of one half of the Garden and Toney the other
half for three years and then to return to my heirs.

Item.   I give to Nathaniel Thomas Esq. a Gold Ring
and to the Rev. Mr. James Gardener of Marshfield a
Ring.   I give to the Rev. Mr. James Colman a spoon
washed with gold marked T. C.   I give to Mr. Richard
Brooks a gold Ring.   I give Madam Usher my Colash
for one year and then to return to my two neices.   And
I constitute my five Cousins Henry Dunster Jonathan
Dunster and David Dunster and Elizabeth Cartrell and
Dorothy Dunster to be executors of this my last will and
Testament and order that none of my estate shall be
prized.   Further and my Bearers shall have gold Rings.
And if the money That I leave at my decease will not

5

Defray all Charges then every One to bear an equal share in the charge.

LYDIA WADE   ELIZABETH THOMAS [seal]
SIMON TUFTS
AMMI RUHAMAH CUTTER.

My mind is That Toney shall have a Black Coat and Toney shall have the Frying Pan two old Pewter Dishes, the biggest Brass Skillet, the old Chairs in the Kitchen, the old saddle and Bridle the little Pot and a pail and his chest and further my mind is that he and Peggy shall have half the Indian Corn and half the Barly and he—that is Toney—a Hogg and Pigg My mind is Peggy shall have the great Pott and the little Brass Skillet and the old Brass Kettle that was my dear Child's, one Pewter Dish six Plates marked E. W. [Elizabeth Wade, her daughter.]

A paper of Directions for my heirs to do as to my funeral—Six Bearers—Coll. Byfield of Boston, Judge Davenport Jonathan Dows of Charlestown, President of the College, Simon Bradstreet Benjamin Colman—all to have a ring if alive at my decease.

These "freedmen" came into her possession by marriage. There is abundant evidence that President Dunster never owned a slave. His whole life would refute such an inference. Her wishes appear to have been fully carried out. Although they seem to have continued to live in the families to whom she was related, they were brought up in moral and religious instruction, and treated as "a brother beloved." We hope none of them were the ones whom the *government* of Charlestown ordered her nephew "that he Entertain them no Longer at the Peril of the Law." "Toney," whose welfare seems to have been the burden of her mind, lived and died in the Dunster family, and reposes in the same cemetery with them, and the record is: "Toney Dunster died March 4 1745 aged 90 years." "Peggy" seems to have lived with "Aunt Carteret" (Elizabeth Dunster Carteret). In Mr. Cooke's Records, 2d Church, Cambridge, are these entries: "Carteret, Pegg, woman servant of Capt. C. died Dec. 10 1757." Also, "Negro

5

Child at Mr. Dunster's died April 2 1750." "Negro boy of Capt. Carteret died April 12 1747 aged 6;" and "Negro Child (girl) of Capt. Carteret died August 15 1753." "Negro child of Mr. Dunster died March 24 1747 aged 7 days." (Honest Mr. Cooke, he wrote in common language, which enthusiasts of this day have intentionally perverted to mean something worse.)

In Bond's History of Watertown, p. 754, it is stated Mahitible Dunster was warned out of town, May 15, 1695.   Much pains have been taken to get a full copy of the record, but without success.   We think she was a liberated slave, living at Jonathan Dunster's.

In looking over this faithful record, so often referred to, our eye caught, almost the next entry to our own grandfather's marriage: "Punch servant of Mr. Samuel Brooks of Medford and Rose servant of William Cutler, Cambridge married June 3, 1754." Tracing the baptisms, we found: "Prince son of Rose Cutler slave b. June 10, bap. June 12 1762;" and further on, "Experience a Mulatto brought by Geo Cutter bap. Nov. 23 1783 by Rev. Mr. Marrett."

One of these unfortunates has made his mark in history.   He was probably the son of Jack and Peggy.   S. A. Drake, (*Historic Fields and Mansions of Middlesex, p.* 358,) after graphically describing the march of Gage's troops from Boston towards Lexington, says: "It is a tradition in Arlington that the first person to give the alarm here was Cuff Cartwright, a negro slave who lived at his master's on the road not far from the pond.   An officer gave the black a dollar to silence him, but as soon as the detachment had passed, Cuffee struck across the fields, and roused the neighborhood."   William R. Cutter writes: "Cuffee Cartwright, colored, (a corruption of 'Carteret') died in West Cambridge, Jan. 25, 1826, aged 77."   "A noted character, and a servant of Revolutionary officers.   He distinguished himself in an exploit at the time of the march to Lexington.   Old Cuff was a great story-teller, and many in Arlington now remember him.   A fuller relation of him can be had among my acquaintances.   He was the last representative, I believe, of the Carteret family in Arlington."

6

How different was the thoughtful and Christ-like action of this good woman from the tumultuous scenes we have just passed through. It seems to us that in God's plan of "development," irresponsible *national* "glorious victories" are only *accountable individual* "struggles for existence." In this struggle, some have survived to exhibit traits learned there, at which they would have shuddered before. Others, boasting of their reckless daring, strive to keep the enmity alive. Many, ponder on the cost, misery and unfathomable mystery of "God's strange work," as war is sometimes called; and a fearful number have fallen, among whom we can count nineteen killed or wounded of our own blood or marital relations. We never intended to say a word on this painful subject—"It slipped out itself."

6. HENRY³ DUNSTER (*Jonathan,*² *Henry,*¹) was born in Cambridge, July 17, 1680. He "owned the covenant and was baptized Feb. 1, 1707–8." From this, it appears that Jonathan Dunster, his father, like President D., neglected to bring his children to the ordinance of baptism. He married Feb. 25, 1707–8, Martha Russell, who had owned the covenant and was baptized Feb. 13, about two weeks before their marriage. They were both admitted to full communion in the First Church, Cambridge, March 11th or 16th, 1710–11. They were both constituent members of the Second Church in Cambridge, now the First Congregational Church in Arlington. To the first pastor of this church, Rev. Samuel Cooke, he gave wood gratis for seven years. He resided on what was then known as Menotomy Field, or more recently as Charlestown Neck, now Arlington. "No vestige of the Dunster residence alluded to remains save the site, which for thirty years and over has been vacant as far as any dwelling or household structure is concerned. It is at this day one of the most sightly, eligible situations for a mansion in the section. Its present pecuniary value could not readily be estimated. A large and thriving village of new houses, with uncommon railroad facilities, is rising around it." (W. R. C.) The division of the paternal estate, and the dissatisfaction of

6

Henry at the valuation of 16s. per acre for this land, has
been alluded to in the settlement of Jonathan Dunster's
estate.   Perhaps this discontent was, in some measure,
owing to the fact that no part of the large landed estate
of Elizabeth Thomas, his aunt, was given to him, but
all of it to his half brothers and sisters.   On the fifth
day of October, "Annoqᵉ Domini" 1744, "Jason Russell," (and his wife, Elizabeth Russell,) "of Cambridge
in the county of Middˣ in his Majesties Province of the
Massachusetts Bay, in New England, yeoman—For and
in consideration of the sum of Two Hundred Pounds in
Bills of Credet in the old Tenor" gave a deed (now in
the writer's possession) to "Henry Dunster of Cambridge aforesd yeoman" "of one certain Piece or Parcel
of land situate in Cambridge aforesaid Containing twelve
acres be it more or less Bounded northeasterly on Charlestown Road Easterly on yᵉ said Dunster's Land partly,
and partly on Land Belonging to ᴹʳ· James Smith south-
westerly on Concord Road and northwesterly on Land of
Jason Winshipp's, reserving the buildings Standing on
the Premises to my own use and the Liberty of taking
of the Same at any time when I shall See Cause."

In the writer's possession, handed down in the family,
on a paper measuring ten by seven inches, and containing sixty lines in the plain handwriting of Rev. Samuel
Cooke, is the following will:

"In the name of God. Amen! I Henry Dunster of
Cambridge in yᵉ county of Middlesex and Province of
yᵉ Massachusetts Bay in New England, Husbandman:
Being Weak in Body, but of perfect mind & memory
blessed be God therefor, and not knowing how soon it
May please God to call me away by Death: Do make &
Ordain This My Last Will & Testament: That is to say
principally & in yᵉ first place I Give and Recommend my
Soul into yᵉ hands of God who gave it and my Body I
recommend to yᵉ Earth to be Buried in a decent Christian Manner at yᵉ discretion of my Executors. Hoping
in the mercy of God thro yᵉ merits of Christ to receive
yᵉ same made like unto Christ's Glorious Body at the
General Resurection. And as touching my Worldly Es-

6

tate wherewith it has pleased God to Bless me in this Life, I Give Demise and Dispose of the same in manner & form as follows (viz)

Imprimis. I give & Bequeath to Martha My Beloved Wife the use & Improvement of ye one half of all my real Estate during her Natural Life and also ye improvement of ye one half of my Dwelling House & Barn Likewise ye improvement of ye one half of my stock of Cattle, Horses, Sheep &c also the use of ye one half of my Carts Ploughs & certain Tackling or any other tools or Implements belonging to Husbandry. I likewise Give to my s^d Wife ye use & improvement of the whole of my Household Stuff as Beding, Pewter, Brass, Iron, Chairs, Linning &c during her Natural Life, as also ye use of my clock and ye whole service & improvement of my Negro Woman Nancy During my sd wife's Life.

Item. I give and Bequeath to My Beloved Son Jason Dunster to him and his heirs forever all my Lands Messuages & tenements together with all my Just Debts, Stock and movable effects of every kind not heretofore disposed of or not hereafter mentioned in this my last Will & Testament. He allowing his mother, my sd wife ye Improvement as above mentioned and paying ye following Legacies herein Mentioned and also all my Just Debts & funeral expenses.

Item. I give to my beloved son Isaiah Dunster (besides what I have done for Him in Giving Him a Liberal Education) the Sum of Two Hundred Pounds in Bills of y^e old Tenor so called or what shall be in value equal at y^e time of Payment to what sd old Tenor Bills now pass for, to be paid within the space of three years after y^e decease of my sd wife Martha Also my Silver Tankard marked _H^D_M to be delivered to him Upon My sd Wife's decease.

Item. I give to my Beloved Son Henry Dunster besides What I have already Given to Him my Large Copper Kettle to be delivered to Him upon y^e decease of my sd wife.

Item. I give to my Beloved Daughter Martha Dickson besides what I have already given to her the sum of one hundred and fifty pounds in bills of the old Tenor— or what shall be equal * * *

6

Item.   I give to my Beloved Daughter Mary Marrat besides what I have already given her y° like sum of one hundred and fifty pounds in Bills of y° old Tenor. * *

Item.   I give to my Beloved Daughter Abigail Cutler besides what she has already received the sum of One Hundred & fifty pounds in Bills of the Old Tenor or what * * * y° above sums or Legacies to be paid to the persons above named or their heirs within three years after y° decease of my sd wife Martha.

Also I give & Bequeath to my D. Daughter Abigail & Her Heirs forever a certain tract of Land containing one acre more or less Lying in Cambridge second precinct bounded Northerly on Concord Road Easterly on the Winshipp's Pasture, on y° other sides on my Land as y° wall now stands She maintaining the whole of y° fence adjoining my Land.   Furthermore I Give & Bequeath to my above named Beloved Son Jason Dunster my above sd negro woman Nancy to him & his heirs after my sd wife's decease and also y° whole of that part of the Stock, Team Tackling &c which I have Given my Wife for improvement during her life and Likewise what shall remain of y° House hold Stuff not already disposed of by me and which my sd wife shall not dispose of in her lifetime He paying y° Legacies & debts as above.   I do likewise Hereby constitute & appoint my Beloved Wife Martha & my Beloved Son Jason Dunster to be executors of this my last Will and Testament Hereby revoking all former Wills * * *

I do hereunto set my hand & seal this eighth day of October Annoq¹ Dom. one thousand seven Hundred and forty eight—and in the twenty Second year of y° reign of George y° Second of Great Britain y° King &c.

Signed Sealed Published, pronounced & Declared by y° sd Henry Dunster to be His Last Will and Testament in presence of us   HENRY DUNSTER." [seal]
         the subscribers

HUBERT RUSSELL
         His
WALTER X RUSSELL
         mark
SAML COOKE.

6

HENRY[3] DUNSTER died at Cambridge (now Arlington), Jan. 28, 1753, as appears from the record in his son Jason's Bible (now in my possession), written by Rev. Samuel Cooke, his pastor, as follows:

> "MR. HENRY DUNSTER
> Dyed Jan[r] 28, 1753 Æt. 73
> be ye also ready for
> at such an hour as ye
> think not of the Son
> of Man Cometh."

The following copy of inscription is taken from the original stone (slate) now standing in a group of graves around a venerable apple tree, near the horizontal slab of the Rev. Samuel Cooke, in the centre of Cambridge second precinct burying yard, now the old cemetery in Arlington:

"Here Lyes Buried the Body of Mr. Henry Dunster who Departed this Life Jan[r] 28 Anno Dom[1] 1753, in the 73rd year of His Age. 'Therefore be ye also ready for in such an Hour as you think not ye Son of Man Cometh.'"

In the same group of graves are buried Mrs. Elizabeth Dunster DeCarteret and her husband, with several of their children. The stones are such as would be erected over persons of family and substance at the time of their erection.

His wife, Martha (Russell), survived him, and married Francis Locke (his 2d wife), March 15, 1759. "She was the daughter of Joseph Russell, who married Mary Belcher, June 23, 1662, and was born July 26, 1691, at Cambridge. Francis Locke, his first wife Elizabeth, and his daughter Elizabeth, were original members of the church in West Cambridge [Arlington], which was founded 1739." (*Book of the Lockes, p.* 24.)

In the "*Cutter Family of New England*" it is stated, p. 380, that "the mother of Jason Dunster [son of Henry] was Martha Russell, daughter of Jason and Mary (Hubbard) Russel, of Cambridge, and born May 2, 1691." The Cutter record is correct. She, Martha

6

(Russel Dunster) Locke, died of the palsy, in Menotomy, June 27, 1771, aged 81 years. (*Dr. B. Cutter's MSS.*)

In the Middlesex probate office is a bond of Martha Dunster, widow, Jason Dunster, Edward Dixon, and Joseph Belknap, to perform the duties of executors to the estate of Henry Dunster, late of Cambridge.

HENRY³ DUNSTER had eleven children by his wife, Martha (Russell):

9 §. i. MARTHA⁴ DUNSTER, b. Feb. 7, bap. Feb. 13, 1708-9, m. Edward Dickson, March 18, 1730-31.

10 §. ii. MARY⁴ DUNSTER, b. July ye 8, bap. July 13, 1712, m. Amos Marrett.

11 §. iii. ABIGAIL⁴ DUNSTER, b. March 18, 1714, bap. March 21, 1713-14, m. James Cutter, Jr.

iv. ELIZABETH⁴ DUNSTER, b. July ye 7, 1716, died Nov. 7, 1716. She was one of the grand-children [It should have been *great* grand-children] referred to in Chaplin's Life of Henry Dunster, page 227. She was buried in Old Cambridge, near President D. The inscription on her head-stone is still plain and distinct, and reads:

> "ELIZABETH DUNSTER,
> Daughter of Henry
> &   Martha Dunster
> aged 4 months.
> Died novemb^er 7 1716."

12 §. v. ISAIAH⁴ DUNSTER, born Oct. 21, 1720, m. first, Hannah Dennis, May 26, 1750, second, Mary Smith, Nov. 13, 1766.

vi. HENRY⁴ DUNSTER, born Feb. 13, bap. Feb. 17, 1722-3. He married April 27, 1748, Abigail Moor. He is mentioned in his father's will of Oct. 21 (?), 1748, as lately deceased. By this, it appears that his father made another will a few days after the one copied on a preceding page. He died Oct. 13, 1748, childless. His wife, Abigail (Moor), had a daughter, March 4, 1749, who lived one-quarter of an hour. (*Rev. S. Cooke's Record.*) He was buried at Arlington. The inscription on his grave stone is:

6

" Here lyes Buried ye Body of Mr. Henry Dunster Junr who Departed this Life October 13, Anno Dom^l 1748 aged 25 years & 8 m^oth."

His widow, then Abigail Harrington, was dismissed from the 2d Church Sept. 15, 1751, to the church in Lexington. She was married to Jonathan Harrington, Aug. 1, 1750, by whom she had eight children, the fourth of whom was Jonathan, who was the last survivor of the battle of Lexington, and to whom she said, on that eventful morning: "Jonathan, get up, the Regulars are coming, and something must be done." She died June 30, 1776. (*Hist. Lexington, Gen. Reg.*, *pp.* 91, 94.)

In the probate records at East Cambridge, the will of *Henry*[4] Dunster, Jr., is recorded, as is also an inventory of his estate, in which is mentioned a beaver hat valued £8 0s. 0d.; a "new wigg" valued £4 0s. 0d.; an "old wigg" valued at £0 10s. 0d.; a fine linen Shirt valued £3 0s. 0d.; a new full trimmed blue Coat valued at £16 0s. 0d.; a pair of leathern Breeches valued at £9 0s. 0d.; a "fustin" Coat valued at £6 0s. 0d.; a blue Jacket valued at £4 0s. 0d.; a "streight" bodied Coat valued at £4 0s. 0d.; a stuff Jacket valued at £3 10s. 0d.

At the time of his death he owned about fifty acres of land in what is now Arlington, which appears to have been sold by his widow to his brothers and sisters. The deed, a copy of which, written by Mr. Cooke, was found among Rev. Isaiah Dunster's papers, is sketched as follows :

" 'To All People to whom these Presents Shall Come Greeting Know Ye That I Abigail Dunster of Cambridge in ye County of Middlesex in ye Province of ye Massachusetts Bay in New England Relict Widow of Mr. Henry Dunster Junr of Cambridge aforesaid Deceased For Divers Good Causes, & Considerations —— Me thereunto Moving But More Especially For & in Consideration of ye Sum of Twelve Hundred & thirty pounds in Good & Passable Bills of Credit of ye Old Tenor to me in hand well & truly paid by Mr. Isaiah Dunster of Harwich in ye county of Barnstable in ye province aforesd Clerk and Jason Dunster Edward Dick-

6

son and James Cutler Jun' all of Cambridge aforesd
Husbandmen and Also in consideration of certain Privi-
liges* & Improvements on ye Estate of my Husband
Decesed by me still to be enjoyed Have Given ———— ————
———— unto the said Isaiah Dunster Jason Dunster Edward
Dickson & James Cutler Jun'. their Heirs & Assigns
forever equally as tenants in common all the Right Title
Interest, Claim Challenge & Demand whatsoever which
I ye sd Abigail Dunster have had or Ought to have (in
& unto ye estate both Real & Personal where of my late
husband Henry Dunster Jun' Died Seized and Possessed)
by virtue of marriage or by any other ways—means
whatsoever.

The Sd estate consisting of about forty acres in the
Homstead with one Dwelling House and a Barn Standing on ye Same   Also about Ten Acres of Pasture Land
on the South easterly side of ye Road over· against sd
Homstead   To Have & to Hold all ye above sd Estate
* * * * *   unto them ye sd Isaiah Dunster Jason
Dunster Edward Dickson & James Cutler their Heirs &
Assigns forever To their only proper use benefit & behoof
forevermore * * * * *   shall & may from time to
time and at all times forever hereafter by force & Virtue
of these presents Lawfully Peaceably & Quietly Have
Hold Use Improve Occupy Possess & Enjoy ye above
Remised & Released Premises without the Lawful Lett
Suit Denyall Contradiction or Expulsion of me ye sd
Abigail Dunster * * *

In Witness Whereof·I ye sd Abigail Dunster have
hereunto set my hand & Seal This Twentieth Day of
December In ye Twenty Third year of his Maj.ᵗʸˢ Reign:
Anno Domini One thousand seven hundred & forty nine.
Signed Sealed & Delivered   ABIGAIL DUNSTER [seal]
      in presence of us
CHARLES MOOR
AARON CUTTER   *Vera Copia.* Attsᵗ SAM'L COOKE.

---

* It is probable that the "certain privileges and improvements" on the estate of Henry Dunster, Jr., "by me still to be
enjoyed," gave rise to the repeated lawsuits between the Dunsters
and Jonathan Harrington, who married the widow of Henry D.
Fragments of the writs are still in the family, by which it appears
that Harrington recovered ninety pounds.

7

MIDDLESEX ss.   Dec 22 1749

Then The Within Named Abigail Dunster appeard &
acknowledged ye within written Instrument to be Her
free Act & Deed before me

WILLIAM LAWRENCE J. PACIS."

On the copy of this deed is the mark of the nails in
the heel of a boot, made probably to *identify* the paper.
Such an act was common in "old times."

vii. ELIZABETH⁴ DUNSTER, b. May 9, bap. May 10,
1724, d. June 27, 172 , [last figure gone.]

13 §. viii. JASON⁴ DUNSTER, b. July 24, 1725, N.
S., bap. July 18, 1725. (For this discrepancy, see note
to Rev. Isaiah Dunster on a subsequent page.) He married Rebecca Cutter Nov. 6, 1749, and died in Mason,
N. H., Feb. 19, 1805.

ix. EUNICE⁴ DUNSTER, born May 21, bap. May 26,
1728, died July 11, same year.

x. JONATHAN⁴ DUNSTER, b. May 27, bap. June 1,
1729, died July 9, same year.

xi. RUTH⁴ DUNSTER, b. Oct. 1, bap. Oct. 7, 1733,
died June 30, 1735. She was the other child referred
to by Chaplin as one of the *grand*-children. Her grave
stone is close to President Dunster's, and is inscribed:

            RUTH DUNSTER,
            Daugᵗʳ of Mr. Henry
    &   Mrs. Martha
            Dunster, Died
            June 30 1735   Ageᵈ
            1 year & 9 months.

7. iv. ELIZABETH³ (DUNSTER) CARTERET (*Jonathan,*² *Henry,*¹) was born about 1699, not Feb. 22,
1681–2, as stated in Life H. D., p. 237, that Elizabeth
died young. She was married Nov. 16, 1727, to Capt.
Philip Carteret, or DeCarteret, a mariner, of Boston.
The record of their marriage in Charlestown is: " Philip
Cartwright of Boston & Elizabeth Dunster of this town
were joyned in marriage by the Reverend Mr. Simon
Bradstreet, November 16, 1727." She was admitted to

*5

7

full communion in Medford Church April 21, 1728, and dismissed to Menotomy Church Sept. 1, 1739. They lived in Charlestown, but the place was called Cambridge Precinct, and is now Arlington. He was master of a vessel sailing from Boston, and was probably born about 1703, in France, as the name would imply. He owned landed property to considerable extent in the vicinity of Cambridge. When absent on voyages his wife signed his name to all necessary papers, as appears by public records. She was evidently a woman of more than ordinary executive ability, and made a prominent impression on her relatives. Every branch of the Dunster family, within our knowledge, has retained a memory of "Aunt Carteret," or, as most of them call her, "Aunt Cartwright."

In 1857, Edward S. Dunster, then a student in Harvard College, visited Westminster and Gardner, Mass., to obtain information of the "Dunster Descendants."

Mrs. Precilla (Dunster) Estabrook, then 70 years old, (a notice of whom will appear farther on,) told him, with other traditions which may be referred to in other pages, and which he copied verbatim: "I used to hear much talk about Aunt Cartwright, sister of my grandfather. She lived in Notomy. When the Regulars were in Boston, she took her silver and hid it in the ash heap; her money she sewed up in a leather apron and threw it into the well. My grandmother often used to talk about Aunt Cartwright, and used to tell the story of President Dunster's laying the Devil."

Capt. Carteret died at Arlington, and the inscription on his grave stone in the Dunster group is: "Here Lyes Buried the Body of Capt. Philip DeCarteret, who departed this Life April 19, 1767. Aged 64 years." She survived him twenty years, and managed the property, which was large, during her life. She, also, was buried in Arlington, and the inscription is: "Erected to the memory of Mrs. Elizabeth DeCarteret widow of Capt. Philip DeCarteret who Died Jany. 25 1787 in the 88 year of her age." She was one of the original members of Cambridge Second Church, organized Sept. 9, 1739.

7

The children of Capt. P. Carteret and Elizabeth³ (Dunster) Carteret were:

i. MARY⁴ CARTERET, born 1730, died Nov. 17, 1751, aged 21 years.

ii. RUTH⁴ CARTERET, born 1736, died June 2, 1754, aged 18 years.

iii. ELIZABETH⁴ CARTERET, born 1737, died June 8, 1751, aged 14 years.

iv. ABIGAIL⁴ CARTERET, born about 1739 or 1740, married Oct. 12, 1758, William Whittemore, who was the son of Samuel* and Elizabeth (Spring) Whittemore. He graduated at Harvard College, 1755, was admitted "full communion to Menotomy Church Oct. 26, 1755." Abigail, his wife, was admitted to the same church July 29, 1781. She died Aug. 27, 1809, aged 70 years. He died in West Cambridge, March 17, 1818, aged 86 years.

* Samuel Whittemore, the father of William Whittemore, (H. C., 1755,) died at Menotomy, Feb. 2, 1793. "When the British troops marched to Lexington he was 81 years old, and one of the first on the parade. He was armed with a gun (*King's Arm*) and horse pistols. After an animated exhortation to the collected militia to the exertion of bravery and courage, he exclaimed, ' If I can only be instrumental of killing one of my country's foes, I shall die in peace.' The prayer of this venerable old man was heard, for on the return of the troops from Lexington he lay behind a stone wall and discharged his gun. A soldier immediately fell. He then discharged his pistol and killed another, at which instant a ball struck his face and shot away part of his cheek bone, on which *a number of soldiers* ran up to the wall and gorged their malice on his wounded head. They were heard to exclaim, ' We have killed the old man.' About four hours after, he was found in a mangled situation His head was covered with blood from the wounds of the bayonet, which were six or eight, but, providentially, none penetrated so far as to destroy him. His hat and clothes were *shot* through in many places, yet he survived to see the complete overthrow of his enemies and his country enjoy all the blessings of peace and independence. His funeral will be to-morrow at four o'clock, P. M., from his house at Menotomy, which his relations and friends are requested to attend." (*Columbian Centinel, Feb.* 6, 1793.)

" This old gentleman was posted in the rear of the house of Hon. James Russell, in West Cambridge, on the road to Woburn, awaiting the return of the enemy from Lexington. On discovering the flank guard (five in number) approaching, a friend who was with him deserted him, but *he* refused to run, saying, ' I am

7

Rev. L. R. Paige, referring to the Cambridge records then in his hand, said the children of Abigail (Carteret) and William Whittemore, A. M., were:

1. ELIZABETH[5] CARTERET WHITTEMORE, b. April 4, 1763, bap. at West Cambridge April 10, 1763. She died Nov. 8, 1763, aged 7 months.

2. ELIZABETH[5] CARTERET WHITTEMORE, b. Oct. 6, bap. Oct. 7, 1764. She married first, Moses Robbins, and second, John Frost, Nov. 9, 1802, published Aug. 14, 1802. Frost's first wife died March 18, 1802. She died May 1, 1813, aged 49 years. She was, probably, also the mother of William Whittemore Frost, who was baptized Nov. 20, 1803, of whom there is no other record. (*Cutter Family, p.* 46.)

3. PHILIP[5] CARTERET WHITTEMORE, b. Sept. 1, bap. Sept. 7, 1766, married Lydia Phelps.

4. WILLIAM[5] WHITTEMORE, b. Jan. 28, bap. Jan. 29, 1769, d. July 3, 1771, aged 2 years, 5 mos. 6 days.

5. WILLIAM[5] WHITTEMORE, b. June 30, bap. July 5, 1772, married Feb. 2, 1796, Anna Cutter, daughter of Samuel and Rebecca (Hill) Cutter, of Menotomy. She was born June 19, 1771. She was baptized, no doubt, on a profession of faith Nov. 24, 1799, at Second Church in Cambridge. At the same time, her husband owned the covenant, and their first child, Ann, was baptized. He was a farmer, residing on his wife's father's homestead, and died in Chelsea, Mass., Oct. 17, 1854. She died Oct. 27, 1849. Had seven children:

(i) ANN[6] WHITTEMORE, b. Oct. 21, bap. at Menotomy, Nov. 24, 1799. She married May 26, 1822, (May

eighty years old and I will not leave, for I am willing to die if I can kill one British red coat.' On the nearer approach of the 'guard' he shot one with his gun and another with his pistol, and while raising his second pistol he received a wound in his face * * * He was taken to the hospital (Cooper's Tavern) on the corner of Medford road, in West Cambridge. Surgeons Welch and Spring dressed his wounds (one shot wound and thirteen bayonet wounds). He was born July 27, 1696, and his tomb stone, now in the burying ground in West Cambridge, has the following inscription, viz.: 'In Memory of Capt. Samuel Whittemore who departed this life Feb. 2 1793 Aged 98 years.' "
(*See Hist. Cutter Family*, N. E., *Supplement p.* 390.)

7

22, *Hist. Lexington*) Samuel Adams, born in West Cambridge, Sept. 28, 1790. They removed to Lexington in 1827. He died Sept. 16, 1866. She died May 14, 1862. They had four children:

(1) ANNAS[7] ADAMS, b. June 5, 1823. She married April 2, 1867, John Beals.

(2) W. FRANK[7] ADAMS, b. April 16, 1829, married Emma C. Balles, of New Jersey.

(3) ROBINSON[7] ADAMS, b. Nov. 24, 1832, went to New York, died 1866.

(4) GEORGIA[7] ADAMS, b. June 6, 1839, m. May 10, 1857, Albert Griffith, of West Cambridge. She died May, 1859. (*Hist. Lexington.*)

(ii) ELEANOR[6] WHITTEMORE, b. June 25, 1801, died Oct. 5, 1805.

(iii) WILLIAM AUGUSTUS[6] WHITTEMORE, b. Nov. 30, 1804, married Abigail C. Tuffts, Jan. 8, 1838. He died in Arlington, April 24, 1867. He resided on his father's homestead. She is living in Arlington, and has six children:

(1) WILLIAM AUGUSTUS[7] WHITTEMORE, b. —, unm.

(2) ABBIE I.[7] WHITTEMORE, b. ——, married Simeon Barker, of Arlington. They have a daughter, Emma Gertrude[8] Barker.

(3) EPHRAIM T.[7] WHITTEMORE, b. ——, unmarried.

(4) BENJAMIN F.[7] WHITTEMORE, b. ——, unmarried.

(5) LIZZIE[7] WHITTEMORE, b. ——, m. Clarence F. Hobbs, of Arlington. They have a daughter, Laura E.[8] Hobbs, b. ——.

(6) GEORGE HENRY[7] WHITTEMORE, b. ——, unm.

(iv) SUSAN FRANCES[6] WHITTEMORE, born May 11, 1807, m. Pascal Sprague, of West Cambridge, April 15, 1832, and died Jan. 17, 1850. They had four children:

(1) GEORGE[7] SPRAGUE, b. ——, m. ——, and died without issue.

(2) HARRIET A.[7] SPRAGUE, b. ——, married George Going, of Boston. They have four children, whose names have not been obtained.

(3) JOHN[7] SPRAGUE, b. ——, now in California.

7

(4) MARY ELLA[7] SPRAGUE, dead. Possibly, others died young.

(v) ELEANOR SOPHIA[6] WHITTEMORE, born Nov. 24, 1809, married John P. Daniels, Oct. 18, 1832, died in Arlington, Dec. 25, 1868. They had children:

(1) ELLEN S.[7] DANIELS, b. ——, m. Edwin Robbins, and had Frank,[8] Henry Parker,[8] Nellie,[8] and Nathan[8] Robbins.

(2) JOHN P.[7] DANIELS, b. ——, m. Sarah Hanson. Have two children.

(3) HARRIET[7] DANIELS, b. ——, unmarried.

(4) SARAH A.[7] DANIELS, b. ——, m. Albert Winn, Jr., of Arlington. They had two children, both died young. The other children of John P. and Eleanor Sophia (Sprague) Daniels died young.

(vi) GEORGE WASHINGTON[6] WHITTEMORE, b. May 5, 1812, m. Cynthia Richardson, and died July 17, 1870. He was proprietor of Wilde's Hotel, Elm street, Boston. Their children were:

(1) GEORGE HENRY[7] WHITTEMORE, b. ——, unm.

(2) FRANK[7] WHITTEMORE, born ——, married, and believed to have two children.

(3) HELEN[7] WHITTEMORE, b.—, unm., and deceased.

(4) FLORENCE[7] WHITTEMORE, b. ——, m. a clergyman, and died within a few days (Dec., 1875).

(5) FRED[7] WHITTEMORE.

(6) WILLIE[7] WHITTEMORE.

(vii) THOMAS[7] WHITTEMORE, b. May 9, 1815, married Clara Richardson, of Fitchburg, Mass., July 27, 1837, resides at Chelsea, and have two children:

(1) THOMAS[6] WHITTEMORE, b. ——, married Abbie Clark, and have two children:

(i) LILLIE[8] WHITTEMORE.

(ii) CORA[8] WHITTEMORE.

(2) CLARA[7] WHITTEMORE, b. ——, m. William W. Viles. No children.

6. ABIGAIL[5] WHITTEMORE, b. Aug. 16, bap. Aug.

8

18, 1776, married John Davenport, both of Cambridge. Presumed, says Mr. Paige, to be the keeper of the Davenport Tavern.

8. vii. DAVID³ DUNSTER (*Jonathan,*² *Henry,*¹) was the seventh and youngest child of Jonathan² and Deborah (Wade) Dunster, and was born in Charlestown about 1706. He was a "Minor" "in the twentyeth year of age" when his father died in 1726. Joseph Hartwell was appointed his guardian. His bond is recorded in Middlesex probate office. In some documents he is called a tanner. He married, about 1730, Mary, daughter of Hubbard and Elizabeth (Dickson) Russell. She was baptized Dec. 14, 1712, and was admitted full communion Sept. 6, 1741, to the Second Church in Cambridge (Mr. Cooke's). Her husband, David,³ was admitted full communion June 13, 1742. He had "owned the covenant" previously. They were "regularly dismissed" from that church "Oct. 17, 1742, to be imbodyed in a church to be gathered at Narraganset No. 2, so called." (*Rev. Mr. Cooke.*) Mary (Russell), wife of David³ Dunster, was a niece of Martha Russell, the wife of Henry³ Dunster.

[Jonathan, Thomas, David, Elizabeth and Dorothy, all children of Jonathan² and Deborah (Wade) Dunster, "owned the covenant," and were baptized in Cambridge First Church, April 14, 1723.]

At the settlement of his father's estate, before referred to, he came into possession of large landed property in Cambridge Precinct, then called Menotomy Field, afterwards West Cambridge, now Arlington.

"In 1646 the Inhabitants of Charlestown granted to Henry Dunster Prest. of the college and his heirs & assigns Wenatomie or Menatomy bounded with Cambridge bounds on one side, Misticke pond & River and Menotomy brook being the bounds of said field on the other side." This tract seems to have comprised the greater part of that interesting section now in Arlington limits, known even till quite lately as Charlestown End, and from its shape was vulgarly y'cleped by fellows of the baser sort as "Squash End." Here, at the head, was the cele-

8

brated Square Sachem Reservation, under the shadow of high hills, whence is now obtained a wonderful view of the surrounding territory.   The mansion house of David Dunster, sold to Joseph Winship, which was torn down in 1798, had a hipped roof, and William R. Cutter, who furnished this sketch, says that it is well remembered by his present living grand-parents, who could tell how many windows there were, and the number of rooms on each floor.   The house was, they believe, unpainted on the outside, like many at that day.

"David Dunster of Charlestown yeoman by Deed March 12 1742 conveyed for £750 to Joseph Winship the younger of Cambridge yeoman the home place north west of the road with the house and barn namely 18 acres of Land in Charlestown bounded E. and N. E. by Medford river and pond N. W. and N. E. on Simon Holden's land W. by a 'drift-way' leading to said Holden's land, South on land of Jonathan Dunster there being a road leading from Medford over the 'wairs' to Menotomy running through said Messuage and understood to be excepted in this deed and also 3 acres of Salt marsh in Medford bounded east on Solomon Page's * Marsh S. on Medford River N. on Ebenezer Cutter's and W. on John Willis marsh, with a dwelling house & barn on the abovesaid 18 acres or homestead.

 Witness   (Signed) DAVID DUNSTER
PHILIP CARTERET   MARY DUNSTER
JONATHAN ROBINSON "

Again, "David Dunster of Narragansett township No. 2 so called in the county of Worcester yeoman for £250 in good bills of the old Tenor conveyed Nov. 18 1742 to Joseph Winship of Charlestown Middlesex county yeoman 11¼ acres of Land in Charlestown bounded N. E. by land of Joseph Winship N. W. on a highway leading to Medford S. W. on a two rod Roadway joining to Geo. Cutter land and S. E. by George Cutter's land and East by Medford River.   Dunster's wife's name Mary.   Signed by him only.   Ephraim Frost and John Cutter witnesses.   Eben Trowbridge Just. Peace."

 * This was the Solomon Page who married his sister.

8

"At a meeting of the proprietors of Narragansett No 2 at the house of Mr. Ebenezer Stedman in Cambridge Dec. 2d 1741 in the division of Upland David Dunster drew a lot No 10 Home lot." In a second division of upland he had the same number of the lots, and also the same in a division of meadow lots.

"At a meeting of the proprietors of Narragansett No. 2 held at the house of Mr. Ebenezer Stedman in Cambridge 1st September 1742 —— —— voted and accepted the Acre of land given by Mr. Dunster for a burying place and chose Mr. Holden, Mr. More, Mr. Hoar, Mr. Bemas, Miller & Bigalow a committee to stake it out and take a deed of Mr. Dunster for the same." (*Westminster Town Records.*)

Mrs. Priscilla[5] (Dunster) Estabrook, to whom reference is made in Elizabeth[3] (Dunster) Carteret, related: " My Grandfather, David, was not a son of President D; of this I am positive.* My Grandfather, David, was the third settler in this town [Westminster]. He had a garrison house near where the Baptist Meeting House now stands." At one time he was directed to put his garrison house in better condition for defence.

The quantity of land in Narragansett No. 2, drawn by David Dunster, must have been large, for Jan. 14, 1744, he sold two lots, of sixty acres each, to William Brattle for 25 pounds lawful money, which "I drew myself upon the tenth lot which I purchased of Wm. Wallace of Medford." There are also four deeds of parts of this tenth lot recorded.

In 1758 he made a will, of which the following is a sketch:

"In the name of God Amen this nineteenth day of May One thousand seven hundred and fifty eight * * * I David Dunster of a place called Nargansett Township No 2 in the county of Worcester * * Husbandman

1st I give and recommend my Soul into the Hands of God that gave it and my body into the Earth * * *

* In the family records of some of the Westminster Dunster's, *Jonathan*[2] had been omitted, making *David*[3] the son of *Henry.*[1] In this Mrs. Estabrook was right.

6

8

nothing doubting I shall receive the same again at the Resurrection by the mighty power of God.

Imprimis. I give unto Mary my beloved wife and unto Hubbard and Thomas my two oldest sons all my real and personal estate and all my utensils for husbandry—goods with claims * * * to my wife whom I constitute and appoint executrix with my oldest son Hubbard, To my wife I say I give and bequeath my house and all my lands during her continuance of my widow —— but if she see cause to marry again to acquit her right to all my Estate.

Item. To Hubbard ⅔ of my real & personal estate after my wife has done with it. To Thomas ⅓ do. To Elizabeth Taylor wife of James Taylor my eldest daughter —— £2 10s. over and above what she has already had and besides what I did for her in her sickness. To Mary Bemis wife of David Bemis my 2nd daughter besides what she had at her setting out and what she had in cash of me I bequeath her 10 shillings.

To Marguary Dunster my third daughter I give & bequeath four pounds.

To Ruhamah my fourth daughter I give and bequeath four pounds.

To Carteret Henry Dunster my youngest son when one and twenty —— Fifty Pounds—to be paid ⅔ by Hubbard and ⅓ by Thomas and I further order that he shall live with his mother and Hubbard till 21 —— —— Hubbard and Thomas to have six years to pay these legacies —— I further add that none of my estate shall be prised [appraised].

Item. To the Rev. Isaiah Dunster of Harwich I give a gold Ring. (Codicil) I give to Marguary & Ruhamah a low chest of Drawers apiece, Three pewter Platters apiece ½ a Doz. Chairs apiece. Recorded Worcester Probate office 4 Oct. 1758."

DAVID[3] DUNSTER died in the summer of 1758.

Mrs. Estabrook says: "My grandfather died in Rutland, in this State,* of the camp disorder. He had gone

---

* Rutland, "*in this State.*" This error was the result of confounding two different events. The prisoners at Rutland, Mass., were British, captured with Burgoyne in 1777.

9

to see his son Thomas, my father, who was a soldier in
the war, and was sick at Rutland with the same disease.
My father got well, but grandfather died." In a subsequent letter her daughter, Miss Betsey Estabrook, states
that her mother says: "He died in Rutland, at the barracks, where he went to care for his sick son, Thomas,
then about twenty years old, stationed there for the exchange of prisoners of war. He recovered. His father
took the camp disorder and died, and was buried in the
barracks there." This must have been at the disastrous
campaign against Ticonderoga in the French war. That
event took place in July, 1758.

His wife, Mary (Russell) Dunster, died after 1772.
They had seven children:

14 §. i. ELIZABETH⁴ (BETTY), baptized April 25,
1730–1, married James Taylor.

15 §. ii. MARY⁴ (MOLLY), baptized March 4, 1732,
married David Bemis.

16 §. iii. HUBBARD,⁴ born 1735? m. Ruth Bailey.

17 §. iv. THOMAS,⁴ baptized May 8, 1737, married
Lidia Peirce.

18 §. v. MARGARY,⁴ baptized Dec. 23, 1739, married Joshua Wilder.

19 §. vi. RUHAMA,⁴ born ——, m. Dudley Bailey.

20 §. vii. CARTERET⁴ HENRY, b. ——, m. ——.

9. i. MARTHA⁴ DUNSTER (*Henry,³ Jonathan,² Henry,¹*)
was born at Cambridge Feb. 7, bap. Feb. 13, 1708–9, and
was admitted to church Jan. 14, 1727–8. She married
March 18, 1730–31, *Edward Dixon,* or *Dickson* as it was
afterwards written. He was the son of John Dixon,
who married Margary Winship, Cambridge, May 12,
1687. She died Oct. 6, 1734, in her 72d year. He died
March 22, 1737, in his 82d year. John Dixon was son
of William D., who was freeman, 1642, and member of
Cambridge Church. The wife of William was Jane, who
died Dec. 4, 1689, aged 73. On William's grave stone
is inscribed:

"The memory of yᵉ Just is blessed." (*Camb. Epitaphs.*)

He, EDWARD, was baptized Jan. 18, 1702, and admitted member of Cambridge First Church June 30, 1728,

9

about six months after Martha[4] Dunster, and died in
Cambridge, May, 1787, aged 86 years. The date of his
wife's death has been doubted. Following the Cambridge Epitaphs, we placed it, in Life H. D., p. 238, in
1800. It is in the Epitaphs, *Mrs.* "Martha Dixon died
1800." In a will of her husband, dated 1753, her name
is mentioned, but in a will of "*Edward Dixon,*" dated
April 6, 1788, there is no mention of her. The latter
will was that of Edward[5] Dixon, her son, who died *unmarried.* They had seven children, baptized at Cambridge First Church:

i. EDWARD[5] DICKSON, baptized April 2, 1732, died
May 3, 1732, aged 1 month, 2 days. Grave stone in Old
Cambridge burying ground. (*Cambridge Epitaphs.*)

ii. MARTHA[5] DICKSON, born Dec. 8, 1734, bap. Dec.
15, 1734, d. in May, 1788, unmarried. (*Camb. Records.*)

iii. EDWARD[5] DIXON, b. in Cambridge June 7, bap.
June 12, 1737. Edward Dixon died 1825. (*Cambridge
Epitaphs, p.* 162.) This date is probably wrong. Mr.
Paige writes: "He was a harness maker, and died Oct.
30, 1820. *No issue.*"

iv. ELIZABETH[5] DIXON, bap. Nov. 4, 1739. Samuel Cook, Jr., and Elizabeth Dickson were married in
First Precinct, Cambridge, April 26, 1764. She was,
probably, this Elizabeth[5] Dixon. She was living July
4, 1817. No record of children.

v. HENRY[5] DICKSON, bap. Nov. 8, 1741, mar. July
24, 1766, Elizabeth Cox. He "owned the covenant"
May 24, 1767, in order to have his children baptized.
Henry Dickson and Sarah Cooke, daughter of Rev. Samuel Cooke, were married in Cambridge Nov. 15, 1774.
[From this, it appears that his first wife, Elizabeth
(Cox), died, leaving children, as he "owned the covenant" to have them baptized.] She died about 1785,
and afterwards he married Mercy ——. He died Sept.
23, 1815. His widow, Mercy, died Dec. 4, 1815, aged
69 or 70. There was a "widow Sarah Dickson (Henry's)
died of a fever Sept. 30, 1780." (*Cooke.*) She could
not have been the widow of *this* Henry. The three
children of Henry[5] Dickson, one by each wife, were:

9

1. ELIZABETH⁶ DICKSON, born 1767, daughter of Elizabeth (Cox) Dixon. She died March 3, 1800. Unm.

2. EUNICE⁶ COOKE DICKSON, dau. of Sarah (Cooke) Dickson, bap. May 17, 1778, m. Dec. 21, 1806, John Goddard, of Cambridge. She died prior to Feb. 14, 1817. They had:

(i) HANNAH⁷ GODDARD. (ii) CHARLES⁷ HENRY GODDARD. (iii) JOHN⁷ GODDARD.

3. HENRY⁷ DICKSON, son of third wife (Mercy), bap. Feb. 21, 1790. He died before his father.

vi. GILBERT⁵ DICKSON, bap. Nov. 18, 1744, married Martha Varnum.

vii. ISAIAH⁵ DICKSON, born or bap. April 12, 1747, owned the covenant, "in order his children be baptized," Feb. 9, 1777. He married Judæ (Judith) Symms, of Woburn, May 15, 1773. She died in Oct., 1783, and he married July 10, 1788, Sarah Cooper. He died Aug., 1805. His children by Judith (first wife) were:

1. JOHN⁶ ELIOT, bap. Feb. 9, 1777, died 1783.

2. JUDITH,⁶ bap. Nov. 10, 1781, died 1783. Both died in the same year with their mother.

By second wife, Sally Cooper:

3. EDWARD⁶ DICKSON. 4. ANN⁵ COOPER DICKSON. 5. ABIGAIL⁶ DICKSON.

The dates of the births of these children are unknown. They were all living in 1820, and are named in their Uncle Edward's will. Edward appears to have come of age in June, 1814. Both of the daughters were born prior to 1800. Ann⁶ Cooper Dickson is thought to have married William Everett. (H. D. B.) Rev. L. R. Paige thinks Edward⁶ Dickson may have been the one who died at Bedford, Mass., March 23, 1825, aged 33.

These items are "based on researches in the Collections of the late Dr. B. Cutter, by W. R. Cutter," and the "Records of Rev. L. R. Paige."

For the record of vi. Gilbert⁵ we are entirely indebted to Henry Dunster Billings. It is given mostly from his MS., but condensed a little where it could be. The

9

descendants are tabulated to correspond with other families.

vi.   GILBERT[5] DICKSON (*Martha,[4] Henry,[3] Jonathan,[2] Henry,[1]*) was born 1743, (?) and married Dec. 3, 1772, Martha Varnum, born July 12, 1750, daughter of Jonas and Lydia (Boyden) Varnum.   She, Lydia, was daughter of Jonathan and Elizabeth Boyden.   He kept a tavern in Acton, and is styled, "a cooper."   He was worth at one time considerable property.   Later, he owned a house in Cambridge, near the College, where he lived till the close of his life.   He died of lock jaw Sept. 15, 1818.   His wife died June 20, 1800, aged 50 years, from a severe cold, contracted while attending Washington's mock funeral in Cambridge.   They had eight children:

1.   HANNAH[6] DICKSON, b. ——, 1771, mar. Thomas Rundle,* born in England.   He arrived in this country with only fifty cents in money; was a cabinet maker and circular stair builder, said to be the first of that trade in the country.   He died in Boston Jan. 5, 1841, aged 64 years.   He was never naturalized.   His wife, Hannah[6] D., died of old age, while on a visit to her sister (Sally Shedd) in Pepperell.   They were childless.   Lived at 21 Warren, now Washington street, and were both buried at Mount Auburn.

There was a John Dickson, who married Elenor "Runel," in Cambridge, June 30, 1781.   (*Cooke.*)

2.   SALLY[6] DICKSON, (*Gilbert,[5] Martha[4] Dunster,*) b. ——, 1775, m. Joshua Shedd.   She spent most of her time in Pepperell with her Aunt Nutting,** her mother's

---

* A letter from Z. Jamison, of Cambridge, Jan. 31, 1837, to Dr. Martin Dunster, says: "Mr. 'Rundlett' married Hannah Dickson.   He was a carpenter, and lived in Pleasant street, Boston."   The same letter says: "Mrs. Hammond lives also in Boston (or did lately), and kept a milliner's shop in Washington street."   The letter also says: "A near neighbor of mine, a Mrs. Sawin, is a descendant of President Dunster, and lives in the house of Mrs. Monroe (Cambridge)."   We have no knowledge of this Mrs. Sawin.   [S. D.]

**The Nuttings were among the early settlers of Groton, which originally contained Pepperell and other towns.   In the papers of Rev. I. Dunster is an "Indenture of an Apprentice," filled out,

9

sister, who, having considerable property and no children, welcomed those of her niece. She was for many years a member of the Orthodox Church, and a devoted Christian woman, beloved by all who knew her. She died in Pepperell, of heart disease, Sept., 1848, leaving seven children:

(i) SARAH[7] SHEDD, unmarried.

(ii) MARTHA[7] DICKSON SHEDD, married Orris T. Chapin, and had:

(1) THOMAS[8] RUNDLE CHAPIN.
(2) AUGUSTINE[8] C. CHAPIN.

(iii) JOHN[7] SHEDD, m. Ruth Elliot, and had three children: (1) MARY[8] EVELINE SHEDD, who m. —— Wilson. (2) MARTHA[8] ANN SHEDD. (3) Unknown.

(iv) SARAH[7] SHEDD, died unmarried.

(v) JOSHUA[7] SHEDD, mar. and has three children.

(vi) MARY[7] EVELINE SHEDD, mar. Leonard Snow, has one child.

(vii) WILLIAM[7] SHEDD, m. and has five children (?)

apparently, in his hand, and probably left with him for safe keeping. This child was made, by this document, a "servant," for whose *security* and that of another class of unfortunates to their masters, the Constitution of the United States made special provision. It is copied for the benefit of our young friends, with the hope that they will never experience what it is to be "bound out":

"THIS INDENTURE WITNESSETH
That Nehemiah Nutting son of Nathaniel Nutting of Groton in ye County of Middlesex Husbandman of his own free Will and Accord and with the Consent of his Father doth put and bind himself to be an Apprentice unto William Nutting of Groton aforesaid Husbandman to learn the Art Trade or Mystery of an Husbandman and with him the said William Nutting after the Manner of an Aprintice to Dwell and Serve from the Day of the Date herof for and during the full & Just Term of Eleven Years next ensuing and fully to be compleat and ended. During all which said Term the said Aprentice, his said Master honestly and faithfully shall Serve—his secrets keep close—his lawful & reasonable Commands every where gladly Do and Perform—Damage to his said Master he shall not wilfully do—his Masters Goods he shall not waste embezel purloine or lend unto others nor suffer the same to be wasted or purloined but to his power shall forthwith discover and make known the same unto his said

9

3.   PATTY[6] DICKSON (*Gilbert,[5] Martha[4] Dunster,*) was
born Feb. 6, 1778.   She was the only child at home
when her father died.   By arrangement with the other
heirs she kept the house, in which she kept scholar
boarders, and living alone, laid aside enough to carry
her through life.   About 1837 she sold her house, and
lived with her different relations.   Enfeebled by a severe
sickness, she fell the entire length of a flight of stairs,
fracturing her hip, and died in Cambridge, Aug. 6, 1868,
aged 90 years and 6 months.   She was buried at Mount
Auburn.   "One of her most cherished possessions was
the Bible of Henry Dunster, which she rarely permitted
to be moved from her chamber.   It was left to the
writer (H. D. B.), on condition that he should be named

Master.   Taverns or Ale-houses he shall not frequent At Cards,
Dice or any other unlawful Game he shall not play.   Fornication
he shall not commit nor Matrimony contract with any person during the said Term.   From his Masters Service he shall not at any
Time unlawfully absent himself but in all Things as a good, honest and faithful Servant and Apprentice shall bear and behave
himself towards his said Master during the full Term of Eleven
Years commencing as aforesaid.

AND THE SAID William Nutting for himself his heirs &c Doth
Covenant Promise Grant and Agree unto and with the said Apprentice in Manner & Form following THAT IS TO SAY, That
he will teach said Apprentice or cause him to be Taught by the
best Ways and Means that he may or can the Trade Art or Mystery of a Husbandman &c & to Read ye English Bible & to write
a Legible hand (if the said Apprentice be capable to learn) and
will Find and Provide for and unto the said Apprentice good and
sufficient Cloathing, Meat Drink Washing & Lodging both In
Sickness and In Health, fitting for an Apprentice during said
Term and at the End of said Term to dismiss said Apprentice
with two Suits of apparrill for all parts of his body one of which
to be suitable for Lord's Day and other such occasions & to pay
said Apprintice Twenty pounds equill to twenty pounds Old
Tenor of this day [$8.88].   *In Testimony Whereof* The said Par-
ties to these presents Indentures have interchangeably set their
Hands and Seals the twenty sixth Day of November in the
Eighteenth year of the Reign of Our Sovereign Lord George ye
Second by the Grace of GOD King of Great *Britain France* and
Ireland and in the year of Our Lord One Thousand Seven Hun-
dred and Forty Four.

Witness   WILLIAM NUTTING   [L. S.]
JACOB NUTTING.
JOHN SHEPLEY Junr."

9

Henry Dunster, with the hope that he would become a Baptist minister, which hope she was permitted to indulge to the last."

4. JOHN[6] H. DICKSON (*Gilbert,[5] Martha[4] Dunster,*) was born 1781. "He was a cabinet maker, (learned his trade in Maine.) He there became engaged to a young lady; but going to New York city on business, was taken sick with yellow fever, and died Sept. 30, 1805."

5. POLLY[6] DICKSON lived with her Aunt Nutting (on her mother's side) when her sister Sally[2] was married. She married Simon Hosley, by whom she had one child: (i) SIMON[7] HOSLEY. He died young. She removed to Boston, and there married Dr. John Hammond, a widower, of Philadelphia. Dr. Hammond practiced in Watertown, Mass., about three years, and then moved to Watertown, N. Y., where he died, leaving four children: (1) CHARLES,[7] died in infancy. (2) CHARLES[7] E. D. (3) THOMAS[7] RUNDLE. (4) C. M.[7] HAMMOND, a daughter, who married Luther Sanderson.

6. LYDIA[6] VARNUM DICKSON was born Sept., 1789. "She devoted her life to charitable purposes, visiting the poor and needy wherever she could find them. Rigidly Orthodox in her religious belief she never united with a church, looking in vain for one whose spirituality rendered a connection desirable." She died unmarried, at Charlestown, July 30, 1868.

7. GILBERT[6] DICKSON, died in early childhood.

8. ABIGAIL[6] DICKSON, born Sept., 1793. At the age of fourteen or fifteen she went to live with her Aunt Nutting. She was a favorite with her uncle and aunt. She there married her second cousin, Walter Fiske, grand-son of Daniel Fiske and Elizabeth Varnum, and the son of Walter and Phebe (Abbott) Fiske. Mr. and Mrs. Nutting settled their home in Pepperell on this young couple, on condition that they should be cared for by them until death, which was rigidly complied with. Both died in their old homestead. On this homestead, the six children of Walter and Abigail[6] (Dickson) Fiske were born. The family was an unusually happy one. But adversity came, and Mr. Fiske

9

was obliged to sell the old place in 1837. They moved to Cambridge, keeping boarders about a year. Thence to Weld, Maine, taking two of their children, Sarah and Henry, with them. They lived on a farm about three years, then moved to Dedham, Mass. While living there, Mrs. Fiske came to Newton to visit her daughter, Mary Ann[7] Billings, where she died, Aug. 24, 1846. Was buried at Mount Auburn.

The six children of Walter and Abigail[6] (Dickson) Fiske are:

(i) MARY ANN[7] FISKE, born June 6, 1813. When about eleven years old she went to live with her Aunt Hammond, in Boston. Here she married John Edgar Billings, born in Boston, July 10, 1810. They removed to Newton, Mass., about 1844. Here Mr. Billings died, after a long sickness, Feb. 18, 1857, was buried at Mount Auburn. His was the only death which has occurred in the family. Mrs. Billings is in perfect health, her sister (Hannah[7] Maria) and two younger children living with her, and the other three in the immediate vicinity. These five children are:

i. CHARLES[8] EDGAR BILLINGS, (*Mary Ann[7] Fiske, Walter,[6] Gilbert[5] Dickson, Martha[4] Dunster,*) born in Boston, Nov. 12, 1834, entered the employ of Brewer, Stevens & Cushing, druggists, in Boston, when he was fifteen, and continued with them and their successors until 1860. He then entered the firm of J. R. Nichols & Co., manufacturing chemists. Soon after the great fire, Dr. Nichols retired, and he formed a new firm, Billings, Clapp & Co. He was superintendent of Dr. Wellman's Sabbath School, in Newton, for three years, but in consequence of an attack of nervous prostration in May, 1873, he resigned this position, and retired from active business, though his name and interest continue in the firm. He spent about a year traveling in Europe for his health. Since his return, 1874, he has been resting at his home. He has for several years been a director of the Newton National Bank. He married Aug. 7, 1861, Mary Murdock, of Newton. They have three children:

9

(i) MARY[9] NICHOLS BILLINGS, born in Newton, June 4, 1868.

(ii) EDGAR[9] FRANCES BILLINGS, born in Newton, May 4, 1871.

(iii) GEORGE[9] BACON BILLINGS, born in Newton, June 7, 1872.

ii. EDWARD[8] TUCKERMAN BILLINGS, (*John Edgar[7] Fiske[6] Dickson,[5] Martha[4] Dunster,*) the second child of John Edgar and Mary Ann Billings, was born in Boston, Dec. 17, 1838, entered the employ of Brewer, Stevens & Cushing, of Boston, when fifteen years old. Upon the failure of their successors, 1860, he established himself at Newton in the apothecary business, which he still conducts. He married Sept. 1, 1870, Abbie Holland Ewings, of Townshend, Vermont, and has one child:

(i) EDWARD[9] ABBOT BILLINGS, born June 7, 1871.

iii. ELLEN[8] FISKE BILLINGS, the third child of John Edgar and Mary Ann Billings, born at Boston, May 24, 1843. She was married May 19, 1868, to James Albert Sullivan, an apothecary, in Watertown, Mass., where they now reside. They have one child:

(i) HARRIET[9] BILLINGS SULLIVAN, b. Nov. 23, 1873.

iv. EMILY[8] LEAVETT BILLINGS, b. at Newton, Mass., Sept. 17, 1845, completed her education at the Newton High School, and is now living at her mother's.

v. HENRY[8] DUNSTER BILLINGS, (*John E.[7] Fiske[6] Dickson,[5] Martha[4] Dunster,*) born at Newton, July 16, 1849, attended the Newton High School for three years, then spent six months at the Lawrence Scientific School at Cambridge. Entered the employ of James R. Nichols & Co. July 9, 1866, and has remained with them and their successors until the present time. He owns the English Bible of Henry Dunster.*

* This Bible is in old English letters, having references in Roman. It has the Litany of Charles I. and Sternhold and Hopkins' version of the Psalms as far as LXVIII., the rest gone. On a blank leaf dark with age, and written in a bold, clear hand, is a record of the children of Henry[3] Dunster, from which I have been enabled to add to the record in Dr. Chaplin's Life of Henry Dunster, pp. 238-9, three children, who died in infancy, also

9

(ii) BENJAMIN⁷ NUTTING FISKE (*Walter,*⁶ *Gilbert*⁵ *Dickson,*) was born in Pepperell, Feb. 29, 1815. He lived at Pepperell till 1837, and then went to Boston. Here he married July 1, 1846, Eliza Pierce Warren, of that city, and moved to Medway, Maine, where he has since resided. They have three children, all living with or near them. No death has occurred in this family.

(1) EMILY⁸ DICKSON FISKE, b. at Medway, Me., m. Charles Moore, and has three children: (1) RACHEL⁹ EMILY. (2) ANNIE.⁹ (3) BERTHA⁹ MOORE.

(2) THEODORE⁸ VARNUM FISKE, b. at Medway, Me., married Augusta Hathaway, and has two children.

(3) HENRY⁸ DUNSTER FISKE, is unmarried.

(iii) SARAH⁷ NUTTING FISKE, born March 31, 1817. After the return of her parents from Weld, Maine, she lived with her Aunt Hannah Rundle and her sister Mary Ann (Billings) until her marriage, at Boston, May 4, 1843, to Isaac Pierce Blood, born at Hollis, N. H., Feb. 17, 1803. She lived at Hollis until her death, of heart disease, April 21, 1865, aged 48 years and 20 days.

They had five children:

(1) HARRIET⁸ MARIA BLOOD, born in Hollis, July 17, 1844.

(2) GEORGE⁸ HENRY BLOOD, born Jan. 7, 1848.

(3) MARY⁸ ANN BLOOD, born June 20, 1851.

(4) ABBIE⁸ LOUISA BLOOD, born July 7, 1853.

(5) CHARLES⁸ WALTER BLOOD, born July 13, 1857.

"Cousin Hattie," to whom I am indebted for the above dates, says: "There is nothing particular to say about us." I will, however, add (says H. D. B.) that

other matter. This record is undoubtedly correct. It is believed to be by Rev. S. Cooke. The binding has been repaired and indorsed, "HOLY BIBLE, 1634, H. DUNSTER." The imprint is: London. Printed by Robert Barker, Printer to the King's most excellent Magistie, and by the Assigns of John Bill, 1634, (old Testament) 1636, (new Testament.) The title page is surrounded by the banners of the twelve tribes of Israel and of the Apostles. On one page is written, "Mary Jonson, hur booke." It is a most valuable antiquity, and from its association a relic of rare merit.

S. D.

9

the girls have been well educated; Mary graduating at the State Normal School in Framingham, and taking an advanced course. George married, in Brookline, N. H., Harriet Augusta Hills, of Hollis, April 8, 1875. Charles learned the apothecary business at J. A. Sullivan's, in Watertown, but is now at home.

(iv) ACHSAH,[7] daughter of Walter and Abigail (Dick-

_____ her
Mary
street,
a dry
ldren:
She
er was
Merrill
ds re-
helsea.

in the
ington

cousin,
GRACE[9]
_____.

arried a
e dying

1822, in
She then
ir years.

_____ mother's remo___ ___ _____ she has
lived with her sister Mary Ann Billings [in Newton].
"To her retentive memory and her sister's (says H. D. B.), this record of their family history is due."

(vi) HENRY[7] WALTER FISKE, b. in Pepperell, June 18, 1827, lived with his father until he was sixteen, when he moved to Medway, Me., where he married Feb. 15, 1852, Harriet Waite, by whom he had: (i) ABIGAIL[8] DICKSON FISKE. (ii) HARRIET[8] ELLEN. After his

7

10

wife's death, he married at Dexter, Me., Sarah Elizabeth
Green, of that place, Dec. 31, 1863.   He moved to Canada, and lived there until 1867, when he moved to Cambridgeport, Vt., and soon after to Mattewamkeag, Me.,
where he has since lived.   He has had: (iii) LAURA[8]
(?) died in infancy.   (iv) CHARLES[8] EDGAR, by his
second wife.

10. ii. MARY[4] DUNSTER, (*Henry,*[3] *Jonathan,*[2] *Henry,*[1]) the second child of Henry and Martha (Russell)
Dunster, was born in Cambridge July 8, bap. at First
Church July 13, 1712.   She was admitted to full communion March 9, 1730–31.   She married Amos Marrett,
of Cambridge, Sept. 21, 1732.   He was born Sept. 5,
1703, and was the *nephew* (not the *son*, as stated in Life
H. D., p. 239,) of Lieut. Amos Marrett, who married
Widow Ruth Eaton (Dunster).

A manuscript, entitled, "A Brief Account or Gen-
ealogy of the Marrets Taken 1773," is in possession of
Samuel Sewell, Esq., a descendant of Mary[4] Dunster.
It has been the subject of some criticism by the Willard
Memoir.   It has never been published, and we copy it
entire, as well as its accompanying paper, "A Brief
Account of the Families of Dunsters, A. D. 1764."
This was the next year after the author of both papers
(John Marrett) graduated at Harvard College.   Both
papers were evidently made up from tradition, as the
language shows, and some of the errors in it, which are
pointed out by Mr. Willard, p. 339, also occur in the
family Bible of Rev. Isaiah Dunster, which have been
referred to, and it is believed corrected.   The "Balehoult" Letter, which was probably in his possession at
the time his nephew, J. Marrett, made this account,
and the public records of their own town, were evidently
not consulted.   They would have corrected some of these
statements.

A SCHEME OF THE DUNSTERS.

"A Scheme of the Families of the Dunsters—From
whom descended my Mother, Mary Marrett."

1st. "Henry Dunster favoured with a liberal Education lived in Old England as it appears by a Letter of

10

his (Dated Balehoult March 20 1640) to his son Henry in N. England at which time it seems he was an aged Man living at y° above ment'ed Place. he had then living four sons and two daughters which see in y° Scheme."

(1) Henry—(2) Henry, Thos, Rich'd, Robt, Faith, Dorothy.

(3) Henry, Jonathan, Elizabeth.

(4) Henry, Jonathan, Thomas, David, Elizabeth, Dorothy.

(5) Isaiah, Jason, Martha, Mary, Henry, Abigail.

"Henry was sent for to N. England to take y° Charge of the College at Cambridge upon him as accordingly he did, and was the 1st President of Harvard Colledge which post he Sustained for a Number of years till inclining to y° Anabaptist Persuasion he left y° College and after y' was ordained at Scituate where he finished his Days."

2d. Thomas, Richard & Robert never came over to N England Their Posterity if they had any Remain on y° other Side of y° Atlantick Faith and Dorothy Came over to N. England after their Brother Henry—Faith married Rice of Sudbury by whom she hath left much Issue Dorothy married to —— Willard of —— by whom she hath left issue

3d. Henry died without Issue a Lawyer in Old England Jonathan lived in Cambridge a farmer, had six children v. Scheme

Elizabeth married Wade of Medford & then Col.° Thomas of Marshfield But left no Issue

4th. Henry lived in Cambridge a farmer had six children v. Scheme

Jonathan & Thomas died at Charlestown without Issue David's Issue are at Westminster or No 2

Elizabeth married to Philip Carteret by Wm. she hath Issue Dorothy married Solomon Page of Easthampton and hath Issue

Isaiah (favored with a Liberal Education) is now an Ordained Minister at Harwich on Cape Cod & hath One Daughter

5th. Henry a Farmer lived at Camb. died without

10

Issue   Jason lives at Camb. a Farmer hath much Issue
[In a later hand]—"Died Jan. 1805 Æ 80."

Martha married Edw. Dickson of Camb. hath Issue

Mary married Amos Marrett of Camb. by whom she
had three sons & three daughters two sons & one daughter now living "Mary died June 29 1795 Æ 83" [Writ-
ten in a later hand.]

Abigail married to James Cutler of Camb. and hath
Issue

"March 2 1766 she died at Newton & buried at Lexington 4th." [In a later hand.]

GENEALOGY OF THE MARRETT FAMILY.

"A Brief Account or Genealogy of the Family of the
Marretts Taken Anno 1773

Marrett is a French name There are now of that
name in France Called French Protestants Family
probably sprung from Normandy

But it matters but little from What Country yy origi-
nated if yy are but honest & good Men.

SCHEME TO JOHN MARRETT.

1st   Thomas Marrett

2d   John

3d   Edward, Amos, Thomas, John, Hannah, Susannah, Abigail, Lydia, Mary.

4th   Amos, Amos, John, Edward, Hannah, Susannah, Abigail, Mary.

5th   Amos, Amos, John, Abigail, Ruth, Mary.

1.   Thomas Marrett is supposed to have come over to
N England Anno. 1635 about the time yt Rev. Mr.
Shepherd & Company came and settled in Cambridge
who succeeded the Rev. Mr Hooker & Company in Cambridge by purchase of their Estate (wn they removed to
Hartford in Connecticut) "Rev Mr Hooker & Co removed June 1636" [In a later hand.] There are records
in Cambridge Town Book of ye said Thomas having purchased of the town Anno. 1639. But he lived in town
before ye date.

2.   John came from England with his father and settled in Cambridge. Succeeded his father in his inheri-

10

tance—his name is several times mentioned in Camb. Town Book for buying & Selling Lands he appears to have been a farmer and of what other occupation I cannot find out—he married Miss Abigail Eddes but whether he married her before he came over or after I cannot tell.

3. Edward lived in Cambridge about half a mile from the College on the Watertown road He was a Glazier and Tanner He died Anno 1754 April 11 he married Hannah Bradish of Cambridge. They both died in one week (she on the 9th) and were both buried at one time in the same grave—both attended meeting the preceding Sabbath. He was 84 & she 85 years of age—left much Issue See Scheme

Amos was a farmer in Cambridge and a Lieutenant in ye foot Company in Cambridge he married Bethiah Langhorn of Cambridge for his first wife and Mrs. Ruth Hays * a widow of Reading for his second wife—he had no children but made his nephew Amos Marrett his heir he died 1739, aged 81 years

Thomas never Married—was killed in Sudbury fight April 20 1675 with the indians

John never married he died att Sea

Hannah married Samuel Hastings of Cambridge wht Issue she left or whether any I cannot tell

Susannah married Amsdel of Camb. a glazier

Abigail married Rice of Sudbury

Lydia died young

Mary married Joseph Hovey of Cambridge by whom she left Issue and afterwards she married 2^u Husband Nath. Parker of Newton

4. Amos the 1st died when about 3 years old

Amos the 2nd lived in Cambridge possessed Lieut. Amos Marrett estate He was a glazier and farmer by occupation Married MARY DUNSTER of Cambridge by whom he had six children. See Scheme. He died 1747 in the month of November aged 46 years

John died of Small Pox in Boston when about 18 years old

* *See ante " Jonathan Dunster."* [S. D.]

*7

10

Edward lives in Cambridge a Taylor by trade or a Merchant Tailor. He was made Capt. of the foot Company in Cambridge. Afterwards the company was divided and on a special Occasion had an independent Captain's commission over both Companies. Soon afterwards laid down his commission. He married for 1st wife Mary Wyatt of Boston by whom he had 5 children but one now living viz Thomas. Capt. Edward Marrett died Sept. 13 1780 aged 67.

[Memo. in a later hand]—Capt Edward Marretts 1st wife died Dec 1787. His 2n wife was Susannah Foster a widow of Boston now living. Deacon Thomas Marrett died at Cambridge June 23 1784 Æ 43 years

Hannah married to Joseph Lawrence of Cambridge, Gunsmith, (afterwards removed into Connecticut Colony) by whom she hath Issue

Susannah married to John Pierce of Boston a carpenter, afterwards he removed to Stowe where he purchased a good farm. He hath been dead some years and his widow is again married to Samuel Witt of Marlboro, a farmer, & for a great number of years a representative to the General Court for yt town She and her 2n husband both living She never had any children [Mrs. Wit died Dec., 1794, aged 96 years.]

Abigail married Judah Monis of Cambridge Hebrew Proffessor at Harvard College, They are both dead and died without Issue

Mary married John Martyn of Boston afterwards a settled minister at Northboro, in the county of Worcester by whom she hath much issue He is dead. She lives yet at Northboro [In a later hand]—"She is dead."

5. Amos ye first died in infancy.

Amos ye 2d lived at Cambridge about a mile from the College married Abigail Tidd of of Lexington afterwards sold att Cambridge to one Capt Ruggles & bot att Lexington where he now lives he hath four children viz Amos, Daniel, Abigail and Ruth (& since John, Thomas & Betsey) John favored with a Liberal Education was Graduated at Harvard College Anno 1763 is a Preacher But unsettled in the ministry as yet He lives at Newton has his home at Mr. John Pidgeons [In a later hand]—

10

"1774 Dec 21 John was ordained Pastor of the 2ᵈ Parish in Woburn."

Abigail died in infancy. Ruth never was married. She died at Newton May 2 1766 and was buried att Lexington aged 31 years Mary died att Cambridge in the fifteenth year of her age Anno 1754 of a consumption

Acct. taken June 1 1773

Thomas Marrett who is favoured with a Liberal education and was graduated at Harvard College 1761 now lives at Cape Ann a trader and is Deacon of the 3ʳᵈ Church in Glocester

N. B. There are but six of yᵉ name of Marrett in the male line of the aforesaid family now living in these parts viz Capt Edward Marrett of Cambridge and his son Thomas of Cape Ann and Amos Marrett of Lexington and his two sons & his brother John four females of yᵉ name viz Capt Marrett wife Amos Marretts wife & their two daughters.

June 1 1773." [End of MS. S. D.]

This list is not made out in the order of birth, but like official papers of that day, the males are named first, and after them the females, according to age. The account is generally correct, and far more reliable than the "Scheme" of the Dunsters. The children of Amos and Mary⁴ (Dunster) Marrett are rearranged to correspond with the plan adopted in other families, and such further notice of them made as is necessary and attainable.

Amos Marrett, husband of Mary⁴ Dunster, died in Cambridge, Nov., 1747, aged 46 years, leaving her a widow with four children, the eldest 12, and youngest 6 years old. These she cared for with great ability, giving her youngest, John,⁵ a college education. In a few years, both her daughters died, her oldest son was married, and her youngest unsettled in the ministry. It is not strange that she was melancholy and dejected. She avoided association with others, preferring the then solitary habitation of her brother, who had just settled on the borders of the wilderness, to the more social comforts to be had in the neighborhood of her birth, still she was

10

not forgotten by her sons, as letters show. She lived a widow almost half a century; and the traditions of "Aunt Mary" are still fresh in memory. She died at her brother's, Jason Dunster, in Mason, N. H., June 29, 1795, aged 83 years, and was the first, we think, to occupy the Dunster group in the cemetery at Mason Centre. For near eighty years her grave was unmarked, when a plain stone was erected at it with this inscription:

"Mary Dunster, widow of Amos Marrett, born at Cambridge July 8, 1712. Died at Mason June 29, 1795, aged 83 years. Ex dono S. Dunster, 1873."

The six children of Amos and Mary (Dunster) Marrett were:

i. AMOS[5] MARRETT, b. ——, died in infancy.

ii. ABIGAIL[5] MARRETT, b. Aug. 25, 1733, died young.

iii. RUTH[5] MARRETT, b. April 30, 1735. She died in Newton, May 2, 1766, and was buried at Lexington on the 4th. Unmarried.

iv. AMOS[5] MARRETT, b. Feb. 4, 1738, mar. Abigail Tidd, of Lexington.

v. MARY[5] MARRETT, born Aug. 20, 1740, died 1754, aged 14.

vi. JOHN[5] MARRETT, born Sept. 10, 1741, (H. C., 1763,) married Martha Jones.

iv. AMOS[5] MARRETT, born Feb. 4, 1738, mar. Dec. 14, 1760, Abigail Tidd, born Jan. 12, 1738, daughter of Daniel and Hepzibah (Reed) Tidd. He married as of Cambridge, where he probably resided some five or six years after his marriage, when he moved to Lexington. They were admitted to the Lexington Church Sept. 15, 1771, from the First Church in Cambridge. He died March 24, (28th, *J. M. Diary*,) 1805, aged 66. He was a soldier in Capt. Parker's company in 1775, and was in the Jerseys three months the year following. He was selectman for Lexington, 1785–86–89 and 91. (*Hist. Lex. Gen., p.* 130.) In July, 1776, he and his two sons and eighteen others were innoculated for small-pox at his own house. (*Rev. J. Marrett's Diary.*)

His children by Abigail Tidd were:

10

1. AMOS,[6] born in Cambridge, Oct. 4, 1763, married Nov. 28, 1786, Patty Reed.

2. ABIGAIL,[6] born in Cambridge, June 4, 1765, mar. Oct. 6, 1788, Jonathan Smith.

3. DANIEL,[6] born in Cambridge, July 18, 1767, mar. July 24, 1796, Mary Muzzy.

4. RUTH,[6] born Nov. 12, 1768, died 1775, buried Oct. 13. (*Rev. John Marrett's Diary.*)

5. BETSEY,[6] bap. Nov. 28, 1773, died Nov. 3, buried 7th, 1797, aged 24.

6. JOHN,[6] baptized July 9, 1775, died Dec. 17, 1797, aged 22½.

7. THOMAS,[6] baptized July 20, 1777, died July 6, 1798, a student of Harvard College.

1. AMOS[6] MARRETT, b. in Cambridge, Oct. 4, 1763, mar. Nov. or Dec. 28, 1786, Patty Reed, born Dec. 5, 1765, daughter of Hammon and Betty (Simonds) Reed. He was in the battle at Lexington, April 19, 1775. He died Nov. 10, 1824, aged 61. She died Oct. 16, 1849, aged 85. They had nine children:

(1) PATTY,[7] born Sept. 9, 1787, mar. Jonas Cutler.

(2) SALLY,[7] born Oct. 1, 1789, mar. June 15, 1823, Benjamin Locke, Jr.

(3) HANNAH,[7] born Dec. 24, 1792.

(4) NABBY,[7] b. Aug. 18, 1795, d. Apr. 6, 1854, unm.

(5) BETSEY,[7] born July 4, 1798, mar. April 30, 1826, Amos Towne.

(6) MARY,[7] born March 18, 1801, m. April 1, 1827, Joel Adams.

(7) JOHN,[7] born Oct. 17, 1803, died 1858, unmarried.

(8) EMILY,[7] born Dec. 26, 1806, mar. King George, Nov. 17, 1830. (This was not the *King George* of whom it was said if he had not been a King he would have made an excellent tailor.)

(9) HARRIET,[7] born Sept. 13, 1809, mar. April 22, 1842, Ivory Sanborn. They have had several children. Of the families of these nine children we have no further record in *Hist. Lexington*, but they are noticed further on.

2. ABIGAIL[6] MARRETT, daughter of Amos and Abigail (Tidd) Marrett, was born in Cambridge, June 4,

10

1765, married Oct. 6, 1788, Jonathan Smith, his second wife. She died at Lexington, March 30, 1794, was buried April 5. She had one child:

(i) HARRIET[7] SMITH, born Jan. 6, 1791, married Jan. 1, 1823, Imla Parker, born Sept. 4, 1791. He was the son of Imla and Hannah (Ames) Parker, of Groton, and died March 20, 1836? aged 44 years. Their only child, named Abigail[8] Marrett Parker, after her great grandmother, was born Aug. 20, 1824, not 1827, as her mother's Bible has it—(*wrong*, said Mrs. P.) She was a school teacher in the primary school, Lane Place, Fort Hill, Boston, for fifteen years. She died in Boston, Aug. 11, 1863, aged 39 years, unmarried. She was placed in the Parker family tomb, in Groton, Mass.

In 1873 Mrs. Imla Parker was visited at her residence, No. 2015 Washington street, Boston Highlands. She was found an amiable and benignant lady, who, though 82 years old, had a wonderful memory, and stated many facts of her relatives, which, it is believed, exist in no record, and hardly in any memory but hers. Among her few papers she had kept a Eulogy on her mother's death, which she permitted to be copied:

"Died in Lexington, on 30th of March, 1794, Abigail Marret, wife of Jonathan Smith, aged 29 years. Being of a placid and even temper she was ever easy and content. Delighted with industry she was always busily employed. Fond of peace she gave no provocation. Averse to contention she received in silence the provocation of others. Kind and tender she worthily sustained the relations of a wife and parent. Amiable in disposition she was beloved by all her acquaintance. Patient under affliction she uttered not a complaint, or expressed the least discomposure of spirits during the course of a lingering, and the latter part of the time a very painful disease; and pious in life, her death was in the greatest composure of mind, and 'tis presumed, glorious and happy."

From her lips we learned that besides

(i) HARRIET[7]—ABIGAIL (MARRET) SMITH had:

10

(ii) CYRUS,[7]   ⎱ Twins, born Oct. 20, 1792, (not
(iii) AUGUSTUS,[7] ⎰ *Dec. 20, as in Hist. Lex., p. 225.*)

(ii) CYRUS[7] SMITH, born Oct. 20, 1792, mar. May, 1825, Mary Porter, daughter of Noah and Mary (Miller) Porter, of Boston, where they had two children:

(1) CYRUS[8] AUGUSTUS SMITH, born July, 1826. He · went to sea when about fifteen years old, which business he continued till about 1868; was mate part of the time. He now, says Mrs. P., lives with his step-mother, at Marlborough, in feeble health, and unmarried.

(2) THOMAS[8] JEFFERSON SMITH, born at Boston, about 1829, was educated for a physician; went into the army as a *soldier;* was under Gen. Butler; was wounded in the battle at —— ——, and died (probably) in hospital. He was unmarried.

(iii) AUGUSTUS[7] SMITH, the other twin, born Oct. 20, 1792, was found drowned in a watering trough, in Lexington, in the year 1839. He was not married.

Mrs. Parker gave other information of the children of Amos[6] and Patty (Reed) Marrett, which we add to the list as numbered above.

P. S.   Mrs. Imla Parker died at her home, April 15, 1876, aged 85 years, 3 months and 18 days. (?)   She was entombed at Groton, beside her husband and daughter, She lived a widow forty years.

(1) PATTY[7] MARRETT, born at Lexington, Sept. 9, 1787, mar. 1811, Jonas Cutler, son of Thomas Cutler, of Lexington, born March 3, 1782. They bought a farm in Westminster, Mass., where he died Jan. 29, 1830, aged 48. She died Nov. 20, 1852.

They had three children:

(1) JONAS[8] CUTLER, born at Lexington, Nov. 15, 1811, mar. at Leominster, April 30, 1855, Martha M. Hager, daughter of Elijah Hager. They live on the old place bought by his father. Have no children.

(2) AMOS[8] MARRETT CUTLER, born at Westminster, July 13, 1816, mar. at Fitchburg, Mary Barnes, of Westminster. Reside at Westminster. Keeps a livery stable. Have two children:

10

(i) ABBY[9] MARIA CUTLER, married Marcus Miller.

(ii) MARY[9] ARDELIA, married George Brooks.

(3) MARTHA[8] CUTLER, born at Westminster, Feb. 28, 1814, mar. at Fitchburg, Jan. 10, 1854, Sanford Sawyer, son of Amos Sawyer. Is a carriage maker. Have had three children:

(i) EMILY[9] SAWYER, died young. (ii) OLIVER[9] SAWYER, d. young. (iii) FRANK[9] MARRETT SAWYER.

(2) SALLY[7] MARRETT, married Benjamin Locke, Jr., June 15, 1823. Had three children:

(i) ELIZABETH[8] LOCKE, born Feb., 1824, married Jeduthan Richardson, of Woburn, now living in East Boston, and has three children, all living.

(ii) BENJAMIN[8] FRANKLIN LOCKE, born 1826? mar. Eliza Hill, of Arlington, have one daughter, Louisa[9] Locke, lives in Arlington.

(iii) ALBERT[8] LOCKE, born 1828? mar. about 1869, Mina Hill, sister to his brother B. Franklin Locke's wife. He (Albert[8]) went to South America. Mrs. P. being asked to what part, could not remember, but said, "where the earthquakes are."

(3) HANNAH[7] MARRETT, born Dec. 24, 1792, died in Lexington, 1823? twenty-five years old, unmarried.

(4) ABIGAIL[7] (NABBY), born Aug. 18, 1795, died April 6, 1854, unmarried.

(5) BETSEY,[7] mar. Amos Towne, of Woburn, April 30, 1826. Two children:

(i) ELIZABETH[8] TOWNE, mar. a Bruce, and lives at Fitchburg, a carpenter, and has three children.

(ii) HARRIET[8] TOWNE, born ——, married Thomas Simonds, who is in the shoe business at Reading. Have three children, Alice,[9] ——, ——.

(6) MARY,[7] born March 18, 1801, mar. Joel Adams, of Shirley, Mass. Have three children, John,[8] Mary Ann,[8] and Albert[8] Adams.

(7) JOHN,[7] born Oct. 17, 1803, died 1858, unmarried.

(8) EMILY,[7] born Dec. 26, 1806, mar. King George, of Sanbornton, N. H., and has two children:

10

(i) ELIAS[8] GEORGE. (ii) MARTHA[8] GEORGE, mar.
—— Baxter, and lives at Lakeville.

[There was a Mr. George, Methodist minister, preached at Springvale, Me., in 1836.]

(9) HARRIET,[7] born Sept. 13, 1809, mar. Ivory Sanborn. Have had six children:

(i) LOUISA,[8] born ——, died young.
(ii) GEORGE[8] SANBORN, mar. Ada ——, of Waltham.
He is a watchmaker at Waltham.
(iii) ABBEY,[8] b.— } both died same day of dysentery.
(iv) LYMAN,[8] b.— }
(v) ELLEN[8] MARIAH, } Twins.
(vi) EMMA[8] MALINDA, }

Ellen died when about 3 months old.

Emma married Charles Swan, of Reading, about 1826.
Have no children.

3. DANIEL[6] MARRETT, (*Amos,[5] Amos and Mary[4] D.,
Henry,[3] Jonathan,[2] Henry,[1]*) the third child of Amos
and Mary (Tidd) Marrett, was born in Cambridge, July
18, 1767, and married first, July 24, (*Feb. 24, Hist. Lex.*)
1796, Mary Muzzy, daughter of Wm. and Lydia (Reed)
Muzzy, of Charlestown, born Jan. 2, bap. Jan. 7, 1770.
He graduated at Harvard College, 1790, and was classmate of Hon. Josiah Quincy and Gov. Crafts, of Vermont. From his class of forty-two there were five members of Congress and two judges. He studied theology
with Dr. Stearns, of Bedford, Mass., and was ordained
pastor of the Congregational Church in Standish, Maine,
Sept. 21, 1796, and continued to hold that relation for
more than thirty-three years, resigning in Dec., 1829.
In addition to his ministerial duties, he engaged in horti-
culture extensively. He had a large orchard of the finest
fruit in the State, and was the first to introduce grafted
fruit; and owned the first covered carriage in that neighborhood. By Mary Muzzy he had six children:

i. DANIEL[7] MARRETT, born July 15, 1797, Saturday
afternoon, at three o'clock. He married Jan. 26, 1825,
Abigail March, daughter of Col. James March, of Gor-

8

10

ham. She died March 15, 1856. He was a merchant. resided in Portland, and died Dec. 3, 1875. Both buried in Westbrook. Three children:

1. EDWIN⁸ AUGUSTUS MARRETT, born March 12, 1826, mar. Mary Louisa Nelson, daughter of Samuel Nelson. He is a merchant in Portland. They are Unitarians. Have no children.

2. JAMES⁸ SULLIVAN MARRETT, (*Daniel,⁷ Daniel,⁶ Amos,⁵ Amos and Mary⁴ D., Henry,³ Jonathan,² Henry,¹*) born May 30, 1827, married Sarah Jennie (?) Gorham, daughter of Hon. Jason Gorham, of Barre, Mass. Resides in Portland, is a merchant and carpet manufacturer. "Never held any political office." "Was councilman several years." "Did nothing towards the late war but to pay money." (*Letter.*) They have two children:

(i) ELIZABETH⁹ MARCH MARRETT, b. Aug. 10, 1856.
(ii) CHARLES⁹ GORHAM MARRETT, b. Feb. 23, 1861.

3. ORLANDO⁸ MELVILLE MARRETT, born May 19, 1829, married Dec. 4, 1851, Louisa Small, daughter of Francis Small, of Windham. He was a merchant ship chandler, and engaged in navigation. He was Orthodox (Congregational) in religion. Filled several offices of local importance; was President of the City Council. For many years President of the Mercantile Library Association, and Vice President of Board of Trade. He died Jan. 9, 1870. Had one child:

(i) JAMES⁹ E. MARRETT, born April 7, 1854, now living in Portland.

ii. JOHN⁷ MARRETT, b. Feb. 1, 1799, Friday morning, at 10 o'clock, died May 3, 1821, at Standish, Me. Unm.

iii. AMOS⁷ MARRETT, born Nov. 27, 1800, Thursday afternoon, at 3 o'clock, Thanksgiving Day, mar. April 12, 1826, Mary S. Strothers, of Bridgeton, Me., and died a few weeks after at Bridgeton, Me. No children.

iv. CAROLINE⁷ MARRETT, born July 3, 1802, 12¼ A. M., Saturday, d. Dec. 27, 1817, aged 15 y., 5 mo., 24 d.

v. WILLIAM⁷ MARRETT, (*Daniel,⁶ Amos,⁵ Mary⁴ Dunster,*) born Sept. 5, 1804, Wednesday, at 2½ o'clock, P. M. He took his medical degree at Bowdoin College in

10

1830, and settled as a physician in Westbrook, Maine. He was for many years a deacon of the Congregational Church at Saccarappa Village. He married Adaline Irish, daughter of Gen. James Irish, of Gorham, Me., and died in 1860 at Westbrook. One child:

(i) MARY[8] MUZZY MARRETT, born Sept. 22, 1834, married Fabius M. Ray, a lawyer in Portland. He is Treasurer of a Savings Bank at Saccarappa. Resides in Westbrook. Has two children, Addie and Willie.

vi. MARY ANN[7] MARRETT, born Feb. 1, 1808, Monday, 1½ P. M. She mar. June 2, 1833, Warren Duren, of Woburn, Mass. She died Oct. 4, 1839, aged 31 years, 9 months and 4 days, and was buried at Woburn. She left one child:

(i) CAROLINE[8] AUGUSTA DUREN, born Oct. 25, 1835, and died May 13, 1852, aged 17 years, unmarried.

Mr. Duren moved to Lexington, where he has been several times in town office. He married 2d Oct., 1848, Mary Chandler. He carries on the shoe business.

MARY (MUZZY) MARRETT, first wife of Daniel[6] Marrett, died March 6, 1810, aged 40 y., 2 mo., 4 d., and was buried at Standish, leaving all her six children living.

REV. DANIEL[6] MARRETT, married second wife, Oct. 8, 1810, Dorcas Hastings, born at Lexington, June 27, 1785 or 6, daughter of Maj. Samuel and Lydia (Nelson) Hastings. Maj. Hastings was taken prisoner with Gen. Lee on Long Island. At the time of his capture a British officer wounded him with a sword in the neck, but his "queue" broke the force of the blow and saved his life. By her he had eight children more, making fourteen.

vii. LEANDER[7] (first child of Dorcas) MARRETT, born Sept. 16, 1811, Monday, at 7 A. M., died July 13, 1814, aged 2 years and 4 months?

viii. LORENZO[7] MARRETT (*Daniel,[6] Amos,[5] Amos and Mary[4] Dunster, Henry,[3] Jonathan,[2] Henry,[1]*) was born at Standish, March 18, 1816, Monday, at 5½ P. M. He graduated at Bowdoin College, Maine, Sept. 1838; was

10

tutor in Jackson College, Columbia, Tenn.; studied law at Dane Law School, Harvard University, and with Nathan Dane Appleton, Alfred, Maine; was admitted to the bar in Cumberland Co., Me., 1842; settled in Cambridge, 1843, where he now resides. To him we are indebted for most of the records of his father's (Daniel[6]) family. He writes: "I think I am the only direct descendant in Cambridge of Thomas Marrett, who settled in Cambridge, 1630." He has some interesting relics of the Marrett family, among which is a copy of the "Spectator," having the autograph of all his ancestors, from Thomas down. He married Eliza Anthony Winsor, of Pawtucket, R. I., Aug. 14, 1845. She died Feb. 25, 1876. No children.

ix. ISABELLA[7] ANNETTE MARRETT, born July 20, 1817, on Sunday, at 6 o'clock, died March 4, 1818, aged 7 months and 7 days.

x. AVERY[7] WILLIAMS MARRETT, born Jan. 19, 1819, on Tuesday, at 5 P. M., mar. Nov. 25, 1847, Elizabeth Bancroft Weston, daughter of Rev. James and Sarah (Chase) Weston, born Jan. 5, 1820, in Augusta, Me. He is a farmer, and lives on the old place. Seven children:

1. HELEN[8] MARIAH MARRETT, born Jan. 20, 1849, graduated at Tilden Female Seminary, class 1869, West Lebanon, N. H., and is now preceptoress of Gorham Seminary, Maine. She is a member of the Orthodox Congregational Church in Standish.

2. WALTER[8] HASTINGS MARRETT, b. Oct. 28, 1850. He is a member of the senior class, 1876, Bowdoin College, and a member of the Congregational Church in Standish.

A GRADUATE'S BIG WALK.

SUMMIT HOUSE, MT. WASHINGTON, N. H., Aug. 25. —Mr. Marratt, graduate of Bowdoin College, who took a prize at Saratoga this summer, walked from the top of this mountain to Portland yesterday. The distance is 90 miles.—*N. Y. Tribune.*

The prize at Saratoga was a very handsomely engraved medal. He had previously taken a number of silver

10

vases, cups and goblets at College field days. Always won them easily. The best time in walking he ever made was half a mile in 3 minutes, 27 seconds. "Have now given up walking altogether, and am giving my whole attention to teaching" at Yarmouth, Me. One of his sisters is his assistant.

 3. MARY[8] ELIZABETH, born Feb. 21, 1852.
 4. CARRIE[8] LOUISA, born Dec. 26, 1855.
 5. HENRY[8] WESTON, born April 19, 1857.
 6. CHARLES[8] NELSON, born Feb. 4, 1860, died July 12, 1872, aged 12 years, buried at Standish.
 7. FANNIE[8] SARAH, born Oct. 10, 1865.

 xi. DANE[7] APPLETON MARRETT, } Twins.
 xii. SAMUEL[7] HASTINGS MARRETT, }

Dane Appleton, born at 3 o'clock, A. M., and Samuel Hastings at noon, on Saturday, Jan. 12, 1822.

 xi. DANE[7] APPLETON MARRETT, married Eliza Ann Locke, of Lancaster, Mass., June 7, 1848, lives at Chelsea, Mass. Three children:

 1. SAMUEL[8] HASTINGS, b. Aug. 10, 1850, d. young.
 2. DANE[8] APPLETON, born July 1, 1855.
 3. AUGUSTUS,[8] born ——, 1858.

 xii. SAMUEL[7] HASTINGS married Francis A. Locke, of Lancaster, Mass., June 7, 1848.

Twin brothers married twin sisters at the same time.

Samuel[7] Hastings and Frances A. (Locke) Marrett had Frances[8] Hastings, born Aug. 27, 1849. She died an infant.

Samuel[7] Hastings Marrett died May 22, 1850, aged 28 years, 4 months and 10 days.

 xiii. HELEN[7] MARIA, born July 3, 1823, at 4 o'clock, P. M. She died March 15, 1846, aged 23 years, 7 mo., 22 days, unmarried, and was buried at Standish.
 xiv. FRANCIS[7] GRENVILLE MARRETT, born Sept. 8, 1826, on Friday, at 6 o'clock, P. M. He was an organ builder, at Detroit, Michigan, died at Cambridge, Mass., unmarried, and was buried at Standish, Maine.

 *8

10

Rev. Daniel⁶ Marrett died at Standish, Maine, April 14, 1836, aged 68 y., 8 mo., 26 d., and was buried there.

Dorcas (Hastings) Marrett, second wife of Rev. Daniel Marrett, was a member of the Congregational Church, and died Aug. 6, 1857, at Standish, aged 72 years, 1 month, 9 days, and was buried beside her husband and his first wife, Mary (Muzzy) Marrett.

vi. JOHN⁵ MARRETT, (*Amos and Mary⁴ (Dunster)*, *Henry,³ Jonathan,² Henry,¹*) was the sixth and youngest child of Amos and Mary⁴ (Dunster) Marrett, and was born in Cambridge, Sept. 10, 1741, O. S., Sept. 21, N. S. He was probably baptized in the First Church of Cambridge, of which his mother, before her marriage, was a member in full communion. His father died Nov., 1747, when he was six years old, and left his mother to watch over and educate her four children. What property was left for that purpose is not now apparent, but from the fact that her daughter, Ruth, died in Newton and was buried in Lexington, and that her youngest son often refers to Newton as a residence, it would seem that she parted with the home residence given her husband by his uncle, and lived in Newton, or elsewhere.

His education was not neglected. He entered Harvard College 1759, when eighteen years old, and graduated 1763, in the class with Timothy Pickering. Of his early religious experience no facts have reached us. After graduation he seems to have resided with his mother in Cambridge, and have had an oversight of the farm. He kept a Diary, which is now the property of his grand-son, Samuel Sewall, of Burlington, Mass. It commenced with the year 1767, and is, excepting 1768, which is missing, attached to the Almanac of each year.

We have been kindly permitted by Mr. Sewall to examine it, and have copied a few items illustrating his life, and regret that our limits compel us to omit many very interesting ones.

He seems to have studied Divinity at Harvard, and was, in 1767, apparently, a member of the "Ministers' Meeting." These meetings were held at each minister's residence, alternately. The one for May of that year is

10

entered " May 5 Ministers meeting to be here." He has also in the calender marked the Sabbaths on which the Sacrament was held.

The Diary for 1769 is dated Cambridge. They all give notes of the weather, his journeys, places of preaching, his work on his farm in detail, and often the expenses, &c.

REV. JOHN MARRETT'S DIARY.

"Jany. 18 1769   Started on my journey to Yarmouth." Here he preached till April 11, when the church gave him a call to settle. This he declined, although given with unusual unanimity. After visiting his uncle, Rev. Isaiah Dunster, by whom he was probably introduced to that people, he preached at Barnstable, then returned to Cambridge, and roomed at the College till Aug. 5, 1770, when he went to Mr. Pidgeons, at Newton.

June 3   Witnessed transit of Venus

Sept 4   Saw the comet   Its tail appears to be 20 rods long.   13th do.   Its tail about 30 degrees

1770 March 8.   —— ——   Went to Boston   Saw ye largest Funeral perhaps that was ever in Boston   8 or 10 thousand present—four men buried in one grave who were shot by the Centry Guard of regulars on Monday night last.   [The Boston massacre, of which he gives a graphic account.]

Oct. 8.   Went to Cambridge in evening.   Made an entertainment for the Gentlemen of the college and quitted living at the college.   Gave up my chamber after possessing it 3 years & 4 mo.

Oct 12   Set out on a journey to see my mother

14   Preached at Mason, 20.   back to Newton " Can go no where else "

1771 July 12.   About three nights agone a mad Dog passed by here   " It is about two years since mad Dogs came into this country "   Preached at Stow 12 Sabbaths.

1772 June 14   preached at Ashby "a new place but good land.   Settles fast." He preached here six Sabbaths.

see "Whitely" p. 41. Dict of Biography.

10

1773 March 31 Very warm the "Silver Tankard filled with Cyder Sweated like Summer"

April 11 Left off my wigg & wear my hair.

Sept. 29. Very hot & dry. At Rhode Island they sell the water in the town for 11s. 3 pence pr. bbl.

Oct 21 One Levi Ames executed at Boston for stealing

    31 preached at Stow the last of my engagement 15 Sabbaths

Dec 16 "A meeting of ye town of Boston & ye neighboring towns about landing a Quantity of Tea In ye eveng about 300 Chests of Tea a Board ye Ships in ye harbor all flung over Board & Destroyed by ye ple. yy mett with no resistance"

1774 May 17 removed from Newton to Lexington to live with my Brother. I have lived at Mr Pidgeons three years & nine months

Sept 2 (P. S.) Abt 3000 of ye country ple assembled at Cambridge with fire Arms & Clubs yy obliged Col. Oliver Judges Danforth & Lee to resign y^r Counsellor ship & Mr Phipps not to act as Sheriff. [Mob law rampant in Massachusetts!]

29 The Church in Topsfield [where he had preached several Sabbaths] gave me a call. He declined this call also.

Oct 11 A provincial Congress at Concord began to day

    12 rode from Lex. to Concord to see ye Congress

Nov 10 gave my answer to the call I received from Woburn Precinct * * * I asked for wood—not granted as yet.

16 Messrs Zach^e Gould & Daniel Bixby lodged here last night & tarried to day. They came as a Comtte about Topsfield affairs

17. Capt Johnson and Dea Reed of Woburn visited me & informed me that the 2nd parish in Woburn had complied with terms for settling with them in the ministry.

29. Rode to Woburn attended parish meeting Ordination appointed to be 21 of Dec.

Dec 21 Last night and to day Exceedingly cold, fair. Themo. 6° A. M. My Ordination at ye 2nd Parish in Woburn. Went into meeting house a little before 12

10

clock came out half past two oclock P. M. Revd Mess^s Cushing of Waltham began with prayer. Clark of Lexington preached from 1 Thess. 2–4. Sermon an hour and ten minutes long. A very good Sermon. Cook of Cambridge prayed and gave the Charge. Stone of Reading prayed after the Charge. Morril of Wilmington gave the Right Hand. Was sung 97 Hymn a stave and a half from the 4 verse—good singing Council Supped at Lieut. Walkers.

Thus he remained *unsettled* for eleven years after his graduation, and at least eight, probably more, after he began to preach. In this interim, certainly the last five years, he preached almost every Sabbath. Most of the time as a substitute for others. He preached in nearly every pulpit in and around Boston. His sermons, the manuscripts of which are now in the possession of Mr. Sewall, at Burlington, are of the Calvinistic faith, yet liberal and free from bigotry. They are artistic in form, systematic in detail, with an evident intention to mould the affections and purify the life, rather than charm the head and dazzle the understanding. A single sentence, written apparently after he had noted "some conversation on points of Divinity at Topsfield," gives an insight into his views. It is copied verbatim:

"The Doctrine of Election, must be consistent with mans free agency so yt wn Gd Judgeth sinners yy shll Stand Condemned, in foro cons^{ce} that is, yy are not condemned because Gd would not Save ym but fr yir own sins & because yy would not attend to & accept of ye offers of salvⁿ."

Very soon after his ordination he moved to Woburn (Jan. 13, 1775). "Board at Madam Jones's for 40s. pr week, and keep my horse myself." Here he staid about a year. Madam Jones was the widow of his predecessor in that church. He afterwards married her daughter. The first Sabbath in that year he "went to meeting on snow shoes." After moving to Woburn he devoted his time to the interests of the parish—visiting the sick, attending funerals, solemnizing marriages, and adminis-

10

tering consolation to the afflicted—all of which are
noted.   He found time, however, to attend to a farm he
had bought in Lexington, which he kept till April 18,
1785, and also to the homestead of Madam Jones, which
ultimately came into his possession through his wife.
The details of these transactions are curious and interesting, embracing daily entries for forty years, excepting a
month, when he "bespoke a 'Birth' in ye Hospital at
Lincoln for ye Small Pox " —— "took 5 small mer-
curial Pills 2 doses of Salts   Whole expense about £40
Old Tenor " ($16.)

On one occasion he writes: "Had a Blister on my
arm for a sore eye."   (This looks like the famous *similia
similibus curantur*, but failed to carry out the formula
of infinitesimal doses.)   On another, he "Bottled 11
Doz & One bottles of Cyder."

The first year of his ministry was the eventful one of
the opening of the Revolution.   In this he took an
active and decided stand against the Mother Country.
On the 9th of Feb., 1775, he attended " a *Lecture* at
Lexington on the *Times* " —— " I began with prayer
Mr. Cushing preached from Ps. 22, 28 ' He is the Governor among the Nations.' "

March 7 attended training at Lexington.   21st training, viewed arms at home   April 4 rode to Reading and
heard Mr Stone preach a sermon to the *Minute Men*

April 8.   People moving out of Boston on account of
the troops

April 19 fair, windy & cold.   "A Distress'g Day.
Abt 800 Regulars marched from Boston to Concord as
yy went up yy killed 8 men at Lex.gton meetg house,
they huzzard & then fired as our men had turned yr
backs, who in number were abt 100 & yn yy proceeded
to Concord.   Ye adjacent Country were alarmed ye later
part of ye night precedg.   Ye action at Lex^n was just
before Sunrise.   Our men pursued ym to and fm Concord on yr retreat back.   Several killed on both sides
but much ye least on our Side as we pickt ym off on yir
retreat.   Ye Regulars were reinforced at Lexgton to aid
yir retreat by 800 wth two three field pieces   they burned

10

3 houses in Lexgton and one barn & did other Mischief to buildings they were pursued to Charlestown Where yy entrenched on a hill just over ye neck. thus Commences an important Period

April 20 rode to Lex^n and saw the mischief the Regulars did

21. rode to Concord. The country coming in fast to our help.

22. All quiet here Our forces gathered at Cambridge and towns about Boston The regulars removed from Charlestown to Boston the day before yesterday

23. S.(abbath) Preached at home. Soldiers travelling down and returning brought their arms with them to meeting with warlike accoutrements. A Dark Day. In the forenoon service just as service was ended Dr. Blodget came in for the People to go with their teams to bring provisions from Marblehead out of the way of the Men of War. Considerable number at Meeting

24. packing up my most valuable effects to be ready to move on any "sudden occasion"

25 rode to Cambridge. Our forces very numerous there

26. returned home via Lexg^n Many houses on the road pillaged by the regulars between Lexington and Charlestown

There was one important personal incident in the affair at Lexington which Mr. Marrett passes without notice, unless the words "sudden occasion" give a hint of it.

It was well known that one of the objects of Gen. Gage was to seize John Hancock and Samuel Adams.

On the night preceding the march to Lexington, these men were lodging at the Clark parsonage, formerly the residence of Rev. John Hancock, in an apartment of which, says Drake, (*Hist. Fields, &c., p.* 366,) there is no doubt Hancock courted Dorothy Quincy, who was then living in the house under the protection of Madam Lydia Hancock, the Governor's Aunt. The people of Lexington were apprised by Revere and others of this object of Gage, and insisted that Hancock and Adams should go

10

to a place of greater safety. "They first repaired to the hill southeast of Mr. Clark's, where they remained until the troops passed. They were afterwards conducted to the house of Madam Jones, widow of Rev. Thomas Jones and Rev. Mr. Marrett, in Burlington" (then Woburn). Mrs. Clark had arranged to have fresh salmon, the first of the season, for the breakfast of her family on the morning of the 19th. The abrupt departure of her guests had disappointed her as well as themselves. On their way they recollected their expected entertainment. They stopped at Mr. Reed's for a short time, sent back the servant to get the rarity, and took it with them for Madam Jones to cook. Upon a new alarm, they were conveyed by Mr. Marrett along a cart-way in the woods to the house of Amos Wyman, in a little clearing, about three miles distant, in the corner of Billerica. The "elegant repast," as Drake calls it, was not quite ready, and they left it untasted.

In the meantime, by Mrs. Jones' directions, the servants had drawn the elegant carriage which had brought the "Patriots" to her house, into the thickly wooded swamp to avoid any trace to their whereabouts.

On arriving at Mr. Wyman's, they asked if they could be supplied with something to eat, saying they had had neither breakfast nor dinner. Mrs. Wyman replied she had nothing in the house except the cold pork and potatoes left of their boiled dinner. Mr. Adams rejoined, please let us have some of them. The patriotic woman, taking down from the kitchen shelf a wooden tray containing the boiled salt pork and unpeeled potatoes left of the family dinner, set it, with some brown bread, before her guests. Woman like, she apologized for the humble fare. Mr. Adams, with his usual courtesy, assured her he had made a hearty meal, and had never tasted anything better. Hancock is reported to have given Mrs. W. a cow in his more prosperous days. (*Family tradition.*)

Dorothy Q., who had refused to have her lover separated from her at Lexington, appears to have been left at Mrs. Jones'. Mr. Marrett constituted himself "Master of Ceremonies" and apprised his proteges of the

10

progress of events.   They came back to Mrs. Jones' the
next day, but appear to have - returned to Wyman's,
where Paul Revere and Dorothy Q. joined them.   They,
with the "women and children of several of the neighboring families who had fled thither for safety, fearing
that if they remained at home 'the Regulars' might
come and murder them or carry them off," made quite a
party, "roughing it in the woods."

On the 4th of September of the same year, Dorothy
Quincy was married at Fairfield, Conn., to John Hancock, afterwards the famous President of the Continental Congress.

On the 12th of June following, Gen. Gage, by procla-
mation, exempted Hancock and Adams from his offer of
a general pardon, and declared all persons who might
give them shelter or aid, rebels and traitors.

We think it was prudent in Mr. Marrett not to commit the part he had taken in the affair to writing.   Had
the rebellion been unsuccessful, his head might have
"graced the hill called Bacon."

The Wyman house was long since torn down.

There is not a doubt of the truth of this matter.   It
is detailed in the histories of Lexington and Woburn.

"Miss Quincy, afterwards Mrs. Hancock, was connected with the Sewall family, and often gave to my father
an account of the affair.   She was one of the party.   He
also doubtless heard it from Madam Jones, who was living after he came to Burlington." (*Samuel Sewall's
Letter.*)

As it has never been published before, we copy here,
in full, a letter of Rev. J. Marrett to his uncle, Isaiah
Dunster, found among the papers of the latter:

"Rev⁰ Hon⁰ & Dear

Sir   I hve yis week recvd yrs of yᵉ 3ᵈ Inst. & think
myself very happy in yᵉ continuation of yr. Friendship
& Correspondence wᶜ I sh'll always endeavour to Culti-
vate & endeavour to Deserve: I acknowledge my past
defficiencies But hope for future amendments —— I hve
sent you a Letter sometime ago wᶜ I hpe by yis time has
reached you.   I am glad you continue Steadfast in yᵉ

9

*The originals of these letters
are in my Library   S. Dunster*

10

Cause of Liberty; but I never entertained y° least Doubt
to y° Contrary knowing y' you are not given to Change
w" you are once established on rational principles.   As
to those around you of different Sent^nts yy will only in-
creas y^r glory by yir opposition—I think with you Concerning y° Drs Serm. y' it is a very good one. as to y°
two men unarmed y' were killed in a house at Menotomy, am not absolutely Certain but take ym to be Jabez
Wyman who used to work for Mr Cook and Jason Winship killed in y° tavern y' Capt Adams formerly owned,
now Cooper at the Corner.   Wyman was certainly killed
yer & I think Winship but am not Certain yy were unarmed; but its likely enough yy were drinking phly°
[flip].   Wyman was warned of y° Danger but says he let
us finish y° mug yy wont come yet he died as a fool
dieth.   the woman you speak of was Dea^cn Adams wife
She had newly been brot to bed a few Days before: ye
Regulars Came into y° house & one of ym presented hs
peice at her but she Screamed for mercy & another prevented his firing but pulled off y° Cloths & told her to
get out of y° way, or to use yir phrase to make herself
Scarce.   So she went off but I know not where.   her
child^n were some of ym under y° bed & I think remained
undiscovered.   yy set y° house on fire But it was soon
put out: yy set John Cutters house on fire But by y°
Activity of our ple it was soon put out; our ple pressed
so hard upon ym y' yy had not time to Excute yir Masters will so fully as yy desired.   Menotomy meetg house
received no other Damage than some of y° windows be'g
broken and some Balls fm Small Arms Shot into it.
Lexgton meetg had a Cannon Ball a six pounder Shot
thro it besides many small arms fired into it.   yy broke y°
windows of Mr Cooks house and fired into it & y° kitchen
y° setty room & y° best room N. E.   yy plundered as
much as y° time would admit; took, broke & Destroyed
wht yy could—Jason Russel y° Old man was y° person
killed & in his house whose Dth I have mentioned in my
other Letter—it was not your Brother Harrington y' was
killed nor his Son It was Moses Harringtons Son it
runs in my mind yre were two of y' name killed but I
forget whose son y° other was.

10

As to ye British Parl^{ats} having ye supremicy over ye American Colonies, as now contended for by y^t Body I hope y^t thro ye help of Divine Providence by next Septr great Britain will be convinced she never did, nor will hold such a Power in her hands.   thus I have Answered ye Several Questions already to ye best of my knowledge I was in ye Army last Sabth & left my ple Destitute in order to promote ye publick good   Several of ye neighboring ministers hve taken yir turns.   Of late it hth been somewhat Sickly in our army—fever & flux.   But not many die.   I hear it is very sickly at Boston both among ye Inhabitants & troops & mortally so.   Our Army appear in good Spits & are under good Regulations.   no prospect of ye Regulars Comg out.   yy, we imagine are more afraid of an attack fm us   two of ye advanced Centry fm Bunker hill deserted to us yesterday Wht yy relate hve not heard.   Our Chief General is much admired   Wish him Good Speed.   We ve had a very dry time   yesterday a fine rain.   I hve Just made inquiry & am informed y^t Jason Winship & Wyman were ye persons killed who were unarmed & had not been in the engagement but were Solacg themselves at ye tavern ye chief of ye day & both died like fools   hve also heard y^t 7 deserters are come over to us from ye enemy who brng an acc^t y^t 5500 troops were ye whole number y^t were in Boston & its environs & its not likely more yan 2200 of ym can performe duty—An officer afterwards came to our advanced Centry on Charleston Side & inquired of our Centry how we treated deserters.   who answered yy were treated as yy ym selves were   y^{ts} well says ye Officer and turned about to go away.   Says our Centry where are you go'ng?   back says ye Offi^r.   Stop says Centry I have a brace of Balls in my Gun & if you Stir another Step you are a ded man.   Come back   Upon y^t ye Offi^r returned and yy took care of him *   Dr Eliot has got out in Disguise.   13 in a week of ye Inhabitants of Boston die. its so sickly   thus you hve it Just as I hve now receved it   how true it will prove know not. —— there is likely to be plenty of Cyder & Indian Corn   yn expect Bread & Cyder—I hve got good Bottle Cyder & pipe & tobacco   will you come and see me?   My Dutiful re-

10

gards to Mrs Dunster & love to your Children—Am not married   From your Dutiful & Obedent Humb¹ Serv't

Shushan July 28 1775   J. MAR [Part of signature and corner of letter gone.]

* P S Since heard y' ys. story is not true
& Dʳ. Eli
of Boston   we dont know
Some days after a thing is fi
Every day hear yᵉ firing of
frequently in yᵉ morning yᵉ reg

SIR   Please to convey yᵉ Inclosed to Mrs Hows when you have opertunity & thereby you' oblige   &c "

"MRS. HOWS. We should Choose to have about 12 15 or 18 yds Linnen Cloth ¾ of a yd wide after it is scunc [shrunk]   yᵉ yarn to be spun so y' 12 or 14 Skeins (7 knots to yᵉ Skein) will weigh 1 lb. before it is Boiled— we expect to pay yᵉ Cash for it as soon as done But should be glad to know before you begin."

The letter was directed:

For—The Rev.d—ᴹʳ·—Isaiah Dunster—Att Harwich. Pr. Favour of Mr. Joseph Nye—
Representative for Harwich.

There are two or three other letters from Mr. Marrett to his uncle, Isaiah Dunster, which are interesting.   All these letters were found in Rev. Isaiah Dunster's papers:

"REVD & HONᴰ SIR   It is so long since we have had any Communication between each other that I know not what to write (and yet you would think I might have collected matter enough by this time to fill a Letter) I have transciently heard from you two or three times which was some Satisfaction   The reason why you have had no Letter from me is owing to yᵉ removal of Mrs Stone from her old place. I have repeatedly endeavored to find her present place of abode but without success I continue at Shushan But my Income is not answerable to so Dignified a Name.   Thro Divine Goodness we are all in health   little Patty (stil yᵉ only one) has entered her 7ᵗʰ year and I dont know but is as likely as yᵉ fair ones of Harwich   The Measles are reif amongst us none of my family but myself have had ym and we are in daily expectation of having ym   your Brother

10

Dunster comes to see me once a quarter & seldom goes away without 6¼ dollars at time its not long since he was here; they were all well; mother as usual. The winter favourable but little snow not enough for transportation.

I had a full View & for Sometime of the President of yᵉ Union upon his Visit amongst us The View was in the College Library; the first time I ever saw him. his Dress was neat & modest, his personal appearance good But not Distinguishingly great. But there is something in his Mein, Behaviour & Address wᶜ commands love & respect & Discovers quietness & penetration of that & observation (with yᵉ greatest ease) of every thing around him He appears affible & pleasant but not lightly so. The Affections & Benevolence of a tender Parent as well as yᵉ qualities & Accomplishments of a Supreme Civil & Military Officer appear to possess his Soul.

We have no Special News But mind our own business & live upon the fruits of last summer's labor. Should be glad to hear from you yᵉ first opportunity. We all unite Duty & Regards to yourself & Lady & Family. Woburn Feby 3 1790 From your old acquaintance
Rev Mr Dunster "   JOHN MARRETT

"REVD SIR—I rote a Letter last winter for you I hve nt had opportunity to send it, not havng been at Boston since last Fall Therefor send it with this Nothing remarkable hath turned up since writ.g of yᵉ foregong—we have not had yᵉ Measles tho yy hve been all round us. it has been Sickly & a time of mortality in many paces this spring. with us in general healthy. The Distemper called yᵉ Influenza has prevailed—I have been confined with it about 10 days. But now well as we all are we hve no news. the Spring appears promising at present for a good Season The apple trees are in yir Glory a fine show of Blossoms Should be very glad to see you or any of yr. fam'y here. Whether I shall ever Come into yr. parts again or not is very uncertain Mr Hilyard of Cambridge continued but a short time in his agreeable Situation—Please give my dutiful Regards to Mrs Dunster & love to yr Children Shld be glad once more to See them—my little Patty is in her Seventh year

10

& grows fast—yr Brother is well for ought I know—my
Mother much so   Mrs Marrett is not present or also
would join in her regards to you & family
May 25 1790   From your old Friend
Rev Mr Dunster "   JOHN MARRETT
   [Directed] Rev Isaiah Dunster Harwich Cape Cod
   The death of Rev. Isaiah Dunster took place Jan. 18,
1791. Rev. Mr. Marrett wrote to his widow a feeling
letter of condolence:

   "DEAR MADAM It is a long time since there has
been any Correspondence between me & your family by
Letters & this on my part for want of Conveyance: But
tho it is a long while since you have heard from me, yet
I have not forgot you.   I sincerly Condole with you &
Family under y° heavy Loss you have sustained in y°
Death of my Uncle. Alas how great is y° Change in
your Family! I have lost a Friend in whom I took great
satisfaction; But y° best of friends must part: we live in
a world of Change; which should teach us to place our
Hopes on better things than Creature Comforts or Earthly Enjoyments.   I heartily wish you & your Family the
Divine Consolations & y° Guidance Protection & Blessing of Divine Providence that your Days on Earth may
be blest & that y° Blessing of y° Just may rest on you &
yours   The first intelligence I had of M^r· Dunsters
Death was by y° Publick Prints   But we knew not what
he died of til M^r· Stone who was up at Election informed
me   I hear y° people of Harwich are well united in M^r·
Simpkins & hope they will be happily provided for in
Another Minister—I dont know M^r· Simpkins.
   If any of your Family should come to Boston I should
be glad to see them at Woburn—I heard y^t one of your
daughters was at Boston last year & sent me a Letter but
I never received it nor heard she was in Boston till some-
time after she returned.   I should be glad to hear from
you   I have received M^r· Mellens Funeral Sermon for
which I thank you—We are all in tollerable good health
M^r· Dunsters family at Mason were all well last April—
         I remain your Sinceer Friend
Woburn July 18 1791.   JOHN MARRETT
Mrs Dunster "   [Directed] Madam Dunster Harwich

10

We resume the Diary:

1775 June 17 S Preached at home very thin meeting the men gone down to the Army on the alam yesterday (P S) Last night 3000 of our army went to Charlestown and entrenched on a hill But before they had prepared their cannon the shipping and Regulars by land attacked them After much fighting we were obliged to quit the entrenchment and the town. Many killed and wounded on both sides The shipping annoyed us much The town laid in Ashes! The adjacent country gone down—1000 of the Regulars killed & wounded not more than 200 of ours.

24—Just heard that our army entrenched last night nearer to the enemy on Bunker's hill—and that the enemy this morning appeared with their horse in Battle array and in readiness at the bottom of the hill to drive our forces away—but after a while they withdrew

Dec 29 Our forces essayed to attack Bunker hill over the ice on the Mill Pond but the Ice was not strong enough.

1776 Aug 15 S Read the Declaration of Independence

1778 Oct 13 removed from Dea Johnson to my place in Lex

1779. Dec 16. Morning Some Snow and then cleared off Was Married to Miss Martha Jones—Mr. Morril officiated

23 Moved into Parish [at Mrs Jones again]

1780 Jan 4 Great Snows—went on Rackets till Feb no roads broken out

1780 May 19 Morning, Thunder & rain at home An uncommon Darkness from ½ past 10 clock A. M. to ½ past one P. M. So dark that I couldnt see to read common print at the window nor see the hour of the clock unless close to it and scarcely to see to read a Bible of large print people left off work in the house and abroad. The fowls, some of them went to roost It was cloudy, wind S. W. The Heavens looked yellowish and gloomy what is the Occasion of it is unknown The moon fulled yesterday Many persons much terrified never known so dark a day People lit candles to see to dine.

1782 June 16 S. Preached at home. My wife

10

brought to bed 5 oclock P M   The child lived about
3 hours   A son

18   Funeral of my child

1783. Nov 2.   S.   My wife brot to bed last night 20
min past 1 oclock of a daughter

Nov 9   Baptized my child [Martha *"little Patty."*]

1786   Great commotion concerning Setting of the
Court at Concord.   The courts at Northampton & Worcester prevented by mobs.

1787   Troops passing here on their way to Worcester

1803. Aug 25   Mrs Marrett Sick for three days past

    30   Mrs M. dangerously Sick of a Fever

Sept 7   Mrs M. remains very weak   Her Senses gone

11   S.   preach'd A. M.—dismissed the People P. M.
¼ past 4 oclock my wife died

Sept 12   Busy in sorrow preparing for the funeral.

    14   fair—The funeral of Mrs Marrett.   Minis-
ters Revd Messrs. Clark, Stone Dr. Cummings Dr. Osgood, Fisk, Adams—A very large collection of People
The procession reachd from meeting house into the
Burying Yard & not all went   The whole conducted
with Great Decency and propriety —— My people exceedingly Kind and helpful   They propose to defray the
funeral Charges

18.   Sabbath   Preached at home Funeral Sermon on
the death of my wife

1806   June 16.   The great and Solar Eclipse.   The
Sun totally covered.   The Stars appeard bright   Dark
as a Moon-Shine night   as the eclipse went off could see
the moon with the sun

1810 March 21   Pidgeons flew in abundance towards
N. E. for two days

1812 March 26   Pidgeons flew in multitudes for three
days.

May 1   Some sore on my foot   Dr Kitteredge here

Nov. 26   Thanksgiving.   preached at home   [This
appears to have been his last sermon.]

Nov 29 S.   no preaching first time omitted on account
of my sore foot   I know not when I shall preach again.

Dec 30   Cloudy   Wind S. W ⎱ [Written with a trem-
    31   do   do   ⎰ bling hand.]

10

This ends his Diary. He died Feb. 18, 1813, of a cancer on his foot, and was buried near, but by a mistake not exactly beside his wife, in the old cemetery at Burlington. A marble stone is erected at his grave with this inscription:

Your fathers, where are they?
And the prophets, do they live forever?

HERE

Lie the Remains of the

Rev. Mr. John Marrett,

Third Pastor of the Church of Christ
in this Place,

Who departed this life

February 18, Anno Domini 1813,

. Æ 72.

A good man, a Just and devout.
In temper mild, in deportment blameless,
In doctrine incorrupt. Grave, sincere,

Given to Hospitality

and eminently Studious of the Things
that make for peace.

He labored 38 years in the Ministry
In active harmony with this people.

He died lamented

as he had lived respected & beloved.

"The Righteous hath Hope in his death."

Remember them that have spoken unto you the Word
of God whose faith follow, considering the end of their

Conversation,

Jesus Christ, the same yesterday, to-day & forever.

10

The Rev. Thomas Jones, the father of Mrs. Marrett, graduated at Harvard College 1741, was settled at Woburn 2nd Parish in 1751. He was the predecessor of Rev. John Marrett. He died March 13, 1774, in the 52d year of his age, and 24th of his ministry. He married Abigail Wiswell, of Dorchester. She was the daughter of —— Wiswell, who owned "Savin Hill, now a favorite place of residence for those who have plenty of money." She died May 24, 1814, aged 92, having lived a widow 40 years. In the Diary, the Wiswell family is often referred to, especially "Lois," whom Mr. Marrett sometimes calls "sister."

Rev. John Marrett, as we have seen, married Dec. 16, 1779, Martha Jones. She died Sept. 11, 1803. They had two children:

1. Infant^6 son, born June 16, Sunday, 1782. He lived about three hours.

2. MARTHA^6 MARRETT, (*John,^{5} Amos and Mary^4 D., Henry,^{3} Jonathan,^{2} Henry,^{1}*) born Nov. 2, Sunday, 1783. She is often called by her father "little Patty." She was an object of tender solicitude, being the only daughter and surviving child. She married Jan. 1, 1818, Samuel Sewall, son of Chief Justice Samuel Sewall and Abigail Devereux. He was born at Marblehead, June 1, 1785, graduated at Harvard College 1804, was settled at Burlington, Mass., (over the 2nd Church in Woburn, as formerly known—Burlington was incorporated 1799), April 13, 1814, where he preached until 1842. He preached several years afterwards as a supply for the society in North Woburn, where he organized a church. He wrote for the American Quarterly Register, in 1838, "A complete list of the churches and ministers of Middlesex * * * " making, in many cases, a history of the churches and their usages. He was distinguished as an antiquary. He deciphered the "Balehoult" Letter, before referred to. He also wrote the History of Woburn, which was his last work. It was in the hands of the printer at the time of his death, Feb. 18, 1868, aged 82 years, 8 months and 17 days. His wife, Martha,^{6} died March 26, 1860, aged 75 years, 4 months and 25 days.

10

They are buried at the new cemetery in Burlington.

They had three children:

(i) SAMUEL' SEWALL, (*Samuel and Patty*⁶ (*Marrett,*⁵) *Amos and Mary*⁴ *D., Henry,*³ *Jonathan,*² *Henry,*¹) born Nov. 29, baptized Dec. 26, 1819. He resides on the old Jones, Marrett, and Sewall parsonage, which he has improved by additions and adornments since those of his Grandfather Marrett. With commendable regard for the memory of his ancestors, he has left untouched by the barbarism called modern architecture, that "best room," where Hancock and Adams were disappointed of their "savory breakfast," and where some of these memoranda were written. Its walls are adorned with the painted portraits of Chief Justice Sewall and other worthies, carrying one back to old times when ministers were not ashamed to walk to meeting on Rackets. Those magnificent elm and chestnut trees, four feet in diameter, which adorn the lawn in front of the house, were mere saplings when Rev. John Marrett first visited his "lady love." On one of those occasions, he tied his horse to one of them. Perceiving this, Mr. Jones' colored servant removed it to a more proper place, and, with a native politeness known only to his race, announced: "I'se fetched the gemmans horse and hitched him where folks allers put um, cause he'd eat up the trees me & Massa planted." Faithful and considerate man, he appears to have been the trusted executive of the estate after Mr. Jones' death. Honorable mention is often made of him in Mr. Marrett's Diary. He now reposes in the adjacent cemetery, borne to his grave by the selectmen of Burlington, personally, as a mark of respect for him and the ministerial families he had served so long; and in the Family Bible it is written of him: "Cuff, the faithful Negro Servant of the above Thomas & Abigail [Jones] died April, 1813, having lived in the family about 60 years."

Mr. Sewall (Samuel) has been much in town business —the settlement of estates, and other trusts. He is now Clerk and Treasurer of the town of Burlington, and Justice of the Peace. To him we are indebted for much

11

information of the Marrett family.   He married March
21, 1844, Elizabeth, daughter of Samuel and Elizabeth
(Tuttle) Brown, of Billerica.   She was born at Carlisle,
Mass., Feb. 6, 1820.   They are both members of the
Congregational Church.   They have two children, born
at the old parsonage:

(1) SAMUEL[8] BROWN SEWALL, (*Samuel,*[7] *Samuel,*[6]
John[5] *Marrett, Amos and Mary*[4] *D., Henry,*[3] *Jonathan,*[2]
Henry,[1]) born Aug. 17, 1846.   He was clerk at Carter
& Wiley's, druggists, Washington street, Boston.   He is
now in business for himself, as druggist and apothecary,
Main street, corner of Oak, Charlestown, Mass.   He
married June 11, 1872, Louisa Elizabeth, daughter of T.
F. Farrington, of Cambridge.   They live in Cambridge.

(2) MARTHA[8] ELIZABETH SEWALL, born Tuesday,
May 18, 1858, is at school at Cambridge, boards with
her brother.   P. S.   She graduated with distinguished
honor, and is now, 1876, at her father's.   She has been
appointed as School Superintendent for the town of Burlington, although but eighteen years of age.

(ii) MARTHA[7] SEWALL, daughter of Samuel and
Martha (little Patty) Sewall, was born Oct. 31, baptized Nov. 1, 1823, married at Burlington, Nov. 26,
1861, Luther P. Martin, of Goffstown, N. H.   He is a
very successful teacher at Windsor Locks, Conn.

(iii) ABIGAIL[7] DEVEREUX SEWALL, daugh. of Samuel and Martha (little Patty) Sewall, was born Sept. 7,
1830, and was baptized 12th.   She is a teacher, with her
brother-in-law, L. P. Martin, and lives with her sister at
Winsor Locks.   Unmarried.

11.   iii.   ABIGAIL[4] DUNSTER, the third child of
Henry[3] and Martha (Russel) Dunster, was born March
18, 1714, and baptized March 21, 1713–14, at First
Church in Cambridge.   This date, 1713–14, is according to the old reckoning, when March commenced the
year, therefore the birth and baptism were really in 1714.
She was admitted to the First Church, Cambridge, with
her sister, Mary (Marrett), March 9, 1729–30, as a member in full communion, and, as she had been baptized,
she was admitted on a profession of faith, and not re-

11

baptized. She married James Cutler, Jr., (not *Cutter*, as is written in the family record of Rev. Isaiah Dunster, and as printed on page 40 of this work, and from that record printed in Life Henry Dunster, p. 239). Of the date of this marriage we have no record, but they were published 29th Oct., 1737. He was probably the son of James Cutler, baptized at Watertown, Jan. 9, 1687, and Alice ——. If so, he was born April 3, 1715, and died in Salem in 1795, aged 80 years. They lived in Menotomy, and she was among the constituent members of Cambridge 2nd Church, 1739. The history of this family is only known to us in fragments, which it is difficult to arrange. In 1750 he was certainly in Cambridge and was an innkeeper, and, without much doubt, at Menotomy, now Arlington. At that time, he conveyed to Jason Dunster, of Cambridge, husbandman, for and in consideration of one hundred and six pounds, thirteen shillings and four pence, lawful money, "One fourth part of a certain piece of Land and the Mansion House and the barn thereon, lying and being in Cambridge aforesaid which land is Bounded South Easterly on Concord Road, Easterly on James Cutlers Land Northerly on Gilboa Road Westerly partly on Winships & partly on Whitmans land Also one fourth part or piece of Pasture Land—in Said Cambridge bounded Northerly on Concord Road Easterly on land of the town of Cambridge, Southerly on Appletons land Westerly on Coopers land containing about ten acres which land and buildings were owned by Henry Dunster Junr. late of Said Cambridge deceased * * *

And that he, the said Jason Dunster, his Heirs and Assigns shall & may from Time to Time and at all times for ever hereafter by force and Virtue of these Presents lawfully, Peacebly and Quietly Have Hold Use Occupy, Possess & Enjoy the said demised and bargained Premises with the Appurtanances free & clear and freely and clearly Acquitted exonerated and discharged of from all and all manner of former Gifts Grants Bargains Sales Leases Mortgages Wills Entails Jointures Dowiers Judgements Executions or Incumberances of What Name or Nature soever —— ——

11

And Abigail the wife of me the said James Cutler doth by these Presents freely, willingly give, yield up and Surrender all her right of dower —— ——

In witness whereof I the above named James Cutler & Abigail my wife have put our hands and seals this twenty fifth day of January Anno Domi 1750—and in the twenty fifth year of the reign of his Majesty King, King, George the Second.

| (Signed &c) | JAMES CUTLER Jun |
| SAMUEL RUSSEL | ABIGAIL CUTLER " |

her
" Widder" ANNA X FESSENDEN
mark

This was the same property conveyed to him, with Edward Dickson, Isaiah Dunster and Jason Dunster, by Abigail (Moor), widow of Henry[4] Dunster, the 20th of December, 1749, which he, James Cutler, Jr., kept only one month.

The next we find of him in a property transaction, is a deed (*Middlesex, Vol.* 101, *p.* 132,) in which he joins with the Dunster heirs, viz.:

"Rev. Isaiah Dunster, Edward Dickson and wife, Martha, James Cutler, of Salem, brickmaker, and wife, Abigail, Amos Marrett, of Lexington, John Marrett, of Newton, Gentlemen, and Jason Dunster, of Mason, 'Heirs at Law to our Late honored Mother, Martha Locke, Cambridge, deceased.'"

This was the property left by Henry[3] Dunster to his wife, who afterwards married Francis Locke. (*V. ante.*)

To this transaction Rev. John Marrett refers in his Diary, Sept. 30, 1771: "Rode to Cambridge and settled Grand Mother Locke estate and lodged at Dixons."

It is pretty clear that they lived in Cambridge in 1755, and probably kept the inn much longer. March 18, 1773, Jonathan Gardner conveyed to James Cutler, of Salem, *Brickmaker*, house and land, bounding east on the highway leading to the Great Pasture. This was at the west end of the town. He appears to have resided there till his death in 1795. He mortgaged the same

11

place, at the time he bought it, to William Cutler, of Cambridge, yeoman, his wife, Abigail, releasing her dower. She made her mark in this deed. This is very significant. We know she could write, and her signature, now before us, much resembles those of President D., her Grandfather, Jonathan, and her father, Henry Dunster—all being much alike. That mortgage was not discharged till Feb. 21, 1795, and then done by Thomas Brooks, administrator. He mortgaged again, May 5, 1789, to William Cutler, of Weston, Middlesex Co. In 1785 he is described as a "victualler," with a slaughter house and bake house standing on his land. In 1789 he mortgaged the same estate to Benjamin Phillips, and in this deed he is described as a "brickmaker of Salem." In this deed his wife, *Huldah*, releases her dower. In 1790 he is styled a *victualler* in one deed, in another, a *butcher*. In 1783 he conveyed part of his land and house to George West, who, at the same time, reconveyed it to his wife, *Abigail*, and in 1793 this land is described as the land of the heirs of his second wife, *Abigail*. This looks like confusion; but on examining the records of intentions of marriages (*City Records*), these entries are found:

"April 6 1776 James Cutler and Widow Abigail Tozzer both of Salem."

"April 28 1787 James Cutler and Huldey Symonds both of Salem."

In the records of deaths, "Feb. 1795 James Cutler victualler died aged 80 years."

In the probate records is found: "Admr. on Estate of James Cutler of Salem, victualler granted to Abraham Foster March 2 1795." The estate was settled and receipts given by Huldah—the widow—George West, son (in-law?) James Johnson, son (in-law?) and Abigail Lander.

For these recorded items we are indebted to William P. Upham, Esq., Harvard College, 1856.

From these scanty records, not a solitary tradition having reached us, we can only *conjecture* that her hus-

11

band, who was innkeeper, brickmaker, butcher, victualler and baker, was not successful in business matters. That his wife, worn out with bearing a large family of children, with grief for the loss of many of them, and the care of the living, was prostrated by sickness, and while unable to leave her bed, was called to surrender even her right of dower. It is not wonderful that she could not command the pen to write her name. She died soon after, and reposes in an unknown grave.*

We look back. She united with the church in the very bloom of womanhood, and before the cares of the world had made their inroads on her mind, as they must have done afterwards. It was done on a profession of faith, therefore deliberate. She could say, "I *know* my Redeemer liveth." Her husband, again, yea, twice, married, and what property he had went to the children of his last wife by a former husband, and his own children, if any lived to maturity, are totally unknown to us.

Should this ever meet the eye of any of Abigail Dunster's descendants, they will relieve anxiety by communicating the fact.

From the records of the 2nd Church in Cambridge, in Mr. Cooke's own hand, we learn that the children of Abigail[4] Dunster and James Cutler, Jr., were

i. JAMES[5] CUTLER, b. May 30, bap. June 10, 1741.

ii. ABIGAIL[5] CUTLER, born Sept. 22, baptized Oct. 3, 1742.

iii. ALICE[5] CUTLER, born April 16, baptized April 21, 1745.

iv. MARTHA[5] CUTLER, born July 14, baptized July 27, 1746.

v. HENRY[5] CUTLER, born May 10, baptized May 15, 1748.

---

* It is stated in "Brief Account of Families of Dunsters," before referred to, in a later hand (probably Rev Mr. Sewall's), that Abigail (Dunster) Cutler died March 2, 1766, at Newton, and was buried at Lexington on the 4th. She certainly was living in 1773. May 2, 1766, her niece, "Ruth[5] Marrett, died at Newton, and was buried at Lexington on the 4th." Was not she the one referred to in that interlineation?

12

vi. BETTY⁵ CUTLER, b. April 17, bap. April 22, 1750, and died July 24, 1754.

vii. SARAH⁵ CUTLER, born Feb. 1, 1753, died July 30, 1754.

viii. WILLIAM⁵ CUTLER, b. April 11, baptized April 13, 1755.

After this we have no knowledge of the children. Perhaps the "Abigail Lander," who signed the receipt at settlement, was ii. Abigail,⁵ born Sept. 22, 1742.

12. ISAIAH⁴ DUNSTER, (*Henry,³ Jonathan,² Henry,¹*) was the fifth child of Henry³ and Martha (Russell) Dunster, born in Cambridge, Oct. 21, 1720, O. S. In the Life of Henry Dunster, p. 238, his birth is stated to have been Nov. 1st. There is really no discrepancy here. For many of the family records we have been indebted to memo. made by Rev. Isaiah Dunster in Family Bibles and other papers. After he was settled in the ministry, 1748, the date of time, style as it is called, was altered by act of Parliament, eleven days being dropped in Sept., 1752, and thence forward chronology was designated N. S. (New Style.) This occurred while he was in active life, and he took the liberty to alter dates to correspond with the new mode of reckoning. This was right as to dates following 1752, but altering those *before* that time, without marking them N. S., makes us liable to some confusion. Hence official records and family ones, in some instances, vary ten or eleven days. He was baptized in the First Church, Cambridge, Oct. 23, 1720. We have no knowledge of his boyhood. At about sixteen he entered Harvard College, from which he graduated A. B., 1741, and A. M., in course. He probably resided in Cambridge, studying for the ministry with Mr. Cooke, of whose church his father was one of the constituent members. When about twenty-four years old, the neighboring ministers gave him a recommendation * in these words:

* This paper was carefully kept in his family until by the death of his daughter, Hannah, that family became extinct. It is now before the writer.

*10

12

"These may certify that Isaiah Dunster Master of Arts having given us satisfaction as to his Qualifications for the work of the Gospel Ministry & of his good Disposition in that Way to Serve & promote the Kingdom of Christ.

We accordingly heartely recomend him to that Sacred Work wherever divine Providence may call him.

Weston May 14 1745

JOHN HANCOCK
WM WILLIAMS
JOHN COTTON
NATHL. APPLETON
WARKAM WILLIAMS
SETH STORER
NICHOLAS BOWER
SAML. COOKE"

He appears to have preached as a candidate for settlement in Sutton, Worcester Co., Mass., where they invited him to settle. To this invitation he replied:

"GENTLEMEN Having I trust duly considered ye Greatness and Importance of the Work of ye Ministry and the Circumstances of the Parish in which you have invited me to Settle & depending on ye Divine Assistance I hereby declare my compliance with your Call provided ye Society think it reasonable and prudent to comply with the following Conditions viz

That immediately after my Ordination upon my Desire you enter into Bonds upon lawful Interest for ye payment of ye sum of Four Hundred Pounds Old Tenor* (which is already voted as an Encouragement for my Settlement) engage to make up for ye Depreciation of money in Said Sum till paid and pay ye Principal as soon as you conveniently can. That at any time upon my Desire you add ye Value of One Hundred Pounds Old Tenor to my Settlement in such Materials for Building & Labour as shall be most agreeable to me at y^e same prices for which I may yn procure ym for ready Money.

That you State the Sum of Two Hundred Pounds Old

---

* The Old Tenor was two-fifteenths of lawful money; so that £400 would equal \$177.78, and the yearly salary, \$88.88.

12

Tenor which is voted for a yearly Sallary upon the Produce of the country in the following or some Such Method viz

That you engage annually to pay me so long as I continue your Minister such a sum in Bills of Public Credit or other General Medium of Trade as shall be Sufficient to purchase as many Bushels of Indian Corn in the month of May as Fifty Pounds Old Ten^r would have done & as shall be Sufficient to Purchase as many bushels of Rye as Fifty Pounds Old Ten^r would have purchased in the Month of May this present year at ye General Price among yourselves. That you annually pay me Such a Sum also as will be sufficient to purchase in ye month of October as many pounds of Beef as Fifty Pounds Old Ten^r shall in ye month of October next & as shall be sufficient to purchase as many pounds of Pork in ye Month of December as Fifty Pounds Old Ten^r will in ye month of December next at ye General Price in Worcester After three years are expired from my Ordination y^t you yearly add unto my Sallary the sum of ten Pounds Old Ten^r till it come to two Hundred and Sixty Pounds Old Ten^r as ye Money is now stated. That if this Sallary be insufficient for My Comfortable Support you make Such farther Additions thereto as my Necessities require and your abilities will permit.

Gentlemen If you can cheerfully comply with these Conditions it Appears to me a Foundation will be laid for my Comfortable Maintainance. But if you think ym Such as you cannot caisly fullfill, I shall be glad to know it.

So expecting to hear farther from you & desiring your Prayers for Me y^t I may be a Vessel of Honour Sanctified & fitted for ye Masters use & Service & Praying y^t ye Society may live in Love & Peace and be directed by ye Great Head of ye Church unto y^t which may be most for his Glory I remain your Friend & Servt.

Cambridge Augt 12 1746   ISAIAH DUNSTER

To Capt. Timothy Carter, Messrs Isaac Barnard, Josiah Bond, Lieut. Sollomon Holman & Messrs Gershom Wait & Richard Singletary Comitte in Sutton Second Precinct. (to be communicated)"

12

These conditions were not complied with, although great personal efforts were made, as the following subscription paper shows, to induce him to settle there:

"SUTTON Sept y° 1 1746

We the subscribers would Show our Willenness to help forwards the Settlement of Mr. Dunster whome this Parish have already voted a Call in order for to settle in y° Gospel Minestry with us in order hereto we have Set our Names and fixed the following Sums which we promas to pay unto Mr Dunster in work or material sutable to carre on his Bulding if he shall settle with us upon his demand "

(Signed by twenty-one individuals, in sums from £10 to 3 shillings, Old Tenor.)

In March, 1747, he had been preaching in Dartmouth, Bristol Co., Mass., for considerable time, and had pleased the church, as shown by this letter:

"MR DUNSTER Sir I was yesterday at the Invitation of the Second Precinct of Dartmouth over there to attend their meeting which was not only to Chuse their Officers for the year as the Law directs but also to see if the Precinct would Concur the Churches Choice of yourself for their minister & never any man could have a more clear & full vote than you had & if Providence should so order that you should be otherwise Ingaged I am afraid they will never unite for a man so again. I hope God will Incline your heart to them as he has united their hearts to yourself, as to your Settlement & to Support you, this is what you may rely upon that It will not bee less than six hundred pounds of the present currency & three for your yearly Salery tho they were not In a Capacity to run their votes so Just now, but will soon do it if they can have any Incouragement that you will come to them the reasons why they could not do it yesterday the bearer Mr. Tupper will render to you and besides the Six Hundred Pound I think you may depend upon considerable help in building if you do build. if Ever you desire to go to a place that the affections of the People are universall to you, this must be It pray sir if you are not Ingaged keep yourself free for

12

them untill all things are brought to your mind which if you will be so good as to let the messenger know I hope It will be soon complyed with which is the needfull   from yours to Serve

TIMOTHY RUGGLES

Roch[ester] 4th March 1747"

Mr. Ruggles (H. C., 1707,) was the minister of Rochester, and took a large interest in the settlement of Mr. D. at Dartmouth. Afterwards he wrote Mr. D. another letter:

"MR DUNSTER Sir yours of 8th present came Safe to hand and I readily Comply with your reasonable request—In order to it, may remind you that Rev. Mr Pierce was no Great favorite of the Petition (as you were knowing) but since it is granted he is as far as I can find Intirely Silent I may add that at the request of a great number of the new Parish I was over at Dartmouth at their meeting—as far as I could observe there was no matter of uneasiness Capt Pope then & since has manifested his Intire Satisfaction In the thing—and as far as I can find those who were ever uneasy. It was lest by that means they should have a man imposed on them by the church which they were opposed to There were three men present at the meeting who at first did not act but when the jealosy they had that it was a contrivance to bring in Mr Willis to be their Minister, was removed & the vote called for the Parishe's concurrance of the Church's choice of yourself they freely acted but did say that they were not reconciled to a maintainance of a minister by *way of Tax* but were free to do their parts to the full with respect to yourself & they were told that that should be all that they would require of them, after which I heard not nor percived either at their meeting or in any other way the least uneasiness & It plainly appears to me that a year or two's gentle treatment of the non Petitioners by the other party will Intirely erase those difficulties I have since I received your letter been over there occasionally & can find nothing of that nature nor anything else that looks discouraging. they have a loving desire of your return to

12

them In general & I question whether they will look
after any Body to preach to them till your time is out at
Harwich & if they do It will be only somebody to preach
for the neighboring ministers & they to them.   There
are many things which might be urged upon you as Inducements to your coming to them again.   Submitting
all to Divine Providence I shall only ad one thing Instead of many that might be said & that is They are Intirely united In yourself & if you reject them there is no
prospect of their being so In another   I am sir your sincere friend & Humble Servant

Timothy Ruggles

Roch. 22 March 1747–8 "

The church in Dartmouth had given him a call, and
the precinct " At an adjourned meeting of yᵉ Inhabitants of the Second Precinct in Dartmouth

Voted on the Second Article Contained in the Warrant that the Precinct Offer Mr Isaiah Dunster Six hundred Pounds Old Tenor for a Settlement to Incourage
him to Come and Settle with us in the Work of the
Ministry

Also Voted that Fifty Pounds Old Tenor be added to
yᵉ former Two hundred and Fifty Pounds Old Tenor
Voted as a Salary for Mr Isaiah Dunster which will be
Three hundred Pounds Old Tenor pr. year

Also Voted that Mr. Quishman be chosen agent to inform Mr. Isaiah Dunster what Steps we have Taken in
Order to Obtain him to Settle with us and to Get a Minister to Preach to us Two Sabbaths

Attest   Paul Mandell
Precinct Clerk "

This vote, the copy of which is written in a free, distinct, and very ornamental hand, was dated after "*Dartmouth,*" " May 16 1748," but it was in Rev. I. Dunster's
hand.   We think it was sooner, probably in April, for
this is the copy of Mr. D.'s reply:

" Sɪʀ   please communicate this to yᵉ Committee
Gentlemen   I have received yours of April 15 in which
you intimate yᵗ your Societies being unable to invite me
to Settle with them in yᵉ Ministry sooner than they did

12

lays me Under an Obligation to Comply with their Invitation.   But I conceive it doth not for after I had tarried near two months with ym purely for the Sake of their forming Some Scheme for a Maintainance, it was thought by Several of their Committee so improbable yᵗ yᵉ Society would come into any Peaccble Method yᵗ yy told me yy could not desire me to tarry any longer with any View thereto altho yy should be glad yᵗ I would tarry if I could See my Way Clear, Upon which I concluded to leave yᵉ place & told them I should engage in any other Place yᵗ Presented.   This Gentlemen some of yourselves undoubtedly remember.   As to the Circumstances of your Society which are mentioned in your Letter you may depend upon it I shall duly consider them but cannot give you any visit as you desire at present for The Church & Congregation in this place have given me an Invitation to Settle with them in yᵉ Work of yᵉ Ministry and tis Thought reasonable yᵗ I preach with ym until I give an Answer   I desire therefore yᵗ you would immediately apply to Some Suitable Person to preach with you till then & remain your Sincere Friend & Servt
Isaiah Dunster

Harwich   ⎱ To Deacon Jenness
May 4th 1748 ⎰ to be communicated "

Although Mr. D. had given the people of Dartmouth so decided an answer, they appear still unwilling to give him up.   The Rev. Richard Pierce, (H. C., 1724,) who was the minister of the First Parish there, interceded in their behalf, and sent this letter:

"Rev. and Dear Sir   I recd yours Dated May 4 1748 in which you tell me that you have an invitation to settle in yᵉ work of the Ministry at Harwich to which I say I am glad to hear that you have met with such a kind reception there but at the same time I am sorry for our misfortune for I hear you intend to settle with them & not with us   but notwithstanding all I hear I must beg one favor of you and that is that you would not proceed any farther with yᵗ People nor give them any farther encouragement than you have already given till I have an opportunity to speak with you which I intend

12

to do with Submission to Providence on or before the 14th of this month—Of this I cannot be Denied—I had almost said y' I will not be Denied of this favor—I have hired a man on purpose to bring this Letter to you therefore I trust you will not deny my Request. I have many things to say to you but am in ye utmost hast, being bound to Boston directly and after my kind Respects to you I Rest your assured friend

Dart^th June 4 1748   RICHD PIERCE"

To this he replied:

"REVD SIR   I have receved yours of 4th instant by which I perceive you have heard y' I intend to settle in this Place. How you had the Information I know not but this I assure you is Truth. I am determined at present to settle in no Place whatsoever unless a foundation may be laid for a suitable Maintainance. What yy have offered in this place for y' End apeares to me insufficent & tis uncertain whether yy will comply with a Sufficiency or not. However I have frequently spoke to some of ye Committee & Others of making proposals and should have done it this week were it not for your Letter, for every thing considered I see no Sufficient Reason at Present why I should not Settle in this place & ye Comitte I am informed have agreed to come to me for an Answer this afternoon   But I will endeavor to convince them y' your Request to defer it till next week may Safely be complied with   But if I cant prevail with them to Consent to this I shall make my proposals for I hardly imagine y' there are any Considerations of Importance to be suggested relating to either place y' I am unacquainted with.   However a visit from yourself as mentioned in yours will be exceedingly agreeable to your Friend & Sevt   ISAIAH DUNSTER

·Harwich June 6, 1748"

This correspondence ended the negotiations at Dartmouth, and he received from the church and people of Harwich, where he had been preaching, apparently, for a year or so, this call to settle with them. That from the church is in the handwriting of the aged Mr. Stone (H. C., 1690), then the pastor of that church:

12

"Sɪʀ We yᵉ Chh of Christ in yᵉ north part of Har-wich being exposed to difficulty in regard of Gospel Ordinances our Pastor being far advanced in years and so enfebled as not to be able to goe through yᵉ Whole of his Work

We also having for some time had experience of your ministerial qualifications wherewith Christ has furnished You as also your good conversation in Christ Jesus: we doe hereupon, Sir invite you, in partnership with Our ancient Pastor to take yᵉ Pastoral care of this Flock; taking yᵉ Oversight thereof according to the Apostolicall command given in I. Pet. 5, 2.

Nᴀᴛʜᴸ· Sᴛᴏɴᴇ Pastor
with the joynt concurrance
of yᵉ Bretheren "

Harwich May
3 1748

To this is added, in Isaiah Dunster's handwriting:

"I Pet. 5, 2 *'·Feed yᵉ flock of God which is among you taking yᵉ oversight thereof not by Constraint but willingly not for filthy Lucre but of a ready mind.'*"

The parish joined in the call:

"Harwich May yᵉ 3, 1748 At a precinct meeting Leagually warned & Assembled Deacon Mayo Modera-tor Voted to concur with yᵉ Church to give Mr. Isaiah Dunster a Call to settle with us in yᵉ Work of yᵉ Minis-try Voted also to give him Six Hundred Pounds Old tenor for his settlement and for his yearly Sallary three hundred and fifty pounds Old tenor as it is now valued and all yᵉ other ministerial priviledges except what is at present Reserved for yᵉ Revⁿ Mr Stone provided he Set-tles with us in yᵉ work of the Ministry

A true copy attest
per Jᴏʜɴ Sɴᴏᴡ Clerk "

To these calls he replied:

"To Deacon Chillingworth Foster, Deacon Joseph Mayo & Thomas Winslow Esq Gentlemen Tis disired yᵗ yᵉ following Lines may be communicated to yᵉ Inhab-itants of yᵉ first Precinct in Harwich

Gᴇɴᴛʟᴇᴍᴇɴ Having duly considered your invitation to me (tho very unworthy) to Settle with you in yᵉ Work

11

12

of y⁰ Gospel Ministry I hereby declare my acceptance of y⁰ Same provided a foundation be laid for a suitable maintenance. What you have proposed for y⁺ End appears to me insufficient. The Settlement I fear is much too small: But doubt not your Rediness to make such an addition as is Reasonable: As to y⁰ Salary I am not at present able to say what is sufficient for I conceive tis for your Interest as well as my own y⁺ some particular method be agreed to by which y⁰ Salary may be regulated yearly and until this is done I know not what y⁰ 350 which you have proposed is equal to. However I must say y⁺ I know not of any method which tis probable you will agree to which will render this sufficient. What I desire therefore at present is y⁺ you would propose some Method to regulate y⁰ Salary by, and y⁰ more particular & clear y⁰ more acceptable it will be to me since there will then be a greater prospect of y⁰ continuance of mutual love & Peace among us which are so frequently inculcated in y⁰ Gospel & which y⁺ it may ever abide in this Society is y⁰ Prayer of your Servant in y⁰ Gospel of Christ.   I. DUNSTER.

Har. June 7 1748 "

The difficulty of "regulating the currency" occasioned *them* much trouble, and again he sent a communication:

"To the Inhabitants of y⁰ first precinct in Harwich:

GENTLEMEN Having received Information that you have stated the Salary voted for me on Silver at fifty shillings pr oz. I hereby Signify that it is agreeable to me & I know of only y⁰ following Particulars relating to that matter which appear necessary for the continuence of Peace viz that y⁰ first years Salary be paid according to Silver as you have stated it And if y⁰ precinct & myself should think differently concerning y⁰ price of Silver in any year hereafter that my Salary be paid in Coined Silver. As to the Proposal which I sent by your Comittee at your last Precinct Meeting for your consideration It is needless I concieve to repeat them since they must be remembered and altho y⁰ whole of what I then proposed is no more than sufficient for a comfortable maintenance as I concieve or than was voted A. D. 1710 as a

12

yearly Salary for Rev Mr Stone Yet since Public Taxes
are likely to be high in this Precinct at present by Reason of yᵉ War & for yᵉ payment of yᵉ Settlement and
since Providence frowns upon you as to yᵉ fruits of yᵉ
Earth I am willing to settle on yᵉ Salary already voted
provided you now engage to add the value of fifty pounds
after three years and of one hundred pounds more as
money is now stated upon the Rev Mr Stones decease
and this to remain a yearly Salary during my continuance in the Ministry in this place.   As to the Settlement I concieve yᵗ as a Precinct you may provide a dwel-
ing House & Land to my acceptance for a less sum than
I can Safely accept off and I am willing to tarry in the
Place untill you have oppertunity therefor & desire that
you would do it.   I hope these Conditions will be complied with in Love & Peace but if they are not I expect
to be informed of it by yᵉ Precinct as soon as Possible &
remain Gentlemen your Friend & Sevt.

ISAIAH DUNSTER.

Harwich June 24 1748 "

There seems to have been still some difficulty in regard
to his salary, and he sent again:

"To yᵉ Inhabitants of yᵉ 1st Precinct in Harwich

GENTLEMEN   I am informed by your Comittee yᵗ several among yourselves are desirous yᵗ I should make
some alterations in yᵉ Salary proposed in my answer &
yᵉ chief Reason is because yᵉ neighboring ministers have
not so much at present.   In answer to which I think it
may be truly said yᵗ by far yᵉ greater number of yᵉ ministers in this county had a Salary when yy first settled
which would have procured as many of yᵉ necessaries of
Life as £500 Old Tenor will do at present & if so that
objection entirely fails.

Tis suggested also yᵗ I am not really desirous of settling here but I can truly say I know of no Place in
which I could more willingly settle than in this.

As to yᵉ Settlement if yᵉ Precinct decline purchasing
one & choose I should mention yᵉ sum which I will accept off I declare myself contented with the addition of
£200 Old Tenor to yᵉ Settlement already voted provided

12

I can dispose of it to my mind and y⁰ precinct will allow me a reasonable time therefor.

As to y⁰ Article which mentions y⁰ payment of Coined Silver in case y⁰ precinct & myself should think differently concerning an equivelent to y⁰ Salary I am willing y⁰ precinct should do anything which may be Safe for y⁰ Precinct & myself.

I trust Gentlemen yᵗ you will do yᵗ as to y⁰ Salary which may be honourable for yourselves & afford Liberty for me to attend y⁰ Work of y⁰ Ministry without Perplexity & remain yours

Harwich July 1 1748.   ISAIAH DUNSTER."

This proposition was complied with by vote of the precinct, and the whole matter appears to have been settled. Still "specie payment" seemed to trouble some of the parishioners, and on the 29th of August Mr. D. sent another letter:

"To the Inhabitants of the first Precinct in Harwich

GENTLEMEN   Although at your last Precinct meeting as a Precinct you fully complied with the Proposals for my Support in y⁰ Work of y⁰ Gospel Ministry which were then laid before you—yet (as I am informed) a considerable number are uneasy on account of the Salary which was then proposed and complied with, and therefore I propose the following Conditions for your Consideration viz: That the precinct engage Four hundred pounds as a yearly Salary for me at present and Four Hundred and Fifty Pounds after the Revd Mr Stone's Decease to be & remain my yearly Salary during the time of my continuance in y⁰ Ministry in this Place—Stated upon Silver at Fifty Shillings pr. Ounce & to be regulated Annually by y⁰ Current Price of Silver that is to say the Salary to rise & fall from the sums now mentioned in proportion as the current price of Silver shall rise or fall from fifty shillings pr. ounce with Merchants in Boston which (as I concieve) is what was intended by a vote passed by yourselves at a former meeting.

And if tis probable that these Conditions will be complied with in Love & Peace or others which some in the Precinct may propose which will as well answer y⁰ End

12

Proposed I am willing & desirous that the vote which was passed at your last Precinct Meeting may be reconsidered as far as it relates to yᵉ Salary and that these conditions may be lawfully Voted and then for yᵉ continuance of Peace it may be convenient for the Precinct to propose some Method by which it may herafter be determined what shall be esteemed yᵉ current price of Silver with yᵉ Merchant in case the Precinct & myself should think differently concerning this in any year herafter. As to yᵉ present year I concieve tis just yᵗ yᵉ Salary be paid according to Silver as you have already stated it for this was the current price of Silver about yᵉ time yᵗ the Precinct gave me an invitation to settle in this place But if there is not a Prospect that yᵉ Precinct will comply with yᵉ conditions above mentioned I desire (if yᵉ Precinct think proper) that I may speedily be released from yᵉ obligations which I have any ways laid myself under of Settling in this Place: for tis undoubted yᵗ yᵉ Gospel hath obliged its Professors to provide a comfortable maintenance for its Ministers and I am unwilling to accept of any Salary whatsoever unless obtained with as much unanimity as is usual in things of this nature. I desire therefore that the matter may be Seriously & Calmly considered & Debated & pray yᵗ you may be directed unto that which will be most for your Peace & Happiness here and hereafter and remain your Sincere Friend & Sevt.

Harwich Aug 29 1748.   ISAIAH DUNSTER."

This letter brought matters to a crisis, as we see by a memo. made on the back of the letter copied above:

"On yᵉ 31 of Augˢᵗ The Precinct at a meeting proposed for yᵉ consideration of what might be laid before them by me after Seriously Considering yᵉ matter signified by their Comittee viz Mr Kenelon Winslow yᵗ they could comply with yᵉ proposals herin mentioned with as much uninimity as was reasonable to expect and desired me to sign yᵉ conditions seperately & signify my acceptance of yᵉ same & yy would vote them & record my letter without Reconsidering the former vote. Accordingly I wrote yᵉ first Paragraph in this letter verbatim & after

12

these words '*which (as I conceive) is what was intended by a vote passed by yourselves at a former meeting*' I added and if these Conditions are Complied with with as much Uninimity as is usual in things of this Nature; for yᵉ Sake of Love & Peace I declare yᵗ I am willing to settle in yᵉ work of yᵉ Gospel Ministry in this place & remain Gentlemen your sincere Friend & Sevt.

Harwich   ISAIAH DUNSTER
Aug 31 1748 "

To this is added: " And the following method agreed to in which to Regulate yᵉ Salary Annually viz Yᵗ The Precinct Choose one man, myself another annually in ye month of March both Inhabitants of this place of good Report & voters in all Town affairs to enquire into yᵉ Price of Silver and determine what yᵉ Salary shall be by yᵉ Price of Silver in yᵉ months of April & May: & if these two cant agree yᵗ yy shall Choose another to assist them & a majority in this case to determine yᵉ Salary for yᵗ year."

Thus the long and tedious negotiations, made necessary, perhaps, by the scarcity of money,* the troublous times of the French war, and the unharmonious views of the people about his salary, which could have been reconciled only by their unusual unanimity in his call, added to a general distrust of man with man, which war always produces, were brought to a close, and Wednesday, the 2d day of Nov., 1748, appointed for his ordination.

A draft of the letters missive, in his handwriting, is found among his old papers, which we copy:

"The Chh. of Christ in yᵉ north part of Harwich To the first Chh of Christ in Cambridge:—Grace, Mercy & Peace be multiplied from God yᵉ Father & from his Son Jesus Christ.

REVD. HOND & BELOVED   Whereas Jesus Christ our King & Head hath of his Grace enclined us Unanimously to invite Mr Isaiah Dunster to take the Pastoral Charge

---

* The next year, "Seventeen cart and truck loads of coined silver and about ten truck loads of coined copper" arrived. (*Coll. Hist. Soc.*, I. 53–58.

12

over us with our Rev. Pastor (who by reason of age is unable to perform y° whole of y° ministerial work) and him to comply with this our invitation. And whereas we have appointed Wednesday y° Second Day of November next to be set apart for his Solemn Ordination. We therefore hereby request & desire y' your Revd Elder and a Messenger chosen by you would come to this place on sd Day to join with y° Rev Elders & Messengers of other Chh's by us invited, in all such Ministerial Acts as y° work of such a Day requires. We also request an Interest in your Prayers to God for us & Commending you to GOD & his Word of Grace Subscribe your Brethren in y° Faith & Fellowship of y° Gospel.

Harwich * Sept 6 1748 "

Thus invested with the authority of pastor, he entered upon its duties with the ardor of a young minister who feels the responsibility of his position and the magnitude of his call. In his sermons he was "thoroughly evangelical," yet he delighted to dwell upon the practical duties of life, and enforced his instructions with a gravity and sincerity which carried conviction to the hearts of his hearers. His sermons, especially, in his early ministry, were written in full, but later in life, he appears to have spoken *ex tempore* in the body of the sermon. There are many fragments, having only the text, introduction and items of doctrine to be illustrated, and duties to be applied. Among many manuscript sermons now in our possession, is one in an excellent state of preservation, which he preached, as shown by a memo. on it, at "Dartmouth July 26, 1747 P. M.," and also at "Cambridge 2nd Church Oct. 18th, 1747 P. M." This was Mr. Cooke's church, and the one to which his father's family belonged, and which from 1739, the date of its organization, he had undoubtedly attended. He also preached it at "Harwich January 31 1748 P. M.," when he was a candidate for settlement. The manuscript is less than six inches long, and is three and a half wide, with the margins carefully ruled off, leaving just three inches for use. On these pages, fifteen in number,

---

* This Parish was set off as a separate town in 1830? and called Brewster.

12

(eight leaves in the MS.) are, on an average, forty lines, with nine words to a line, making over 5000 words in the discourse.   The text, Matthew 5, 43, 44, 45, written in full, begins the second page.   On the blank page is written the Psalms to be sung, all taking just half an inch of the page, thus:

PS. 35 from v. 13 to end of 2nd ph.	PS. 133 2nd Metre
But as for me when yy. were sick	How good it is to see
my cloathing yn of sackcloth was	& how it pleaseth well
my soul I bowed with Fasts, my prayers	together ev'n in Unity
did back into my bosom pass. *	for Brethren so to dwell

There were several of his sermons published.   He was evidently in advance of his times in liberality.   He disclaimed all interference of the ministry with civil authority.   In a sermon preached Sept. 15, 1762, at the "instalment" of Rev. Mr. Joseph Green, Jr., as pastor of the First Church in Yarmouth, from Heb. 13, 17, he said: "Altho an awful Degree of Power hath been claimed, and through various Arts maintained by some who are stiled the Ministers of Christ yet private Christians have no cause to dread the Authority which really belongs to the Christian Ministry.   It clasheth not with civil Government being so far from curtailing the Authority of the civil Magistrate and from infringing the Rights of private Persons that ministers are peculiarly obliged to obey Magistrates in all lawful Things and not to break in on the Rights of private Persons   The Ministerial Authority is purely Spiritual & Ecclesiastical   A spirit of Domination in the Clergy is of the most Pernicious Tendency   Now tis easy to gather what that Obedience & Subjection is which private Christians are required to yield unto those who are placed over them in the Lord. It respects nothing purely of a Civil Nature.   In things relating merely to Civil Society & Government the

---

* This is from a version in common use at that day of "The PSALMS of DAVID in Metre, newly translated and diligently compared with the original Text and former Translations. More plain, smooth and agreeable to the Text than any heretofore. Allowed by the Authority of the General Assembly of the Kirk of SCOTLAND and appointed to be sung in Congregations and Families." Slightly altered in a new edition.

12

Authority wherewith Ministers are vested, leaves Men
entirely at Liberty."

As was the custom of those days, passing events were
fruitful themes of discourse.   He preached in commem-
oration of the achievements in the French war and the
opening of the Revolution.   At that time his views
agreed with the clergy and people in general.

In a MS. sermon, which is without date, but which is
endorsed "Mr Bascom's * 1775," showing that. it was
preached at that time, from Luke IV., 18, 19, in which
he has underlined *" to set at Liberty ym yt are bruised,"*
he said: "Our Saviour left men with respect to their
Civil rights where he found yᵐ so doth Christianity
The Apostles & first Christians did not claim any civil
Privileges *as* Christians.   They obeyed the magistrates in
things lawful even altho those magistrates were heathen
and thus ought Christians in every age to do.   They
ought not to be disturbers of yᵉ peace but exemplary in
obeying laws & magistrates of yᵉ country to which they
belong so far as those magistrates are the ministers of
God for good to their People.

But doth it thence follow that tis agreeable to Christianity yᵗ the followers of Christ should never find fault
with nor oppose their Rulers?   By no means.   If Kings,
if Rulers, if Magistrates enact Laws which are not just,
which are not for yᵉ good of yᵉ People in General it is
Sinful to obey ym.   If yᵉ ·Authority under which I am,
becomes Tyrannical, If yᵉ Great Men make it their chief
Design to oppress yᵉ common P.ple, I know no Law of
God which can justify me in submitting to, or joining
with them therein.   If instead of being a Terror to Evil
Doers magistrates encourage them they are yn not yᵉ
ministers of God for Good but yᵉ Instruments of yᵉ Evil
One and ought by all prudent methods to be opposed
and resisted.   To submit to such things and much more
to countenance, to encourage, to plead for ym is to deal
unjustly, to do what yᵉ Gospel absolutely forbids.   Let
us all stand up for our rights, but at yᵉ same time let us
not speak evil or oppose any Authority which is of God
when duly administered."

* Mr. Bascomb (H. C., 1768,) was minister at Eastham.

12

Among his papers found at Pembroke, is an original Declaration of Independence.

The council of the "Province" of Massachusetts ordered, July 17, 1776, "a copy sent to the Ministers of every Denomination within this STATE* and that they severally be *required* to read the same to their respective Congregations as soon as divine Service is ended in the afternoon on the first Lord's Day after they shall have received it."

This Declaration is directed, "Revd. Mr. Dunster, Harwich." There is not a doubt that he read it from the pulpit, and from the very paper now before me.

Mr. D. was a close student and a good classical scholar. To the numerous notes made by President Dunster in an interleaved book, "A Concent of Scriptvre," which has come down through the family to the present time, and from which the photograph fac-simile which precedes this record of the Dunster family was taken, he added a number of additional ones.

He possessed, in a remarkable degree, a vigor of intellect and clearness of perception which well fitted him for his station, but had not what at this day would be called "brilliant talents," fitted to shine as an eloquent orator, capable of captivating the extravagant enthusiasm of a fashionable audience. His judgment was solid, mature, deliberate, and weighty, and his position among his cotemporaries appears to have been an honorable one. He was genial, and at times even humorous.

Among his papers is found an amorous production, written in a fine and distinct hand which characterized his early manuscripts, containing 1200 words, or more, in eighty-five lines, on a single page of paper six by twelve inches. We think it must have been written for his own amusement, as a trial of skill in composition, perhaps in his college days. It is introduced by a quotation from Ovid's Pastoral Elegy on the death of Delia, and proceeds, sometimes in his own poetry, to enumerate the endearing charms which delighted his imagination, until he had exhausted, as it would seem, the terms of

* Was this the first time the word *State* was used instead of *Bay?*

12

blandiloquence with the fascination of "Dear Maddam" to whom it is addressed.

He was often entrusted with the settlement of estates and other business, which he did with a minuteness of accounts which appears almost ridiculous.* In an old account book is the entry, "Edward Clark cut of ye Oak & Eastern wood all except 6 feet cut by myself."

This was wood voted by the parish, 1788, for his

* A reason for this exactness may perhaps be found in the annoyance to which Rev. Henry Dunster, his great grandfather, had been subjected by the lawsuits which John Glover, his step-son, had instituted for the "recovery of property alleged to be in the possession of Mr. D." This matter is referred to by Dr. Chaplin (p. 209, Life H. D.). There are fourteen writs recorded in Middlesex County about it.

In the language of a letter from Joseph Willard to Librarian Harris, 1854, now on file at Harvard College, "This controversy was somewhat angry. It had been continued in one form or another for some years. It had become complex, and every day it became more difficult of adjustment. It was a misfortune, resulting perhaps incidentally from the early marriage of Dunster with 'Josse's' widow, that no executor or administrator of the estate in this country had ever been appointed, and Dunster went on rather more trustingly than wisely, not with the wisdom of a business man. I find *no* reason to suppose that the charges against Dunster to which I have alluded were sustained by any evidence."

In the course of litigation, Mr. D. was required to file a "bill of particulars," to which he replied that the court required an impossibility, "for how should your petitioner, unless a Joseph or a Daniel, give an account of a Gentleman's estate dead above 16 years agoe, whom nor whose estate he never knew." President D. had taken care of all the five children, giving the eldest a college education, and declared his willingness to give a faithful and fatherly account to the full content of the two children that have not fully received their childs' portion. The claims were settled by referees, who reduced them from £1447 to £117, "leaving £57 to be further *cleared* by sd Henry." Danforth, Mr. Glover's lawyer, seems to have kept that for his fee.

Rev. Isaiah Dunster must have known of this trouble, and seems to have accounted for everything, however small, to avoid a like difficulty. Some of the descendants of Mr. D. appear to have taken the other extreme, and forbid the appraisal of any of their estates.

To the will of President D., which was dated Feb. 8, (not 18, as on page 16,) an inventory of his estate was annexed by his executors, which was particular even to the baby's wardrobe, some little things being called by a name not now fashionable.

12

use. He appears to have been always active, and for many years dealt in merchandise.

To show the mixing up of spiritual and temporal things of that day, we transcribe a letter and bill dated

"CHARLEST'N Dec 31 1759

SR. Yours of Nov[r] 23 and Dec[r] 12 have receved and should have answered sooner had it not been for the afflicting Stroke of Divine Providence in taking away our Eldest Son   I pray God it may be Sanctified unto us for our everlasting Good have Sent pr. Sears the Tea, Cups & Saucers and Allspice   have neither Brown Bowles nor Powder Sugar or would have Sent them   I remain yr Most H. Servant   ISAAC FOSTER

20 lbs of Tea at 50s.	50	
12 Doz Cups & Saucers at 7s. 6d.	4	10
12 lbs Allspice at 7s. 6d.	4	10
O.d T.nd	59	
By Cash of Capt Sears,	50	
O.d T.nd	9	

To Reverend Mr. Isaiah Dunster at Harwich pr. Sears."

He owned a large landed estate, the boundary of one tract of which, in Yarmouth, began at the "Fox Hole." He took a large interest in the education of children, and delighted to assist in imparting personally to them the benefits of knowledge.

His popularity among the people may perhaps be measured by the number of marriages he solemnized, for young people love to be married by a popular minister.   He had been ordained but a few days, when Moody Howe and Hannah Sears presented themselves and were joined in wedlock, and paid a fee of one pound, lawful money; and he has recorded three hundred and ninety-five more couple married during his ministry, with a fee of six shillings, as a general rule, which is equal to one dollar.   Mr. Samuel Cobb paid £3 10s. for being united to Mrs. Sarah Bangs.   Many of the marriages in 1776

12

to 1778 are marked p., which probable means paper—
"Continental money"—which was then at a large dis-
count, though the nominal fee was not increased. In
the summer of 1778 two are marked "6 shillings silver."
The lowest fee is two shillings—equal to 33⅓ cents—
paid by Joseph Robbins and Desire Ham, Indians, of
whom he married several couple, they paying from two
shillings upward, to James Oliver, who married Hope
Ralph, and paid the usual dollar. Mingo Eoney paid
3s. 7d. for the hand of Zilpha Cuffey.

His library, to which that of Rev. Mr. Dennis' was
added, was a large one for those days, and valuable as
historic records. Mr. Barry, a historian of Massachusetts, who had a large part of it, says he has seen many
specimens of his poetry, and they are creditable evi-
dences of his skill in that department of literature. He
also mentions many commendable traits in his character.

Yet, there was a scandal. Ministers even now do not
all escape. A negro *servant* [there were never any
slaves in Massachusetts!—*Anti-Slavery statement*] tied
up to a tree in the Bay State and whipped! That convenient myth "Somebody told," — Mehetebel Clark
"sizzled" on Lord's day. Susannah Bangs and Mrs.
Bloomer blowed the story. The good people down on
the Cape were dismayed. The official report, found
among his old papers, reads:

"Whereas I the Subscriber to diverse Persons have
represented yᵉ Conduct of yᵉ Rev. Mr. Dunster as bar-
barous & Cruel to his Negro Servant on yᵉ 19th Day of
July last, saying yᵗ I saw sd negro tied up to a tree·so yᵗ
she could not touch anything but by yᵉ ends of her Toes;
& represented it yᵗ she was cruelly whipped by her Master (having received this account from others) all of
which I now am fully Convinced was false altho I verily
believed it to be true when I said it and am now fully
convinced yᵗ sd negro was not used or corrected by her
Master with any Undue Severity—Whereas I reported
some or all of these things on yᵉ Lords Day following to
Mrs. Bleamour & Mrs. Susannah Bangs near yᵉ Widow
Bangs' House at Noon im⁻idiately after I came from yᵉ

12

Lords Table: & to diverse Persons in My own House between yᵉ Sacriment & yᵉ Afternoon Service & to other Persons & at other Times without ever informing Mr. Dunster of any uneasiness on my mind toward him By which means his character Suffers as I am informed in this & yᵉ Neighboring Towns.

ᴦ. I am sensible yᵗ my Conduct therein was very unchristian & Injurious to Mr. Dunster & to yᵉ Interest of Religion & I Sincerely ask yᵉ forgiveness of God, Mr. Dunster & of all others to wm I have given offence & hope by the grace of God yᵗ for yᵉ time to come my Conduct will be more agreeable to yᵉ Gospel & particularly yᵗ I shall never Spread an Evil Report to yᵉ Disadvantage of any Person before I have in yᵉ first Place taken Pains to inform them of it.

 Harwich Augˢᵗ 27 1777 MEHETEBEL CLARK
Signed in Presence of us
 JOSEPH SNOW
 JOSEPH NYE."

In the back end of an old account book, written upside down in a hand not his own, is this entry:

"Received of Mr Isaiah Dunster one Guinney if taken I the Subscriber are to have the whole of the money Iff not taken to Deliver the Whole of the Neat Proceeds to Sd Dunster as witness my hand
 April 6 1779. JOSHUA WINSLOW."

We know not what the stake was about, but if it related to the taking of Charleston, S. C., then besieged by the British army, Joshua lost his "Guinney."

Isaiah⁴ Dunster was twice married. The record of his whole family is taken from his Family Bible, and is written by himself to the birth of his fifth daughter, inclusive. The record is introduced by the statement that "Henry Dunster, President of Harvard College N. England came from Old England about yᵉ year 1638. He was yᵉ son of Henry Dunster & left behind him in Old England his father & two Brothers. The children of this President were I. *Henry* who returned to England & as yᵉ family tradition is died

ᴦ. *A manuscript Sermon is in my library preached the next day (aᵗ day) after Mehetebel Cla..*

12

without Issue, a Lawyer in Greys Inn, and Jonathan who died at Charlestown about yᵉ year 1727, whose children were I. Henry yᵉ father of Martha Dixon Mary Marret Abigail Cutter—Isaiah yᵉ writer, Henry who died childless & Jason who hath several children now living, 1765."

It was *this* introduction that misled many who sought the record of President D. and his posterity, to which allusion has been made.

He then proceeds: "Isaiah Dunster born at Cambridge Nov. 1, 1720 N. S. ordained at Harwich Nov. 2, 1748." "Hannah Dennis born at Yarmouth Oct. 15. 1730 N. S. married at Yarmouth May 26, 1750 N. S."

She, Hannah Dennis, was the daughter of Rev. Josiah and Abigail? Dennis. He, Josiah Dennis, graduated at Harvard College, 1723, and though the poorest scholar of the class became a useful and prominent minister in Yarmouth. He gave the right hand of fellowship at the installation of Joseph Green, at which Rev. Isaiah Dunster preached the sermon.

Among Mr. Dennis' classmates were Samuel Mather, Samuel Willard, John Collender and Habijah Weld.*

---

* Habijah Weld settled in Attleboro, Mass., 1727. He was rigidly precise in everything; not a bed was made or a room swept on the Sabbath, and the food for that day was prepared on Saturday. He married Mary Fox, of Woburn, by whom he had fifteen children—eleven daughters, who were not allowed to entertain company after nine o'clock. They mostly married ministers. He had a slave whom he used to send with presents to the poor of the parish who had entertained him. "Bristol" used to say on delivering the gifts, "Master always sends the best chicken to thank folks for a dry crust." Mr. W. felt the wrong of slavery, and offered Bristol his freedom, but he indignantly replied that he "had done nothing to merit such an act from his master, and if *anybody* had got to be turned away, the geese and the sheep and not himself were the ones to go." (*Annals Am. Pulpit, p.* 353.)

He built the house for a parsonage where the writer now lives. On removing the chimney (about ten feet square), filled in solid, having a fire-place eight feet long, and an oven that would have done for a western barbacue, a fragment of a grave stone, having the inscription, "Samuel Weld 167—," surmounted by a hideous face adorned with wings, was found; also a brick having the impression of the foot of a goose. Neither Bristol or the geese were turned away. The house, large for those days, is framed and

12

From this marriage, after thirteen years, "their first child a Daughter named Martha was born Friday 2 of y° clock A. M. Oct 7, 1763 N. S."

"Hannah (Dennis) Dunster," wife of Rev. I. D., "died May 22 1766 after about 4 months languishment being satisfied with Life and in a Comfortable Hope of a better."

boarded with oak, filled between the boarding and plastering with brick laid in mortar, and covered with clapboards *split* from the logs, and fastened with wrought nails made in better style than those Stephen Burroughs says he made while serving out his time in prison.   There is a tradition that Stephen, in pursuit of his *calling*, waited on Mr. Weld, by whom he was asked to preach.   Of course he did not decline.   On Monday, Eunice, the youngest daughter, invited her lady friends to call and be introduced to the brilliant young minister who had captivated her heart.   They came, and were delighted.   It was proposed to visit a pear tree then loaded with ripe fruit.   The pears lying on the ground being exhausted, it was suggested that he climb the tree for more.   He accepted.   Removing his well black-balled boots, Eunice perceived they contained no stockings.   He was *not* invited to stay that night even *till nine* o'clock.   He left—but not without stealing some of the old gentleman's sermons to set up business elsewhere.

Part of a letter found among papers of Isaiah D., no doubt sent to Mr. Dennis, is introduced to show the "doings" at College.

"BOSTON December 17 1728

REV SIR   After respects I would just manifest to you a sence of my love & regards by a line or two though you account it not worth while to write or come to see me or anything of yt nature wn personally so near as Boston   *   *   *   Give my service to Col John Paddock & tell him my study of Physick will be no damage to his brother if he makes a doctor of him and commend suitable respects to all.   *   *   *   *   Its like you hear of transactions at College yt is.   A great though not a *good* number of scholars found out to have stole geese & a turkey and roguery beside, your classmate Bosson is one of the worst its said Mr Walters son of Roxy is sent home,   Sir Lovel Senr and many under graduates with ym were only some punished 10 s:and some admonished, Frost the head of a class degraded 3rd   Iniquity abounds and the College is full of sin   *   *   *

DAVID HALL."

Frost was restored.   He was a classmate of Solomon Page, who married Dorothy Dunster.   "Sir" Lovel probably relented his conduct, and graduated 1728.   Mr. Walters' son got back, and graduated 1729, and made a minister.

12

MARTHA⁵ DUNSTER, (*Isaiah,⁴ Henry,³ Jonathan,² Henry,¹*) lost her mother when about three years old, but she appears to have been well cared for by her step-mother. In addition to the tuition given by her father and common schools, she was sent to school at Barn-stable. The property of her grandfather, Josiah Den-nis, who died 1762, went to his daughters, Jane and Abigail. It was mutually agreed by Isaiah Dunster, his wife, Hannah, and Abigail and Jane Dennis, who were then "single women," that the property of their father, Josiah Dennis, should be equally divided between those three daughters, without regard to his will. One of these aunts died before 1767, and by her will her prop-erty was given to Martha⁵ Dunster, and Martha's father was made her guardian. He took out letters, Aug. 11, 1767, and then "pd cash to yᵉ Judge 2s. & Do. pd Reg-ister 3s" L. M.; and on the 19th, charges "½ a day at Nobscusset to view yᵉ Library & take delivery thereof and Patty's Legacy in her Aunt Abigail's will." He took a minute account of all the goods, and a catalogue of the library, which was for that time large and valu-able, mostly of religious publications, among which was a copy of the New England Psalm Book. To that item he has added "worn out by Martha." In the list of wearing apparel, which was exceedingly extensive, was "2 pair Leather Gloves used by Martha 1774 wn at school in Barnstable." "1 pr womans Mitts 1773" "2 pr do. used by sd minor 1775." "13 shifts (numbered seriatim of which the 11 & 12 were) used by Martha 1775."

There is also a list of "Things Taken out of the In-ventory of the goods of Mrs. Jane Dennis and out of the acct of yᵉ Legacy of Mrs. Abigail Dennis to Martha Dunster and put into yᵉ trunk with her mothers Cloath-ing among which are 3 Gold Rings, 1 pr Gold Buttons, 1 Gold Necklace, old Gold, ½ Doz large Silver Spoons, Silver Tea Tongs, Silk Damask Gown, 1 Silver Por-ringer, Yellow Silk Quilted Coat, a flowered Apron (yellow silk), and a Gauze Curtain turned into an apron for Martha's wear."

There were also "a Brown Taffitee Gown, best Chince

*12

12

Gown, another Chince Gown, a Red Calimanco Gown, a Crape Gown, a plaid Gown, a striped Gown, a Silk Damask Gown, Best Chince Gown A. D. [Abigail Dennis] a black Crape Gown, a striped Linen Gown, a Red White & Blue Gown, a pale Blue Camlet Gown, a man's Gown, and a 'Full suit of Black Pady-osway.'" Some of these were "Reserved for Martha," others sold. The *Padyosway* suit bringing six dollars. Six yards of Red Quality were sold to a squaw "for 7 pence 1 farthing; to Aunt Howe an old tea cup & 2 saucers 1 shilling; Rev. Nathan Stone an old meet barrell 1s 2d 1 farthing; 5 old maps much tattered but sold Jany 7 1773 to Aaron Crowell for white Leather to y° value of 3 shillings; 'a pillow case & remnants.' N. B. These Remnants were put & sold with y° Gowns yy belonged to so far as y' could be known, so y' one way or other y° minor hath the benefit of ym except remnant of Calimanco used by & charged to y° child." Thus he accounted for every article except a few books lent and not *returned*, and a "cheese press left at Nobscusset." A receipt was taken for them.

"HARWICH Sept 22 1785

Then received of Isaiah Dunster by us the subscribers the sum of Fifty three pounds thirteen shillings & nine Pence which with what we have formerly received is in full of all demands from him as guardian to Martha Foster formerly Martha Dunster.

JAMES FOSTER.
MARTHA FOSTER."

Martha⁵ Dunster married Dr. James Foster, of Rochester, Mass. The date of this marriage has not been obtained. Nothing further was known of her family, except on a little scrap of paper was written, "Dr. James Foster Died 1811 30th of June." "Dr. Josiah Dennis Foster Died Aug. 11th 1812 at Detroit." "Dr. Isaiah Dunster Foster Died April 7th 1813 at Montagues on the river Rappahannock, Virginia."

A letter addressed to the "Oldest Physician" in Rochester, Mass., was responded to as follows:

12

"ROCHESTER, Aug. 2, 1872.

MY DEAR SIR: Dr. James Foster was a teacher of mine, and I was intimate with the family. The record in your letter [copied above] of the deaths of his sons I think is correct. Neither of them were married, and they have no connections in this town.

Respectfully yours,

JOSEPH HASKELL."

A second letter was also answered:

"ROCHESTER, Aug. 30, 1872.

TO SAML. DUNSTER,—MY DEAR SIR: Dr. James Foster and Martha, his wife, never had but two children, both born in Rochester, Mass. There was but one Dr. *James* Foster. Dr. Josiah Dennis Foster, their eldest son, was born Feb. 24, 1784; Dr. Isaiah Dunster Foster, Feb. 2d, 1791. Neither of these sons were ever married. Dr. James Foster was a good physician, and well beloved. He was not very well calculated to meet the trials of this life, and depended very much on the energy and good judgement of his wife, who was a Superior Lady. Tilly Foster liked to spend money, but had but little. He tried all he could to get the funds from his brother, James, but this Mrs. Foster prevented in a great measure during her life. After Mrs. Foster's death, Tilly succeeded in obtaining a good deal of his brother's property, which Dr. James lost entirely, causing him to become partially deranged, which ended in his committing suicide in 1812 or 13, I think. Nathan Willis, of this town, settled his estate, which was rendered insolvent. The good Doctor never had even a tombstone. * * * *   Very truly yours,

JOS. HASKELL."

Rev. L. R. Paige, D. D., of Cambridgeport, said, Oct. 19, 1872, that when Dr. Foster was buried the funeral procession was over a mile and a quarter long. He also remarked that he had a letter from a brother in which the death of Josiah[6] Dennis Foster was announced.

"MARTHA[5] DUNSTER FOSTER died Dec. 19, A. D. 1808," leaving only those two sons. Both died unmar-

12

ried. Both were doctors. Were they surgeons in the war of 1812? It is understood that Dr. James Foster erected a suitable monument over his wife's grave prior to his unhappy end.

The record in Rev. I. Dunster's Bible, after the death of his first wife, continues:

" *Mary Smith* born at Yarmouth May 29 1735 N. S.* married ISAIAH DUNSTER Nov. 13 1766 at Pembroke."

"Their first child a daughter named *Hannah* born Friday Feb. 26 at 5 of the clock A. M. 1768."

"Their second daughter *Judith Miller* born Wednesday Dec. 6 1769 between 12 & 1 of the clock A. M."

"Their third Daughter *Mary* born Lord's Day May 17 1772 at 3 oclock."

"Their Fourth Daughter *Catherine*, Born Tuesday March 1st 1774 between 5 & 6 oclock P. M."

"Their fifth Daughter *Abigail*, born Monday July 29 3 of yᵉ clock in the morning 1775."

This ends the record written by himself. The precision as to the hour of their birth seems to indicate a lingering regard for the aspect of the heavens claimed by Astrology over the destiny of the little one who makes its advent at that time.

The record, written by other hands, concludes:

"The Revd Isaiah Dunster died Jany 18—1791 after a short and distressing sickness."

"Mrs. Mary Dunster died Dec. 23 1796 after 8 days sickness."

"Martha Foster died December 19 A. D. 1808."

"Catherine Dunster died May 1 A. D. 1811."

"Abigail Dunster died May 13 1816."

"Judith M. Dunster Died March 22 1843."

"Mary Dunster died April 27th 1850."

"Hannah Dunster Died May 9 1853."

* She was the daughter of Rev. Thomas Smith, (H. C., 1720,) of Pembroke.

12

Over the grave of Isaiah Dunster was placed a stone with this inscription:

"To the Memory of the

Revd. ISAIAH DUNSTER,

the pious and beloved Pastor of the First Church in Harwich.

He was educated at the University in Cambridge, his native town.

Was ordained Nov. 13, 1748.

After a judicious, pertinent and faithful discharge · of relative and ministerial duties,

Satisfied with Life and Confident of Immortality,

He Died Jan. 18th, 1791,

In the 71st year of his Age, and 43d of his Ministry."

In the loose papers is a receipt, dated

"PEMBROKE, June yᵉ 10th, 1797.
Then Received of Miss Hannah Dunster Eleven Dollars in ful for a Pair of Gravestones.
I say Received By Me,
ASAPH SOULE."

These, we take it, were, with filial affection, placed over her mother's grave. She survived her husband almost seven years, removing to Pembroke, where it is thought some of her relatives still live. Her five daughters, none of whom were ever married, appear to have gone with her. Hannah, the oldest, received this certificate, and taught school:

"PEMBROKE, the 28th of May, 1792.
To all whom it may concern, this may Certify that Hannah Dunster is a Person of Sober Life & Conversation, and well qualified to Instruct Children in the more Early Stages of Life.
JOSIAH SMITH,   } Selectmen of
JOSIAH CUSHING, } Pembroke."

12

Mary also received a similar paper, in which it is certified that "Molly Dunster who proposes to keep School in the town of Pembroke for the education of Children in the most early stages of life, is a Person of Sober life and Conversation, and well qualified for keeping such a school.

Given under our hands this 2d day of July, 1798.

JOHN TURNER,) Selectmen of
NATH. SMITH,) Pembroke."

Here in loneliness they lived.   In 1841, when Hannah, Mary and Judith were living, they gave to Harvard College the "Bible of President Dunster, of which the Old Testament is in Hebrew and the New Testament is in Greek."   Mr. Eliot (*His. Har. Col., p.* 183,) says, "the Misses Dunster are the only descendants of *President* Dunster."   It should have been Rev. *Isaiah* Dunster. This Bible is carefully kept in a case made on purpose, and without a special request few there be that find it.

This gift was remembered, and their scanty means and grateful hearts were enlarged by a generous donation from the College.

"HARVARD COLLEGE, 31st October, 1848.

TO THE MISSES DUNSTER: LADIES,—In conveying to you a small remittance about this time last year, I expressed a hope that it would be in our power to continue the payment of a similar sum as a regular annuity. I have now the pleasure of transmitting to you the sum of one hundred and fifty dollars, which you will be pleased to accept as a tribute of veneration for the memory of your honored ancestor, the first President of the University in this place, and as a token of respectful interest in the welfare of his descendants.

I remain, Ladies, with high respect,

Your obedient, faithful servant,
EDWARD EVERETT, President."

At this time Judith had gone to the grave, and Mary followed in about eighteen months, leaving Hannah, although the oldest, the only one living.

In 1852, Edward' Swift Dunster, who had passed an unconditional examination and was awaiting active du-

Edward Everett letter is in the "Dunster papers" at Auburn

12

ties as a student of Harvard College, visited this old lady at Pembroke, to learn from her own lips the history of her family. He found her the solitary occupant of a humble dwelling. Her house, facing the south, was a little old-fashioned one, a story and a half high, with gambrel roof, door in the middle of the front, two rooms only in the main part. She occupied the room which looked to the east and south, giving sunny exposure. This was her sleeping and sitting room. The kitchen, in the rear, she used for her comparatively little cooking, &c. In appearance the old lady was quite stout, and rather tall, before being bent with age. She was not very chatty, but communicated freely and, I believe, without reserve all she knew of her ancestors. Her affection for her cats was manifested all the time of my visit. (E. S. D.)

With her, the house and its scanty furniture had grown old, but the courtesies of her early days had not departed, nor her sensibilities become impaired. He was kindly received.

Denied by fate of a recipient for the adult affections of the heart, she had transferred them to her three domestic pets, allowing them the freedom of her bed, and purchasing for them their favorite food, of which at times she deprived herself. Their well developed limbs and glossy fur showed that they realized her care.

On making known his name and the object of his visit, she was much surprised, for she firmly believed that *she* was the only living descendant of the first President of Harvard, whose name she bore. She gave him a few books of her father's, some of which had come down in the family from the earliest time.

He then inquired if she had any old papers which she would let him see. She replied that she had none of any interest to any one, but, pointing to a shelf near the the top of a closet in the hall, said, "there were some old ones there, but no one can read them." The permission to search the house was gladly received. On removing some of her well preserved things, he found beneath them a pile of old papers, which proved to be the "Balehoult Letter," and other papers of President

12

Dunster and her father, some of them in Latin; among these was the "broadside" Declaration of Independence, before referred to. Becoming interested in meeting a relative who bore her name, and probably feeling that there were no others who could preserve the relics of the family, she gave him other papers. Among them was a small package, which she had neatly folded and carefully pinned together.

This little treasure contained both school certificates, the bill of her mother's grave stones, the love letter before referred to, her father's epitaph, the records of the death of her sister Martha's husband and his sons, and other scraps of writing, in which no interest can be *now* perceived. Among them was this:

"Elkanah Fauman Lately Returned from Sea Desires to Return thanks to God for him & again Bound Desires Prayers."

It can easily be imagined how such a "note" should be in her father's papers, but what influence should have prompted its preservation must ever be a mystery. It will be preserved with the same fastening put there by her hand.

Hannah[5] Dunster died May 9, 1853, aged 85 years, 2 months and 13 days.

With the death of this old lady, *that* branch of the family became extinct. Rev. Mr. Allen, of Pembroke, preached her funeral sermon, which is reported in the Christian Register of June 11, 1853, from which we make a few extracts:

"The funeral of a person more than four-score years old is an occasion that seldom occurs, especially in a sparse population. —— —— ——

"The person, whose remains are now before us, was the descendant of one of the early settled and highly respected families in this community. Henry Dunster, a minister in England, came to Boston in the year 1640, and was immediately chosen President of Cambridge College, in which situation he remained, with distinguished reputation, fourteen years, when, in consequence of dif-

12

ferences of opinion between him and the overseers on the subject of infant baptism, he was dismissed. ——

"The father of our deceased friend, it appears, was son of one of the President's grand-sons. He was born in Cambridge, Nov., 1720. Was educated and settled in the ministry. In Nov., 1766, he took for his second wife Mary Smith, daughter of Rev. Thomas Smith, of Pembroke. The person whose funeral we are solemnizing, was the first child of this marriage, born Feb. 26, 1768. We may reasonably suppose, that in early life Hannah Dunster received all the advice and good instruction which sincere piety would dictate. We are happy in believing that parental and pious labors for her good were not fruitless. As she advanced in life, good evidence was given of steadfast purpose of walking in the footsteps of pious friends who had preceded her. At an early period her name was enrolled among professed believers and followers of Jesus Christ. There were some peculiarities in her views and manners, but nothing to justify doubts of the sincerity of her Christian profession. She embraced the views and took rank with those called liberal Christians; this was the title given in her early days, and this she was willing should be applied, but would admit no other. Nothing would sooner disturb her feelings and provoke resentment than a request to receive a paper or a book with the modern title commonly given liberal discourses. —— ——

" At an early period of life, and when her sisters were quite young, she lost both of her parents. She assumed the chief direction of the family, and in her solicitude to guard younger sisters against error and guide them in right paths, it is not wonderful if she frequently exposed herself to the just charge of unreasonable precision, and too much exactitude in her demands. Females when advanced in life, who have not been mothers of families, generally have some views and plans of life which look strange to others. —— —— We must think, with some admiration, of her provident care for sisters and wisdom in keeping them so comfortable on so scanty means. She cherished a remarkable independence of temper. This, in a measure, is always praiseworthy, but

13

12

may be carried to an extreme. We think the deceased was too averse to receiving aid from friends, able and disposed to lighten her burdens. It was only after long and earnest solicitations, that she would consent to participate in the benefaction of charitable institutions, established specially for the relief of persons in precisely her situation. —— ——

"The preceding sketch shows many difficulties which the deceased was obliged to encounter; yet amid them all, she was unwavering in her attentions to means of moral and spiritual improvement. Till the weaknesses and infirmities of age had greatly increased, very seldom was her place in the house of worship or the church found vacant. —— ——

"We have taken from yonder house the last member of a family, and the only inhabitant of it. We have come up here to perform the last offices of earthly friendship. Soon shall we return mortal remains to kindred dust, and thus extinguish among ourselves a name long known and respected. Can we perform this service? Can we look at the desolated house, or into the open grave, without thinking how rapid the approach of the hour when our houses must be left, and all the places on earth which once knew us shall know us no more?

"Earnestly let us all inquire what manner of persons we ought to be. Through the influence of means a wise Being is employing, may all be induced to walk in holy conversation and godliness, looking steadfastly for the second appearance of Jesus Christ. When he shall appear, through mercy, may these vile bodies be changed and fashioned like unto His glorious body."

13. JASON⁴ DUNSTER, (*Henry,*³ *Jonathan,*² *Henry,*¹) the eighth child of Henry and Martha (Russell) Dunster, was born in Cambridge, "July yᵉ 14, O. S., July 24, 1725–6, N. S.," and baptized July 18, 1725, and not 1726, as in Life H. D., p. 238. He married Oct. 26, 1749, Rebecca, daughter of Samuel and Anne (Harrington) Cutter, born March 3, 1731–3 (*Charlestown Records*). Her father died when she was about six years old. Nath. Francis, of Medford, and Joseph Adams, a member of

13

Mr. Cooke's church, were appointed her guardians, Oct. 12, 1744. The year before (March 31, 1743), her mother, who had owned the covenant at the formation of Cambridge Second Church, was married by Simon Tufts, Esq., to Mr. Francis. Mr. F. died Sept. 2, 1764, and she appears to have lived with her daughter (Mrs. Dunster) afterwards. In one record of Mr. Cooke, kept apparently to note his income from marriages, the entry is, " Jason Dunster and daughter of Mrs. Francis, 1749, of Charlestown precinct—marriage fee £4." She appears to have gone to Mason with Mr. D.'s family, 1769. In Mr. Cooke's record of deaths is " widow Ann Francis, of *Mason*, was buried in Menotomy, Jan. 1, 1778, aged 76." Her grave stone is standing in Arlington. She was baptized March 31, 1700. (*Bond's His. Watertown, p.* 274.) This agrees nearly with her age as recorded by Cooke. She, Rebecca, was a member of Menotomy Church June 2, 1749, about five months before her marriage. In the Bible of his father, Henry[3] Dunster, in the handwriting of Rev. Isaiah[4] Dunster, the record is, " Jason Dunster, born July 24, 1726, New Stile. Rebeccah Cutter, born March 19, 1732, New Stile [altered in a later hand to 1731.] They were married Nov. 6, 1749, New Style." These discrepancies are referred to in Isaiah[4] Dunster (*ante p.* 103), and there explained. They have been a source of much trouble. He, Jason,[4] was a member in full communion of the Second Church in Cambridge (now Arlington) March 18, 1753.

It is not clear, with present investigation, whether he united with Cambridge First Church and received letters to Mr. Cooke's, or whether he united with the Menotomy Church on a profession of faith. It is certain that they were married by Rev. Mr. Cooke, and his marriage record is, "1749, Oct. 26, Jason Dunster, of Cambridge, and Rebecca Cutter of this Precinct, Charlestown." He lived at the old Dunster homestead, bounded northerly by the "Gilboa road" and easterly on Concord road. We have seen that he bought the portion of his sister, Abigail[4] (Dunster) Cutler, and was already in possession of the property of Henry, his brother, given to his widow by his will.

13

For about eighteen years he lived there, and there all his children were born.   What should have induced him to sell that almost sacred place and remove to the wilds of New Hampshire? January 28, 1769, we find him taxed in the town of Mason, N. H., for the first time. His tax was 9s. 6d., the highest being Thomas Tarbell, £1 10s. 10d., and the lowest, Widow Mary Jefts, 8d. 2qrs. This land was sold by Timothy Whitney, of Shrewsbury, in Worcester County, for £121 6s. 8d.— "containing 190 acres, in two tracts, lying partly in the Province of Massachusetts Bay and partly in New Hampshire, beginning at a stake & stones which is on the southwest corner of the premises being in Townsend, by a corner of land owned by Jonathan Wallace; from thence northerly about one hundred and sixty rods to a pitch Pine by Jos. Herrick's land. —— ——

The other tract is meadow, about five acres—southerly on Hezakiah Richardson's land —— —— to Jason Dunster of Cambridge, Co. Middlesex, Massachusetts Bay.

Signed 23d April, 1767.   TIMOTHY WHITNEY.
Witnessed:
JOSEPH ESTABROOK.
SAM. HOBART.

Acknowledged May 21, 1767, by Samuel Hobert."

This deed was not recorded till April 23, 1769, the year in which he was taxed. The property (two lots) was split in two by the survey in 1741, by which New Hampshire obtained from Massachusetts a strip of land fourteen miles wide and more than fifty miles long. (*Farmer.*) It was chicanery on both sides. *Governments* are applauded for acts that would condemn a *man* to infamy. Belcher, who was Governor of both provinces at the time, was accused of bribing that "Irish Dog of a Surveyor." He retorted, that the "People were too poor to be taxed, and had solicited him to allow them to issue paper money without any fund for its redemption!" (*Belknap's History New Hampshire.*)

The town was incorporated Aug. 26, 1768, and the tax list referred to was the first under the corporate authority. Whether he had been here before is not certain. There had been a meeting house erected by the

For the quarrel about this line see N. H. Provincial papers vol V p 712-19   also vol IX. pp 153, 233 Dunstable-

13

proprietors before a church was organized, and it was given to the town in 1769. There was preaching in it, for we find a vote, passed Jan. 11, 1770, "To pay John Swallow two shillings and eight pence for boarding Mr. Nathan Bond's horse while preaching in 1769." (We trust it was Mr. Bond, not his horse who preached.)

Soon after his settlement in Mason a church was organized, in which he took an active part. The records of this church commence:

"A Book of Records belonging to the Church of Christ in Mason, began Oct. 13, 1772, when yᵉ Brethren were incorporated into a distinct Chh. Society by yᵉ advice and Assistance of an Ecclesiastical Council."

Then follows the covenant, in which it is declared:

"As to matter of faith we cordially adhere to the principles of religion (at least the substance of them) contained in the Shorter Catechism of the Assembly of Divines —— —— not as supposing there is any authority much less infallibility in human Creeds or forms —— —— hereby declaring our utter dislike of the Armenian Principles vulgarly so called."

In a note it is said, "by '*the Substance of them*' we intend to govern ourselves by the platform, so far as it agrees with the word of God."

(Signed)

JONATHAN SEARLE,	OBEDIAH PARKER,
ENOSH LAWRENCE,	NATHAN COBURN,
NATHAN HALL,	JOSIAH WHEELER,
JOHN ELIOT,	SAMUEL SMITH,*
JASON DUNSTER,	JOSHUA DAVIS,
AMOS DAKIN,	WILLIAM ELIOT.

The church was then declared by the council to be "now a Visible, distinct Church, regularly and scripturally embodied." The same date, Oct. 13, 1772, they unanimously "Voted to receive yᵉ hereafter mentioned sisters as standing in full Chh. membership with yᵐ."

* Samuel Smith was dismissed from the church in Lexington to Mason, in order to aid the gathering of a church there. (*History Lex. Gen.*, 223.)

*13

13

This is followed by nine names, of which the fourth is "Rebecca, ye wife of Jason Dunster."

Feb. 8, 1773. "Voted that Brother Jason Dunster and Bro. Nathan Hall serve the Table for a time until the church shall proceed to make choice of Deacons."

Oct. 13, 1789. "Voted that Dea. Hall, Jason Dunster and Samuel Smith be a committee to wait on Ebenezer Hill and invite him to be their Pastor."

When Mr. Hill (H. C., 1786,) first came to preach at Mason, provision had been made for him to board at Mr. Dunster's. On his way there he was accompanied by Rev. Mr. Dix, of Townsend. Coming to two obscure roads in the woods, they doubted which to take. Soon a man came along of whom Mr. Dix inquired the way. The man, either from uncouth manners or studied perverseness, replied, "I have got two sheep, a cow, a pig and a whole lot of chickens, and hay enough to keep them." "We wish to go to Mr. Dunster's," says Mr. Dix;" "will you please direct us which road to take?" Mr. Squeer's returned the same answer as before. "Well, my friend," said Mr. Dix, who never let the opportunity slip to make an "application," "you seem to be pretty well provided for in the things of this world; how is it with you in the world to come?" "That is the road to Mr. Dunster's," replied S., and, turning on his heel, left the unwelcome question unanswered.

Oct. 14, 1790. "Voted that Hobart Russel and Jason Dunster be a committee to wait on the Honorable Council at the Ordination of Mr. Ebenezer Hill."

July 1, 1802. "Jason Dunster and wife by virtue of a letter from the Chh. in Ashburnham to which they were lately recommended by us and now received back again." (*Church Records.*)

In 1773 he was Surveyor of Highway, and in 1774 was Constable, i. e., Collector of Taxes, and in that year his Province (State) tax was 2 farthings! equal to one-third of one cent. Taxes soon increased. In 1780 his "Beef Rate"* was £131 14s. 10d. 3qrs.; and in 1781 his "War

---

* This was to purchase beef for the Continental army.

13

Rate" was £2 5s. 5d. 3qrs., and his "Rum Rate" 3s. 5d. 1qr. The same year, the records show that "Jos. Herrick was paid £56 8s. for two and a half bushels of rye delivered to Jason Dunster for part of his sons hire for six months service in the year 1781." ($42.67 a bushel!) There is also recorded an order "to pay Nathan Wood £25 10s. ($83.33) for a pair of overhals delivered to Deacon Dakin for one of the soldiers." These prices were in Continental money. "Greenbacks" were never so low as that. New Hampshire tried to remedy this state of affairs by issuing bills of her own. These went down one-half.

Light is thrown on these enormous prices by reference to a list of prices fixed by law in the next town, where West India Rum is set down £6 11s. per gallon, New England Rum £4 18s., Men's Shoes £6, Women's do. £4, W. I. Phlip 15 shillings, and New England Phlip 12 shillings (two dollars) "a mug." "In short," says Hon. John B. Hill, (*Hist. of Mason*,) "so worthless was the currency that it would take a sack full of paper notes to pay for a pipe full of tobacco."

The bubble burst; but not before the town voted, Feb. 12, 1782, that the Selectmen "strain on the Treasurer amediately." Prices went down so that rye came within the means of the common people; and the town voted, May 26, 1783, "To pay Capt. Wm. Chambers 4 shillings Lawful money, it being for two mugs of Philp (33 cents a mug) that the arbitrators had that set on the dispute that the town had with Ens. Joseph Ball, and for two mugs that the selectmen had when they vendued the shingles and nails that blew from the meeting house."

An intelligent old gentleman, Thomas ... Wilson, who belonged to the same church with him, and who married the writer's aunt, and was brother to the Samuel Wilson from whom the interpretation of U. S. to mean "Uncle Sam," which so often does duty in print, was derived, related about twenty-five years ago, that Mr. Dunster was a devoted Christian, and a prominent member of Mason Church, and further said: "He was a tall, slim man, about six feet high and wore a white linen cap under his 'three cornered hat,' which he exchanged

13

for a green one when he went to 'meeting.' He was very amiable and of a uniform temperament, and much attached to children, especially his grand-children. His wife also was a church member, but more irritable and easily excited. His farm was in the extreme southeast corner of Mason, touching Brookline (then Raby) and Townsend, Mass., then spelled Townshend."*

In 1798 his son Samuel came to Mason and bought the farm. Soon after (1801?) he removed to Ashburnham, taking the "old folks" with him. They were discontented, and returned to Mason, where, as we have seen, they applied for readmission to their old spiritual home, and were gladly welcomed back. They spent the remnant of their days with their son, Jason[5] Dunster, at the west part of the town, afterwards called Mason Village.

He died Feb. 19, 1805, and was buried at Mason Centre. A slate stone at his grave is inscribed:

"Sacred—to the Memory of—JASON DUNSTER—who died Feb. 19, 1805, in the 79th year of his age."

"Great God, I own the sentence just,
 And yield my body to the dust;
 Yet by Thy Grace I hope to rise
 And dwell with Christ above the skies."

His wife died Feb. 16, 1806, not 1816, as stated in *Hist. Mason, p.* 182, (the error was on her grave stone, but is now corrected,) and was buried beside her husband in the Dunster group. The inscription is:

"Sacred—to the Memory—of—REBECCAH DUNSTER, wife of Jason Dunster—who died Feb. 16, 1806—in the 72d year of her age."

"In faith she died, in dust she lies;
 But faith foresees that dust shall rise
 When Jesus calls; while hope assumes
 And boasts her joy among the tombs."

* We think this was a mistake. *Shadrack Whitney* was the original owner of lot No. 1 in the *third* range, and Mr. Dunster bought of *Timothy W.,* perhaps his son. The lot in the *corner* of the town was No. 1 in range one.

14

The eight children of Jason⁴ and Rebecca (Cutter) Dunster were:

21 §. i. RUTH⁵ DUNSTER, born at Cambridge, Aug. 21, 1750, N. S., married Joseph Blood.

ii. REBECCA⁵ DUNSTER, born Aug. 18, bap. 23, 1752. She died at Cambridge, June 5, 1753, aged 10 months.

22 §. iii. HENRY⁵ DUNSTER, born Aug. 4, baptized 11, 1754.

23 §. iv. REBECCA⁵ DUNSTER, born June 18, baptized 20, 1756, married John Swallow.

24 §. v. MARTHA⁵ DUNSTER, baptized Sept. 3, 1758. married Oliver Wright.

25 §. vi. ISAIAH⁵ DUNSTER, bap. April 12, 1761.

26 §. vii. JASON⁵ DUNSTER, born March 27, baptized April 3, 1763.

27 §. viii. SAMUEL⁵ CUTTER DUNSTER, baptized April 27, 1766.

These children were all baptized at Cambridge Second Church.

14. i. ELIZABETH⁴ DUNSTER, familiarly known as *Betty*, (*David,³ Jonathan,² Henry,¹*) called in her father's will "Elizabeth, my eldest daughter," was baptized in Cambridge First Church, April 25, 1730–31. She married, at Westminster, James Taylor. They both lived and died there. Very little of their history is known; Westminster records have not been searched for it. They had a very large family of children, thirteen or fourteen in number, most of whom died in infancy. There is no register of these children to be found, nor sufficient data to classify them, and they are given as alluded to in a letter of Mrs. Estabrook:

RUTH⁵ TAYLOR, born and died in Westminster, unm.
REBECCA⁵ TAYLOR, born and died in W., "single."
A daughter,⁵ —— —— married.
JONATHAN⁵ TAYLOR, born in Westminster, married and lived in Ludlow, Vt.; from thence removed to Chittendon, Vt., afterwards to Ohio. It is believed he had a family, but nothing further is known of him.

14

JOSEPH[5] TAYLOR, the youngest child of Jàmes and Betty[4] (Dunster) Taylor, was born May 7, 1778, in Westminster. He married Betsey Green, of Westminster, Sept., 1802, was a farmer, and resided in Ludlow, Vt. He was a member of the Baptist Church, as was also his wife. She died of heart disease, and was buried at Ludlow. He died Nov. 5, 1869, of "old age and infirmity incident thereto," aged 91 years, 6 months, and was buried at Ludlow.

"They had nine children, of whom I am the youngest and only living one. All but three died in infancy or early childhood." (*Ora J. Taylor.—Letter.*)

(i) ARDAIN[6] GREEN TAYLOR, the oldest child of Joseph and Betsey (Green) Taylor, was born in Ludlow, Vt., July 12, 1803. He graduated at Castleton Medical College, Vt., and practiced medicine in Ludlow and Plymouth. He was a self-educated man, and a successful physician; took an active interest in education and temperance; was Justice of the Peace, and highly respected in the community. He was twice married. 1st, July 13, 1828, to Ruth Pettigrew, daughter of Deacon Andrew Pettigrew, of Plymouth. She died June 5, 1839. By her he had four children:

(1) RUTH[7] ANN TAYLOR, born Oct. 18, 1829, died in infancy.

(2) ANN[7] ELIZA TAYLOR, born Jan. 29, 1834, now living in Ludlow. ⸺

(3) AMANDA[7] B. TAYLOR, born Aug. 7, 1836, living in Missouri, married?

(4) ORINDA[7] L. TAYLOR, born Aug. 22, 1838, living in New York city, married?

Dr. Ardain[6] G. Taylor married 2d, March 29, 1840, Orinda Elisabeth Walker, daughter of Deacon Rufus Walker, of Williamstown, Vt. She is still living. He died at Ludlow, June 3, 1846, aged 43, and was buried there. By her he had three children:

(5) RUTH[7] PETTIGREW TAYLOR, born Aug. 20, 1841, died March 12, 1855.

P. Ann E. Taylor man Hon Wm H Walker
State senator from Ludlow Vt.
Had a son Frank Ardain Walker
student in Middlebury Coll. 1878

14

(6) SUSANNA[7] M. TAYLOR, born Feb. 1, 1845, died Aug. 27, 1875, in California, married, and believed to have had children.

(7) EMILY[7] M. TAYLOR, born Sept. 8, 1846, about three months after her father died. She is living in Rutland, Vt., married?

(ii) AMANDA[6] TAYLOR, (*Joseph,[5] James and Betty[4] D., David,[3] Jona.[2] Henry,[1]*) the second child of Joseph and Betsey (Green) Taylor, born Oct. 25, 1805, in Ludlow, married John Tyrrell, son of John Tyrrell, of Andover, Vt. He was a farmer. They both died in 1840, at Andover, Vt. They had six children:

(1) ALMIRA[7] AMANDA TYRRELL, born Aug. 10, 1828, now living at Sherberne, Vt., married.

(2) ARDAIN[7] AUGUSTUS TYRRELL, born March 22, 1830, went to the "far West," married, and died there.

(3) ELISABETH[7] ANN TYRRELL, born June 11, 1832, died unmarried.

(4) LUCINDA[7] SMITH TYRRELL, born April 27, 1834, married, lived and died in Cavendish, Vt.

(5) OSCAR[7] OLDEN TYRRELL, born Feb. 20, 1836, "married, went to the Union army in the rebellion, and died there."

(6) MELINTHA[7] TAYLOR TYRRELL, born Feb. 18, 1838, married, and is living in Mount Holly, Vt.

(iii) ORISON[6] TAYLOR, born Nov. 27, 1808.
(iv) REUBEN[6] BEMIS, born Nov. 2, 1811.
(v) MELINTHA[6] ——, born Aug. 7, 1814.
(vi) MERIAH[6] ——, born April 22, 1817.
(vii) —— ——, born Feb. 19, 1820.
(viii) —— ——, born Jan. 8, 1823.

These six children of Joseph and Betsey (Green) Taylor, all died in infancy or early childhood.

(ix) ORA[6] JAMES TAYLOR, (*Joseph,[5] James and Betty[4] Dunster, David,[3] Jona.[2] Henry,[1]*) the ninth and youngest child of Joseph and Betsey (Green) Taylor, born Aug. 5, 1825, at Ludlow, Vt., married Jan. 1, 1849, Abby Patience? Taylor, daughter of Nathan Taylor, of Sherberne, Vt. They were not related before marriage. He

Ora James Taylor was a Baptist minister in Plymouth Vt 1878

15

is a farmer, and resides in Ludlow. To him the credit of most of the history of " Betty " Dunster's descendants belongs. Being pressed with the inquiry if he had held official station, he replied: " I have the usual history of a small farmer, except, perhaps, that I have been Justice of the Peace for ten or twelve years, and am Deacon of the Baptist Church to which I belong; but would prefer neither of these should appear." Such modesty, in these days of official effrontery, ought not to be suppressed. Disclaiming any discourtesy, in printers' phrase, " It must go in." They had two sons and two daughters, born in Ludlow:

(1) JASON⁷ DANIEL TAYLOR, born July 17, 1852. He was drowned in the Indian Territory, June 16, 1875. Unmarried.

(2) LIDA⁷ MARIAH TAYLOR, born March 26, 1857.

(3) ARTHUR⁷ ORISON TAYLOR, born Oct. 28, 1858.

(4) RUBY⁷ ALMIRA TAYLOR, born July 12, 1860.

15. ii. MOLLY⁴ DUNSTER, (*David,³ Jona.² Henry,¹*) called in the will " Mary Bemis, my 2nd daughter," was baptized at Cambridge First Church, March 4, 1732–3, and went with her father's family to Westminster, in 1742. She married, probably at W., David Bemis. He was deacon of the Baptist Church. " She was a capable and efficient woman, doing good, and was well beloved." They settled in Brattleboro', Vt., on a farm. Had nine children: 1. John. 2. Joseph. 3. Benjamin. 4. Elias. 5. Abner. 6. Levi. 7. Asa. 8. Samuel. 9. Sarah.

1. JOHN⁵ BEMIS was a soldier in the war of the Revolution. He married first, —— Tubbs, by whom he had three children: Benjamin, Lucy, Nabby. His wife died, and he married second, Jemima Whipple, who had nine more, making twelve. He died in Dummerston, Vt.

(i) BENJAMIN⁶ BEMIS, (*John,⁵ David and Molly⁴ D.*) married Rebecca Dickinson. Resided at Bath, Vt. Enlisted in the regular service, and died there. No children.

(ii) LUCY⁶ BEMIS, resided in Littleton, N. H.

15

(iii) NABBY[6] BEMIS, married Joseph Hildreth. Reside in Dummerston, Vt. Two children: (1) George[7] Hildreth, married Mary Clark, of Dummerston, and reside there. (2) Alzina[7] Hildreth, married Humphery Barrett. Have two children.

(iv) JOHN[6] BEMIS, (by 2d wife,) married at Dummerston, —— Knight. Two children:

(1) ROXANNA[7] BEMIS. (2) BRADLEY[7] BEMIS.

(v) MELINDA[6] BEMIS, married Nathan Applebee, of Littleton, N. H.

(vi) ASA[6] BEMIS, enlisted in the war of 1812, died in the service, unmarried.

(vii) DANIEL[6] BEMIS, married Melinda Goddard, reside in Dummerston. Four children: Melinda, Anna, Orpha, Sumner—all dead.

(viii) KATIE[6] BEMIS, mar. Dr. Sewell Walker, of D.

(ix) EMELINE[6] BEMIS, mar. —— Applebee, went to Littleton, N. H.

(x) DAVID[6] BEMIS, married —— Burnham, reside in Dummerston. Four children:

(1) ERASTUS[7] BEMIS, was a physician, died in Michigan?

(2) DANIEL[7] BEMIS, was killed by the falling of a tree, unmarried.

(3) SAMUEL[7] N. BEMIS, is a physician at Dummerston, married Louisa Miller.

(4) HORACE[7] BEMIS, is a lawyer in Alleghany Co., New York.

(xi) STEPHEN[7] and (xii) WILLIAM[7] BEMIS, both died in Dummerston, Vt.

The date of the births of this family is not known. They were mostly Universalists.

2. JOSEPH[5] BEMIS, the second child of David and Molly (Dunster) Bemis, enlisted into the Continental service when between 16 and 17 years of age. Wintered at Valley Forge with Washington's army. He stood guard one night over a house in which General Washington was an inmate. At daybreak, the General came

14

15

out and said, "Pretty cold morning, isn't it, soldier?
Do you suppose a little peach brandy would hurt you?"
Mr. Bemis replied, "I think not." The General returned to the house and sent his servant out with a flask.
At another time, while on guard, General Washington
wished to pass into camp. He presented his gun, and
called for the countersign. General W. told him that
he could let *him* pass; he was one of his officers. Mr.
B. told him he must give the password first. The General then said, "You have a fine gun there, soldier."
B. replied, "Guess I can kill an Indian six or eight rods
off. Stand out there; you can tell. The General held
out his hat and showed the countersign in it, which was
obliged to be given in a whisper, or written. As he
passed, the General slapped him on the shoulder, and
said, "I wish I had a whole regiment of soldiers like
you." He married Jemima Stoddard; was a farmer, in
Dummerston, Vt. The family are Baptists. He died
at Dummerston. Had six children:

(i) POLLY[6] BEMIS, married Nathaniel Attridge, a
farmer, reside in Ellisburg, Jefferson Co., N. Y. She
died Dec. 25, 1864, aged 82 years. Had nine children:

(1) CYNTHIA[7] ATTRIDGE, married Artemas Halley,
of Ellisburg. Two children: Charles[8] Hally, who died
in the late war, and a daughter, who is also dead.

(2) ANNA[7] ATTRIDGE, married Elias Dickinson, died
at Ellisburg.

(3) OSCAR[7] ATTRIDGE, married Relief Pratt, res.
Ellisburg, and died there. Had four children, names
unknown.

(4) LAURA[7] ATTRIDGE, d. at Springfield, Mass., unm.

(5) NATHANIEL[7] ATTRIDGE, mar. Pamelia Marshall.
Is a horticulturist in Wisconsin. Two children, both
dead.

(6) AMANDA[7] ATTRIDGE, married Cyrus Taylor, of
Ellisburg. She died in the Insane Asylum in Adams,
Jefferson Co., N. Y. Had five children:

i. DON[8] TAYLOR, was in the service in the late war,
has since gone West.

15

ii. ADELBERT[8] TAYLOR, is a merchant in Adams, Jefferson Co., N. Y. Three daughters—have no account of them.

(7) POLLY[7] ATTRIDGE, married Seth Griggs, of Ellisburg. No children.

(8) LUCY[7] ATTRIDGE, married Benjamin Dickinson, reside in Brookfield, Missouri. He was the son of Paul Dickinson, who married Sarah Bemis. They have one daughter, married, and lives with them.

(9) JOSEPH[7] ATTRIDGE, died in Dummerston, when about nine years old. Family all Baptists.

(ii) CYNTHIA[6] BEMIS, second child of Joseph and Jemima (Stoddard) Bemis, mar. in 1803, Joel Chandler. She died Nov., 1864, aged 80. Were Baptists. Had three children: Elam, Maria, Jerusha.

(1) ELAM[7] CHANDLER, born at Petersham, Mass., married first, Maria Foster, of Dummerston. She had:

i. ELIZABETH[8] CHANDLER, who mar. Martin Wiltre, a farmer, reside at Yorkshire Corners, Cattaraugus Co., N. Y. Have two children: Eddie[9] and Henry[9] Ward B. Wiltre. Baptists.

He married second, and had: ii. Murrey[8] and iii. Ella[8] Chandler.

(2) MARIA[7] CHANDLER, married Daniel Babcock, of Newfane, Vt. Has two children: Maynard[8] Babcock, res. Michigan. Salina[8] Babcock, married Hiram Hall, lives in Springville, Erie Co., N. Y., and has a large family. Mrs. Maria Babcock resides in Yorkshire, N. Y. Baptists.

(3) JERUSHA[7] CHANDLER, born in Dummerston, Vt., Jan. 29, 1818, married June, 1846, C. M. Hadley. Three children:

i. AMBROSE[8] W. HADLEY, married Emma Holden, res. Yorkshire, farmer. Two children: Howard[9] and Zelna[9] Holden Hadley.

ii. EDWIN[8] S. HADLEY, married Elmira Smith, res. East Ashford, Cattaraugus Co., N. Y., farmer. They have one child: Cornelius[9] Hadley.

15

iii. FRANK [8] C. HADLEY, married Dora Evarts, res. East Ashford, farmers. The Hadley families are all Methodists.

(iii) JOSEPH [6] BEMIS, the third child of Joseph and Jemima (Stoddard) Bemis, born at Dummerston, Vt., Aug. 5, 1786, married Dec. 3, 1807, Abigail Hadley; farmer; res. East Ashford, N. Y. Methodists. They had ten children:

(1) PRISCILLA [7] BEMIS, married George Dickinson, farmer, res. Ellisburg, N. Y. He was a son of Sarah [7] (Bemis) Dickinson, the ninth child of David and Molly D. Bemis. Four children:

i. GEORGE [8] DICKINSON, is a Methodist minister somewhere out West.
ii. EDWIN [8] DICKINSON, lives at Ellisburg.
iii. JOSEPH [8] DICKINSON, not living.
iv. WESLEY [8] DICKINSON, res. Ellisburg. Served in the late war.

(2) EDWIN [7] BEMIS, married first, Eliza Duncan, of Dummerston; second, Ann Crossfield; reside in East Ashford, N. Y.; farmer. Two children:

i. CHARLES [8] BEMIS, married Lavonia Nemires. Had three children. He died in the late war from sickness.
ii. JULIA [8] BEMIS, married Hudson Chamberlain. Two children. Res. West Valley, Cattaraugus Co., N. Y.

(3) EMILY [7] BEMIS, born at Dummerston, married Alander Dickinson. She died at Ellisburg, Sept., 1849. Had six children. Nothing is known of them, except "Ashell [8] Dickinson, who served as a ranger during the late war; went through thirty or forty engagements, and came out without injury."

(4) LEWIS [7] M. BEMIS, mar. Naomi Cushman. Three children: *i.* Harriet [8] Bemis, married, and living at Pleasant Valley, Oclair Co., Wis. Two others dead.

(5) JESSE [7] H. BEMIS, born 1818, at Dummerston, Vt., mar. Pamelia Cole. Res. E. Ashford. Methodists.

(6) MARY ANN [7] BEMIS, born at Dummerston, 1824, married John Emerson, of Ellisburg. Three children:

15

i. Annette.[8] *ii.* Ossian.[8] *iii.* A son,[8] who died at Big Prairie, Minnesota.

(7) ABIGAIL[7] BEMIS, unknown.

(8) HARRIET[7] BEMIS, unknown.

(9) JANE[7] BEMIS, born 1829, at Dummerston, Vt., mar. James Peabody. Res. West Valley, Cattaraugus Co., N. Y. Three children: James,[8] Frank,[8] Charles.[8] Family are United Brethren.

(10) SARAH[7] BEMIS, born at Dummerston, Sept., 1834, married Dennison Wilson. She died at Spring Brook, Erie Co., N. Y. Two children: *i.* Ida[8] Wilson. *ii.* Clara[8] Wilson.

(iv) SYBIL[6] BEMIS, (*Joseph*,[5] *David and Molly*[4] *Dunster, David*,[3] *Jona.*[2] *Henry*,[1]) born at Dummerston, Vt., Nov., 1789, married 1814, Ebenezer Hadley. Res. East Ashford, N. Y. She died Feb. 17, 1864. Nine children, all born at Dummerston, Vt.:

(1) GEORGE[7] HADLEY, married first, Nov., 1839, Sarah A. Wellman; second, Sallie Weast. Two children:

i. MARTHA[8] A. HADLEY, mar. Jeremiah Vaughan. Res. Iowa, about fifty miles from Omaha, Neb. Two children: Ida[9] and Alonzo[9] Vaughan.

ii. SARAH[8] A. HADLEY, died young.

By second wife he had:

iii. WILLIE[8] HADLEY. *iv.* HATTIE[8] HADLEY. Res. Yorkshire, N. Y. Farmers. Methodists.

(2) ADALINE[7] L. HADLEY, died young.

(3) OSCAR[7] HADLEY, born March, 1818, mar. Jan. 1, 1840, Elvira Davenport. Res. East Ashford. Three children: Marion,[8] Fred.,[8] Helen[8]—two latter dead. Marion married Ebenezer Sherman, Sept., 1866. Three children: Fred.,[9] Helen,[9] (son[9]) Sherman.

(4) CORNELIUS[7] M. HADLEY, born Dec. 10, 1819, married June, 1846, (3) Jerusha[7] Chandler, daughter of ii. Cynthia[6] (Bemis) Chandler. Had three children. See page 150. Methodists.

(5) EBENEZER[7] BEMIS HADLEY, born Dec. 8, 1822, married Jan. 2, 1848, Miranda Hill. Reside in East

*14

15

Ashford. Are Methodists and farmers. From him we obtained, through Miss J. R. Wilder, this record of the Bemis family. Have had three children, the youngest, Luella,[8] only living.

(6) SELMA[7] HADLEY, died young.

(7) HENRY[7] HADLEY, no record.

(8) HORACE[7] HADLEY, born May 17, 1829, married Oct., 1852, Sarah W. Thomas. Reside in East Ashford. Farmer. One child: Warren[8] Hadley.

(9) LESTINA[7] S. HADLEY, born April 5, 1832, mar. Oct., 1852, Andrew Studley, died 1873. Res. Yorkshire, N. Y. Three children: Alice,[8] Wilber,[8] Elmer[8] Studley. Alice[8] Studley married Dec. 24, 1874, Edwin Hammond, a cheesemaker.

(v) ASA[6] BEMIS, was the fifth child of Joseph and Jemima (Stoddard) Bemis. No account of him has been obtained.

(vi) JOANNA[6] BEMIS, the sixth child of Joseph and Jemima (Stoddard) Bemis, born 1797, mar. Feb., 1824, Rufus Hadley. She died at Dummerston, Jan. 4, 1840. Methodists. Seven children, all born at Dummerston:

(1) LAURELLA[7] J. HADLEY, born May 9, 1825, mar. E. M. Wiltre. One child: Nettie,[8] who died Feb. 25, 1875. Res. East Ashford. Presbyterians.

(2) EDWARD[7] L. HADLEY, born April 26, 1827, mar. Harriette Clark, of Westminster. Reside near Whitewater, Walworth Co., Wis. Farmer. No children.

(3) CHARLES[7] N. HADLEY, born Nov. 2, 1830, mar. June 21, 1857, Lorancy Wilder. Res. East Ashford. Farmer. Four children: Agnes,[8] Charles[8] M., Valentine[8] R., Laura[8] Hadley.

(4) LAURA[7] A. HADLEY, born Oct. 1, 1832. Res. Ypsilanti, Wishtenaw Co., Mich. She is a bookkeeper. Presbyterian. Unmarried.

(5) HORACE[7] W. HADLEY, born Sept. 10, 1835, mar. Sedelia Boleyn, of Hinsdale, N. H. Res. Ypsilanti. A druggist. Presbyterian.

(6) WARREN[7] J. HADLEY, born Dec. 28, 1837. Methodist. He enlisted in the summer of 1862; was

15

taken prisoner at Gettysburg, July, 1863; died on Belle Island, near Richmond, Va., Jan. 10, 1864. Unm.

(7) EVALINE[7] J. HADLEY, born Oct. 19, 1839, mar. C. W. Sherman, Jan. 1, 1873. Res. East Ashford. Methodist.

3. BENJAMIN[5] BEMIS, was the third child of David and Molly (Dunster) Bemis. Of him we have no knowledge, except that "he went West."

4. ELIAS[5] BEMIS, (*David and Molly[4] D., David,[3] Jonathan,[2] Henry,[1]*) born July 15, 1767, mar. Jan. 11, 1789, Experience Hendrick. He owned the best farm in Brattleboro. He died June 2, 1806, from exposure after having had the measles. Her grief for his death made her partially insane. They had six children:

(i) LEMUEL[6] K. BEMIS, born Oct. 22, 1790, at Dummerston, Vt., married Betsey Buck, of D. He was a blacksmith. Died at Brattleboro, July 30, 1854. Unitarian. Had six children:

(1) MANDANA[7] BEMIS, married William Chase, of Brattleboro. She died, leaving three children: .

i. ANNIE[8] CHASE, who married John Whiting, a merchant, at Waterbury, Conn.

ii. ALICE[8] CHASE, married Albert Boyden, hotel keeper, Brattleboro.

iii. WILLIS[8] BEMIS CHASE, who res. in Brattleboro.

(2) BETSEY[7] BEMIS, mar. Charles Lawrence, hotel keeper. Two sons:

i. ALBERT[8] LAWRENCE, gone to Australia.

ii. FRANK[8] LAWRENCE, is clerk in a dry goods store at Brattleboro.

(3) MARIA[7] BEMIS, married Lewis Burdit, of Brattleboro. She died, leaving a daughter.

(4) CYRENE[7] BEMIS, is a blacksmith, an excellent and ingenious workman, in Brattleboro.

(5) WILLIS[7] BEMIS, married Eliza Day, of Chesterfield. She died, leaving two children, a son and daughter. The son[8] is express agent from North Adams to

15

Boston. The daughter at home. Willis' B. married second, the widow of a soldier, an amiable woman. He (Willis') has been for fifteen years express agent at Brattleboro.

(6) LEMUEL' BEMIS, the youngest child of Lemuel K. B., went with seven other young men prospecting years ago in California, and has not been heard of since. Family Congregationalists.

(ii) ABNER⁶ BEMIS, born March 8, 1792, mar. March 5, 1818, Boliva Tracy. He died Jan. 8, 1854. Was a Congregationalist. Had six children:

(1) JAMES' BEMIS, was a nail maker. A machine for making nails was invented by him. He married Mary Chipman, of Shoreham, Vt., died in Pittsburgh, Pa., leaving a son and daughter.

(2) ANN ELIZA' BEMIS, died young.

(3) JUNIETTE' BEMIS, mar. a custom house officer at Rouse Point. Have one son and four daughters.

(4) ERSKINE' BEMIS, is a rich farmer in Norfolk, New York.

(5) MAKENSIE' BEMIS, is a carriage maker at Saxon River, Vt. Has two children.

(6) MARY' BEMIS, married Alfred Wright, a merchant, in Brattleboro. He is deacon of the Congregational Church. Four children.

(iii) CLARISSA⁶ BEMIS, born March 28, 1794, mar. Jonathan French, nephew of William French, the first man killed in the Revolution. Four children:

(1) CLARISSA' FRENCH, mar. Joel Miller, of Dummerston. They have: *i.* Henry⁸ French, who married Hellen Dutton, of Dummerston, and lives with her father. They are farmers.

(2) HENRY' FRENCH, is unmarried, and lives on the beautiful farm in Dummerston, where his father and mother died.

(3) WARREN' FRENCH, went to California, and died of the cholera soon after.

(4) SARAH' FRENCH, married John Day, of Chesterfield, N. H., died July 8, 1864. Family Congregationalists. No children.

15

(iv) SALLY⁶ BEMIS, born March 18, 1796, married Sept., 1820, Asa Miller, of Dummerston. ˙ He was a carriage maker. Congregationalists. She died Feb. 14, 1870. Two children:

(1) CATHERINE⁷ MILLER, married Orrin Slate, a merchant. He sold his store in Brattleboro, and went to Winstead, Conn., to establish another. He arrived on Saturday; went to church three times on Sunday, and was as well as usual when he went to his room in the second story of the public house. He was found in the morning *under* his window dead. She has two daughters: Genevieve⁸ Slate, who lives with her mother, and Emily⁸ Slate, who married Henry Thompson, a goldsmith, of Brattleboro. His widow, after four years' widowhood, married April, 1876, Alfred Stevens, a Congregational minister for 35 years in Westminster West Parish, Vt.

(2) SIDNEY⁷ MILLER, is a first rate carriage maker. He married first, Emily Dickinson, daughter of Asehel Dickinson; second, a daughter of Rev. W. S. Balch, a Universalist minister. One son,⁸ ten years old. Family Unitarians.

(v) LAVINA⁶ BEMIS, born Aug. 16, 1798, married Edward Whitney, hotel keeper in Keene, N. H., Jan., 1822. She died Aug. 25, 1854. They had seven children—all Unitarians:

(1) ELIAS⁷ WHITNEY, has been twice married, and now lives in Boston; clerk in Martin, Bates & Son's fur store, Elm street.

(2) ELIZABETH⁷ WHITNEY, married George Sawyer, a hatter, Keene, N. H.

(3) LEMUEL⁷ WHITNEY, was killed in a building blown up in Hague street, New York.

(4) CHARLES⁷ WHITNEY, married Delia Safford, of St. Albans, Vt. Reside in LaCrosse, Wis. Is in the mercantile business.

(5) EDWARD⁷ WHITNEY, died at Fort Covington years ago. He left a wife, who has since died. Had no children.

15

(6) MARY[7] JANE WHITNEY, married Edward Upham, merchant at Waukegan, Ill. Has one son,[8] —— Upham, who is about to. enter college.

(7) HATTIE[7] WHITNEY, married —— Robinson. He is a sealer of weights and measures in New York city. Have no children.

(vi) ELIZA[6] BEMIS, (*Elias,*[5] *David and Molly*[4] *D., David,*[3] *Jona.*[2] *Henry,*[1]) born Aug. 3, 1804, mar. Dec. 19, 1822, Loran Smith, of Monkton, Vt. In 1848 removed to Illinois. Presbyterians. From Mrs. Smith we had the foregoing record of 4. Elias[5] Bemis' family. She res. in Galesburg, Ill. They have had six children, four daughters and two sons—both sons died young.

(1) BETSEY[7] SMITH, married Milo D. Cooke, a lawyer, of Cornwall, Vt. They had one son, ——[8] Cooke. He is a lawyer, and is in business in Galesburg with his father. He went a three months' man to Cairo, Ill., to guard that place; was absent six months. He is a graduate of Knox College, Galesburg. He married a lady in Ogdensburg, N. Y., and has a daughter.[8] "So you see," adds Mrs. Smith, "that I am great-grandmother."

(2) LAURA[7] SMITH, mar. Jan., 1852, Henry White, of Dresden, Ohio, a millwright. He was with the army two years, building bridges and mills in Tennessee. Mr. White has just built the first flouring mill in Galveston, Texas, a city of 40,000 inhabitants. They reside in Omaha, Neb., but will soon remove to Texas. They have one son, Harold[8] White, who is a graduate of the Business College in Omaha, and three daughters, Annie,[8] Helena[8] and Bessie[8] White, who are at school at Omaha.

(3) URSULA[7] SMITH, married Charles Norton, a farmer, of Addison? Vt. Three children:

i. HENRY[8] NORTON, is a station agent at Duncan, Ill., on the C. B. & Q. R. R.

ii. JENNIE[8] NORTON, is a teacher in the graded school at Galesburg.

iii. HERRICK[8] NORTON, is at school in Galesburg.

(4) MARY[7] SMITH, married Lothar Becker, of Henderson, Ill. They reside in Galveston, Texas. He is in

15

company with Mr. White. They are doing a large business in a flouring mill. He was four years with the army; stationed at Clarkesville, Tenn.; was Lieutenant of artillery. His wife, with her children, was with him two years. Have four children:

i. FRED.[8] BECKER, is a pianist. He took the gold medal at the Chicago College of Music.

ii. FRANK[8] BECKER, works in his father's mill.

iii. LOUIS,[8] and *iv.* PAULINE[8] BECKER, are at school.

5. ABNER[5] BEMIS, the fifth child of David and Molly[4] (Dunster) Bemis, was a Baptist minister. He married Katie Freeman; was settled in Halifax, Vt. He died at that place, and willed his property to that church. They now have the benefit of it. He was much beloved by all. They had no children.

6. LEVI[5] BEMIS, (*David and Molly[4] D.*) married, and removed into New York State. No further knowledge of him. Mrs. Loran Smith thinks he died in Dummerston, Vt.

7. ASA[5] BEMIS, the seventh child of David and Molly[4] (Dunster) Bemis, went West, but returned and died in Dummerston. He was born in Brattleboro.

8. SAMUEL[5] BEMIS, (*David and Molly[4] D.*,) went West also. Nothing further known of him.

9. SARAH[5] BEMIS, the youngest child of David and Molly (Dunster) Bemis, married Paul Dickinson. Res. Ellisburg, Jefferson Co., N. Y., where she died. They had six children:

(i) ELIAS[6] DICKINSON, mar. Anna Attridge. Had six children. "Cannot even tell their names." (E.B.H.)

(ii) GEORGE[6] DICKINSON, mar. (1) Priscilla[7] Bemis, daughter of Joseph and Jemima (S.) Bemis. Four children: George, Edwin, Joseph, Wesley. (*See ante.*)

(iii) BENJAMIN[6] DICKINSON, was formerly a sailor; was on a whaling vessel some years; visited every seaport of importance in the world; spent two years in South America; has visited Greenland and Palestine; was gone from home seventeen years; is now a farmer; resides in Brookfield, Missouri. He mar. Lucy Attridge, daugh-

16

ter of Nath. and Polly (Bemis) Attridge. Have one daughter, married, and lives at Brookfield.

(iv) ASA[6] DICKINSON, d. young, at Dummerston, Vt.

(v) ALCANDER[6] DICKINSON, resides in Bellville, is a merchant. He married Emily[7] Bemis, daughter of Jos. and Abigail (Hadley) Bemis. (*See ante.*)

(vi) SALLY[6] DICKINSON, mar. Barney Poole. She became insane, was sent to the almshouse. She was drowned in Black River, whether accidental or otherwise was never known. Five children:

(1) Asa[7]. (2) LIONEL[7]. (3) ELIZA[7]. (4)–(5) Names unknown. "I think there are none living." (E. B. H.)

16. iii. HUBBARD[4] DUNSTER, (*David,[3] Jonathan,[2] Henry,[1]*) the third child of David and Mary (Russel) Dunster, was born in Cambridge (Menotomy), probably in 1735. He inherited two-thirds of his father's real estate at the decease of his mother. He bought of Mary Dunster (probably his mother), for £10, "a tract of upland and meadow in the easterly part of Westminster, and is part of the original house lot No. 76, and it begins at a stake and stones at the corner of Henry 'Cartrite' Dunster's land, containing about thirty acres." This deed was given May 13, 1772, but was not recorded till Aug. 26, 1805. He also bought, Aug. 26, 1781, of John Bailey, of Sterling, and Dudley Bailey, of Westminster, for £25, one-half of a tract of land in the southeasterly part of Westminster, containing eighteen acres. This deed was not recorded till Sept. 14, 1805. "He was pressed into the army, but refused to go. He concealed himself at the house of a man named Lyon, and when inquiry was made for him, the reply was, that if he was not in the lion's den, they did not know where he was." (*Mrs. Estabrook.*) He married Aug. 31, 1769, published Aug. 2, Ruth Bailey, probably a sister of John and Dudley, of whom he purchased the half tract of land. They were married by Rev. A. Rice. In the record at Westminster, her name is "Ruth Baley." She died March 19, 1788. He died —— ——, intestate. The estate was appraised at $692.07. The inventory was

16

sworn to Oct. 15, 1805, by Hubbard Dunster, his son, who was administrator. They had six children:

1. EPHRAIM DUNSTER, born April 18, 1770.
2. HUBBARD DUNSTER, born Oct. 4, 1772 or 3.
3. REBECKAH DUNSTER, born April 3, 1775.
4. JASON DUNSTER, born April 3, 1778.
5. NATHAN DUNSTER, born May 23, 1780.
6. JONATHAN DUNSTER, b. Sept. 19, 1784, d. young.

1. EPHRAIM[5] DUNSTER, (*Hubbard,[4] David,[3] Jona.,[2] Henry,[1]*) the first child of Hubbard and Ruth (Bailey) Dunster, was born at Westminster, April 18, 1770. It is believed he married and had children. He appears to have been unsuccessful in the race for riches, and applied to public beneficence, and was provided for. He was living in Westminster in Aug., 1857.

2. HUBBARD[5] DUNSTER, (*Hubbard,[4] David,[3] Jona.,[2] Henry,[1]*) the second child of Hubbard and Ruth (Bailey) Dunster, born at Westminster, Oct. 4, 1772, married at Gardner, May 1, 1797, "Becca" Kendall, of that place, born Aug. 1, 1774. They were published April 11, 1797. He went to Gardner as early as 1796, the year before his marriage. Here he purchased, in 1801, of Sally and Jonas Eaton, about fifty acres of land, for which he paid $432. A part of this land lay on "Otter River." The turnpike divided the estate; Sally's part being on the south and Jonas' part on the north side. It was their portion of their father's (Ebenezer Eaton) estate. In these deeds he is called a cooper. He was also a box maker, and tradition says he was a drummer. At Gardner he accumulated a handsome property, and occupied a fair position among the wealthy people of that town. Adversity came. He lost the whole or a great part of his careful earnings, which appear to have gone into the hands of Josiah Howe, of Templeton. Giving up to despondency, he died at Gardner, Dec. 3, 1818. His widow did the most she could for the children. She died at Melrose, Mass., Aug., 1839. They left eight children.

The other children of Hubbard and Ruth (Bailey) Dunster were:

15

16

3. REBECKAH[5] DUNSTER, born April 3, 1775. We have no authentic account of her. Among the Dunster papers we find a manuscript of about seventy pages, written very closely, and in a hand somewhat resembling President Dunster's. The first part is gone. It is a catechism, with Calvin's views fully stated. The date of the MS. is not in it, but the use of *v* for *u*, and the peculiarity of the J, indicate a great age. It has the signature "Richard Harrison," in ink and letters like the MS. It has also "David Dunster," in a later hand. In Aug., 1857, this MS. was given to Edward S. Dunster by "an old lady in Westminster, Mass., whose maiden name was 'Dunster,' as being an old family relic." The tradition of it is not remembered, and we can refer to Rebeckah[5] Dunster only as answering his description.

4. JASON[5] DUNSTER, born April 3, 1778. Of him nothing further is now known.

5. NATHAN[5] DUNSTER, (*Hubbard,[4] David,[3] Jona.,[2] Henry,[1]*) born May 23, 1780, was published July 7, mar. July 22, 1810, to Hannah Darby, of Fitchburg. He died Aug. 18, 1850. (*Westminster Records.*) Further search of the records in Westminster ought to be made for these families.

6. JONATHAN[5] DUNSTER, born Sept. 19, 1784, died when five or six years old. (*Mrs. Estabrook.*)

These four children of Hubbard[4] Dunster are interpolated for convenient reference before the eight children of Hubbard[5] and Becca (Kendall) Dunster, who were:

i.   MARTIN[6] DUNSTER, born Jan. 3, 1798.
ii.   PRUDA[6] DUNSTER, born Jan. 23, 1800.
iii. REBECCA[6] DUNSTER, born Feb. 11, 1802.
iv.   LOUISA[6] DUNSTER, born Feb. 18, 1805.
v.   ASAPH[6] DUNSTER, born July 6, 1807.
vi.   MARY[6] JANE DUNSTER, born Nov. 12, 1809.
vii. LYDIA[6] DUNSTER, born Jan. 24, 1816.
viii. DAPHENY[6] LELAND DUNSTER, b. July 18, 1818.

i.   MARTIN[6] DUNSTER, (*Hubbard,[5] Hubbard,[4] David,[3] Jonathan,[2] Henry,[1]*) was born in Gardner, Jan. 3, 1798.

16

He lived in Gardner, was a physician, and practiced medicine there. He received his medical diploma from the Electic Medical College at Cincinnati, Ohio, but at what date is not ascertained. He bought for $750, Nov. 14, 1821, of Joseph Howe, the estate his father formerly lived on, and owned other land in the westerly part of Gardner. He was a prominent citizen, having filled many town offices. In 1837 he represented the town of Gardner in the General Court. He married Feb. 13, 1823, Sarah Nichols, born Sept. 14, 1800, at Westminster. She died July 2, 1845, leaving no heirs. After the death of his wife he went to Boston, and was in a drug store for a few years. "In 1850 (his second wife says) he went to Rochester, Vt., to Asa Whitney's. His mother was sister to my husband's first wife, and Asa Whitney's wife is my sister, and that is where I became acquainted with him. We were married in Rochester, Vt., June 9, 1852. Our union was a happy one."

Emma C. Chamberlain, Martin Dunster's second wife, was born in Bethel, Vt., Feb. 5, 1820. In 1853 they removed to Quincy, Ill., where he practiced medicine until his death, Dec. 2, 1854, leaving no children by either wife. From other sources we learn that he was an "affectionate husband, and a highly respected citizen, was a man of sterling integrity, very influential, for many years a zealous member of the School Committee in Gardner, and represented the town in the State Legislature for several years." "He was liberal in religious sentiments. His religion consisted in dealing justly, loving mercy, and walking humbly before God. This he lived up to." After his death his widow, Emma (Chamberlain) Dunster, married Stephen G. Tyler, of Quincy, his second wife. Mr. Tyler was the same who married Mary⁶ Jane, sister of Martin Dunster. She has since deceased, and was buried at Quincy.

ii.   Pruda⁶ Dunster, born Jan. 23, 1800, at Gardner, married ——, 1818, Isaac Fitts, Jr. In a Bible belonging to Mr. Withington, of Mason, N. H., who married a Miss Fitts, is this record: "Isaac Fitts, Jr., and Prudy Dunster married 1818, by Rev. Mr. Osgood." Mr. S. Osgood was minister at Springfield, Mass. Mr.

16

W.. says that the Fitts who married Prudy Dunster went "West" several years ago. She died at Rochester, Vt., or N. Y.? about 1830. Had no children.

iii. REBECCA⁶ DUNSTER, born Feb. 11, 1802, mar. March 4? 1827, Gilman Robbins, of Leominster, Mass. He is still living, a farmer and gardener, in Leominster. She died June 24 or 26, 1854, at Melrose, Mass., and was buried at the new cemetery in Leominster. They had six children:

1. GEORGE⁷ ROBBINS, (*Gilman and Rebecca⁶ D., Hubbard,⁵ Hubbard,⁴ David,³ Jonathan,² Henry,¹*) born Dec. 5, 1827, in Leominster, is a tin and sheet iron worker, and dealer in stoves. Resides in Fitchburg, Mass. He married Charlotte M. Dennis, daughter of Thomas and Ruth — Dennis, a farmer, of Barre, Mass. They have three children:

(i) CHARLES⁸ ROBBINS, born Nov. 19, 1859, died Jan. 28, 1860.
(ii) HENRY⁸ DENNIS ROBBINS, born Nov. 3, 1864.
(iii) FREDDIE⁸ ROBBINS, born Jan. 11, 1869, died Sept. 4, same year.

2. CHARLES⁷ ROBBINS, born May 9, 1830, at Leominster, by trade is a mason. He mar. May 22, 1851, Angeline Kinsman Wilson, daughter of John Bucknam and Mary Goodwin Wilson, both of Bedford, Mass. He is a mason by trade also. They have two children:

(i) JOSEPH⁸ ROBBINS, born May 20, 1856.
(ii) CARRIE⁸ LOUISA ROBBINS, born Jan. 23, 1859.

3. SARAH⁷ BROWN ROBBINS, born June 8, 1833, at Leominster, was named for her uncle Asaph Dunster's wife. She resided some years in Boston. She was mar. Oct. 5, 1875, to Martin Hatch, son of Isaac and Lavina (Allen) Hatch, of Pembroke. He had been engaged in manufacturing for considerable time, but has now retired to a farm in East Pembroke, Mass. We are much indebted to Mrs. Hatch for memo. of her father's family and their descendants.

4. JOSEPH⁷ ROBBINS, (*Gilman and Rebecca⁶ D., Hubbard,⁵ Hubbard,⁴ David,³ Jonathan,² Henry,¹*) the

16

fourth child of Gilman and Rebecca (Dunster) Robbins, was born Sept. 12, 1834, at Leominster. He graduated at the Jefferson Medical College, Philadelphia, and in 1858 settled at Quincy, Illinois, where he has an extensive practice. He is President of the Adams County Medical Society, and also President of the Medical Pathological Society in Quincy, and a member of the American Medical Society. Is a prominent politician in that city, and much engaged in public enterprises; takes very high rank in Masonic institutions, and is 2d officer of the Illinois Grand Lodge. He married at Melrose, Mass., June 4, 1863, Louisa Amelia, daughter of Henry A. and Elizabeth (Temple) Norris, of Melrose. In religious views an Unitarian. Have no children.

5. CAROLINE[7] AUGUSTA ROBBINS, born Feb. 16, 1840, at Leominster, married at Fitchburg, Dec. 29, 1863, Reuben Dow, of Nantucket, Mass. He is a tin plate worker, and trader in stoves and such materials. They reside in Fitchburg. Have two children:

(i) WALTER[8] GILMAN DOW, born Dec. 30, 1869.
(ii) CHARLOTTE[8] REBECCA DOW, born April 4, 1873.

6. JEROME[7] AUGUSTINE ROBBINS, born Nov. 13, 1844, is a baker by trade, and resides in Charlestown, Mass., unmarried.

iv. LOUISA[6] DUNSTER, the fourth child of Hubbard and Becca (Kendall) Dunster, was born at Gardner, Feb. 18, 1805. She died there, 1875, unmarried.

v. ASAPH[6] DUNSTER, (*Hubbard*,[5] *Hubbard*,[4] *David*,[3] *Jona.*,[2] *Henry*,[1]) the fifth child of Hubbard and Becca (Kendall) Dunster, was born July 6, 1807. At the time of his father's death he was eleven years old. The family had been kept together until that time; but the loss of property and his untimely end appear to have broken it up. The family struggled on as best they could. He learned the trade of a mason, and a trace of him is found in Acton and Malden, Mass., and soon after at Boston. In 1837 his name is found in the Boston Directory as a mason living at 604 Washington street. This was three years after his marriage, and two years after the birth of

*15

16

their first child.   Where he was in the interim is uncertain, possibly at Hingham, the residence of his father-in-law.   From Boston he went to Quincy, Ill., where he carried on his business till 1863 or 4, when he removed to Chicago.   He married at Hingham, Mass., Jan. 2, 1834, Sarah Brown Stoddard, daughter of Marshall and Anna Stoddard.   She, Anna, was born June 20, 1781, and died June 20, 1842.   Sarah Brown (Stoddard), wife of Asaph Dunster, died Dec. 22, 1870, aged 63, having been born July 13, 1807, at Hingham.   He died in Chicago, Sept. 1, 1867.   They had six children:

1.   LYDIA⁷ ANN DUNSTER, born at ——, March 30, 1835.   She married Dec. 4, 1867, Ambrose Kinley. They live in Mendota, Illinois.   Have had two children:

(i)   SARAH⁸ ANN KINLEY, born Nov. 30, 1868.   She died March 14, 1869.

(ii)   MAY⁸ CORETTA KINLEY, born Feb. 15, 1870.

2.   SARAH⁷ CAROLINE DUNSTER, b. Sept. 12, 1836, at Gardner? mar. April 28, 1859, Warren M. Brown, of Quincy, Ill.   They went to Chicago in 1861; thence to Aurora, Ill., two years; thence to Chicago again; thence to St. Louis; thence back to Chicago again.   At these places he had followed his trade—painting.   He is now, 1872, President of the Metalic Roofing Co., Chicago, and lives at 519 Hubbard street.   They are both Universalists in religious belief.   Have had four children:

(i)   ELMER⁸ WARREN BROWN, born May 26, 1861, died Feb. 22, 1870.

(ii)   EMMA⁸ CARRIE BROWN, born Aug. 4, 1863.

(iii)   FREEMAN⁸ EDWIN BROWN, born Sept. 20, 1865.

(iv)   SARAH⁸ GRACIE BROWN, born May 28, 1869.

3.   REBECKAH⁷ HENRIETTA DUNSTER, (*Asaph,*⁶) was born Aug. 4, 1838, at Gardner.   She married James Elmore Coe, at Quincy, Oct. 6, 1861.   He is a painter, and worked in Quincy, Aurora, and 1863 in Chicago, at that business.   In 1872 he had billiard rooms and saloon at his residence, No. 809 West Madison street, Chicago. They are Universalists.   Have had five children:

16

(i) CHARLIE[8] COE, born April 20, 1863, died Aug. 22, same year.

(ii) WILLIE[8] EARNEST COE, born May 20, 1864, died Nov. 23, 1866.

(iii) MARY[8] JANE COE, born Dec. 29, 1866.

(iv) LUCY[8] FRANCIS COE, born Oct. 21, 1868.

(v) EDGAR[8] ANDREW COE, born Jan. 21, 1872.

4. BENJAMIN[7] CURTIS DUNSTER, born April 6, 1842, died Aug. 19, same year.

5. Infant,[7] daughter, b. Sept. 20, 1843, d. next day.

6. LUCY[7] FRANCES DUNSTER, born in Malden or Melrose, Dec. 16, 1847. When her father removed to Quincy she accompanied them, where she attended the splendid public schools of that city, and was an accomplished scholar of amiable deportment. A young lady from Providence, R. I., taught in Quincy, and Lucy was her pupil. This young lady was an intimate friend of ours, and mentioned that a Lucy Dunster lived in Quincy and attended her school. This gave us a clue. Being in Quincy in 1872, and having a spare day, we spent it in trying to hunt up the family to which she belonged. We applied to the directory, public records, school departments, an ex-Governor of the State, who had always lived in Quincy, but no trace of a *Dunster* was to be found. Being about to give up the search and abandon our efforts, we met an elderly lady of whom we inquired if she had known any such people. She replied that she had; but they were all gone from Quincy. She added that Dr. Robbins' mother was a relation of them, and referred to him. We found him, and he contributed much information of Hubbard Dunster's family.

Lucy Frances Dunster died in Chicago, Oct. 27, 1865, unmarried.

vi. MARY[6] JANE DUNSTER, the sixth child of Hubbard[5] and Becca Dunster, was born in Gardner, Nov. 12, 1809, married Stephen G. Tyler, of Shirley, Mass. They moved to Quincy, Illinois, about 1830. She died about 1855. He married second, Emma C. Dunster, the widow of Dr. Martin Dunster. She died at Quincy, and was buried there. He is still living at Quincy.

16

Stephen G. and Mary Jane (Dunster) Tyler had two children:

1.   MARY[7] JANE TYLER, born ——, married ——, Edward Weisenberger, of Quincy.   He died about 1860, and she has married second, —— Blakeslee.   She had by first husband:

(i)   A son,[8] born ——, at Quincy.   He was drowned at Quincy, after his mother was widowed.

2.   ADALINE[7] TYLER, born ——, married Samuel Dodd, a machinist, at Quincy.   In 1861 or 2, they removed to Denver, Colorado, where they still reside. They have: (i) ADALINE[8] HUBBARD DODD.

vii.   LYDIA[6] DUNSTER, (*Hubbard,[5] Hubbard,[4]*) born in Gardner, Jan. 24, 1816, married Sept., 1838, Joel Nichols, of Westminster.   He was a nephew of Dr. Martin Dunster's first wife, Sarah Nichols.   He is living in Gardner, and is a chair maker.   She died April 3, 1863; buried at Gardner.   They have three children:

1.   ELIZA[7] ANN NICHOLS, born at Gardner, Sept. 26, 1842, married Aug. 8, 1862, Joseph Heywood, a chair maker.   She died Aug. 20, 1867; buried at Gardner. Had no children.

2.   FRANK[7] EDMUND NICHOLS, (*Joel[6] and Lydia D.*) born April 26, 1848, at Gardner, is a chair maker.   He married Oct. 10, 1870, Ada L. Sargent, of Brattleboro, Vt., daughter of Willard and Lavina Sargent.   They have one child:

(i)   BERTHA[8] NICHOLS, born March 1, 1875.

3.   EMMA[7] PARSON NICHOLS, born at Gardner, Aug. 28, 1850, married Oct. 11, 1872, James E. Newton, of Phillipston, Mass., a chair maker, resides in Gardner. He is the son of Ira and Elizabeth Newton.

viii.   DAPHENY[6] LELAND DUNSTER, was the youngest child of Hubbard and Becca Dunster.   She was born in Gardner, July 18, 1818, married Sept. 19, 1849, John Parson, M. D., of Quincy, Ill.   They removed to Denver City, Colorado, several years since.   Three children (history traditional):

17

1. WARREN⁷ PARSON, born at Quincy, married.
2. CHARLES⁷ PARSON, b. ——, d. young, at Colorado.
3. HELLEN⁷ MINNIE PARSON, born ——, 1862, living at Denver, Colorado, 1872, unmarried.

17. iv. THOMAS⁴ DUNSTER, (*David,³ Jonathan,² Henry,¹*) the fourth child and second son of David and Molly (Russell) Dunster, born at West Cambridge, now Arlington, was baptized May 8, 1737, at Medford. With the rest of the family he went to Westminster in 1742. Unlike his brother, he went into the army in the French war, and was taken prisoner in the disastrous campaign against Canada, then a French province. From the memory of Mrs. Estabrook it is related that he was held a prisoner at Rutland, Mass., ("this State.") This is improbable. No account of prisoners of war at that date and place have been found; but in 1777 there were prisoners of Burgoyne's army held there. The "Rutland" was probably Vermont. That will reconcile all the events known of his army life. Here, he was taken sick of the "camp disorder,"—horrors of too recent date to need description,—was visited by his father, who, as we have seen, fell a victim to the disease while on a mission of affection and kindness to his sick son. He returned to Westminster, and inherited one-third of his father's real estate, as provided in the will. Being a younger son, the custom of the times and the law required that his brother should have a double portion. No records of his transactions of a business kind have been found. He appears to have led a quiet life. There is a tradition that he was called a "Pigeon Catcher." He married Feb., 1768, Lidia Pierce, of Fitchburg. He died July 18, 1819. She died March 22, 1832. In the record of her death she is called "Mrs. Lydia Dunster." They had seven children:

i. DAVID DUNSTER, born March 14, 1770.
ii. KEZIAH DUNSTER, born April 8, 1772.
iii. ANNA DUNSTER, born Aug. 3, 1775.
iv. THOMAS DUNSTER, born Aug. 13, 1780.
v. LYDIA DUNSTER, born July 19, 1784.
vi. PRECILLA DUNSTER, born March 4, 1787.
vii. HENRY DUNSTER, born May 21, 1792.

17

i. David[5] Dunster, born March 14, 1770, married
Nov. 24, published Nov. 10, 1798, Lucy Mundon, of
Hubbardston.   He died at Westminster, July 10, 1839,
(*Family Record,*) July 24, 1840, (*Westminster Record*).

They had two children:

1.   Lucy[6] Dunster, mar. —— Root, of Hubbardston.
2.   Hannah[6] Dunster, mar. —— Parker, of H.

David married again, but had no children by his
second wife.

ii.   Keziah[5] Dunster, the second child of Thomas
and Lydia (Pierce) Dunster, was born in Westminster,
April 8, 1772, married Daniel Montjoy, of Westminster.
He was the "Montjoy" mentioned in the History of
Westminster.   "In 1738 Philip Beamis, of Cambridge,
moved to the township; was the third family of six or
seven persons.   Among them was an infant by the name
of Daniel Montjoy, who died in 1835, in the hundredth
year of his age.   He was our father.   He was in the
army, under Washington, but never received any pension.
The children were all kind to him.   He is buried in
Westminster." (*Myles Wood's Letter.*)   She died in the
winter of 1838.   They had seven children:

1.   Charlotte[6] Montjoy, born at Westminster, July
19, 1799.   She married first, Nov. 27, 1819, Asher
Brown Cutler.   He died May 22, 1828.   They had two
children:

(i)   Edmund[7] Winslow Cutler, born May 2, 1821,
married April 7, 1842, Hannah C. P. Higgins, of Dedham, Mass.   He died April 27, 1873; interred at Northboro.   They had two children:

(1)   Charlotte[8] E. Cutler, born at Sterling, Mass.,
Feb. 7, 1843, not married.

(2)   James[8] E. Cutler, born at Fitchburg, May 14,
1850, married May 14, 1872, Mrs. Mary J. Austin.

(ii)   Silas[7] Alonzo Cutler, born at Sterling, Dec.
6, 1823, married May 19, 1844, Maria Hale, of Northboro.   Had one child:

17

(1) MARY[8] J. CUTLER, born March 20, 1849. She died April 6, 1854. "A pretty girl; she lives in Heaven, where I hope we may all find our home when God, our Heavenly Father, has done with us in these homes we now enjoy so much." (*Myles Wood.*)

Charlotte[6] Montjoy, after the death of Mr. Cutler, married April 11, 1839, Nathan Burfee, of Sterling. "He dropped down in the door-yard and expired, Sept. 13, 1856." She now, 1875, lives with Myles Wood, Northboro, having been twice widowed.

2. LUCINDA[6] MONTJOY, the second child of Daniel and Keziah (Dunster) Montjoy, was born at Westminster, Dec. 1, 1801. She married Lafayette Willard, son of Joshua Willard, of Sterling. They had:

(i) MARTHA[7] WILLARD, born ——, married Barney Pratt, of Fitchburg, reside there. They have one boy:

(1) ——[8] Pratt, born about 1867.

3. BENJAMIN[6] MONTJOY, the third child of Daniel and Keziah (Dunster) Montjoy, was born in Westminster, June 26, 1804, mar. May 9, 1826, at Westminster, Dolly Perry, daughter of Joseph and Betsey (Pierce) Perry, who lived on a tract of land formerly called " No Town," now Fitchburg. "Same religious views as my ancestor; that is, the teaching of God's word as I understand it." They had nine children:

(i) EDWIN[7] MONTJOY, born Sept. 17, 1827, at Westminster, married March, 1856, Louisa Kelly, daughter of Daniel Kelly. Resides in Fitchburg. They have one daughter:

(1) HENRIETTA[8] MONTJOY, born April 13, 1857.

(ii) FRANCIS[7] MONTJOY, the second child of Benjamin and Dolly (P.) Montjoy, was born Nov. 13, 1832, married —— Poole, of ——, New York State. He enlisted in Co. D., 10th Regiment of Infantry, and was killed at North Anna? River, June 17, 1864.

(iii) CALVIN[7] MONTJOY, born at Westminster, Oct. 25, 1835, unmarried.

(iv) SARAH[7] MONTJOY, born at Westminster, June 25, 1838, unmarried.

17

(v) DANIEL⁷ PORTER MONTJOY, born March 19, 1842, married June 10, 1868, Melissa Newhall, daughter of Augustus Newhall. Resides in Fitchburg. Have one child: (1) CHARLOTTE⁸ MONTJOY.

(vi) HARRIET⁷ E. MONTJOY, born Nov. 20, 1845, in Westminster, married Jan. 2, 1871, Samuel J. Jewett, son of Zenas and Claramond (Myrick) Jewett, of Princeton, Mass.; reside there; is a farmer. No children.

In addition to these six children, Benjamin and Dolly Montjoy had three whose births, names and deaths are not obtained—they all died young.

4. ELIZA⁶ MONTJOY, born Aug. 9, 1806, now lives with her sister, Melinda, unmarried.

5. MELINDA⁶ MONTJOY, (*Daniel and Keziah⁵ D., Thomas,⁴ David,³ Jona.² Henry,¹*) born at Westminster, Feb. 26, 1809, mar. at W., Dec. 25, 1828, Myles Wood, born May 11, 1807, son of Robert and Ester Wood, of Saddleworth, Yorkshire, England. He came to Boston, Aug. 12, 1824; worked in cotton mills for thirty years. He writes: " When I look back and see the changes in manufacturing, it seems as if I ought to be more than a century old. I know the times when there was not a power loom, speeder or picker, in England. I have seen girls winding roping with a spinning-wheel. I tended the first speeder that came to Ashton, ᵛ . It was built at Bolton, near Manchester, Eng." For the last twenty five years he has.lived on a farm in Northboro. His wife's sisters, Charlotte and Eliza, live with him. They have had seven children:

(i) MARY⁷ MELINDA WOOD, born at Philipston, Mass., Sept. 26, 1829, married Benjamin Hopkins. Reside at Newton Upper Falls. He is a mechanic, and owns a house near the Railroad Station. They have two children:

(1) JOSIE⁸ MAY HOPKINS, born at Ashland, Oct. 14, 1858.

(2) JAMES⁸ FREDERIC HOPKINS, born at Newton Upper Falls, Feb. 26, 1868.

17

(ii) JOHN[7] MYLES WOOD, born in Westminster, Sept. 27, 1831, mar. April 23, 1857, Listina Plympton, of Craftsbury, Vt. They had: ELLA[8] AUGUSTA WOOD, b. Feb. 2, 1861. She died Aug. 16, same year. His wife, Listina, died Sept. 26, 1861, at Milford, aged 26 years. He mar. second, Aug. 23, 1865, Mary Johnson, of Clinton, Mass., the sister of Joseph P. Johnson, who was mortally wounded at Antietam. No children by last wife. They reside at Milford, Mass. He is a cabinet-maker, but for the last sixteen or eighteen years has worked at burial caskets, &c.

(iii) GEORGE[7] BLODGET WOOD, born at Northboro, May 6, 1833, married May 6, 1857, Mary S. Warren, of Northboro, resides near his father. "Owns a small farm; works at shoemaking when he can get work. He can turn his hand at most all kinds of work, same as many Americans can. Keeps a good cow and a good horse. Has a small grove, near 'Solomon's Pond,' where they hold picnics in summer."

They have two children:

(1) HERBERT[8] WARREN WOOD, born May 27, 1859.
(2) AMY[8] GERTRUDE WOOD, born July 7, 1867.

(iv) KEZIAH[7] WOOD, daughter of Myles and Melinda Wood, was born at Hopkinton, now Ashland, Mass., Oct. 17, 1838. She married May 3, 1857, Joseph P. Johnson, of Clinton, Mass. He was son of Nathaniel and Almira Johnson. By occupation was a comb maker. "He served in 9th Co., 15th Mass. Vol., and was one of those boys who swam across the Potomac, near Balls' Bluff. He was mortally wounded at Antietam, Sept. 17, 1862, was carried to Washington, where the good soldier died in hospital, Oct. 4, same year. He was buried at Northboro, with great military honors. He was a good husband and loved his family much. I took his family to my house in those dark days, and their mother went to work in a shoe shop in Marlboro, about four miles away. She married a second time, June 1, 1870, Charles H. Brigham, son of Hastings and Nancy Brigham, of Boston. He is an engineer. He had by his first wife

16

17

three boys.   Mr. B. is a good man, and very indulgent father.   Owns a nice house, and has a salary of $1200 a year."   (*Myles Wood's Letter.*)

Keziah⁷ Wood had by J. P. Johnson, first husband:

(1)   FRANK⁸ MYLES JOHNSON, born Oct. 24, 1858.
(2)   MABEL⁸ NELLIE JOHNSON, born May 18, 1860.

By second husband:

(3)   ELBERT⁸ IRVING BRIGHAM, born July 12, 1871.
(4)   RUTH⁸ MAY BRIGHAM, born March 28, 1874.

(v)   CHARLOTTE⁷ WOOD, born in Ashland, Dec. 11, 1840, married at Northboro, June 19, 1873, Samuel Townsend, his second wife.   He had four children by his first wife; was a farmer, but now engaged in the shoe business.   By Charlotte (Wood) he has had no children.

(vi)   JAMES⁷ JACKSON WOOD, (named for James Jackson, of Ashland, formerly of Attleboro, Mass., who was the employer of Myles Wood for many years,) was born at Westminster, Nov. 11, 1844, at the farm his father bought at that place when he left the factory business. This farm is now owned by the town of Westminster, as a Town Asylum.   "When I was there four years ago, the town's poor thanked me for setting out those good fruit trees."   (*M. Wood.*)   He married May 31, 1870, Hattie L. Litchfield, of Leominster, Mass.   Resided in Berlin, Mass., but now lives on his father's farm at Northboro.   One child:

(1)   RALPH⁸ SAWYER WOOD, born Feb. 25, 1871.

(vii) GERTRUDE⁷ ELLEN WOOD, their youngest child, was born at Northboro, Jan. 31, 1850.   She died June 25, 1865, was interred at Northboro.

6.   GEORGE⁶ WASHINGTON, ⎫ Twins, born Oct. 17,
7.   MARTHA⁶ WASHINGTON, ⎬ 1813, in Westminster.

6.   GEORGE⁶ WASHINGTON MONTJOY, mar. Catherine Merryfield, of West Boylston, Mass.   They have had seven children, whose record is very imperfect.   Two only are now living:

17

(i) HENRIETTE⁷ MONTJOY, born in Westminster, married Benjamin Bartlett, and resides in Boston.

(ii) HERBERT⁷ MONTJOY, born in Fitchburg.

(?) "CHARLES⁷ MONTJOY, a fine young man, was lost in the last war—son of George W. Montjoy."

7. MARTHA⁶ WASHINGTON MONTJOY, the twin to George Washington, born Oct. 17, 1813, married Elias Blodget. Reside in South Ashburnham, Mass. No children.

iii. ANNA⁵ DUNSTER, (*Thomas,⁴ David,³ Jonathan,² Henry,¹*)· born Aug. 3, 1775, (*Westminster Records,*) Aug. 10, 1776, (*Mrs. Bennett,*) the third child of Thos. and Lidia (Pierce) Dunster, married Aug. 10, 1803, Aaron Beard, born May 16, 1778, at Westminster. They settled at once at Bromly, since called Peru, Vt., where they spent their days: They lived together sixty-nine years and four months. She died Dec. 17, 1871, aged 95 years, 4 mo. and 7 days, (*Mrs. B.*) 96 years, 4 mo. and 14 days, (*West'r.*) He died Nov. 22, 1873, aged 95 years and 7 months. "She was a woman of great moral courage and excellence of mind. She was the mother of nine children of her own and one adopted—eight daughters and one son. They were all born in Peru, Vt. All lived to be married, and the youngest one was thirty-five years old before there was a death in the family. They were both members of the Congregational Church. Six of their children belong to the same church, two belong to the Methodist, one died without uniting with any church, but as we hoped died in the same faith, trusting in the same Saviour." (*Mrs. Bennett's Letter.*) They had nine children:

i. BEATRICE⁶ BYARD (as now written), born Jan. 18, 1804, married Reuben Tarbell, Sept. 8, 1825. He is a dealer in lumber. They had nine children:

1. ACHSA⁷ ANN TARBELL, born Jan. 23, 1826. She married April 3, 1844, Ezekiel Cudworth, born Aug. 8, 1820, son of Ezekiel and Lydia (Lewis) Cudworth, of Rindge, N. H. They had eight children:

(i) ELIZA⁸ ANN CUDWORTH, born Dec. 27, 1846, died Sept. 22, 1849, at Rindge.

17

(ii)   ELLA⁸ ANNETTE CUDWORTH, born Oct. 1, 1851.
(iii) CHARLIE⁸ MARSHALL CUDWORTH, } Twins.
(iv)   CARRIE⁸ MARIA CUDWORTH,   }
Born July 28, 1854.
(v)   EMMA⁸ TARBELL CUDWORTH, born Feb. 7, 1857.
(vi)   SARAH⁸ ANGIE CUDWORTH, born Nov. 21, 1862,
died Jan. 17, 1865, at Rindge.
(vii) ELSIE⁸ ADDISON CUDWORTH, b. Oct. 23, 1865.
(viii) BEATRICE⁸ DAY CUDWORTH, b. Aug. 26, 1868.

2.   RUSINA⁷ JUAN TARBELL, born Nov. 4, 1827, mar.
Sept. 24, 1851, at Bellows Falls, Vt., George Sidney
Brewer, born Nov. 18, 1828, son of Asa and Rachel
(Knight) Brewer.   She died at Boston, Nov. 20, 1871.
Two children:

(i)   ARTHUR⁸ DUANE BREWER, born April 9, 1854.
(ii) ANDREW⁸ SIDNEY BREWER, born April 12, 1859.

3. } Twins,⁷ b. June 3, 1829.   Both died same day.
4. }

5.   AARON⁷ MARSHALL TARBELL, b. April 24, 1830,
died in Royalston, Mass., July 11, 1836.

6.   CHARLES⁷ DUANE TARBELL, born July 20, 1832,
mar. Nov. 18, 1856, in Marlboro, N. H., Elmira Frances
Whitney, born Jan. 18, 1836, daughter of Benjamin and
Elmira (Stimson) Whitney.   Now living in Littleton,
N. H.   A lumber merchant.   Four children:

(i)   FRANK⁸ LESLIE TARBELL, born March 20, 1859,
died at South Keene, N. H., Feb. 7, 1867.
(ii) MARY⁸ EDITH TARBELL, born March 17, 1861.
(iii) ANNE⁸ MABEL TARBELL, born Sept. 6, 1868.
(iv) FLORA⁸ ELMIRA TARBELL, born March 6, 1871.

7.   LAURA⁷ ANN TARBELL, born Dec. 25, 1834, died
Sept. 8, 1837, at Royalston, Mass.

8.   CALISTA⁷ FAY TARBELL, born May 31, 1837, mar.
at Rindge, N. H., Dec. 1, 1859, Nathan Andrew Fitch,
born Sept. 9, 1835, son of Nathan and Louisa (Burnham) Fitch.   Two children:

(i)   NELLA⁸ LOUISA FITCH, born Dec. 23, 1860.
(ii) HENRY⁸ WARREN FITCH, born Jan. 25, 1866.

17

9. SARAH[7] MARIA TARBELL, born July 3, 1840, married in Boston, Jan. 28, 1864, George B. Day, born Jan. 11, 1838, son of Alvin and Anna Maria (Stebbins) Day. One child:

(i) FLORENCE[8] NATHALIE DAY, born Sept. 6, 1869.

ii. POLLY[6] BYARD, (*Aaron and Anna*[5] (*Dunster*) *Beard*,) born April 27, 1805, married Dec. 1, 1825, Parmason Tarbell. He was a carpenter. She died Aug. 28, 1857. They had three children—two sons and one daughter—one son only now living:

FRANK[7] N. TARBELL, born April 6, 1831, mar.. Nov. 24, 1856, Mary A. Hasting, born June 14, 1838? He is Captain of Police at Green Island, N. Y. He is the youngest of their children. Of the others we have no record. Four children:

(i) CHARLES[8] F. TARBELL, born Jan. 25, 1859, died July 16, 1874.
(ii) WALTER[8] F. TARBELL, born Nov. 7, 1860, died Jan. 14, 1861.
(iii) HERBERT[8] F. TARBELL, born Dec. 12, 1864.
(iv) OLEN?[8] F. TARBELL, born Dec. 31, 1867.

iii. LYDIA[6] BYARD, born Feb. 18, 1807, mar. Nov. 8, 1827, Parker Wyman, a farmer. They had ten children—three sons and seven daughters—all living, 1874. "They are so scattered abroad that I cannot tell much about them. They are in seven different States. Two of the sons were in the army." (*Mrs. Bennett.*)

After the above was written, Mrs. B. furnished memo. of Lydia[6] (Byard) Wyman's children.

1. LYDIA[7] AMANDA WYMAN, born at Peru, Vt., Sept. 24, 1829? 1828, both dates appear. She was mar. by Rev. Mr. Crowley, Sept. 10, 1848, to Edward A. Weeks, of Manchester, Vt. They have three children:

(i) ALICE[8] GERTRUDE WEEKS, born at Manchester, Dec. 8, 1849. She was married at Crestline, Ohio, by Rev. D. I. Foust, Sept. 12, 1869, to Charles Wheeler. He died at Grand Travarse City, Michigan, Feb. 11,

*16

17

1872, of consumption, leaving no children. She was married again, by Rev. J. H. Forbes, Aug. 25, 1875, to M. E. Gaul, of New York.

(ii) ISAAC⁸ WEBSTER WEEKS, born at Rutland, Vt., Nov. 18, 1858.

(iii) JENNIE⁸ ROANA WEEKS, born at Rutland, Vt., Dec. 19, 1864.

2. ALVIN⁷ W. WYMAN, born April 30, 1830. Resides at North Adams, Mass.

3. CHARLES⁷ M. WYMAN, born March 24, 1832, married April 4, 1853, Adaline T. Smith. Have seven children, all born at Manchester, Vt.:

(i) ELLA⁸ A. WYMAN, born March 15, 1854. She married Dec. 28, 1874, George Romig, in Frenchtown, Nebraska. Have one child:

(1) MAY⁹ A. ROMIG, born Nov. 24, 1875.

(ii) MORRILL⁸ C. WYMAN, born April 27, 1856.
(iii) LEMUEL⁸ J. WYMAN, born June 5, 1859.
(iv) LYDIA⁸ A. WYMAN, born Dec. 22, 1861.
(v) LUCINDA⁸ A. WYMAN, born April 3, 1865.
(vi) AARON⁸ DUNSTER WYMAN, born Sept. 6, 1867.
(vii) LORD⁸ A. WYMAN, born March 20, 1870.

4. ABBA⁷ J. WYMAN, born June 24, 1834, 1835? (both dates appear,) mar. Jan. 8, 1855, Orlando Bourn, born Sept. 30, 1834. Have five children:

(i) FLORA⁸ J. BOURN, born Feb. 5, 1856.
(ii) FRED.⁸ O. BOURN, born April 29, 1858.
(iii) CHARLES⁸ W. BOURN, born March 13, 1860, died March 29, 1864.
(iv) THOMAS⁸ W. BOURN, born Aug. 25, 1862.
(v) CHARLES⁸ A. BOURN, born Oct. 22, 1872.

5. JULIA⁷ ANN WYMAN, born Oct. 14, 1836. She married Oct. 19, 1854, John Rising. They have seven children:

(i) CARRIE⁸ RISING, born Aug. 29, 1856. She married June 14, 1874, Simeon Willey.
(ii) FRANK⁸ RISING, born July 16, 1859.

17

(iii) AGGIE[8] RISING, born July 25, 1861.
(iv) ADDA[8] RISING, born June 1, 1864.
(v) JENNIE[8] RISING, born Oct. 12, 1867.
(vi) FREDDIE[8] RISING, born July 20, 1870.
(vii) WALLACE[8] RISING, born June 17, 1874.

6. VERONA[7] A. WYMAN, born Sept. 20, 1838, mar. May 22, 1862, Oscar F. Mattison. Reside in North Barrington, Vt. Two children:

(i) EDMUND[8] J. MATTISON, born Aug. 22, 1863.
(ii) CHARLOTTE[8] C. MATTISON, born March 6, 1870.

7. WARREN[7] M. WYMAN, born Sept. 20, 1840.
8. MARIA[7] L. WYMAN, born Nov. 3, 1842, married Nov. 2, 1869, —— Wells. Have two children:

(i) AURTHER[8] E. WELLS, born Nov. 11, 1870.
(ii) FRANK[8] A. WELLS, born June 22, 1873.

9. MARY[7] R. WYMAN, born Aug. 13, 1845, married July 30, 1863, Myron C. Raymond. He died Aug. 29, 1871, at Geneva Lake, Wisconsin, aged 31 years. Had three children:

(i) JANE[8] C. RAYMOND, born July 30, 1864.
(ii) MARY[8] A. RAYMOND, born April 8, 1868, died at Geneva Lake, May 9, 1869.
(iii) MABEL[8] L. RAYMOND, born March 7, 1871.

10. FANNY[7] A. WYMAN, born March 27, 1849, mar. June 13, 1869, Plynn A. Vanderlip. Two children:

(i) CARRIE[8] A. VANDERLIP, born at Manchester, Vt., Feb. 11, 1870.
(ii) MINNIE[8] E. VANDERLIP, born at Joliet, Illinois, July 31, 1874.

iv. ANNA[6] BYARD, (*Aaron and Anna*[5] *Dunster, Thos.*[4] *David,*[3] *Jona.*[2] *Henry,*[1]) the fourth child of Aaron and Anna (Dunster) Beard, born May 18, 1809, married Dec. 1, 1833, Jonas Bennett, joiner and house carpenter. Reside in Manchester, Vt. Almost the whole history of Anna (Dunster) Beard's descendants was given by Mrs. Anna (Byard) Bennett.

They have had five children:

17

1. GEORGE[7] WALTER BENNETT, born Feb. 6, 1835, is a fresco painter. He married Oct. 20, 1858, Julia F. Reynold, of Troy, N. Y. Three children:

   (i) WILLARD[8] K. BENNETT, born Jan. 24, 1864.
   (ii) OTTO[8] R. BENNETT, born Aug. 14, 1866.
   (iii) CLAUD[8] A. BENNETT, born June 30, 1869.

2. ELECTA[7] M. BENNETT, born Nov. 16, 1836, mar. June 25, 1855, William McFarland, of Jackson, N. Y. Died Dec. 28, 1855.

3. WILLARD[7] K. BENNETT, was born Nov. 1, 1838. He fell in M'Clellan's retreat at Savage Station, June 29, 1862. He was First Sergeant in Co. E., 5th Regiment Vermont Volunteers. Aged 23 years and 7 months.

4. HARRISON[7] T. BENNETT, born Sept. 4, 1840, is a house painter. "He was in the navy one year in the war." He married Sept. 1, 1864, Caroline A. Crofut. Three children:

   (i) ANNA[8] L. BENNETT, born Dec. 17, 1865.
   (ii) WILLIAM[8] W. BENNETT, born Feb. 17, 1868?
   (iii) ALICE[8] E. BENNETT, born July 8, 1871.

5. NANCY[7] A. BENNETT, born Aug. 9, 1842, died June 8, 1849.

v. HEPSEY[6] BYARD, born Jan. 11, 1811, married Feb. —, 1832? Feb. 21, 1831? Charles Childs. He is a cooper. Reside in North Fairfield, Huron Co., Ohio. They had eight children:

1. JAMES[7] F. CHILDS, born Dec. 6, 1832, mar. July 4, 1854. He died May 4, 1863, leaving two children.

2. ROENA[7] CHILDS, born Oct. 9, 1834, died July 20, 1844.

3. CALVIN[7] CHILDS, born Sept. 15, 1836, mar. Nov. 9, 1857. They have six children.

4. JOHN[7] CHILDS, born Oct. 10, 1838, married Dec. 24, 1860. Three children.

5. MARY[7] A. CHILDS, born Oct. 25, 1841, married April 15, 1861.

6. MARCUS[7] CHILDS, born Dec. 22, 1843, mar. ——. Have one child.

17

(No record of any of Hepsey B. Childs' grand-children.)

7. ELLEN⁷ M. CHILDS, born March 1, 1846, died Oct. 5, 1866.

8. CYNTHIA⁷ A. CHILDS, born June 6, 1849, died Aug. 9, 1870.

vi. DORCASANA⁶ BYARD, the sixth child of Aaron and Anna (Dunster) Beard, born Sept. 22, 1812, mar. James Peirce, Feb. 23, 1842. He was connected with C. A. Peirce & Co., printers and bookbinders, Banner office, Bennington, Vt. She died Sept. 10, 1875, of consumption. They have had three children:

1. MARIA⁷ A. PEIRCE, born Feb. 22, 1843, died May 22, 1865.

2. EVERETT⁷ W. PEIRCE, born July 9, 1845. He was in the 5th Regt. Vermont Vols. two or three years.

3. STELLA⁷ C. PEIRCE, born May 22, 1854, died Aug. 29, 1855.

vii. LUCY⁶ B. BYARD, (*Aaron and Anna⁵ Dunster, Thomas,⁴ David,³ Jonathan,² Henry,¹*) born April 16, 1815, mar. Oct. 27, 1835, John W. Farnum, a farmer. They had eight children:

"Six sons, two daughters. The sons are all farmers but one. He is a carpenter. Not one of these six sons use tea, coffee, tobacco, or ardent spirits: good, honest, upright men. Three are members of the Congregational Church. We almost feel proud of them. They are an honor to the family to whom they belong." (*Mrs. B.*) So say we.

1. DAVID⁷ H. FARNUM, born Aug. 19, 1837, mar. Nov. 13, 1862, Frances M. Burton. Two children:

(i) CARRIE⁸ A. FARNUM, born Nov. 25, 1863.
(ii) ALBERT⁸ B. FARNUM, born June 7, 1870.

2. AARON⁷ B. FARNUM, born June 2, 1839. He was killed Nov. 17, 1867, by the bursting of a millstone, at Arlington, Vermont.

3. HENRY⁷ M. FARNUM, born Feb. 29, 1841, mar. Dec. 13, 1865, Betsey Benedict. One child:

(i) FRED.⁸ K. FARNUM, born Aug. 4, 1868.

17

4.   MARION[7] E. FARNUM, born March 8, 1843, mar. Dec. 5, 1864, Edwin B. Simonds.   Two children:

(i)   ARTHUR[8] E. SIMONDS, born Dec. 5. 1865.
(ii) LUCY[8] BELLE SIMONDS, born Dec. 22, 1867.

5.   EDWIN[7] D. FARNUM, born April 29, 1845, mar. Nov. 29, 1869, Ellen M. Smith.   One child:

(i)   HENRY[8] A. FARNUM, born Feb. 1, 1873.

6.   LYCENNIA[7] J. FARNUM, born July 2, 1847.

7.   AMANDIE[7] L. FARNUM, born March 22, 1849, married March 11, 1874, Frank T. Rand.   One child:

(i)   HATTIE[8] L. RAND, born Dec. 12, 1874.

8.   FREDERICK[7] M. FARNUM, born Oct. 6, 1857.

viii. LUCINDA[6] M. BYARD, born June 18, 1818, mar. Dexter French, a farmer, March 28, 1849.   Two children:

1.   JOSIAH[7] A. FRENCH, b. Jan. 24, 1850, is a farmer.
2.   MARION[7] L. FRENCH, born Nov. 17, 1853, mar. Jan. 24, 1874, Myron Taylor, of Manchester, Vt.

ix.   AARON[6] T. BYARD, born May 13, 1823, was the youngest child and only son of Aaron and Anna (Dunster) Beard.   He married Jane M. Muller, Nov. 18, 1845. She was born July 6, 1828.   He was a farmer, and lived on the "old place" in Peru, Vt.   He took care of the old folks, who lived to see forty-one grand-children and sixty-two great grand-children.   They have since increased to fifty-six grand-children, and an "unknown quantity" of great grand-children.   "They fulfilled their Maker's command to multiply and replenish the earth." (*Mrs. Bennett.*)   He has of late years given up farming, and devoted his whole attention to the lumber business, of which he did considerable while farming. They have six children:

1.   ANDREW[7] A. BYARD, born Feb. 28, 1847, married Laura M. Butler.   Have two daughters, names unknown.

2.   FANNIE[7] ANNA BYARD, born Sept. 26, 1850, married Oct. 15? 1872, John G. Miller, of Williamsburgh, Mass.   One child:

(i)   FRED.[8] MILLER, born Oct. 31, 1873.

17

3. JOHN[7] L. BYARD, born Aug. 14, 1853.
4. STELLA[7] E. BYARD, born Sept. 29, 1857.
5. WILLARD[7] H. BYARD, born Nov. 2, 1861.
6. MARY[7] J. BYARD, born Jan. 30, 1865.

iv. THOMAS[5] DUNSTER, (*Thomas,[4] David,[3] Jona.,[2] Henry,[1]*) the fourth child of Thomas and Lidia (Pierce) Dunster, born in Westminster, Aug. 13, 1780, (*West. Records,*) 1772, (*Family Bible,*) married July 17, 1810, Rebeccah Harrington, of Dublin, N.H., (*West. Records,*) Feb. 25, 1811, (*Family Bible*). She was born Feb. 25, 1790. He was a farmer, and lived in Windsor, Vt. He died at Weathersfield Upper Falls, at his son's residence, March 11, 1874, aged, by *West. Record,* 93 years, 7 months, by *Family Record,* 101 years and 7 months. She is living, 1874, at her son's. They had five children:

1. HANNAH[6] DUNSTER, born April 18, 1813, mar. ———, 1830, Joel Nason, now living at East Windsor, Vt.
2. AMOS[6] DUNSTER, born Nov. 1, 1816, died at Londonderry, Vt., Aug. 7, 1838.
3. ESTHER[6] DUNSTER, born Sept. 10, 1820, married 1840, Joel Nichols, of Weston, Vt. They had one child:

(i) AMOS[7] NICHOLS, born June 11, 1842.

John Nichols died ———. She married second, James Bryant, of Reading, Vt. Reside there.

4. EMILY[6] DUNSTER, born Aug. 15, ———? married Dec. 18, 1859, Daniel Bryant, of Weathersfield, Vt. She died June 12, 1869 or 70? at Windsor Corners, Vt.

This record of Thomas[5] Dunster's family was taken from the "*Old Family Bible,*" by A. B. Dunster.

5. AARON[6] B. DUNSTER, (*Thomas,[5] Thomas,[4] David,[3] Jona.,[2] Henry,[1]*) the fifth child of Thomas and Rebeccah (Harrington) Dunster, born Jan. 23, 1823, married Feb. 6, 1850, Sophia Cory, daughter of Charles and Silinda Cory, of Danby, Vt. He is a farmer. Resides at Weathersfield Upper Falls, Vt. Family Congregationalists. They have had eight children:

(i) AMOS[7] P. DUNSTER, born June 2, 1852, a farmer, resides in Weathersfield, unmarried.

17

(ii) LYDIA[7] DUNSTER, b. Nov. 5, 1853, d. in infancy.

(iii) EMILY[7] DUNSTER, born April 19, 1855, living at home.

(iv) AARON[7] W. DUNSTER, born Nov. 2, 1856, a farmer, lives at Cavendish, Vt., unmarried.

(v) ANDREW[7] DUNSTER, born March 11, 1858, died when two years old.

(vi) ESTHER[7] DUNSTER, born July 4, 1860, died when one year old.

(vii) CHARLES[7] DUNSTER, born May 2, 1862, died when three years old.

(viii) EDWIN[7] DUNSTER, born Oct. 8, 1864, lives at home.

This family is the only one by the name of *Dunster* descended from David[5] Dunster, and also from Jonathan[2] and *Deborah (Wade)* Dunster. All their other living descendants are in the *female* line.

v. LYDIA[5] DUNSTER, (*Thomas,[4] David,[3] Jonathan,[2] Henry,[1]*) the fifth child of Thomas and Lidia (Pierce) Dunster, born July 19, 1784, married about 1805, John Wood, of Boston. He enlisted in the war of 1812, and died in the army soon after, on "Boston Island," (Fort Independence). His wife, Lydia, died July, 1814? leaving three children:

1. JOSEPH[6] WOOD, born Jan., 1807, "married Lucy Sawyer—first wife. He is a farmer, lives in Holden, six miles from Worcester. Has no children."

2. PATTY[6] (MARTHA) WOOD, born Aug. 10, 1808, married April 6, 1828, Samuel Shattuck, born April 21, 1804. Had six children:

(i) ELIZA[7] P. SHATTUCK, born Dec. 3, 1829, married William P. Smith.

(ii) LEVI[7] L. SHATTUCK, born Aug. 10, 1831, died Jan. 14, 1865.

(iii) WARREN[7] SHATTUCK, born July 13, 1833, mar. first, Maria Jones, mar. second, Mary McIntire. One child:

(1) IDA[8] JANE SHATTUCK, born Nov. 6, 1864.

17

(iv) SARAH⁷ JANE SHATTUCK, born Jan. 3, 1836, died May 3, 1854.

(v) CHARLES⁷ W. SHATTUCK, born May 23, 1838, married Martha Scott. One child:

(1) LUCIUS⁸ EUGENE SHATTUCK, b. Nov. 23, 1862.

(vi) WILLIAM⁷ HENRY HARRISON SHATTUCK, born Oct. 7, 1841.

Mrs. Martha Shattuck now lives with her two sons in North street, Fitchburg. "Her husband died in 1860. She was only four years old when her mother died, and was taken away from her relatives when very young, consequently knows but little about them."

3. NANCY⁶ WOOD, "the youngest child, died when young."

vi. PRICILLA⁵ DUNSTER, (*Thomas,⁴ David,³ Jona.,²ͫ Henry,¹*) the sixth child of Thomas and Lidia (Pierce) Dunster, born March 4, 1787, at Westminster, married Sept. 6, 1810, Isaac Estabrook, born Aug. 31, 1778. He died at Westminster, 1849. She died at Westminster (Wachusett Village), March 6, 1875, at the residence of her son, aged 88 years and 2 days. She was the last survivor of Thomas⁴ and Lidia (Pierce) Dunster's children. She was a woman of wonderful memory, even to the last. "She was stricken with paralysis in June, 1873, but recovered so as to read and sew at times as well as common." She spent her last days with her son, Charles⁶ A. Estabrook. "She was a very industrious woman. Her husband died many years ago. All the girls of that family (Thomas⁴) were better workers than the men were; for if the men had done right, the land in their possession would not all have got out of it." (*Myles Wood's Letter.*)

To Mrs. Estabrook we are indebted for the foundations of the history of David³ Dunster's descendants. She communicated them twenty years ago to Prof. E. S. Dunster, M. D., then a student in Harvard College.

They had seven children:

1. ISAAC⁶ ESTABROOK, born Feb. 11, 1811, died May 11, same year.

17

17

2. BETSEY[6] ESTABROOK, born June 19, 1812, now living, unmarried, at Wachusett Village, Westminster.

3. ISAAC[6] ESTABROOK, born Feb. 18, 1815. He served three years in the Florida war; then volunteered under Col. Harney three months; returned to Westminster; went about three months afterwards to Savannah, Georgia, where he died, June 12, 1843. Unmarried.

4. CHARLES[6] ASHER ESTABROOK, (*Isaac and Pricilla[5] Dunster,*) born May 24, 1817, married Nov. 23, 1846, Caroline H. Dow. He adds an *s* to their name. Resides at Wachusett Village. They have had seven children:

(i) CAROLINE[7] F. ESTABROOKS, born July 14, 1847, died Aug. 6, 1849.

(ii) ISADORE[7] P. ESTABROOKS, born May 10, 1851.

(iii) CHARLES[7] F. ESTABROOKS, born Oct. 26, 1854.

(iv) AREANNA[7] ESTABROOKS, born Oct. 31, 1857.

(v) ISAAC[7] L. ESTABROOKS, born Feb. 7, 1860, died April 29, 1865.

(vi) HENRY[7] Dow ESTABROOKS, born Dec. 9, 1863.

(vii) CAROLINE[7] G. ESTABROOKS, born July 10, 1871, died Sept. 9, same year.

5. SAMUEL[6] ESTABROOK, born Dec. 19, 1821, died ——, 1833.

6. Infant,[6] born ——, 1823.

7. SARAH[6] ANN, born Sept. 13, 1827, died May 14, 1845, unmarried.

vii. HENRY[5] DUNSTER, (*Thomas,[4] David,[3] Jona.,[2] Henry,[1]*) the seventh child of Thomas and Lidia (Pierce) Dunster, born May 21, 1792, published Sept. 21, married Oct. 7, 1815, Mary Bemis, of Chesterfield, N. H. He died in the army, at Baton Rouge, Louisiana, prior to 1823. They had two children:

1. JASON[6] DUNSTER, born Aug.? 14, 1816, in Westminster. He was a laborer. Married by Rev. C. Mason, March 27, (published 4th and 18th), 1839, Sarah Perry. He died Jan. 19, 1850, of consumption, aged 33 years, 8 months and 5 days. She died Sept., 1861. They had four children:

18

(i) SYLVESTER⁷ DUNSTER, born ———, died when three years old.

(ii) JASON⁷ ALBERT, } Twins, born July 12, 1844.
(iii) SARAH⁷ ADALADE, }

(ii) JASON⁷ ALBERT DUNSTER, enlisted as a volunteer, at Worcester, in 1863, died July same year. Taken sick in the army, but got home to die.

(iii) SARAH⁷ ADALADE DUNSTER, married Thomas Locke, in the fall of 1867. They live in South Saginaw, Mich. They have one daughter: (1) CARRIE⁸ LOCKE.

(iv) MARY⁷ CAROLINE DUNSTER, born Aug. 5, 1846, married first, Nov. —, 1863, Lewis G. Chaffin. He was killed Oct., 1864, at Pond's Iron Works, in Worcester, whilst hoisting machinery. The chain gave way and struck him in the temple. She had a son after her husband's death:

(1) LEWIS⁸ G. CHAFFIN, born Jan., 1865. He lives in Worcester, Mass., with his mother, now Mrs. Jones.

Mary⁷ Caroline married second, May 12, 1867, George W. Jones, born Jan. 4, 1848, at Norwich, Conn. He is a carpenter. Reside at 42 Cutler street, Worcester. They have had four children:

(2) GERTIE⁸ CARRIE JONES, born Dec. 22, 1868.
(3) GEORGE⁸ T. JONES, born 1869, died when five weeks old. (4) Infant.⁸
(5) GEORGE⁸ THOMAS JONES, born Aug. 22, 1875.

2. SYLVESTER⁶ DUNSTER, born June 16, 1819, died May 11, 1842. Not married.

18. v. MARGARY⁴ DUNSTER, (*David,³ Jonathan,² Henry,¹*) the fifth child of David and Mary (Molly) (Russell) Dunster, was born at West Cambridge, (Arlington), and was baptized at Cambridge Second Church, Rev. S. Cooke, Dec. 23, 1739. Mr. Cooke wrote her name "Magire." She was the first child by the name of *Dunster* baptized at that church, which was organized Sept. 9, 1739. Her parents removed to Westminster in 1742, where she was brought up. She married June 17, 1760, Joshua Wilder. The record of her mar-

18

riage in Westminster Town Records is, "Joshua Wilder
and Margary Dunster, both of Westminster, 'was' joined
in marriage June 17, 1760, by Oliver Wilder, Justice
of the Peace." In their Family Bible the record is,
"Joshua Wilder and Margery, his wife, were married in
the year 1760, June the 14th." In a record furnished
by Miss Jane R. Wilder, their marriage is, "June 11th,
1760." In her father's will, she is called "Marguary,
my third daughter." They resided in Westminster till
the spring of 1765, when they bought a farm in Brattleboro, Vt., about a mile from the village, on which they
lived and died. He was a deacon of the early church in
Brattleboro; bought and lived on the farm now occupied
by George A. and Marshall Wilder, and their sister,
Jane R. Wilder.

Joshua and Margary⁴ (Dunster) Wilder had twelve
children, whose births we give from the Family Bible,
adding only the generation and surname, and place of
birth:

i. SARAH⁵ WILDER, "was born unto them Saturday,
March 28, 1761," in Westminster. She died Sept. 16,
1764.

ii. MARY⁵ E. WILDER, "was born unto them Thursday, Sept. 9, 1763." She died Sept. 19, 1764, three
days after her sister; both died in Westminster, and no
doubt were buried there.

iii. SARAH⁵ WILDER, "was born Friday, the 16th of
August, 1765," at Brattleboro. She married (date not
found) Henry Willard. They lived in Dummerston,
and had eight children, the dates of whose births have
not been found. Seven of them were married, but their
record is not further known to us. Their children were:

1. SALLIE,⁶ married William Barnes.
2. POLLY,⁶   "   Isaac Cutler.
3. MARGERY,⁶ "   John Whipple.
4. EUNICE,⁶   "   Josiah Goddard.
5. OLIVE,⁶ - "   Nat. Taft.
6. NANCY,⁶   "   Davis Rand.
7. LEWIS,⁶ was a bachelor.
8. BEN,⁶ married Lydia Bennet.

18

Miss Jane R. Wilder, who gave this record, adds: "These children are all dead. I have not the dates of their deaths, neither that of Uncle and Aunt Wilder."

iv. POLLY[5] WILDER, was born Friday, the 22d day of July, 1768, at Brattleboro. She married Luther Sargeant, and lived at Brattleboro. They had one child, who died young. "I have no date of its death, but can find it on the grave stone, about a mile from us." (*J. R. Wilder.*) In the Family Bible is this entry:

"ANNA SARGEANT, daughter of Luther and Polly (Wilder) Sargeant, was born Sunday, Oct. 12, 1788,"—"gran-child;" and in a memo. by Miss Wilder, is added: "Married Samuel Duncan, and died at Northfield, N. Y., Jan. 8, 1875." This record is not very clear, and may be found erroneous. It is believed she left descendants in Northfield,—perhaps Fay Duncan, and others, who are referred to in a letter, but we cannot classify them.

v. JOHN[5] WILDER, (*Joshua and Margary[4] Dunster, David,[3] Jonathan,[2] Henry,[1]*) was born Thursday, the 4th of Oct., 1770, married Rebecca Chamberlain, of Chesterfield, N. H., in 1795. They lived in Brattleboro. Removed to Newfane, in 1802, where she died Nov. 15, 1811. He removed, in 1840, to Gill, Mass., where he died Jan. 31, 1867. They had eight children:

1. HEPSEBAH[6] WILDER, born 1796, died 1798.

2. LYMAN[6] WILDER, (*John,[5] Joshua and Margary[4] (Dunster), David,[3] Jona.,[2] Henry,[1]*) the second child of John and Rebecca (Chamberlain) Wilder, was born in Brattleboro, Vt., June 28, 1798. He has favored us with a sketch of his life, from which a few items we deemed of interest are extracted: "He commenced life a poor boy. His mother died when he was thirteen years of age. He lived with his father, on a small, stony farm," where he continued till nineteen years of age, working in summer, and going to school from two to three months in the winter. He afterward taught winters till of age; in the meantime studying with a view to a college education. About the time he was beginning

*17

18

the languages his eyesight failed, by reason of too much
study by the "old candle light." Having no means but
his own earnings, his friends dissuaded him from that
course, which they thought would be his ruin. He
yielded to their advice, but at the same time resolved
(D. V.) that he would have as good an education, if his
life was spared, as was then given at a college, by apply-
ing himself in his spare moments closely to study. These
moments are often flung away; but not so in his case.
He felt that his day labor must be devoted to procuring
a living. He began the study of architecture, under a
Boston architect, and was soon master of the business.
His sight gradually returned, and he continued the study
of the higher mathematics until 1831, when he engaged
in building machinery at Hoosick Falls, N. Y., which
he still carries on. He still pursued Natural Science,
mineralogy, geology, paleontology, conchology, &c. In
each of these he has collected largely, so that his cabinet
numbers forty thousand specimens, mostly of his own
collection. These he has worked out almost single-
handed. It is one of the best private cabinets in the
country. He is on the most intimate terms with the
officers and faculty of Williams College, which conferred
on him the honory degree of A. M., and belongs to the
Natural History Society at that College. He has done
all this while carrying on a large and perplexing business
without neglecting it.

He has been a member of the Legislature, and helped
through the railroad from Troy to Hoosac Tunnel, in
which he has been a director more than twenty years.
He has been connected with and at the head of many
other enterprises. He adds: "I have spent a very busy
life. Had half I was worth burned in 1860, and many
other reverses in business, but keep along with a comfortable living. I am yet in active life, but cannot endure as much as I could twenty-five years ago." He
was at this time 78 years old.

He united with the Congregational Church in Brattleboro when nineteen years old. In 1832 he removed his
church relations to Hoosick Falls Presbyterian Church,
and was soon after elected elder. He has held that office

18

ever since (44 years). "I have outlived the elders then in office, and four others elected since. There are not a great many clergymen in the Wilder family, but a good many elders and deacons. There have been two or more elders all the time since I can remember, from my grand-father down. He and my father both were deacons. I have a brother-in-law and a cousin who are deacons."

Lyman⁶ Wilder is descended in the Wilder lineage from John,⁷ Joshua,⁶ Joshua,⁵ Nathaniel,⁴ Nathaniel,³ Thomas,² Martha.¹ He is collecting the family history. It is hoped he will be able to supply the deficiencies of Marguary⁴ (Dunster) Wilder's descendants which appear in this sketch. He removed to Hoosick Falls in March, 1826. He married first, at Hoosick Falls, Jan. 15, 1829, Virtue Ball, of that place, born Aug. 7, 1802. They had six children:

(i) JONATHAN⁷ BALL WILDER, born Dec. 6, 1829, died June 6, 1834.

(ii) A son,⁷ not named, born May 16, 1832, died June 16, same year.

(iii) LYMAN⁷ CHAMBERLAIN WILDER, born May 17, 1833, is a member of the Presbyterian Church. Is a civil engineer, and at present, 1876, employed by the State of New York, surveying and examining the canals. He is not married.

(iv) MARTHA⁷ LOUISA WILDER, born Sept. 2, 1835, married March 10, 1859, Edward Clark, of Weston, Mass. He was a farmer. They moved (from Weston?) to Malta, Ill., from there to Seneca, Kansas, where he died Feb. 1, 1872, leaving three children:

(1) ELLA⁸ M. CLARK, born Feb. 24, 1860, died Sept. 25, same year.

(2) EDWARD⁸ W. CLARK, born Dec. 23, 1861.

(3) IRWIN⁸ M. CLARK, born Sept. 10, 1865, died March 14, 1875.

(v) JOHN⁷ JAMES WILDER, born Jan. 10, 1839, was an elder, with his father, in the Presbyterian Church at Hoosick. On account of his health, he left there in the fall of 1875, and resides in Nordhoff, Ventura County, California, where he is engaged in the bee business. He

18

married Oct. 24, 1865, Marion R. Renwick, of Trenton, N. J. They have four children:

(1) LYMAN[8] RENWICK WILDER, born Nov. 4, 1866, died Jan. 30, 1870.

(2) MARION[8] LYDIA WILDER, born Sept. 5, 1869.

(3) JOHN[8] ARCHIE WILDER, born Aug. 1, 1871.

(4) CHARLES[8] NEWTON WILDER, b. April 29, 1873.

(vi) PHILANDER[7] NEWTON WILDER, (*Lyman,[6] John,[5] Joshua and Margary[4] D.*,) the sixth child of Lyman and Virtue (Ball) Wilder, was born June 6, 1841. He is a member of the Presbyterian Church, resides at Hoosick Falls, and is engaged with his father in the business of manufacturing machinery. He married Oct. 14, 1868, Emma E. Hastings, of South Hadley, Mass. They have three children:

(1) MARTHA[8] VIRTUE WILDER, born March 1, 1871.

(2) MARY[8] EVELINE WILDER, born July 9, 1873.

(3) EDWARD[8] LYMAN WILDER, born Nov. 3, 1875.

Virtue (Ball), wife of Lyman[6] Wilder, died Feb. 18, 1850. He married second, C. Elizabeth Haswell, Jan. 29, 1851. She was born at Hoosick, May 19, 1819. By her he has three children:

(vii) WILLARD[7] HASWELL WILDER, born Nov. 10, 1852, died July 30, 1855.

(viii) ELIZABETH[7] HARPER WILDER, born Aug. 24, 1854, died May 3, 1855.

(ix) CHARLES[7] TEN BROOCK WILDER, born Oct., 1856, died March 7, 1857.

3. MARY[6] WILDER, the third child of John and Rebecca (Chamberlain) Wilder, born July 16, 1800, married Franklin Cook, of Newfane, June 17, 1824. Mr. Cook died Jan. 15, 1829. She married second, William Lovering, June 11, 1834. He is a farmer. They live in Gill, Mass. Mary (W.) and Franklin Cook had two children:

(i) MARIA[7] A. COOK, born Sept. 17, 1826. She married Dec. 31, 1846, Asa Stoughton. They are farmers in Gill. Have one child:

18

(1) FRANKLIN[6] F. STOUGHTON, born Feb. 3, 1855.

(ii) ELIZA[7] C. COOK, born Aug. 4, 1828, married July 17, 1855, Rev. R. Dexter Miller, of Dummerston. They live in Hartland, Vt. Have had six children:

(1) MARY[8] L. MILLER, born Sept. 29, 1856, died Feb. 28, 1865.

(2) CHARLES[8] M. MILLER, born May 2, 1858, died July 21, 1874.

(3) JOHN[8] C. MILLER, born April 4, 1861.

(4) STELLA[8] M. MILLER, } Twins, born Nov. 21, 1863.
(5) ELLA[8] E. MILLER, }

Stella died Aug. 10, 1865; Ella died April 5, 1864.

(6) FLORENCE[8] BELL MILLER, born Feb. 11, 1871.

4. ITHAMER[6] C. WILDER, the fourth child of John and Rebecca (C.) Wilder, born July 19, 1802, married Marshia Miller, the first Thursday in Dec., 1831. Lived in Dummerston. Had one child:

(i) ELIZA[7] WILDER, born Oct. 5, 1832, married in 1852, Robert Arthur. Six children:

(1) ROBERT.[8] (2) GEORGE.[8] (3) JENNIE.[8] (4) ERNEST.[8] (5) FRANK.[8] (6) ALICE[8] ARTHUR.

Mr. Arthur died May 3, 1866.

5. JOHN[6] WILDER, (*John,[5] Joshua and Margary[4] D., David,[3] Jona.,[2] Henry,[1]*) born June 22, 1805, married Jan. 14, 1835, Sarah Kidder, of Wardsboro, Vt. He died in Gill, April 26, 1861. Six children:

(i) PASCAL[7] P. WILDER, born Dec. 21, 1835, died March 6, 1837.

(ii) ABBOTT[7] P. WILDER, born Jan. 13, 1838, married July 23, 1862, Adelia Namoi? Brown. Have one child:

(1) ETHEL[8] MAY WILDER, born at Eau Clair, Wis., Jan. 24, 1875.

(iii) SARAH[7] CORBIN WILDER, born Aug. 13, 1839, died July 29, 1857.

(iv) THEODORE[7] S. WILDER, born April 15, 1842, died Dec. 6, 1846.

18

(v) SEDGWICK [7] PORTER WILDER, born May 28, 1847, married Oct. 13, 1875, Jennie A. Watson. He is a Congregational minister, and is now (1876) preaching at Springfield, Mass.

(vi) ALBAONA [7] K. WILDER, born April 4, 1851, died next day.

6. REBECCA [6] WILDER, (*John,* [5] *Joshua and Margary* [4] *D.,*) born June 22, 1807, married Hiram Newell, March 15, 1827. They lived in Townshend, Vt. In 1837 removed to Dudley, Mass. Five children:

(i) PHILLIP [7] W. NEWELL, born Dec. 12, 1827, married Aug. —, 1868, Harriet L. Perry, of Webster, Mass. One child: (1) GEORGE [8] P. NEWELL, b. July, 1869.

(ii) AMANDA [7] NEWELL, born May 29, 1830, married Aug. 1, 1855, Levi Clark. They live in Centralia, Kansas. Four children:

(1) MARTHA [8] E. CLARK. (2) IDA [8] A. CLARK, died in infancy. (3) LILIAN [8] M. CLARK, died in infancy. (4) LILIAN [8] E. CLARK.

(iii) RUSSEL [7] S. NEWELL, born Aug. 10, 1832, married Nov. 6, 1865, Anna Edwards. They live in Frankford, Kansas. One child:

(1) EFFIE [8] F. NEWELL, born Oct. 28, 1866.

(iv) PASCAL [7] J. NEWELL, born Aug. 27, 1839, married April 28, 1859, Nancy E. Tenney, of Gill. They live in Willimanset, Mass. Have had two children:

(1) J. HIRAM [8] NEWELL. (2) EDWARD [8] P. NEWELL. Both died in infancy.

(v) ELIZABETH [7] NEWELL, born Sept. 25, 1845, died March 20, 1855.

vi. SOLOMON [5] WILDER, (*Joshua and Margary* [4] *Dunster,*) the sixth child of Joshua and Margary (Dunster) Wilder, was born Sunday, Oct. 11, 1772, at Brattleboro, Vt. He married Sunday, Feb. 23, 1806, Levinia Miller, daughter of Vespatian and Abigail (Church) Miller, born March 5, 1782, in Dummerston, Vt. They lived on the old place of their father's. He died in Brattle-

18

boro, March 16, 1832.   She died April 9, 1868.   Had nine children: one account says ten:

1.   GEORGE⁶ MILLER WILDER, born Jan. 9, 1807, died Aug. 9, 1811.

2.   SUSAN⁶ WILDER, born Dec. 2, 1808, married in Brattleboro, April 21, 1845, Asahel Clapp.   She died June 18, 1861.   They had two children:

(i)   GEORGE⁷ HUNTINGTON CLAPP, born April 20, 1846.   He is a bookseller (Cheney & Clapp), in Brattleboro Village.   He married March 24, 1875, Clara A. Town, of Marlboro, N. H.

(ii)   ARTHUR⁷ BRAINARD CLAPP, born Jan. 22, 1851.

3.   MARY⁶ WILDER, born Feb. 5, 1811, died Nov. 29, 1875, unmarried.

4.   JOSEPH⁶ WILDER, born Oct. 13, 1812, married in Newfane, Vt., Dec. 6, 1843, Delia Ann Merrifield.   Four children:

(i)   JULIA⁷ VIRGINIA WILDER, born Nov. 13, 1844, died Dec. 4, 1861.

(ii)   EMMA⁷ LEWIS WILDER, born ——, died ——.

(iii)   ELLA⁷ LOUISA WILDER, born Nov. 30, 1854, died Jan. 8, 1863.

(iv)   JENNIE⁷ ELLEN WILDER, born July 4, 1863.

5.   SARAH⁶ WILDER, born April 2, 1815, died Sept. 30, 1818.

6.   GEORGE⁶ ANSON WILDER, b. May 26, 1817, unm.

7.   MARSHALL⁶ WILDER, born Oct. 25, 1819, unm.

8.   JANE⁶ REBECCA WILDER, born May 14, 1823, lives with her two brothers, George A. and Marshall Wilder, on the farm settled more than a hundred years ago by their grandfather.   She is unmarried.   Much information of the Wilder family came from her.

9.   RUSSEL⁶ KEYES WILDER, born April 27, 1826, died Aug. 31, 1828.

vii.   MARGERY⁵ WILDER, born Thursday, Oct. 20, 1774, was the seventh child of Joshua and Margary (Dunster) Wilder.   "She married David Harron, and was living, the last I heard of her (some ten years since),

18

in Batavia, New York. I know of no one to refer you to for their record." (*Jane R. Wilder.*) They lived formerly in Colerain. She died in Pembrook, N. Y. (*L. Wilder.*)

viii. CHARISSE[5] WILDER, (*Joshua and Margary[4] Dunster, David,[8] Jonathan,[2] Henry,[1]*) the eighth child of Joshua and Margary (Dunster) Wilder, was born Saturday, the 19th of Oct., 1776. She married Oct. 26, 1797, William Farr, Jr., of Brattleboro, a farmer. She died at Carthage, Ill., July 15, 1841. He died at the same place, Dec. 7, same year. They had eleven children:

1. EUNICE[6] FARR, born at Brattleboro, May 3, 1798, married March 5, 1822, Jacob Boyce, son of Nathan Boyce. They lived in Fayston, Vt. He was a farmer, and a member of the Methodist Church. They had eight children, all born and married in Fayston:

(i) DANIEL[7] BOYCE, born ——, mar. ——. The family are Methodists. Had three children:

(1) EUGENE[8] BOYCE.) No further record. There
(2) SARAH[8] BOYCE. } is one child of the 9th
(3) ANNA[8] BOYCE.) generation.

(ii) MARIA[7] BOYCE, born ——, married ——, —— Carrol. He is a farmer, lives in Waitsfield, Vt. The family are Methodists. They have two children:

(1) FRED.[8] CARROL. (2) GEORGE[8] CARROL.

(iii) MARY[7] BOYCE, married ——, James P. Boyce? Is a farmer, lives in Fayston. Have seven children (8th generation), and ten grand-children (9th generation). No record of them.

(iv) SETH[7] BOYCE, married Caroline Hills. Is a farmer. Resides in Fayston. No children.

(v) CARRISSA[7] BOYCE, married Walter Porter. He is a farmer. The family are Adventists. They have two children:

(1) CARRIE[8] PORTER. (2) LILIAN[8] PORTER.

(vi) TARAH?[7] BOYCE, married William Chipman. Adventists. They have three children.

18

(vii) HIRAM[7] BOYCE, married Betsey Eaton. Is a farmer. Six children. Family Methodists.

(viii) GUY[7] BOYCE, married Tamar Porter. No children. Episcopalians. Resides in Giles, N. Y. He enlisted in 1861, in Co. K, 44th Regt. Mass. Vols.

2. MARGARY[6] FARR, born at Dummerston, Vt., Nov. 22, 1800, married March 31, 1822, Philo Talcott. She died at Louisville, N. Y., 1870 or 71. Had three children—five grand-children.

3. THOMAS[6] GRISWOLD WAIT FARR, born at Fayston, Vt., Oct. 16, 1802, was the first male child born in that town. He married, at Waitsfield, June 7, 1840, Fanny Hatch. Is a farmer. He furnished the record of the Farr family. They have one child.

4. ANNA[6] FARR, born Jan. 19, 1805, married May 1, 1824, Peter Drew, a farmer. Universalists. Have had four children:

(i) HANNAH[7] DREW, married David Belding. Has two children:

(1) FRANK[8] BELDING. (2) ANNA[8] BELDING.

(ii) ANNA[7] DREW, dead. (iii) Infant.[7] (iv) Infant.[7]

5. WILLIAM[6] FARR, born Feb. 12, 1807, died Nov. 21, 1809.

6. POLLY[6] FARR, born at Williston, Vt., Feb. 16, 1809, married March 30, 1828, Jonas Hobert. He is a "natural mechanic," lives at Carthage, Ill. Congregationalists. Have ten children: Harriet, Eliza, Caroline, Emaline, Annette, Pardon, Thomas. Three, names unknown.

7. MARTHA[6] FARR, born Feb. 14, 1811, at Richmond, Vt., married Jan. 25, 1829, Russell Drew, a farmer. Universalists. Live in Waitsfield. Four children:

(i) WILLIAM[7] S. DREW, mar.—— Has four children.

(ii) LAURIA[7] DREW, mar. —— Holden. Are Congregationalists. Had five children—two living.

(iii) ELIZA[7] DREW, married —— Palmer. Universalists. Have five children.

18

18

(iv) MARIA' DREW, married —— Avery.   She is dead.   Had two children.

These four families are all farmers.

8. ELECTA⁶ FARR, born at Williston, Vt., Jan. 11, 1813, married Feb. 14, 1836, Sidney S. Hills, of Duxbury.   He is a farmer.   They have five children:

(i) LEAH' HILLS.   She is dead.   (ii) CAROLINE' HILLS.   (iii) ORIN' HILLS, dead.   (iv) ORIN' W. HILLS.   (v)   MASTEN' HILLS.

9. ELIZA⁶ FARR, born at Williston, May 7, 1815, died at Fayston, March 30, 1832.

10. LYDIA⁶ FARR, born at Williston, May 10, 1817, married March 4, 1841, Peter Comer, of Carthage, Ill. He is a cooper.   The family are Seventh Day Adventists. They had six children:

(i) JOSEPH' COMER.   He is a Surveyor and Postmaster.   Married ——.   Has three children.

(ii) THOMAS' COMER, married ——.   Two children.

(iii) MILDRETH' COMER, dead.   (iv) WM.' COMER.

11. JOSEPH⁶ FARR, born June 27, 1820, at Hinesburgh, mar. at Waitsfield, Oct. 9, 1856, Eliza A. Thayer. Have five children: Lewis, Albert, Marthy and Adda (twins), Anna Farr.

ix. JOSEPH⁵ WILDER, the ninth child of Joshua and Margary (Dunster) Wilder, born Wednesday, Jan. 13th or 18th, 1779, married Alice Stoddard.   Lived in Chesterfield, N. H.   He died of cholera in 1833, at Genesee or Buffalo.

x. DAMARIS⁵ WILDER, (*Joshua and Margary⁴ D., David,³ Jona.,² Henry,¹*) born March 10, 1781, in Brattleboro, Vt., married Dec. 7, 1797, Samuel Chamberlain, born in Chesterfield, N. H., Aug. 22, 1773.   She died Sept. 25, 1843.   He died March 3, 1852.   They had seven children, all born in Chesterfield:

1. JOSHUA⁶ WILDER CHAMBERLAIN, born Jan. 29, 1799, married Sept. 20, 1823, Mary Wilson, born May 17, 1807.   She died May 5, 1871.   Had four children:

18

(i)   MARY[7] ANN CHAMBERLAIN, born April 2, 1824. She married Dec. 17, 1844, John Harris, born Oct. 20, 1820.   She died July 23, 1863.

(ii)   OLIVE[7] CHAMBERLAIN, born June 13, 1826, died July 6, 1841.

(iii) JOSHUA[7] W. CHAMBERLAIN, Jr., born June 24, 1829, married March 26, 1854, Mrs. Harriet M. (Johnson) Swan, born May 4, 1822.   Had four children:

(1)   ANNA[8] CHAMBERLAIN, born April 4, 1855.

(2)   GERTRUDE[8] O. CHAMBERLAIN, born March 2, 1858, died March 4, 1862.

(3)   D.[8] WILDER CHAMBERLAIN, born April 19, 1860.

(4)   RICHARD[8] J. CHAMBERLAIN, born May 6, 1863, died Oct. 4, 1873.

(iv)   JOSIAH[7] CHAMBERLAIN, born Oct. 4, 1831, married first, June 18, 1855, Ellen S. Goodrich, born Feb. 15, 1833.   She had:

(1)   CHARLES[8] W. CHAMBERLAIN, born April 14, 1856.   She (Ellen) died Feb. 12, 1857, and he married second, Aug. 10, 1858, Lena Bowman, born Sept. 5, 1835.   She had three children:

(2)   ARTHUR[8] B. CHAMBERLAIN, born Jan. 18, 1860.
(3)   RALPH[8] W. CHAMBERLAIN, born Jan. 5, 1861.
(4)   JUDITH[8] M. CHAMBERLAIN, born May 20, 1865.

Josiah[7] Chamberlain died Jan. 18, 1867.

2.   ALANSON[6] CHAMBERLAIN, the second child of Samuel and Damaris (Wilder) C., born March 24, 1801, married first, Nov. 2, 1831, Eliza A. Thompson, born Jan. 27, 1807.   She had three children:

(i)   ITHAMAR[7] CHAMBERLAIN, born Oct. 20, 1832, died Sept. 17, 1855.

(ii)   ASA[7] T. CHAMBERLAIN, born Feb. 26, 1834, died Jan. 26, 1852.

(iii) WILLIAM[7] CHAMBERLAIN, born Oct. 29, 1837.

She (Eliza A.) died Jan. 4, 1839, and Alanson C. married second, July 7, 1844, Abigail Pierce, born Dec. 12, 1800.   She died April 29, 1858.

18

3. JOSIAH[6] CHAMBERLAIN, born Oct. 26, 1803, died June 5, 1827.

4. ALFRED[6] CHAMBERLAIN, born Oct. 14, 1806, married March 20, 1834, Emily H. Farr, born April 25, 1815. Reside in Newark, Vt. Had four children:

(i) HELEN[7] E. CHAMBERLAIN, born Feb. 21, 1836, married Sept. 19, 1854, Frank A. Way, born July 7, 1834. Two children:

(1) ADA[8] E. WAY, born May 18, 1859.
(2) WILLIAM[8] C. WAY, born May 22, 1862.

(ii) OLIVE[7] A. CHAMBERLAIN, born Jan. 15, 1844, married Sept. 16, 1869, Edward A. Turner, born March 6, 1844. Two children:

(1) MABEL[8] E. TURNER, born Nov. 1, 1871.
(2) EDWIN[8] O. TURNER, born May 30, 1875.

(iii)• NORMAN[7] F. CHAMBERLAIN, born Dec. 12, 1846, died Feb. 21, 1852.

(iv) EMMA[7] H. CHAMBERLAIN, born Feb. 26, 1851, died Feb. 28, 1852.

5. GEORGE[6] CHAMBERLAIN, (*Samuel[5] and Damaris (Wilder), Joshua and Margary[4] (Dunster), David,[3] Jona.[2] Henry,[1]*) the fifth child of Samuel and Damaris (Wilder) Chamberlain, was born May 23, 1811, married Dec. 14, 1837, Diantha Thompson, born Jan. 25, 1812. Resides in West Chesterfield, *NH* He furnished the facts here recorded of Damaris (Wilder) Chamberlain's family. No items of their history, business or profession, were given, unless the closing sentence of this paragraph furnishes a hint of his profession: "As to our religious belief I will say, we all as one, believe in and worship an unchangeable Being of Love, who punishes the sins of all his children through love, and for the good of the punished. We do not believe in creeds, but in one common God of Love; and when his children shall return to goodness, all will be love and happiness. You may use what name you think applicable to such a belief. I will further say, we have a religious meeting one half of the time in West Chesterfield, whose pastor acknowledges our frailties, and prays for all mankind as brothers."

18

6. SAMUEL⁶ CHAMBERLAIN, Jr., born Jan. 28, 1813, married Dec. 22, 1841, Elmira Thompson, born Sept. 29, 1813. She died Aug. 28, 1844. He married second, Aug. 15, 1858, Mrs. Laura T. (Barrett) Atherton, born May 26, 1826. She had one child:

(i) MARTHA⁷ E. CHAMBERLAIN, born Sept. 9, 1859, died Dec. 9, 1860.

Laura T. Chamberlain, second wife of Samuel C., Jr., died Nov. 18, 1860. He married third, Nov. 27, 1862, Mrs. Mary E. (Swan) Holden, born July 22, 1832. They had two children:

(ii) ALICE⁷ E. CHAMBERLAIN, born Sept. 20, 1863, died Sept. 14, 1865.

(iii) LAURA⁷ S. CHAMBERLAIN, born Sept. 3, 1866.

7. ELIZABETH⁶ DAMARIS CHAMBERLAIN, the youngest child of Samuel and Damaris (Wilder) Chamberlain, born March 3, 1823, married April 17, 1849, Shubel H. Randall, born June 27, 1824. Reside at Bellows Falls, Vt. Five children:

(i) URBAN⁷ S. RANDALL, born Oct. 23, 1850, died Aug. 23, 1853.

(ii) GEORGE⁷ C. RANDALL, born July 19, 1854, died Oct. 5, 1862.

(iii) SIDNEY⁷ S. RANDALL, born June 9, 1856, died Feb. 22, 1857.

(iv) HENRY⁷ L. RANDALL, born Oct. 30, 1858.

(v) JESSIE⁷ E. RANDALL, born Aug. 12, 1865.

xi. PHENICA⁵ WILDER, the eleventh child of Joshua and Margary⁴ (Dunster) Wilder, born Wednesday, May 5, 1784, married ——, James Wait. No farther record. It is thought she died in Michigan.

xii. EUNICE⁵ WILDER, the twelfth and last child of Joshua and Margary (Dunster) Wilder, born July 11, 1788, married Nov. 30, 1806, Simeon Duncan. They lived in Dummerston, Vt., about two years, then removed to Brattleboro for a short time. In June, 1810, they removed to Sandy Creek, then called Richland,

18-19

Oswego County, N. Y. They were farmers. He was a deacon of the Congregational (Orthodox) Church. He died Nov. 21, 1842. She died Feb. 2, 1855, of consumption, brought on by grief for the death of her daughter Charrissa. They and their deceased children are buried at Sandy Creek Cemetery. They had five children:

1.   MARY⁶ ANN DUNCAN, born at Dummerston, Vt., Feb. 29, 1808. She resides at Sandy Creek, on the farm bought by her father in 1810. To her, the credit of this record of Simeon and Eunice (Wilder) Duncan's family belongs. She is unmarried.

2.   ANSON⁶ MALTBY DUNCAN, born at Sandy Creek, Aug. 28, 1810, married June 10, 1840, Angeline T. Warner; married by Rev. C. B. Pond, at Sandy Creek. They lived there, then at Pulaski. In Oct., 1855, removed to Beloit, Wis., where he resides, with a second wife. Had three children:

(i)   MARY⁷ E. DUNCAN, "died five or six years ago. She was a graduate of Fox Lake Seminary."
(ii)   EUNICE⁷ R. DUNCAN, "married, and lives in California."
(iii)   ELLEN⁷ B. DUNCAN, "lives with her father, and attends school." These daughters, *Eunice* and *Ellen*, are the extent of Eunice (Wilder) Duncan's lineage.

3.   ELECTA⁶ DUNCAN, the third child of Simeon and Eunice (Wilder) Duncan, was born at Sandy Creek, Jan. 12, 1814. She lives with her sister Mary Ann. Unm.

4.   GEORGE⁶ WASHINGTON DUNCAN, born June 13, 1821, died July 28, 1827.

5.   SUSAN⁶ CHARRISSA DUNCAN, born Nov. 16, 1830, "was a teacher at Pulaski. She was taken sick with typhus fever, brought home, and died in two weeks, Oct. 11, 1854."

The family of S. Duncan "are Calvinists in their religious views; and all who came to maturity, united with the Congregational Church at Sandy Creek."

19.   vi.   RUHAMAH⁴ DUNSTER, (*David,³ Jonathan,² Henry,¹*) was the sixth child and fourth daughter of

19

David and Mary (Russell) Dunster. She was probably born in Westminster, but the date of her birth has not been found. She is called in the will, "Ruhamah, my fourth daughter." Had she been born in Cambridge, her baptism would have been recorded by Mr. Cooke. She married ——, Dudley Bailey. They appear to have settled in Dummerston, Vt., and lived on a farm. He died in Dummerston, March 8, 1812. She died there, also, March 8, 1835, having lived a widow just twenty-three years. They had five children:

i. POLLY[5] BAILEY, born ——, married Joel French, born ——. Both died at Dummerston. They had six children:

    1. JOEL[6] FRENCH.   2. DAVID[6] FRENCH.
    3. SOLOMON[6] FRENCH.   4. HENRY[6] FRENCH.
    5. NATHANIEL[6] FRENCH, now living in Pennsylvania.
    6. WILLIAM[6] FRENCH, died young.

ii. LEVI[5] BAILEY, born ——, died March 13, 1851.

iii. DAVID[5] BAILEY, married Lydia Allen, of Marlboro. He died March 19, 1867. They had twelve children:

    1. ELECTA[6] BAILEY, married William Merriam. She died at Peterboro, N. H., when 21 years and 8 months old. Her husband died soon after. They had one son:

    (i) JOSEPH[7] MERRIAM.

After half of the MS. was printed, and this part was being reviewed, an interest was felt in the welfare of this child, bereaved so early of both parents, and the more so as he had on our record the same name as our own maternal grandfather.

Recollecting an old chum, William B. Kimball, residing in Peterboro, with whom, in our apprenticeship, we became "skillful at sawing planks," with a hand-saw—hard wood, well seasoned, and three inches thick—we wrote, and he replied that:

"There was a William Merriam, who came from Chester, Vt., about 1825, who had one child by his first wife, whose name was William Henry Merriam. His first wife

19

died, and he afterwards married again, but did not live more than a year or two after his second marriage. He and his first wife were both buried in Peterboro. His son, William H. Merriam, is in Boston. He is deacon of the Berkeley Street Church. I cannot find any other William M. who lived in P. His son's name was. William H. instead of Joseph."

Following this trail, a response came dated

"No. 172 Washington street,
BOSTON, Feb. 26, 1877.

"DEAR SIR:—Your favor of 21st inst., came to hand on Saturday. In reply, I hardly have reason to suppose that I can be the missing link of your chain. The record left by my father, William Merriam, states that he married Electa Bailey, Sept. 11, 1825. I (William H. Merriam) was born July 16, 1826, at Peterboro, N. H., and my own mother, Electa, died 28th of same month, when I was less than two weeks old. My father married again, in Peterboro, having a daughter by second marriage, and he died in 1831, when I was only five years old. I left Peterboro at nine years of age, and have never been able to trace *any* relative on my mother's side, or learn anything whatever of her parentage or her native place. I was told by my step-mother and her friends, when I made inquiries in regard to my mother's family, that they did not know anything further about her than the simple record of the date of her birth, marriage, and death, written by my father in the Family Bible. My grandmother, my father's *step-mother*, told me, several years ago, that some gentlemen called on her, then living at Ware, Mass., to inquire about me, a few years after my father's death, saying they were brothers of my mother, their name not being Bailey, but what it was she could not recollect; and that was the only time she ever saw or heard from them.

"I never knew that my father lived in Chester, Vt.; but one thing struck me strangely, and that was, the name you bear—'Dunster'—in connection with a memory I have of being told by some one, when I was about fourteen years old, that they had heard that my own mother came from or had relatives in *Dummerston.* I wrote to Dummerston, but could find no trace of any Bailey family ever residing there; and now this information from you that William Merriam (my father, possibly) came from Chester, and married a *Dunster,* has raised a query in my mind if the Dummerston story could have grown from *Chester* and the name *Dunster,* and the long mystery to me of my mother's parentage can possibly be solved in this way. I presume it will hardly be possible to trace this matter out, if it be traceable at all, in season to be printed with the manuscript you have prepared.

"If there be the slightest probability that my mother may have been a Dunster, or a descendant of that family, the difficulties in the way of ascertaining anything certain about it, at this late day, would be formidable. I would feel obliged ,if you would give me any information of the members of the family into which my father is supposed to have married. —— —— ——

Very respectfully yours,
WILLIAM H. MERRIAM."

Mr. M., by referring to the record above, will find that instead of being without relatives, as he supposed, his grandfather, David[5] Bailey, married Lydia Allen, and they had twelve children, ten of whom were married, and seven had children, and that his mother, Electa,[6] was the oldest of their family; and he himself has announced that his grandfather on the other side had *twenty-three* children. These, we have no authority to hunt up. A subsequent letter said:

"I am both greatly surprised and extremely gratified to catch a glimpse, through your researches, behind the cloud that has so long obscured from me any trace of my maternal kindred. I am most happy to receive such assuring and agreeable testimony from you of the status of my mother and her relatives, the subject of so many imaginings, not to say forebodings, with me in the long past.

"My father, William Merriam, [the husband of 1. Electa[6] Bailey] was the son of James and Lucy —. Merriam, and was one of a family of twenty-three children.

19

He was a mechanic and an overseer in a cotton mill at Peterboro, at the time of my birth. In religious faith he was a Unitarian, and in evidence of his faith he desired his pastor, Rev. Mr. Abbot, to baptize his two little children at his bedside, in his last hours on earth. He was born April 27, 1802, and died Oct. 28, 1831, aged 29 years and 5 months. My mother, Electa Bailey, was born Nov. 25, 1804. They were married Sept. 11, 1825. She died July 28, 1826."

(i) WILLIAM[7] HENRY MERRIAM, (*William and Electa[6] Bailey, David,[5] Dudley and Ruhamah[4] Dunster, David,[3] Jona.,[2] Henry,[1]*) the only child of William and Electa (Bailey) Merriam, was born in Peterboro, N. H., July 16, 1826. After the death of his father, he remained under the care of his step-mother, Betsey (Taplin) Merriam, "a most estimable woman," (married to Mr. M. Dec. 4, 1829, and by whom she had Elizabeth Merriam, born Jan. 3, 1831,) until he was nine years old, "when he was placed on a farm in Lempster, N. H., under the care of a family who were what they professed to be,—*Christian people*, of the Orthodox Congregational denomination." At fourteen, he graduated from the farm to a country store, finding his way to Boston in 1848, at the age of twenty-two. From a clerkship in an auction house in Boston, he succeeded, in 1854, to the extensive business of the house on his own account, continuing the same till 1872. In religious faith he is an Orthodox Congregationalist. On removing from the city proper, in 1873, he resigned his office in the Berkeley Street Church, and took membership in the Walnut Avenue Congregational Church. His business is Auctioneer and Real Estate Broker; and as he resides at No. 28 Greenville street, Boston Highlands, we take it he is reckoned among the "solid men" of Boston. He married, at Boston, Feb. 24, 1851, Maria Antoinette Buel, daughter of Matthew and Fanny P. Buel, of Newport, N. H., who was born June 30, 1830. They have had three children:

(1) WILLIAM[8] LORING MERRIAM, born March 25, 1859, died Dec. 7, same year.

19

(2) FANNIE[8] ELISABETH MERRIAM, born in Boston, July 3, 1864—their only surviving child.

(3) NELLIE[8] MARIA MERRIAM, born April 5, 1866, died Sept. 5, same year.

2. ANNA[6] BAILEY, "married Daniel Baldwin, of Wardsboro. She is now a widow, living in Dummerston, near her grandfather's place. From her I learned this history of the Bailey family. She has no children." (*Jane R. Wilder.*)

3. LEVI[6] BAILEY, married Elizabeth Bryant. Resides in Dummerston. No children.

4. JASON[6] RUSSEL BAILEY, mar.—— Emily Bryant. Resides in Shoply, Canada East. Have five children:

(i) RUSSEL[7] BAILEY. (iv.) POLLY ANN[7] BAILEY.
(ii) MELISSA[7] BAILEY. (v.) DAVID[7] BAILEY.
(iii) HANNAH[7] BAILEY.

5. EPHRAIM[6] BAILEY, married Harriet Sibley, of Newfane, Vt. Resides at Shoply, Canada East. Have five daughters:

(i) LYDIA[7] BAILEY. (iv) BETSEY[7] BAILEY.
(ii) EMILY[7] ALMEDAS BAILEY. (v) LUCY[7] BAILEY.
(iii) ANNA[7] BAILEY.

6. SILAS[6] BAILEY, mar.—— Arvilla Jackson. Lives on the farm settled by his grandfather 75 years ago. Have one son: (i) DAVID[7] BAILEY.

7. CHESTER[6] BAILEY, mar. Beulah Gove, of Strafford, Vt. Lives in Brattleboro. Two children:

(i) JULIA[7] BAILEY. (ii) ISAAC[7] BAILEY.

8. ABNER[6] BAILEY, mar. Caroline Huntley. Res. in West Dummerston. No children.

9. WILLIAM[6] BAILEY, married first, Lois Gould; married second, Caroline Smith. Resides in Worcester, Mass. Have had five children, two living:

EMMA[7] EUGENE BAILEY, KATE[7] ANTOINETTE BAILEY.

10. JOHN[6] BAILEY, born ——, died, aged 20 years.

11. LAWSON[6] BAILEY, born ——, died, aged 5 years and 6 months.

20-21

12. ORRA⁶ BAILEY, married Julia Pettee.   Reside in Michigan.   Two children:

(i) FRED.⁷ BAILEY.   (ii) FRANK⁷ BAILEY.

iv. HENRY⁵ BAILEY, (son of Dudley and Ruhamah (Dunster) Bailey,) married Sally Dill, of Plainfield. Resides in Peterboro, N. Y.   Have several children.

v. EPHRAIM⁵ BAILEY, born ——, died June, 1803.

20. vii. HENRY⁴ DUNSTER, (*David,³ Jonathan,² Henry,¹*) is called in his father's will, "Carteret Henry, my youngest son."   The date of his birth has not been found.   He certainly was not twenty-one years of age in 1758, the date of the will.   He has uniformly been called the youngest child.   We have no data of his history, except that he married Nov. —, 1778, Anna Peirce, of Leominster, Mass., and sold his farm, which adjoined that of Hubbard Dunster, to —— Woods.

Mrs. Estabrook said: "My Uncle Henry died in Princeton, Mass., in a fit.   He was married, but had no children."

21. i. RUTH⁵ DUNSTER, (*Jason,⁴ Henry,³ Jona.,² Henry,¹*) the first child of Jason and Rebecca (Cutter) Dunster, was born in Cambridge, Aug. 10, (Aug. 21, N. S.,) and baptized by Rev. Samuel Cooke, Aug. 12, 1750. She married (probably in Mason, N. H., but we can find no record of it,) Joseph Blood, the son of Joseph and Hannah ——. Blood, of Groton, Mass.   He was born July 29, 1743, and resided in Mason at the time her father moved there, and not far from his farm.   He was chosen Fence Viewer and Surveyor of Highway in 1768.   Their marriage must have been soon after she went to Mason. He enlisted in Captain Mann's company soon after the battle at Lexington, and joined the army at Cambridge. He was killed at the battle of Bunker Hill.   Mrs. Imla Parker, referred to in the record of the Marrett family, page 72, stated that Joseph Blood, on his way down from Mason, staid at her Grandfather Marrett's the night before the battle.   Her grandfather was Amos Marrett, who married Mary⁴ Dunster.   She was aunt to Joseph Blood's wife.   That he started in the morning in high

21

spirits, and went by the way of Cambridge. That he was killed very early in the battle by a cannon ball striking him in the neck. She did not know where he was buried.

His wife, Ruth[5] (Dunster) Blood, kept the family together as well as she could, on the farm of her husband, till her death in 1787. On the 3d of May, 1787, her father took out letters of administration on the estate, which did not quite pay the debts. The enumeration of *small* articles (*Probate Records Hillsboro Co., May* 8, 1787,) is shameful, though "according to law." Her father, however, stopped a *public* sale of them by charging himself with the whole inventory, and enough besides to pay all the debts. At the end of the inventory is added, after the footing of the articles, "One gold ring, 7 shillings." Was that handed down in the family for generations, and then wrested "by law" from her children? It was their "mother's gold ring." Jan. 8, 1787, Jason Dunster, her father, was appointed guardian of Joseph and Sylvanus Blood. July 10, 1790, Jotham Webber was appointed "guardian of William Cutter Blood, of Mason, being upwards of fourteen years old."

The place of her burial is not certainly identified. In 1770, the town "voted to have but *one* grave yard, and voted to accept of that piece of ground for a grave yard which the committee that was appointed to lay out grave yards have laid out at the west end of lot 6 in 9th range, on the west side of the road that goeth to Townshend." In 1776, the town "voted to procure a grave yard for the use of the town, and that Lieut. Swallow and Mr. John Whitaker dig the graves that are 'reasonably' needed in said town." (*Mason Records.*) This cemetery is at Mason Centre. There was a more ancient one in the east part of the town, and as Thomas Tarbell, who lived near it, and in 1773 gave the land for it, was paid for digging her grave, it is probable she was buried there, although two unrecognized graves were to be seen in the Dunster group. Her unknown grave remained for almost ninety years, when a plain stone was set up at Mason Centre, inscribed:

"Ruth Dunster, widow of Joseph Blood, (killed at
19

21

Bunker Hill,) born in Cambridge, Aug. 21, 1750, N. S.,
died at Mason, 1787, aged 37. Ex dono S. Dunster,
1873."

A Bible is among the Dunster papers, in which is
written: "Joseph Blood, Junr.,—His Bibel, the Price
0—4—0—Shillings Lawfull money—and it was Given
Him by—His Honored Father—August y° 20th, A. D.
1767." And on another leaf is written, but in a different
hand, both being bold and plain, and in ink that more
than a century has not faded: "Joseph Blood—His
Book God give—him grace therein—to look that he—
may Run that—Blessed Race that—Heaven may be—
His Dwelling place.

August y° 28th, 1767."

Was the former written by his father's minister in
Groton, and the latter after he received the gift in
Mason?

The children of Joseph and Ruth⁵ (Dunster) Blood
were:

1. Joseph⁶ Blood, (*Joseph and Ruth⁵ Dunster,
Jason,⁴ Henry,³ Jona.,² Henry,¹*) born in Mason, June
17, 1769. He was placed under the guardianship of his
grandfather, Jan. 8, 1787, being then about eighteen
years old. He married Sally Priest, of New Ipswich, N.
H. They had four children, all born in Townsend, Mass.

i. Ruthy⁷ Blood, born Jan. 12, 1798, married Benjamin Smith, of Townsend, and died there. They had
no children.

ii. Joseph⁷ Blood, born Feb. 17, 1800, married
Sept. 24, 1825 or 6, Emma Martin, of Mason, N. H.
She was the niece of Samuel C. Dunster's wives, and
daughter of George and Zilpha (Townsend) Martin. He
died about seven months afterwards. He was sick when
he married. No children.

iii. Walter⁷ Blood, born Jan. 10, 1803, married
Lucy Wadsworth, of Brookline, N. H. She was a niece
of Rev. Mr. Wadsworth. She died, leaving no children.
He married second, Hannah Wadsworth, sister of his
first wife. "She went off and left him," said our in-

21

formant. Had no children. Married third, Eliza Wyn, of Townsend. No children. "She now (1873) lives in the same house with him."

iv. ISAIAH⁷ BLOOD, born May 17, 1805, married Rebecca Jenkins, April 4, 1831. She was born June 14, 1806. He died at West Townsend, Jan. 20, 1847. His widow is now Mrs. Conant. Her second husband is dead. She lives at West Townsend. Had seven children:

1. JOSEPH⁸ PALMER BLOOD, (*Isaiah,⁷ Joseph,⁶ Ruth⁵ Dunster,*) was born in Townsend, July 23, 1832. He married Oct. 26, 1857, Emeline C. Blood, born 1836, the daughter of Calvin and (India) Blood, of Mason. He has been the Superintendent of the Town Farm in Townsend for a long time. Three children, all born in Mason:

(i) FRANK⁹ PALMER BLOOD, born Sept. 27, 1858, died same day.

(ii) ELVA⁹ EUGENIA BLOOD, born March 6, 1860, died Jan. 24, 1864.

(iii) LIDA⁹ MABELLE BLOOD, born Jan. 9, 1866.

2. SARAH⁸ F. BLOOD, born July 24, 1835, in Townsend, married William Amesden, of Mason, by whom she had:

(i) MARY⁹ JANE AMESDEN, born June 30, 1850. She married Frederick Fay, of Westboro, Mass. They have one child—10th generation—if record be correct.

(ii) An infant.⁹

3. CHARLES⁸ L. BLOOD, born Aug. 9, 1836, married Betsey Green (?). Her maiden name was Elizabeth Shattuck. They have three children—births, names and residence not known.

4. DANIEL⁸ A. BLOOD, born March 8 or 18, 1838, died April 4, 1838.

5. HARRIET⁸ A. BLOOD, born Sept. 10, 1840, married first, Andrew J. Fuller, by whom she had one child, who died in infancy. She married second, Luther A. Blood, and by him had:

(i) LILLEIAN⁹ A. BLOOD. (ii) EADER⁹ M. BLOOD. (iii) INER⁹ B. BLOOD. Age and residence not known.

21

6. MARY[8] E. BLOOD, born Oct. 1842, married May 14, 1857, Charles O. Calester. Two children:

(i) ESTELLA[9] M. CALESTER, born July 8, 1860.
(ii) CHARLES[9] E. CALESTER, born Dec. 13, 1861, died June 13, 1862.

"Charles O. Calester, husband of Mary[8] E. Blood, enlisted a private in the Second N. H. Regt. Volunteers; was at the first battle of Bull Run, and in every battle except one in which that regiment was engaged (thirteen, I think), until they had the second Bull Run fight, in which he was killed, Aug. 29, 1862.

"P. S. Charles O. Calester lies in Southern soil. After being wounded, he lay three days before being taken up or cared for in the least, but died soon after being taken up." (*Joseph P. Blood's Letter.*)

She, Mary[8] E. (Blood) Calester, married second, Oct. 10, 1863, W. W. Greenwood.

7. OLIVE[8] A. BLOOD, born Jan. 18, 1846, died Feb. 18, 1855, aged 9 years and 1 month.

2. SYLVANUS[6] BLOOD, the second child of Joseph and Ruth[5] (Dunster) Blood, was born May 8, 1771. He was put under the guardianship of Jason Dunster, his grandfather, at the same time his brother Joseph was. When about twenty years old he, with his brothers, Joseph and William Cutter, sold by the consent of their guardians, the farm belonging to them as the heirs of Joseph Blood. It was bought by Jason[5] Dunster, Jr., and is described as Lot No. 4, in the 5th Range. The deed, now in our possession, is dated April 1, 1791, and is signed by Joseph Blood, whose signature (a very plain and good one) was witnessed by Robert Taylor and "Abijh" Tarbell. Signed also by Sylvanus Blood, whose witnesses were Thomas Clarke and William Wood. Sylvanus Blood's signature is in very large and crooked letters, and occupies a space two and a half inches long by one and a half wide, being in two lines. It is also signed by William Cutter Blood, whose witnesses were Jotham Webber (his guardian) and Elizabeth Webber (Jotham's wife). After this transaction we have no knowledge of

21

Sylvanus. It is noticeable, however, that his acknowledgement of the deed was in Suffolk, ss. Mass., May 14, 1792, and before Thomas Clarke, Justice Peace. There is a tradition that he married, lived in Cambridge, and had at least one child, named Samuel Dunster Blood.

3. WILLIAM⁶ CUTTER BLOOD, (*Ruth⁵ Dunster, Jason⁴ Henry,³ Jona.,² Henry,¹*) was born March 22, 1773, in Mason, and named for his grandmother's brother, William Cutter, whose epitaph is:

> "Come Come, you children, near & view this Stone
> For in the Grave God Saith you Must ly Down.
> You that do Fear ye Lord & honor Parents too
> Christ from his Throne will surely Welcome You
> And after Death assuredly you Will
> In Heavenly Mensions Praise your Maker Stil."

He was put under the guardianship of Jotham Webber, who was deacon of the First Baptist Church in Mason. He married March 11, 1800, Sally Townsend; the sister of his Uncle Samuel⁶ Dunster's two wives. She was the daughter of Samuel and Hannah (Lawrence) Townsend, born Sept. 1, 1777, and heir to that "great estate (?) in England, belonging to the Lawrences!" He removed to Rumney, N. H., where they had four children. About 1820 they removed to Derby, Vermont, where they both died "the same winter, very near each other," about 1867. He is understood to have been a farmer. In the deed referred to he is called a laborer. At Derby they had six or seven more children. For the most of the tradition of them we are indebted to Mrs. Lizzie⁸ R. Bixby, of West Danville, Vt. She was grand-daughter of William Cutter and Sally (Sarah) (Townsend) Blood.

Mrs. Bixby thinks that William C. Blood died in Derby about 1858, and his wife about 1860. Four children:

i. POLLY⁷ BLOOD, born in Rumney, mar. Hezekiah Ingerson, and had four sons and two daughters. The parents are both dead, and were buried in Derby.

ii. SAMUEL⁷ DUNSTER BLOOD, born at Rumney, married ———, and died about 1864, in Kentucky, says his

*19

21

Aunt Dunster,—"I think," says Mrs. B., "in Michigan,"—leaving a wife and one child—a daughter. His Aunt D. says: "They were in Cambridge the last I heard from them. He lived in South Boston, and owned an hourly coach." The writer has tried to find this widow and daughter of Samuel Dunster Blood, but without success, and only conjectures that he left Vermont, came to Boston, was married, perhaps in Cambridge, was engaged in stageing, left that business, went West and died.

Mrs. Bixby adds that "S. D. Blood married Lydia Washburn for his first wife, and Mary Ann Grey for his second, by whom he had two children. The son died in infancy, the daughter still living, so far as I know. She married G. W. Park."

iii. HANNAH[7] BLOOD, born in Rumney, married William Mansur. She died Sept., 1871; buried in Morgan, Vt. They had seven children—three sons and four daughters. Husband and three daughters still living, 1874.

iv. ELIZA[7] Y. BLOOD, born in Rumney, ——, 1807, married Courtland Bovee, in 1825; both died about same time. They had ten children—five sons and five daughters—"of whom," says Lizzie R. Bixby, "your humble servant is one;" thus leaving us entirely at a loss for the further history of her mother's family.

v. HARRIET[7] BLOOD, born in Derby, Vt., died when 16 or 17 years of age, buried in Derby.

vi. WILLIAM[7] CUTTER BLOOD, born in Derby, Vt., "married Sarah Cutter for his first wife, by whom he had one son; Lucy Harvey for his second wife, and Lucinda Courrier for his third wife; all dead. No children by any but first? (*L. R. B.*)

In answer to a letter, John C. Clough, Esq., of Enfield, N. H., wrote: "There was a man by the name of William C. Blood that lived in the village here, near me, who died the 24th day of June, 1862, aged, I should think, 45 or 50 years. He was a traveling physician, and done quite an extensive business in this State and Vermont. I was administrator and settled his accounts.

21

—— —— His first wife I don't know anything about. I have understood that he lived some twelve years or more after her death before he was married again. His second wife was Lucinda W. Courrier, a resident of this town. They were married in the fall of 1860. After the death of his first wife, he had no particular residence, but made his stopping place at Wells River, Vt. At the time of his death he had no children, and I don't know as he ever had any. —— ——

"After the Doctor married his second wife, he and his family went to Wells River and lived until two months of his death, when they returned to this place (Enfield, N. H.), and moved into a house that belonged to his wife. About five days before his death he told his wife that he was going to Chelsa, Vt., to attend a court, where he had some business to settle. He went there, settled his business, started and went to Brownington, in the northern part of the State of Vermont, about 100 miles from here, tied his team at the side of the road, and went into a clump of bushes three or four rods, and there committed suicide."

James[8] Kimball, who lived at Enfield at the time, says that Dr. Blood killed himself by an incision made with a penknife into the jugular vein.

Dr. Blood was buried at Enfield, N. H.

His aunt wrote that "he first practiced 'Tomsonan,' and had very good success, but afterwards 'homepatha.' Why he should commit that deed none ever knew."

vii. Lucy[7] Blood, born at Derby, married Nathaniel Ruggles. They are both dead. She lived a widow some years, and left three daughters. She was buried at Derby.

viii. Edward[7] Blood, born at Derby, married Sarah Leland; dead; buried at Holliston, Mass. They never had any children.

ix. Caroline[7] Celestia Blood, the youngest child of William C. and Sally (Townsend) Blood, was born in Derby, Vt., and at an early age "left home to live with an older brother." [Was it Samuel[7] Dunster Blood?] She married O. W. Merriam. We have an impression

21

that he was a furniture dealer, near Boston, and accumulated a good property. They removed to San Francisco, Cal., where she certainly resided in May, 1874. They have, it is understood, one daughter, who is married, and lives in San Francisco. Mrs. M. can give no records of her father's family. She is evidently in easy, and, probably, in wealthy circumstances. Like all ladies, she ends her letter with a P. S.: "If you should find it convenient to visit this lovely State, I should be happy to see you at my house, 1106 Bush street."

x.   There was another child, named Betsey, who died in infancy.

4.   The fourth child of Joseph and Ruth[5] Dunster Blood was born Jan. 8, 1775. She is named RUTH. We have no further authentic knowledge of her. There is a tradition that she married—when and whom is not known—and that she died, but had no children. There are families who claim descent from the daughter of Ruth (Dunster) Blood, but they say her name was RACHEL. There is no mention of any daughter in the settlement of the estate. There is one fact that possibly may have something to do in this matter.

Jason[4] Dunster brought up a child by the name of *Rachel* Mason. She married a Withington. (*Book of the Lockes.*)

If she was the traditional Ruth, and her name became confounded with the recorded Ruth, it might help us. We give the tradition as it is related by an intelligent lady, who is acquainted with some of the later offspring.

She says: "Rachel's mother was a Dunster. She was brought up, however, by her Grandmother Dunster, and inherited the family loom. (In the inventory of Ruth[5] Dunster Blood's estate, is "One Loom and warping bars, 18 shillings.") She married Jonathan Blood, of Pepperell, a very intemperate man, and his sons followed in his footsteps. They lived in Sharon, N. H. They, Jonathan and Rachel,[6] had six children—two boys and four girls: (i) NAHUM.[7] (ii) JOSIAH.[7] Josiah never married, and is dead. Nahum married a widow woman, from Pepperell. They had one son, who is still living."

Mr & Mrs O W Merriam decd Chelsea Mess,— were both urd in one grave May 9 1887

21

Another tradition, related by an old lady, says that the boys were Nahum and *Cyrus*, (by nicknames then in common use, easily confounded with Josiah—*Cy*-rus, Jo-*si*-ah,) and that neither of them ever married. The daughters were:

iii. REBECAH.[7] She was born April 1, 1803, and married April 20, 1826, Jonathan Russell, of Mason. They had: (1) One boy,[8] name and birth unknown, and three girls:

(2) RACHEL,[8] married, and lives in New Ipswich, and has one or two children.

(3) REBECCA,[8] died in the poor house.

(4) JOANNA,[8] was an intelligent and worthy member of Mason Village (Orthodox) Church in 1853, and is believed to have married very respectably, and lives in Manchester, N. H.

iv. RACHEL[7] BLOOD, married Moses Merriam, son of Ezra Merriam, of Mason. They had no children. Are both living in West Boylston.

v. ROXANNA[7] BLOOD, married July, 1832, Sargent Bohanon, of Peterboro, N. H. She died Jan. 24, 1870, aged 59 years, 6 months and 20 days. One child:

1. MARY[8] ELIZABETH BOHANON. She mar. Giles T. Larkin, of Hancock, N. H. She died July 24, 1864. One child, dead.

vi. OLIVE[7] BLOOD, the sixth child of Jonathan and Rachel, was born at Sharon, N. H., Dec. 25, 1823. She married Simon H. Ralf, or Rolf, born in Jaffrey, March 30, 1820. She died at Jaffrey, N. H., March 4, 1869. They had four children:

1. JOHN[8] S. RALF, born at New Ipswich, N. H., Jan. 28, 1840. "He enlisted in Co. H, Second Regt. N. H. Vols., and was killed at the second battle of Bull Run, and buried on the battle field. This was the first battle in which he was engaged."

2. WILLIAM[8] H. RALF, born at Sharon, Jan. 16, 1842, married ——, ——. His wife is dead. They had four children.

21-22

3. SARAH[7] E. RALF, born at Jaffrey, March 6, 1845, died Aug. 25, 1852.

4. ANGELINE[7] JOSEPHINE RALF, born at Jaffrey, Dec. 31, 1853, married Jan. 9, 1873, Edward Felt, of Peterboro, N. H., born Nov. 27, 1847. They had a son, ELMER[8] MORRISON FELT, who died an infant. No other children.

22. iii. HENRY[5] DUNSTER, (*Jason,[4] Henry,[3] Jona.[2] Henry,[1]*) the third child of Jason[4] and Rebecca (Cutter) Dunster, was born in Cambridge (Menotomy), Aug. 4, baptized by Rev. Samuel Cooke, Aug. 11, 1754. He came to Mason with his father's family in 1769, being then 14 years old. No farther record of him is found till 1774, when he was taxed for the first time, being then only 20 years old. With the exception of 1776, he was taxed every year till 1780, in which year he was taxed as a non-resident. This year his "Beef rate" was £3 10s. 10d. 2qrs., while his father's was £131 and over. He is named in the History of Mason as having done service in the Revolutionary war—probably in 1776, when he was not taxed. He could not have been the son of Jason Dunster for whose "hire" Joseph Herrick was paid for the rye, for at that time he was 27 years old, and his father would hardly have claimed his "hire" at that age. It is almost certain that he went from Mason and lived with a Mr. Sharp in Brookline, Mass., whose daughter Sally he afterwards married, and by her he had twins. These were their only children. No further knowledge is had of him till his death in 1794, in or near Boston, probably in Brookline.

HENRY[6] DUNSTER,) the twins, were born in Brook-
SALLY[6] DUNSTER,)   line, March 25, 1782.

Their mother, Sally (Sharp) Dunster, appears to have died soon after their birth.

Abiel Wright, whose genealogy will be found in Martha[5] (Dunster) Wright's, says in a letter (1854): "Henry Dunster had two children—a son and a daughter—twins. The son's name was Henry, the girl's name, Sally. Their parents died when they were quite young. They died in

22

Brookline, or Roxbury, Mass. Henry was brought up by Stephen Sharp, Esq., of Brookline. My mother brought up the girl. Henry, when he became of age, went into Boston and drove a team, and from that went to work in a distillery. He was married and had some children, and died near forty years since."

Polly (M.) Dunster, his aunt, said Henry was brought up by his "grandfather." A daughter of this twin, Henry, said he was brought up by his Grandfather *Dunster*. We think she was mistaken as to *which* grandfather brought him up. It is almost positive that his Grandfather Dunster did not. If we substitute "Sharp" for "Dunster" it confirms all the traditions, and proves that Henry[5] Dunster married Sally Sharp, which we thought questionable in Life H. D., page 243. Abiel Wright was only 8 years younger than Henry and Sally Dunster. She was an adopted sister, lived and died at his father's.

SALLY[6] DUNSTER, twin to Henry, born March 25, 1782, was brought up by her Aunt Martha[5] (Dunster) Wright, and died of consumption, at the age of 26, April 22, 1808, unmarried, was buried at Nelson, N. H., then Packersfield. She was a member of the Congregationalist Church (Orthodox), and an exemplary woman.

HENRY[6] DUNSTER, the other twin, married Rhoda Jackson, of Bridgewater, Mass., and died July 9, 1818, not in 1813, as in Life H. D., page 243. They had six children, all born in Boston:

i. SARAH[7] DUNSTER, (*Henry,[6] Henry,[5] Jason,[4] Henry,[3] Jona.,[2] Henry,[1]*) was born Dec. 28, 1808. She married July 28, 1833, Joseph Ferrin, born Aug. 10, 1808. He died in California, Aug. 20, 1850, aged 42 years and 10 days. They had four children:

1. JOSEPH[8] WILLIAM FERRIN, born ——, 1834, died Oct. 13, 1834, an infant.

2. SARAH[8] JANE FERRIN, born March 19, 1835, married Aug. 20, 1854, William O. Sumner; living at 34th street, 8th Avenue, New York. They had:

(i) SARAH[9] JANE SUMNER, born Oct. 12, 1859, died Sept. 1, 1860.

22

(ii) JENNY[9] ISADORE SUMNER, born Jan. 20, 1862, died August same year.

3. CHARLES[8] FERRIN, born Sept. 13, 1840, died "in the war," in 1865, aged 24 years, 8 months. Unm.

4. SUSAN[8] ANN FERRIN, born June 15, 1842, died Oct. 12, 1842.

ii. HENRY[7] JACKSON DUNSTER, was born Sept. 24, 1810. "In childhood he had a fall and injured his hip, which disabled him for seven years. In 1828 he went to G. & J. Lorings, Boston, to learn the printers' trade." In a note to *History of Scituate*, he is referred to as a pressman, working on that book. He married May 6, 1834, Mary B. Savery, of Plymouth, Mass. She lived at the time of his marriage in the next house to his mother's, in South street, Boston. Being out of health, he went to Georgetown, South Carolina, in June, 1838, and there died, July 7, 1839, of consumption? His wife never went South. She returned to her father's, in Plymouth, where she is now, 1871, living with her fourth husband. Nothing further was known of this family, and it was fully believed that this branch became extinct, as it was understood he left no children. In 1871, a paragraph appeared in the newspapers stating that *Henry Dunster*, of Duxbury, had been injured by the caving in of his well. This gave a clue to further knowledge of the family, which will be found in Henry[8] Jackson Dunster.

iii. WILLIAM[7] DUNSTER, born April 22, 1812, was a sailor. He was taken sick in Liverpool, attempted a voyage home, but died on the passage, and was buried at sea, when about 18 years old.

iv. "LITTLE RHODA[7]," born ——, 1813, lived only about two hours.

v. JANE[7] LYDIA DAMON DUNSTER, was born Jan. 22, 1815. She lived with her mother in South street, Boston, until she married, July 13, 1834, Charles Johnston, who built the house where she now lives, No. 763 Broadway, South Boston. Mr. Johnston died Aug. 17, 1864. Seven children:

22

1. EMMA[8] JANE JOHNSTON, born May 7, 1835, died March 16, 1836.

2. EMMA[8] JANE JOHNSTON, born Sept. 26, 1836, married John H. Locke, a bookkeeper, and has four children, all living in Boston:

(i) EMMA[9] JANE LOCKE, born July 30, 1860.
(ii) MINNIE[9] LOUISA LOCKE, born Dec. 3, 1861.
(iii) ADDIE[9] WILMAN LOCKE, born June 28, 1864.
(iv) GERTRUDE[9] LILLIAN LOCKE, born Jan. 29, 1869.

3. CHARLES[8] HENRY JOHNSTON, the third child of Jane[7] L. D. (D.) Johnston, born Feb. 12, 1838, died Dec. 16, 1839.

4. ADALINE[8] ADELIA JOHNSTON, born May 1, 1840, is a teacher or bookkeeper, in Boston, not married.

5. SARAH[8] ELIZABETH JOHNSTON, born Nov. 4, 1842, married June 15, 1871, Benjamin M. Campbell, a clerk in Boston. Have two children:

(i) CHARLES[9] BENJAMIN CAMPBELL, born Aug. 13, 1872, died June 5, 1873.

(ii) EMMA[9] FLORENCE CAMPBELL, born June 18, 1874.

6. CHARLES[8] WILLIAM JOHNSTON, born Oct. 13, 1844, is a seaman by occupation.

7. HENRY[8] DUNSTER JOHNSTON, born March 7, 1847, was drowned in South Boston Bay, while bathing, Aug. 30, 1860.

vi. EPHRAIM[7] JACKSON DUNSTER, born May 22, 1817, died Sept. 9, 1818.

In April, 1871, Henry[8] Jackson Dunster, who had been "buried in his well," had so far recovered as to be able to visit. By an express invitation he called on us, and we accompanied him to Boston to see his Aunt Johnston, who, he said, knew more of the family than any one else. We were not introduced by name, which was rather pleasing, as it gave us opportunity to pass incognito. After talking awhile, we told the object of our visit. She remarked that her nephew and his boy were the only "Dunsters" living; and further said that, some

20

22

thirty-five years ago, there was a Dunster who called on her mother's family and said he was their relation. He promised to call again; said he was a calico printer, and lived away down East, somewhere; but as he had never called, she presumed he was dead, and they were the only descendants of President Dunster. We replied, much to her surprise, that we *now* had the pleasure of making the promised call, although somewhat delayed. She was very communicative, and, with wonderful memory, told off-hand and without hesitation, or record, the particulars of the descendants of Henry⁶ Dunster, which we have tabulated above. She added to what is related of Henry, the twin, her father:

"On the very day that Sarah, his twin-sister, died, (April 22, 1808,) he was brought home sick, and although he lived near ten years afterwards, he was sick all the time so as not to be able to work, and died of consumption, on the 9th day of July, 1818, and was buried in the cemetery on Roxbury Neck, now *nearly all dug away.*" Enlightened nations and Christian communities, *only,* disturb the ashes of the dead.

The Boston Directory, 1807, has Henry Dunster, laborer, Elliot street; Rhoda Dunster, 1818, South street Court; Rhoda Dunster, washer, 1820, Hoskins' wharf; Rhoda Dunster, "widow," 1821 to 1825, same place; 1826 to 1834, Rhoda Dunster, widow, South street Place; 1855, Henry J. Dunster, *printer,* house South street Place, and Rhoda at Barry wharf; 1836, Rhoda, South street Place; also Essex Place.

HENRY⁷ J. DUNSTER, (the printer,) (*Henry,⁶ twin Henry,⁵ Jason,⁴ Henry,³ Jona.,² Henry,¹*) married Mary B. Savery, of Plymouth, and we cannot improve her history of their children: "My husband was born in Boston, Sept. 24, 1810. We were united in marriage, in Boston, by Rev. Mr. Streeter, March 6, 1834. My first child was born in Charlestown, Oct. 7, 1834, named (i) HENRY⁸ JACKSON DUNSTER, died Jan. 1, 1835. The second was also a boy, which we called (ii) ANDREW⁸ JACKSON DUNSTER, born in Boston, Nov. 30, 1836. The next was another boy, whom we named after

22

his father, (iii) HENRY 8 JACKSON DUNSTER, born in Plymouth, Aug. 18, 1838, died in the same town, Sept. 5, 1839. Mr. Dunster (her husband) was in Georgetown, South Carolina, where he died, July 7, 1839, of yellow fever. After burying my husband and infant, wishing still to preserve the name (Henry), I changed my only remaining child's name, (ii) Andrew 8 Jackson Dunster to HENRY 8 JACKSON DUNSTER. The only living representative that we know of in the male line, directly or indirectly.

"My native place was Plymouth; name, Mary B. Savery; born Aug. 23, 1813. My husband never professed religion, but we always attended the Methodist Church together. I remember perfectly well the day, now that you have brought it to mind, in which you called at his office, although it had passed entirely from my mind.

MARY B. SAMPSON,
East Marshfield, Mass."

HENRY 8 JACKSON DUNSTER, (*Henry,*7 *Henry,*6 *Henry,*5 *Jason,*4 *Henry,*3 *Jona.,*2 *Henry,*1) was born in Boston, Nov. 30, 1836, (*Mrs. Sampson's Letter,*) 1835, by another account. He is employed in the fishing business, for Boston market. He married Jan. 1, 1857, Mary Anna Brewster, a descendant of "Elder Brewster." She was born August, 1837. They have four children, all born in Duxbury, Mass., all living. No death in their family.

i. HENRY 9 LOYD DUNSTER, (*Henry,*8 *Henry,*7 *Henry,*6 *Henry,*5 *Jason,*4 *Henry,*3 *Jona.,*2 *Henry,*1) was born Dec. 24, 1857. He assists his father at times, but is mainly employed in getting an education fitted for entrance into Harvard College,—his most cherished desire. We trust he will be remembered as a worthy descendant of their first President. To him belongs the distinction of having more Henry Dunsters for ancestors than any other person.

ii. LOUISA 9 ANN DUNSTER, born March 28, 1861, living at home, being well educated.

iii. ELIZABETH 9 WATSON DUNSTER, b. Nov. 30, 1864.

iv. JANE 9 JOHNSTON DUNSTER, born Dec. 24, 1866.

The notice before referred to in relation to Henry[6] Jackson Dunster was: "Mr. Henry Dunster, of Duxbury, had a very narrow escape from death on Monday, 16th Feb., 1871, by the caving in of the walls of a well in which he was at work. He was not rescued from his perilous position until six hours after the alarm was given. At first he could be distinctly heard beneath the fallen earth and rocks with which he was covered to the depth of many feet; but all hopes of rescuing him alive had vanished many hours before he was finally taken out. Perseverance at last succeeded in reaching him, when it was found that he was still alive. Fair hopes are entertained of his recovery. Mr. Dunster is a lineal descendant of the first President of Harvard College."

We cannot better close the sketch of this branch of the Dunster family than by an article we find in the Christian Era, of Boston, Jan. 2, 1873. We know not its author.

1654. HENRY DUNSTER AND HARVARD 1872. COLLEGE.

How good and how pleasant a thing it would be if Harvard College could gratefully and gracefully atone for the martyrdom of the excellent and learned President DUNSTER by giving to his lineal descendant the benefits of the institution to whose development and success he brought his intellectual power and moral influence with such efficient devotion.   And is not the opportunity for such a felicity, of itself, an obligation to improve it? That such an opportunity does exist, appears from the following incident in a wayfarer's note-book:

"April 29, 1872. Duxbury, on the side of 'Captain's Hill.' Off in Plymouth Harbor—in a few minutes she will be out of sight beyond Clarke's Island—scuds a tiny sailboat before the morning breeze: a mere speck on the blue water. Down the hill, with a leap over the stone wall, comes a lad of fourteen on his way to the old house at the foot of the hill, there to pass the summer with his Grandmother Brewster. His name is Henry Dunster, a likely boy, and he says, 'in that boat are my father,

23

Henry Dunster, my mother, and two of the children. My father is going to the Gurnett for the summer to take lobsters for the Boston market.' In his own cottage by the water side, the evening before, Dunster had told me of his lowly life. 'My father,' said he, 'was a printer in Lincoln & Edmond's shop, in Boston. He died early, leaving me an orphan boy, two years old.' A while since, his own self-control and calmness in extreme danger saved his life. Buried beneath the falling walls of the well he was clearing, he coolly directed the movements of the frightened men above, and to his words of cheer and caution the bystanders attributed the care which saved him from premature burial. They both, father and son, showed the aptitude of language and calm decision amid peril—the story of which is so well told by Dr. Chaplin. Now, after two centuries of Dunster's rest in Old Cambridge grave yard—two centuries after the flagrant wrongs which drove him from the College and the colony—occurs a fitting opportunity to make the *amende honorable* by adoption of Henry Dunster, Jr., of Duxbury, as a child of Harvard College, thereby to give him the education of which he is capable. This would be a noble tribute to the public service and private worth of President Dunster.

' J. W. T."

23. iv. REBECCA[5] DUNSTER, (*Jason,*[4] *Henry,*[3] *Jona.*[2] *Henry,*[1]) born June 18, baptized June 20, 1756, was named after Rebecca, her sister, who had died when ten months old. When about twelve years old, her father removed to Mason, N. H. She married (date not found) John Swallow, 3d, born Jan. 3, 1757, the oldest son of Lieut. John, 2d, and Sarah (Lawrence) Swallow. He was the oldest son of John, 1st, and Deborah (Lawrence) Swallow, of Groton, Mass. Of "Lieut." John it is said (*History Mason*), while residing in his father's family in Dunstable, he commenced clearing up his farm in Mason, about 1751. At that time there was no road from Dunstable to No. 1 (Mason). He would start on Monday morning with a pack load of provisions on his back, and finding his way by marked trees to his clearing, would fill the forest echoes with lusty blows of his

*20

John Wingate Thornton "
See John Langdon, Sibly, letter
(Dec 25 1880

23

axe, from sun to sun, till his stock of provisions was
exhausted; and then starting a few hours before sunset
he would wend his solitary way through the forest twenty-two miles to his Dunstable home to replenish his
stock, and after a brief resting would again renew his
journey and labors. Thus he subdued the forest, built
his log cabin, and set up his household. In this log
cabin, a house of one small room, he lived till after the
birth of his eleventh child, 1778, when he removed into
a new two-story frame house, in which he spent the re-
mainder of his days, extended to the good old age of 86
years. He never knew what it was to be sick, or even
tasted of anything called medicine, until past his 75th
year. His death was occasioned by a fall and a broken
bone, the pain of which wore out his life, Nov. 23, 1815.

John Swallow, 3d, the husband of Rebecca Dunster,
was the first to bless this log cabin by a birth. After
him followed fourteen more, making fifteen in all. . No
wonder that that "house of one small room" needed
colonization. After the marriage of John, 3d, with Rebecca, he built a house near the two-story house of his
father, and in it all their children were born; but they
fell short in numbers full fifty per cent. The husband
was a hard-working man and the wife was a similar help-
mate. He was remembered by some of the little boys of
his wife's brother, whom he used to call his little white
'headed "sogers" when, in Indian file, they carried the
dinners to the choppers down in the woods, on the Souhegan River, by the spring beyond the Elliot Pasture.
Time and the Peterboro and Shirley Railroad have taken
all the romance out of that happy locality.

His wife, Rebecca (Dunster) Swallow, died Aug. 3,
1811, aged 56 years, and was buried at Mason Centre, in
the large Swallow group. She was admitted a member,
in full communion, of Mason Congregational Church,
Nov. 1, 1801.

Her husband, in his old age, became totally dependent,
and was long maintained by his brother-in-law, Josiah
Winship. Finding that Winship intended to call on the
town to take care of him, he started on foot, although

in feeble health, and walked to Ashburnham, fourteen or sixteen miles, to Samuel C. Dunster's (his wife's brother), and died there, Jan. —, 1830, aged 73 years. His remains were interred at Mason Centre.

They had seven children, all born in Mason:

i. JOHN[6] SWALLOW, born March 1, 1783, died March 13, same year.

ii. JOHN[6] SWALLOW, (*Rebecca[5] D., Jason,[4] Henry,[3] Jona.,[2] Henry,[1]*) born Feb. 3, 1785, married Jan. 13, 1811, Sally Wood, the daughter of Joseph and Mary (Waugh) Wood, who was born April 19, 1790. She was a member of Mason Church. They lived on the place with his father until the death of his wife. He was employed most of the time in teaming to and from Boston. He then removed to Peterboro, N. H., farming some of the time, making his home at his son's, John[7] Swallow (twin to Sarah). He died at Peterboro, May 24, 1862, was brought to Mason Village and buried beside his wife, who died in that village, Oct. 7, 1852, aged 64 years. They had ten children:

1. ELMIRA[7] SWALLOW, born Sept. 2, 1811, in Mason, married May 7, 1835, Ephraim M. Dudley, son of Ebenezer Dudley, born May 23, 1808, at Roxbury, Mass., where they are now living, 1876. Four children, all born at West Roxbury:

(i) EZRA[8] SWALLOW DUDLEY, born Oct. 7, 1836, died Jan. 26, 1863, unmarried.

(ii) ELMIRA[8] J. DUDLEY, born Nov. 10, 1838, died Jan. 16, 1839.

(iii) ELLEN[8] M. DUDLEY, born Aug. 14, 1840.

(iv) EUGENE[8] B. DUDLEY, born June 3, 1848.

2. MALINDA[7] SWALLOW, b. May 27, 1813, in Mason, married Sept. 22, 1836, Joseph Pollard Felt, of Temple, N. H., his second wife. She was a member of Mason Village Church. She died Aug. 20, 1837, aged 24 years. They had one child, who died about the same time, aged 8 months.

3. CALVIN[7] SWALLOW, (*John,[6] John and Rebecca[5] D., Jason,[4] Henry,[3] Jona.,[2] Henry,[1]*) the third child of

23

John and Sally (Wood) Swallow, born at Mason, April
19, 1817, lived with his father till about twelve years old;
afterwards bought his time of his father. In 1835, went
into the West India goods business for two years. In
1837, visited most of the Western country. He bought
at Berwick, Warren Co., Ill., a section of land, which he
still owns. After about a year's residence there he returned to Boston. In 1841, went into the provision
business, which he continued ten years. Being out of
health, he retired for a couple of years, and was then appointed Inspector of Transportation in Bond for Canada,
at the U. S. Custom House in Boston. This office he
held during the administration of President Pierce.
From 1856 to 1863 he was engaged in building houses,
for sale, in the southern part of Boston, near Chester
Park. About 1863 he engaged in the wholesale pork
business. Since then he has been in the building and
real estate business. He was once robbed of his pocket-
book in New York street cars. Lives at 786 Tremont
street, Boston. He married March 3, 1842, Sarah Bick-
ford Huff, of Kennebunk Port, Maine. Six children:

(i) SARAH[8] MATILDA SWALLOW, born Jan. 2, 1843?
mar. John A. Jones, of Boston. She died June 2, 1872,
leaving two children, who are living with her father: .

(1) GERTA[9] ADILADE JONES. (2) JOHN[9] C. JONES.

(ii) GEORGE[8] EZRA SWALLOW, born in Boston, lives
with his father, unmarried.

(iii) EMMA[8] ADALADE SWALLOW, born in Boston, lives
with her father, unmarried.

(iv) THOMAS[8] JEFFERSON SWALLOW, born in Boston,
went to Buffalo, N. Y., 1872, to learn telegraphy.

(v)
(vi) } Twins.[8] One died in infancy; one lived 18 mo. .

4.   JOHN,) Twins of John and Sally (Wood) Swal-
5.   SARAH, ∫ low, b. in Peterboro, N. H., Jan. 28, 1820.

4.   JOHN[7] SWALLOW (twin), married at Peterboro,
Nov. 14, 1844, Elizabeth Nelson, died Aug. 28, 1869.
Two children:

(i) JOHN[8] CALVIN SWALLOW, born ——, at Peterboro, married there.

(ii) ELLA[8] SWALLOW, born ——, at Peterboro, living with her mother in the house where she was born, unm.

5. SARAH[7] SWALLOW (twin), born Jan. 28, 1820, married April 22, 1838, Joseph Pollard Felt, (his third wife). She died at Mason Village, Nov. 7, 1841, aged 21 years. Had one child, who died in Mason, Feb. 5, 1840.

6. JOSEPH, } Twins (second pair) of John and Sally
7. MARY, } (Wood) Swallow, born Aug. 24, 1822.

6. JOSEPH[7] SWALLOW (twin), married Nov. 24, 1845, Aderathy Woods, of Brookfield. Have one daughter, married ——, 1872, lives at Newton? Have buried two children?

7. MARY[7] SWALLOW (twin to Joseph), mar. Horace W. Pierce, (second wife). Mr. Pierce is the same who married Louisa H. Swallow, daughter of Ezra[6] Swallow. She resides with her step-children in Brighton. She had no children.

8. ELIZABETH[7] SWALLOW, born at Mason, April 7, 1825, united with the Baptist Church at Mason Village, married Seneca Lynch, Aug. 26, 1845. Reside in Berwick, Warren Co., Illinois, on her brother Calvin's land. Have had four children: Two died young. EDWIN[8] LYNCH, WILLIE[8] LYNCH, both now living.

9. ADDISON[7] SWALLOW, born at Townsend, Mass., April 27, 1827, married at Boston, Nov. —, 1852, Sarah Leavy. Resides in Boston. Have two children:

(i) FRANK[8] SWALLOW. (ii) WILLIE[8] SWALLOW.

10. ELLEN[7] REBECCA SWALLOW, born at Mason, May 31, 1829, died Jan. 31, 1842, aged 13 years, buried at Mason Village.

iii. ISAIAH[6] DUNSTER SWALLOW, (*John and Rebecca[5] D., Jason,[4] Henry,[3] Jona.,[2] Henry,[1]*) the third child of John and Rebecca (Dunster) Swallow, born March 29, 1787, married May 30, 1813, Zibiah Davis, of Roxbury, daughter of Noah and Elizabeth (Weld) Davis. Zibiah

23

Davis was a sister of Mary Davis, wife of Isaiah[5] Dunster. They lived in Roxbury till April, 1816, when they bought a farm in Templeton, Mass. His wife died May 7, 1848. He died Sept. 6, 1861. They had eight children:

1. ELLEN[7] ZIBIAH SWALLOW, born at Roxbury, Feb. 7, 1814. After the death of her mother, she appears to have assumed the care of the family, and still resides at Templeton Centre, unmarried. In furnishing a record of her father's family she adds: "There is nothing remarkable about the family that would be interesting." We think the fact that she has lived sixty years and "has not been sick since she was eight years old," is a very remarkable fact, and one that does not often occur.

2. SARAH[7] WOOD SWALLOW, born Oct. 26, 1815, in Roxbury, married Jan. 21, 1846, Edson Higley, of Templeton. He died there, Feb. 9, 1848. Since then she has lived with her sister, Ellen Z., at Templeton Centre.

3. ISAIAH[7] DUNSTER SWALLOW, born Sept. 7, 1817, married April 22, 1847, Esther J. Gates. He was employed in a factory. Feb. 9, 1848, he went to the mill to work before any other hand was in, and it is supposed that he attempted to adjust a belt and was entangled in it and carried round the drum, killing him instantly. They had one child:

(i) LYMAN[8] A. SWALLOW, born Jan. 1, 1848, died April 3, 1851.

4. WILLIAM[7] ALFRED SWALLOW, born April 12, 1819, married April 13, 1845, Azubah H. Hager; was a machinist in Worcester many years. He died April 15, 1866. She died Nov. 1, 1873. Had two children:

(i) ABBIE[8] A. SWALLOW, born Oct. 19, 1846, married Dec. 1, 1868, William B. Allyn. Live in Baldwin, Wisconsin. Have three children:

(1) MARY[9] A. ALLYN, born Oct. 16, 1869.

(2) WILLIAM[9] ALFRED ALLYN, born Dec. 18, 1871.

(3) SYBIL[9] R. ALLYN, born March 26, 1874, died Sept. 12, same year.

(ii) MARTHA[8] ZIBIAH SWALLOW, born Aug. 14, 1849,

23

mar. Feb. 22, 1876, William F. Scribner. They are now in Worcester, but intend to go West this spring (1876).

5. ELIZABETH[7] R. SWALLOW, born Jan. 10, 1821, married Dec. 12, 1861, James H. Bond. They reside in Leicester, Mass. No children.

6. Infant[7] daughter, b. Jan. 18, 1822, died same day.

7. MARY[7] J. SWALLOW, born April 3, 1823, died May 1, 1855, unmarried.

8. LUCY[7] A. SWALLOW, born May 28, 1826, married May 22, 1866, Davight McFarland. Reside in Leicester, Mass.

A part of the family of Isaiah and Zibiah (Davis) Swallow are Unitarians, the rest are Orthodox Congregationalists.

iv. ABEL[6] SWALLOW, (*John and Rebecca[5] D., Jason,[4] Henry,[3] Jona.,[2] Henry,[1]*) the fourth child of John and Rebecca (Dunster) Swallow, born at Mason, Nov. 3, 1789, went to Sudbury, Mass., where he married June 8, 1814, Dorcas Parmenter, born Jan. 9, 1788, at Sudbury. He lived after his marriage in Roxbury, Brookline, Leominster, Marlboro and Framingham. He was a farmer and fruit grower, selling generally in Boston. "He died of heart disease, Aug. 26, 1853, at Framingham. He was handing a box of fine plums, which he had raised, to his market man, when he fell back and never moved a muscle after." They had five children:

1. GEORGE[7] E. SWALLOW, born at Roxbury, July 11, died July 23, 1815.

2. ADALINE[7] E. SWALLOW, born at Brookline, June 24, 1817, married March 14, 1838, in Framingham, Addison Belknap, born Jan. 20, 1811. They are farmers, living in the south part of Framingham. One child:

(i) ADDISON[8] COMER BELKNAP, born Oct. 25, 1844, in Framingham, is a farmer with his father. He married May 31, 1865, Rebecca Jane Hosmer, born Nov. 17, 1846, in Framingham. They have one child:

(1) ARTHUR[9] T. BELKNAP, born Feb. 8, 1872, at Framingham.

23

3. JOSEPH [7] HENRY SWALLOW, born at Brookline, Aug. 9, 1819, is a farmer, and resides in the north part of Framingham. He married at Danvers, Mass, March .19, 1845, Clarinda J. Ordway, born Dec. 9, 1824, in Hopkinton, N. H. They have had three children:

(i) HENRY [8] CLAY SWALLOW, born at Merrimac, N. H., June 3, 1846, died at Framingham, Aug. 10, 1850.

(ii) HENRIETTA [8] SUSAN SWALLOW, born at Danvers, Sept. 23, 1849.

(iii) CARRIE [8] JANE SWALLOW, born at Framingham, May 19, 1861.

4. SUSAN [7] R. SWALLOW, born Feb. 14, 1823, at Leominster, died July 10, 1844, at Framingham, unm.

5. SARAH [7] H. SWALLOW, born at Marlboro, Sept. 19, 1830, married Oct. 19, 1847, at Framingham, Francis Hosmer, born at Bolton, Mass., June 8, 1826. He is a farmer in the north part of Framingham. Have two children:

(i) FREDERIC [8] H. HOSMER, born Oct. 5, 1854, is a bookkeeper in Quincy Market, resides in Boston, married Oct. 14, 1875, E. Ella Winch, born June 24, 1855, in Framingham.

(ii) WILLIE [8] T. HOSMER, born Nov. 20, 1860, in Framingham.

v. NEHEMIAH [6] SWALLOW, the fifth child of John and Rebecca (Dunster) Swallow, born in Mason, May 22, 1792, went to Western New York, afterwards to Ohio, where he died of a fever in 1826. Unmarried.

vi. EZRA [6] SWALLOW, the sixth child of John and Rebecca (Dunster) Swallow, born at Mason, Dec. 22, 1794, in early manhood lived with his Uncle Isaiah Dunster in Roxbury, driving his market wagon to Boston, and attending to the agricultural affairs of the farm generally. After his uncle's death he carried on the tavern and subsequently bought it. He married May 22, 1820, Nancy Shortlift, born April 17, 1799, in Sudbury. She died Sept. 17, 1841. He died at Roxbury, Oct. 21, 1832. They had one child:

23-24

1. LOUISA[7] H. SWALLOW, born at Roxbury, March 24, 1821. She married at Brighton, Dec. 24, 1848, Horace W. Pearce, or Pierce, son of Horace Pierce. They had:

(i) WILLIE[8] H. PEARCE, born Jan. 3, 1850.
(ii) FRED.[8] A. PEARCE, born March 1, 1852.
(iii) CORA[8] C. PEARCE, born Nov. 19, 1854.

. All reside in Brighton.

His wife (Louisa) died May 24, 1859, and he married second, Mary Swallow, daughter of John[6] Swallow (twin to Joseph). Mr. Pearce is dead, and his widow lives with her step-children, at Brighton.

vii. REBECCA[6] SWALLOW, born in Mason, May 3, 1799, lived with the old folks until her mother died (1811), when her father broke up housekeeping. She then lived with her brother Ezra, in Roxbury. Here she married Abram Sanborn, born ——, in New Hampshire. They lived near the Dunster (Swallow) Tavern. She died there Feb. 21, 1832. Her husband married again, and moved to Canada, and took a part or all of the children with him, some of whom are living. They had three children:

1. ELIZA[7] SANBORN. 2. GEORGE[7] SANBORN, lives in Illinois. 3. ELMIRA[7] SANBORN, called, after her mother's death, REBECCA SANBORN. Both daughters are married in South Roxton, Canada East.

24. v. MARTHA[5] DUNSTER, (*Jason,*[4] *Henry,*[3] *Jona.*[2] *Henry,*[1]) the fifth child of Jason and Rebecca (Cutter) Dunster, was born at Cambridge (Precinct), Aug. 28, baptized Sept. 3, 1758, by Rev. Samuel Cooke, Second Church. She removed with her father's family, 1769, to Mason, N. H. She did not live with her father all of the time, but went "out to service," as we call it now, which then meant an assistant in the family equal with the children. She lived at Major Abbot's, in Wilton. Here she became acquainted with Oliver Wright, the son of John Wright, of Dunstable, now Nashua. He was born in Westford, Mass., and died "the year after

21

24

1725 Martha married," aged 92, consequently he must have been born in ~~1692~~. We give the record of his children as remarkable instances of longevity in one family. (*William P. Wright's Bible.*)

JOHN, Jr., born May 4, 1748, died March 1, 1836, aged 88 years, 7 months.

ZEBEDEE, born July 19, 1749, died Jan. 1, 1823, aged 73 years, 5 months.

BENJAMIN, born Oct. 12, 1751, died Aug. 29, 1833, aged 81 years, 10 months.

ISAAC, born Sept. 4, 1754, died Feb. 11, 1837, aged 82 years, 4 months.

NEHEMIAH, born Oct. 12, 1756, died Feb. 18, 1842, aged 85 years, 4 months.

OLIVER, born Sept. 14, 1758, died Sept. 3, 1847, aged 89 years.

SARAH, born Sept. 4, 1762, died Dec. 22, 1838, aged 66 years, 3 months.

Oliver, the son, was born in Westford, Sept. 14, 1758. Martha "fixed her things," as her only living daughter said, at Major Abbot's, and they were married Sept. 7, 1783. Her husband had not been unmindful of the responsibilities he was about to assume. With his brother, Nehemiah, he had purchased two lots of land in Monadnock No. 6, then called Packer's field, now Nelson, lying about forty miles from his father's residence and thirty from her's, among the mountains of the Monadnock range. Here he had "fixed his things," which consisted of a small house and a little "opening" in the solitary wilderness. As soon as married they made their "wedding trip." It was to this little home. Here they lived, here all their children were born, here they died.

They were both members of the Orthodox Congregational Church, and maintained a Christian and consistent life, blameless to the end. A visit to their home in 1837, is vividly remembered. They were alone. Their children had all been married, or died. They were then about 80 years old. That family altar had never been

1725 91 was Martha Wright's (Mensey to which Mrs Butterfield refers on Martha (Dunster) Wright hence the mis-understanding

24

neglected; and kneeling around it seemed almost "Holy ground." They were prudent and hard-working. On the 19th of March, 1821, the house which they had erected and made comfortable in furniture and conveniences by their united labor of forty years, was burned. Nothing of consequence was saved. It was before the days of general insurance, and all was lost. A new home was built by them, assisted by their friends, and again they were cheerful and happy.

She died Sept. 2, 1838, being 80 years, 5 months, 19 days old. He died Sept. 3, 1847, nine years after his wife, aged 89 years. In their Family Bible, at William P. Wright's, Chicago, his birth is April 14, 1758, and his death is Sept. 3, 1846, age 88 years, 4 months, 19 days. They were both buried in Nelson. They raised a large and enterprising family, having had ten children:

i. OLIVER WRIGHT, born June 5, 1786, died Oct. 11, 1850. Twice married.

ii. KENDALL WRIGHT, born March 6, 1788. When four years old he was playing about the wood-pile, then being prepared for burning, when a log rolled from it killing him instantly, April 19, 1792.

iii., ABIEL WRIGHT, born March 27, 1790, married Patty Baker, still living, in Hartland, Vt.

iv. JASON WRIGHT, born April 21, 1792, died Aug. 25, the same year, 4 months old, buried at Nelson.

v. PATTY WRIGHT, born March 28, 1794, mar. Oliver Heald, (1st wife,) died Aug. 19, 1854, at Milford, N. H.

vi. HENRY WRIGHT, born Sept. 17, 1795, mar. Lois Kimball, died in Clinton, Mass., Aug. 26, 1852.

vii. ANNA WRIGHT, born July 9, 1797, married Cyrus Greenwood, died Nov. 12, 1816.

viii. LUCY WRIGHT, born Aug. 28, 1799, mar. Leonard Butterfield, still living, in Dunstable, N. H.

ix. IRA WRIGHT, born Oct. 26, 1801, died Feb. 7, 1802, buried at Nelson.

x. MYRA WRIGHT, born Dec. 30, 1802, mar. Edwin Jewel, died Oct. 7, 1849.

24

i. OLIVER[6] WRIGHT, (*Oliver and Martha*[5] *D., Jason,*[4] *Henry,*[3] *Jonathan,*[2] *Henry,*[1]) was the first child of Oliver and Martha (Dunster) Wright, born June 5, 1786. He lived with his father until of suitable age to learn the trade of cabinet-maker with Col. James Wood, of Mason. While an apprentice he made the black cherry tree case to the clock of his Uncle Dunster—about 1803—the works of which were bought of "Billings, the clock maker," of Acton. It is now as good as new, and is quietly ticking away at the "old parsonage," asking no favors except to be wound up at the close of the week's work. After finishing his trade he established himself at Tyngsboro, N. H. In Mason he became acquainted with Hannah Wheeler, the seventh child of Timothy and and Sarah (Hubbard) Wheeler, who had a fine farm near that of Col. Wood. She was born May 7, 1789. They were married by Rev. E. Hill, May 25, 1809, and went at once to Tyngsboro. They staid but a short time there. He removed to Nelson in 1810, and set up a shop for cabinet making, &c. Here he had machinery of his own contrivance propelled by water power. One of his then little cousins remembers a top turned by him which, being his first one, he considered a marvel of skill.

As early as 1812, and we think before, he conceived the idea of *sawing* shingles from the log. He carried his plan into practice, and set his machine to work. It did all that was expected of it. Everything needed to complete its success and consequent remuneration was a suitable person to dispose of the shingles. The country traders then did most of the business of buying and selling. He applied to them to aid him in selling, and was assured that they would take the matter into consideration and see him again. The one in whom he had placed the most confidence *did see* him. He exhibited the machine and explained its construction, and showed its working. After a full examination and clear conception of its arrangements, he saw its ultimate results. It would interfere with much of the business of his other customers, and therefore reduce his own profits, so he began to belittle its utility and discourage the inventor. This had its intended effect. He was "talked out of it."

24

Modest and confiding, he believed the story. His machine was taken to pieces and stowed away among the "old lumber in the garret;" and he gave up his cherished desire. Such is the fate of many real inventors.

Sometime afterwards, that very man who had "considered" the plan put a "machine for sawing shingles" into full operation, for which he obtained a patent, making oath that it was his own invention, although it embraced exactly the same principles in exact detail. He made a handsome property out of it. We mention this at some length on account of the wrong done the real inventor, and to certify to its priority. We saw it in operation, and, although a child at that time, can now remember the automic contrivance by which it was made to saw the butt and top of shingles alternately. This only was patentable, as we saw in after years, when the *principles* of mechanics were better studied.

He also invented a machine for sawing ship timber. He was at one time an overseer in the Columbian Factories at Mason Village, and spent most of his active life in making steam and cotton machinery.

He married second, Aug. 16, 1818, Rhoda Taylor, of Dunstable, the daughter of Samuel and Ruth (Parker) Taylor, born Aug. 24, 1787. He was the first deacon of the First Baptist Church in Dunstable. She (Rhoda) united with that church about 1805, was afterwards an active member of the first Sabbath School in Dr. Sharpe's Church, Boston, in 1817. "She read the Bible through *annually* for near thirty years." She died at Nunda, N. Y., July 11, 1868, aged 80 years and 10 months, and was buried at Mount Hope Cemetery, Rochester, N. Y.

Oliver Wright united with the Congregational Church in Nelson, on profession of faith, in 1817. He removed to New Ipswich, 1823, and to Mason Village, 1829. Here he united with the Baptist Church in 1830, and was baptized by immersion. He removed with his family to Nunda, Livingston Co., N. Y., 1835, thence to Rochester, N. Y., 1846. "He lived a consistent Christian life, and died in the hope of a glorious resurrection, Oct. 12, 1850, aged 64 years." He was buried at Mount Hope Cemetery, Rochester, N. Y.

*21

24

Hannah (Wheeler), his first wife, died March 4, 1817, when Kendall, their fifth child was ten days old, aged 28 years, was buried at Nelson. She was a woman of good character and deservedly beloved. Her eldest daughter, Caroline, has furnished an interesting sketch of her life and religious experience which we would gladly insert. For want of space we can only say that on her death bed she named her infant child, and with an earnest desire for the conversion of her associates, selected Amos, vi., 3, as a text from which she requested her pastor, Rev. Gad Newell, to preach her funeral sermon. To her friends she said, I am alive, and shall live again; old things are done away; all things have become new. I can now say, "Oh, death, where is thy sting? Oh, grave, where is thy victory?"

Oliver[6] Wright had eight children: By his first wife, Hannah, five; by his second wife, Rhoda, three:

i. CAROLINE[7] WRIGHT, the oldest child, was born in Tyngsboro, N. H., March 5, 1810. Her father went to Nelson when she was about six months old. Here she lived until the death of her mother, when she was adopted by her Aunt Lucy (Wheeler) Stone, of Townsend. She united with the Orthodox Congregational Church, when sixteen years old, on recent profession in Townsend (Rev. Mr. Palmer). Her uncle, Samuel Stone, who had just erected a new house, died Aug. 29, 1830. His widow lived at the new residence until her death, Dec. 28, 1861, aged 77 years, 27 days. By her will, the property was given to Caroline, on which she lived— housekeeping—till about 1868. Her history, though a painful one, is interesting, and we extend it as related by her letters, which have been numerous, and at times written by an amanuensis.

She had often, in her childhood, heard of her Aunt Stone, her mother's sister, but had only seen her in infancy. When her mother died, she felt a desire to go and live with them. At the funeral she asked her aunt if she might go home with her. The reply was an encouraging one; and the same month Caroline went to Townsend as their adopted daughter. For a time she

24

was discontented and unhappy at being separated from father, brothers and sisters. Her uncle and aunt were very kind, and soon she became attached to them. After Mr. Stone died she taught school, occasionally, for some years. In 1842 she was disabled by lameness, hereditary in the family of her Grandfather Wheeler. The disability has been so great that she has been unable to walk for more than twenty-five years; but has been able in later years, generally, to trundle herself about her room in a chair. Sometimes she can use her hands for writing, reading, or other things not requiring much physical strength; at others, she is unable to write, or even feed herself. Since 1868 she has boarded—most of the time in the families of her friends and relations—for the last five or six years at her cousin's, Samuel H. Wheeler, Mason Centre.

She adds that, "in these later years, she views the circumstance of her going to live with her uncle and aunt as a good Providence, by which a more ample provision was made for her comfort and happiness than perhaps would otherwise have been during these years of suffering and disability; and she would most gratefully remember the continued loving kindness of her Heavenly Father, who has so mercifully sustained her under affliction, and so bountifully provided every needed blessing."

Her last letter, written by another hand, says: "I am unusually ill, confined to my bed almost entirely, and have been for the last year. I can generally write five or six lines in a day; when I have more to do, I am obliged to have some one write for me.

ii. The second child of Oliver and Hannah (Wheeler) Wright was SARAH,[7] or SALLY WRIGHT, born in Nelson, Feb. 24, 1812, and died March 16, same year.

iii. ALMIRA[7] DUNSTER WRIGHT, their third child, was born in Nelson, Feb. 8, 1813. She went to Mason Village with her father, 1829. Here she professed religion, and joined the Baptist Church there. She went in 1835 to Nunda, N. Y. She married, at Warsaw, N. Y., May 25, 1837, Mordan Stilman Wright, of Washington County. He was a carpenter, resided at Nunda. He

24

made a profession of religion there.   They were not related to each other.   They moved to Ann Arbor, Michigan, in 1855, and appear to have lived at Mount Morris.
He sold his place in Ann Arbor, in the spring of 1873,
and removed to Eaton Rapids, to live with their son.
He died there prior to Sept. 17, 1873, and his widow returned to Ann Arbor, and lives on property they owned
there.   They had four children:

1. WALTER⁸ STILMAN WRIGHT, born at Nunda,
April 22, 1838, married Sept. 8, 1869, Mrs. Louisa C.
Spoor, at Detroit, Mich.   She had had three daughters
by her former husband.   He is a farmer, and resides at
Eaton Rapids.

2. CARRIE⁸ ELIZABETH? WRIGHT, was born at Nunda, Sept. 14, 1843.   Professed religion at Ann Arbor,
March 17, 1871.

3. ELLA⁸ S. WRIGHT, (ALTHEA in one record,) born
at Mount Morris, April 9, 1846, professed religion at
Ann Arbor, with her sister.

4. HANNAH⁸ ELIZABETH TAYLOR WRIGHT, born at
Mount Morris, New York, Oct. 17, 1848.

iv. TIMOTHY⁷ WHEELER WRIGHT, was born in Nelson, Nov. 29, 1814.   "Possessing an amiable disposition, his affectionate treatment of his younger brothers
and sister left an undying impression on their young
hearts.   Previous to his last sickness he had sought the
Lord, and his dying bed was made soft by his Saviour's
sustaining hand.   He labored to lead all who visited him
to repentance and faith."   (*Caroline Wright.*)   He died
in New Ipswich, N. H., Dec. 6, 1827, aged 13 years and
1 week; was interred in Nelson.

v. OLIVER⁷ KENDALL WRIGHT, was born in Nelson,
Feb. 21, 1817.   His mother died when he was ten days
old.   She named him on her death bed, Oliver, (his own
father) and Kendall, who had been so suddenly killed
while a child.   "He possessed a decided talent for me-
chanical pursuits, and was successful in accomplishing
some, for one so young, difficult pieces of work."   He
died at Nelson, Dec. 2, 1835, aged 18 years, 9 mo. 11 d.

24

vi. HANNAH⁷ ELIZABETH TAYLOR WRIGHT, (*Oliver,*⁶ *Martha*⁵ *D., Jason,*⁴ *Henry,*³ *Jona.,*² *Henry,*¹) the sixth child of Oliver and the first of Rhoda (Taylor) Wright, was born in Nelson, Sept. 21, 1820. "In infancy she was an invalid. Deprived of the ordinary amusements of children she devoted her time, even at that early age, to reading. Imbibing from her mother, who had been no stranger to sickness and casualties, a love of religious reading, she made that her pleasure. When less than seven years old, and during a sickness in which her life was despaired of, it pleased God to manifest his converting grace and implant a love for the Bible and religious literature, and thus shape her after life. At the early age of nine years, while reading the thrilling stories from the Missionary Magazine, a conviction of duty to prepare for work among the heathen was felt. To that object her aim was directed. She had recovered the use of her limbs. On the 7th of Sept., 1834, she united with the Baptist Church in Mason Village, and in the May following removed with her father to Nunda, N. Y. She taught school in Warsaw, N. Y., some portion of each year for ten years.

"In 1846, her father having removed to Rochester, she accepted a situation as teacher in the public schools of that city. During these passing years, the allurements of society, with the pleasure of teaching, had chilled the ardor of early consecration to the cause of Missions. But chastisements [the death of her father, probably] awoke the slumbering conviction and led to a renewed consecration to that work. Induced by the advice of her pastor, Dr. Church, she offered herself to the Board of American Baptist Mission Union, and was appointed teacher in the Karen Normal School, in charge of Rev. Mr. and Mrs. Binney, Maulmain, Burmah. With other missionaries she sailed from Boston, Oct. 18, 1849, in the ship Arab, and arrived March 18, 1850, and assumed the charge of one of the departments of the school the following day.

"Mrs. Binney's health having failed, her husband soon left for America, leaving the school in the charge of Miss Wright, with Mrs. Miranda Vinton as assistant.

24

The oft recurring failure in the health of missionaries prostrated her, and obliged her to leave her much loved and flourishing school, and she returned to her native land in 1853.   Health was again restored; and she married July 15, 1858, in Rochester, Rev. Lyman Stilson, formerly Missionary to the Burmans, of Arracan and Maulmain.   He was born in Merideth, Delaware Co., N. Y., Jan. 29, 1815; sailed for Burmah in 1837; labored in the preparation of books and maps, and teaching, during his stay of fourteen years.

"In Sept., 1847, while treasurer of the Missions, an attempt was made by three Burmans to rob him.   They entered his study late in the evening, while he was alone and unarmed.   A struggle ensued, in which he was severely wounded in his face, head, arm and right hand, which was badly mutilated.   These wounds caused a failure of health, and a return to America in 1853."

Mrs. Stilson contributed, Jan. 11, 1877, to the Baptist Beacon, Des Moines, Iowa, an interesting sketch of President Dunster.

Two children:

1.   CHARLIE⁸ LYMAN STILSON, born at Nunda, N. Y., Feb. 28, 1860.

2.   EDWIN⁸ PARKER STILSON, born at Nunda, May 4, 1861.

The present (1873) residence of this family is at Jefferson, Greene County, Iowa.

vii.   WILLIAM⁷ PARKER WRIGHT, (*Oliver,⁶ Oliver and Martha⁵ D.,*) was the seventh child of Oliver and second of Rhoda (Taylor) Wright.   He was born at Nelson, N. H., Jan. 6, 1823; went to New Ipswich, thence to Mason Village, thence followed all the various removals made by his father till 1852, when he and his brother, Charles B. Wright, established themselves in the business of building fire engines, which they continued till 1859. They then both enlisted in the army.   He enlisted as a private, and went to Washington.   Here he was detailed as nurse in one of the hospitals.   His attention to the sick and wounded made him a favorite confidant with

24

them. Authority at Washington had forbidden these distressed victims of violence to inform their friends of their condition, "lest it should discourage enlistments." Disregarding these orders, and being a ready writer, he made glad the heart of many of them, and their consequent hope of recovery, by sending to their friends such messages as they dictated.

In 1872 he lived at 660 Butterfield street, Chicago, being in the employ of the Rock Island Engine Works, as a machinist, but now resides at the works. He married June 14, 1866, at Port Byron, Illinois, Gertrude E. Simonson. She is descended from the family who owned the property where "rich" Trinity Church, in New York, now stands. It is claimed that "Trinity" never paid for it. They have two children:

1.   ABBOT[8] LAWRENCE WRIGHT, b. at Chicago, May 18, 1869, named by his father for Abbot Lawrence, of Boston, Mass., who was a cousin of his "sainted mother."

2.   A daughter,[8] her name not recollected, born about 1873, at the Rock Island Engine Works, about four miles from Chicago proper.

viii.   CHARLES[7] BATEMAN WRIGHT, was born in New Ipswich, N. H., Aug. 8, 1828. At Mason Village he began his education at the common school; removed with his father to Nunda; removed to Warsaw, N. Y., 1838; back to Nunda in 1840. Here he carried on a more extended business of machine building than he had done at Nunda or Warsaw, till 1846, when he removed to Rochester, N. Y., but was in no business for himself. He learned the trade of machinist of his father. In 1852 he and his brother, William[7] P. Wright, engaged in the business of building fire engines at Rochester? which they continued till 1859.

At the breaking out of the war he enlisted in the army, and on arriving at Washington was transferred to the navy yard, to work in the ordinance department as a machinist. In May, 1863, he was appointed an engineer in the navy, and served two years. At the close of the war he removed to Rochester, and from that place, in 1865, established the machine business with

24

William E. Leard, at Pithole (oil regions), in Pennsylvania. From Pithole they removed to Chattanooga, in Tennessee, where they now carry on the same business.

He married, in Rochester, Oct. 18, 1854, Mary Littlefield, born Jan. 22, 1838, in that city. They both belong to the Episcopalian Church in Chattanooga. Four children:

1. CHARLES[8] PARKER WRIGHT, born in Rochester, N. Y., April 3, 1856.

2. ELLIOT[8] OLIVER WRIGHT, born in Rochester, Jan. 2, 1859.

3. NELLIE[8] WRIGHT, b. in Rochester, Aug. 12, 1860.

4. GENEVRA[8]? or GENEVA? LEARD WRIGHT, born at Pithole, Penn., ——, died Sept. 23, 1868, aged 5 months.

iii. ABIEL[6] WRIGHT, (*Oliver and Martha*[5] *D., Jason,*[4] *Henry,*[3] *Jona.,*[2] *Henry,*[1]) was born in Nelson, March 27, 1790. He lived with his father till about the time of his marriage, June 9, 1818, to Patty (Martha) Baker, daughter of Thomas and Sally (Temple) Baker, of Marlboro, N. H., and then bought a place at Harrisville, a village in Nelson, about four miles from his father's. It is now, we think, a separate town. He was a much respected man; was Captain of the Dublin and Nelson Cavalry Co. for six years; was first Selectman near twenty years, and did much other town business. He was a social, genial, and religious man, but not a church member. After the death of his wife, Dec. 8, 1855, he removed with his daughter, Julian, to Hartland, Vermont, where he now resides. Is in his 87th year of age, and as last heard from, is in good health. His wife was buried in Nelson. They had seven children, all born in Nelson:

1. FRANCIS[7] WALTER WRIGHT, (*Abiel,*[6] *Oliver and Martha*[5] *Dunster,*) born Sept. 27, 1819, lived with his father till 1839, then went with Melville & Nims, merchants, for about three and a half years. Then traded for himself, in Marlow, N. H., about six months, when he removed his goods to Ashby, Mass., April 16, 1844, and traded there about four years. Since 1848 he has been trading in stock, real estate, and nearly everything else;

24

and now (1874) pays the largest tax of any man in Ashby. (This we did not learn from himself.) He has been an Auctioneer, Assessor, one of the Selectmen and Treasurer of the town, Overseer of the Poor, and Collector of Taxes for twenty years. He married July 5, 1845, Caroline Lydia Melville, born Jan. 17, 1823, daughter of Henry and Caroline Lydia (Whitney) Melville, of Nelson. He was born Aug. 27, 1794, and was killed April 3, 1836, while blasting rocks in his door yard. She was born July 6, 1795, died Jan. 8, 1864.

Francis W. Wright's wife died Jan. 4, 1864, at Ashby, was buried at Nelson. He married second, Augusta H. Holden, Nov. 24, 1864, daughter of Edward Hosmer and Dorcas Barrett (Cragin) Holden, of New Ipswich, N. H. She was born in New Ipswich, July 26, 1811. He was born March 26, 1811. Augusta Hosmer Holden was born Sept. 13, 1838, educated at Ashby and Bradford Academy, and Townsend Academy. She taught school sixteen terms in Ashburnham, Townsend and Ashby, and is a member of the Orthodox Congregational Church, which she and her husband joined at the same time. She is prominent in organizing societies, and other means of supporting the church, one of which was a newspaper got up by her, giving an address on the hundredth anniversary of the incorporation of Ashby, Sept. 4, 1867, with poetical and other compositions of her own. She has contributed largely to the periodical literature of the day.

Frank Walter Wright had three children:

(i)   HENRY[8] MELVILLE WRIGHT, born at Ashby, Dec. 15, 1848, died Feb. 27, 1849.

(ii)   FRANCIS[8] DASCOMB WRIGHT, born March 25, 1848, in Ashby. He has been well educated, is a member of the church, and was married Jan. 25, 1875, to Alice M. Haywood, daughter of P. A. and Martha Haywood, of Ashby.

(iii)   CARRIE[8] AUGUSTA WRIGHT, born Aug. 26, 1867, was the third child of Francis W. and the first of Augusta (Holden) Wright.

24

2. ABBIE[7] BAKER WRIGHT, was the second child of Abiel and Patty (Baker) Wright, born June 19, 1821, married Luther Cobb, of Nelson, Nov. 16, 1848. Have no children. Have resided a short time in each of several States, east and west, and finally settled at Big Rapids, Michigan, where they now reside. Mr. Cobb has held the office of Supervisor of the township for some years, also Register of Deeds for the county.

3. WALLACE[7] WRIGHT, born April 23, 1823, died Dec. 23, 1826.

4. JULIA[7] ANN WRIGHT, born Dec. 31, 1824, married July 13, 1848, Calvin Rand Greene, of Hillsboro, N. H. He was born March 30, 1823. They lived at Harrisville, Peterboro, N. H., and afterwards at Hartland, Vt., where her father and husband purchased a large farm, on which they now reside. Her father still lives with them, in good health, but very deaf. Their children are:

(i) ALICE[8] JULIA GREENE, born at Harrisville, Nov. 14, 1853.

(ii) ANNIE[8] MARIA GREENE, born March 11, 1863, at Hartland.

5. ALMEDA[7] WRIGHT, born Feb. 19, 1829, married June 3, 1856, Benjamin W. Plummer, of Northfield, N. H. They resided in Bennington, N. H., and had one child, who died an infant. She died Sept. 7, 1859, aged 30 years and 7 months.

6. DASCOMB[7] WALLACE WRIGHT, born Feb. 6, 1834, died Jan. 30, 1841.

7. MARTHA[7] ELZINA WRIGHT, born July 5, 1838, married March 3, 1870, Lucian Webster Rice, of Hartland, Vt. They resided a short time in Providence, R. I., afterward at Vermont, and now reside on a large milk farm in Lebanon, N. H. They have:

(i) LILLIAN[8] EMILY RICE, born June 1, 1871.

v. MARTHA[6] (PATTY) WRIGHT, (*Oliver and Martha[5] Dunster, Jason,[4] Henry,[3] Jona.,[2] Henry,[1]*) the fifth child of Oliver and Martha (Dunster) Wright, was born March 28, 1794. She married April 30, 1816, at Nelson, Oliver

24

Heald (Hale in the old Family Bible), of Dublin, N. H. His occupation was that of a wool carder and clothier. He was in the war of 1812. He was a Justice of the Peace, and was repeatedly honored by his townsmen, who elected him to places of trust. Moved to Milford in 1849. Patty[6] died Aug. 19, 1854, at Milford. He was married again, to Relief Little, of Peterboro, N. H., March, 1857. He died at Peterboro, Oct. 5, 1867. The ten children of Oliver and Patty (Wright) Heald were all born in Nelson:

1. ADDISON[7] HEALD, born Feb. 25, 1817, married Jane E. French, daughter of Rev. Daniel French, of Bedford, N. H., (Congregationalist.) She was born July 25, 1824. He was educated for the ministry, and licensed to preach, but was never ordained. He had charge of a colored school in Mercer Co., Ohio, from 1850, about four years. He is now (1873) manufacturing furniture, and has planing works, with his son, at Milford, N. H. They have four children:

(i) DANIEL[8] MILTON HEALD, born in Ohio, Jan. 9, 1852, is with his father, manufacturing wood work, at the establishment of his Uncle David[7] Heald.

(ii) MARY[8] JANE HEALD, born in Ohio, July 5, 1853, married June 24, 1872, J. Lewis Merril, a teacher in the Lake Forest Academy, Illinois. One child:

(1) QUINCY[9] MERRIL, born Sept., 1874.

(iii) WILLIAM[8] ADDISON HEALD, born Feb. 22, 1857, died April 9, 1857.

(iv) SARAH[8] MARIA HEALD, born June 4, 1858, at Hudson, N. H.

2. ALBERT[7] HEALD, (*Oliver,*[6] *Martha*[5] *D.,* *Jason,*[4] *Henry,*[3] *Jona.,*[2] *Henry,*[1]) the second child of Oliver and Patty (Wright) Heald, was born Dec. 14, 1818. He married Harriet Munson, born in Whately, Mass., Sept. 15, 1820. He was educated for the ministry, and graduated at New Hampton (N. H.) Theological Institution; was ordained June 15, 1848, at Lyman, Maine, as pastor of the Kennebunk and Lyman Baptist Church; left Maine in March, 1851, and settled at East Washington,

24

N. H., May 1, 1851, at which place he preached until March 1, 1865, when he settled in Warner, N. H., and continued there until August, 1870. In November of that year, he settled as pastor of the Baptist Church in Amherst, N. H. He furnished much of the record of the Heald family. They had but one child:

(i) HATTIE[8] G. HEALD, born at Lyman, Maine, June 1, 1850, married George K. Walker, of Amherst, Dec. 25, 1871. He is a druggist, and lives at No. 3 Buckingham Place, Boston. They have a daughter:

(1) GRACIE[9] MAY WALKER, born May 6, 1874.

3. SARAH[7] DUNSTER HEALD, born Nov. 14, 1820, married April 20, 1848, William Crosby, at Milford, N. H., his second wife. He was the son of Othni Crosby, who was the occupant of the Clothiers' Works at Mason Village, (then called Mason Harbor,) about 1810. They live in Milford. Have no children.

4. EMILY[7] HEALD, born Dec., 1823, was the fourth child of Oliver and Patty (Wright) Heald. She married John Quincy Adams Ware, born Dec. 17, 1822, at Gilsum, N. H. He graduated at the New Hampton Theological Institution, 1850; was ordained over the Baptist Church at Marlboro, N. H., 1852; removed to Sanbornton Bay, where he remained about three years; then removed to Addison, Vt., 1858; thence to Whiting, Vt., 1860. Died at Derry, N. H., Aug. 29, 1865, while on a visit to his friends there. His family all being at Whiting at the time, and expecting his return, went to the depot to meet him, when a messenger came announcing his death. They had six children:

(i) EDWIN[8] CHAPIN WARE, born Oct. 8, 1852, at Marlboro.

(ii) MARTHA[8] JANE WARE, born Dec. 25, 1853, at Sanbornton, N. H. She married Sept. 11, 1874, Willis K. Emerson, of Cleveland, Ohio. They have removed and settled there.

(iii) LAVINA[8] MARIA WARE, born July 19, 1855, at Sanbornton. She has lived since 1866 with her Aunt Lydia Harris, at Harrisville.

24

(iv) WALTER[8] HENRY WARE, born April 25, 1859, at Addison, Vt.

(v) MARY[8] FRANCES WARE, born May 30, 1860, at Whiting, Vt., died at Whiting, May 6, 1862.

(vi) MARY[8] EMILY WARE, born March 6, 1866. Her mother has resided in Milford, where this child was born, since her husband's death.

5. HENRY[7] HEALD, born Dec. 23, 1825, married May 5, 1852, Frances Marshall, born July 9, 1828. Their children were:

(i) JOHN[8] HENRY HEALD, born Aug. 9, 1861, died 19th same month.

(ii) ARTHER[8] CHASE HEALD, born May 14, 1863, died Dec. 15, 1868.

(iii) ESTELLA[8] FRANCES HEALD, born April 27, 1869.

Mrs. Frances (Marshall) Heald died Sept. 28, 1869. He married second, Mrs. Lucy Jane (McKean) Hill, Aug. 24, 1872, born May 31, 1824.

6. LYDIA[7] HEALD, born Feb. 7, 1828, married Sept. 14, 1847, Milan Walter Harris. He is the son of Milan Harris, woolen manufacturer at Harrisville, N. H., and is in company with his father, brother, and Gen. S. G. Griffin. She, Lydia, died Aug. 24, 1873. They had three children:

(i) EDGAR[8] CARLTON HARRIS, born July 17, 1849, at Harrisville. In 1873 was a clerk in a wholesale dry goods store in Boston.

(ii) ARTHER[8] LE WELLER HARRIS, born Jan. 15, 1857, at South Royalston, Mass., died Aug. 4, 1858, aged 1 year, 6 months and 19 days.

(iii) KATE[8] WINFIELD HARRIS, born July 30, 1863, at Harrisville. "She has been very sick for the last ten months (Feb. 15, 1873), and not expected to live twenty-four hours. A bright and charming little girl; but 'Death loves a shining mark.'" (*Albert Heald.*) She died Feb. 25, 1873.

7. WILLIAM[7] HEALD, born June 14, 1830, died Feb. 25, 1831.

*22

24

8. DAVID[7] HEALD, the eighth child of Oliver and Patty (Wright) Heald, was born Oct. 6, 1832. He married first, at Milford, Nov. 27, 1856, Mary Susan Frost, born March —, 1833, at Ashburnham. She died Nov. 9, 1858. They had one child:

(i) ELLA[8] FRANCES HEALD, born at Milford, April 15, 1858, died Sept. 21, same year.

He married second, Oct. 22, 1862, Mary Elizabeth Stone, born June 19, 1840, daughter of Calvin, born June 10, 1801, and Elvira (Wallingford) Stone, born Aug. 24, 1804, all born at Marlboro. She was educated at Marlboro and Dublin; taught school at Marlboro when sixteen years old; came to Milford in 1858, and taught in public school there until her marriage. She is much devoted to religious interests, and prominent in efforts for the welfare of the young. Mr. Heald is largely engaged in the manufacture of furniture, employing at times 75 or 80 hands. He sells mostly in Boston, and is absent a portion of the time for that purpose. During these times family religion is not neglected at home. They have had five children:

(ii) EDWARD[8] STONE HEALD, born Jan. 31, 1864, at Milford. He was (i) of Mary Elizabeth (Stone) Heald.

(iii) FRANK[8] HERBERT HEALD, born June 19, 1866.

(iv) FLORENCE[8] MABEL HEALD, born Nov. 11, 1867.

(v) CLARA[8] MAY HEALD, born Dec. 15, 1870, died Aug. 1, 1871, at Milford, buried there.

(vi) MARY[8] SUSAN HEALD, born at Milford, May 20, 1873.

9. ALMIRA[7] HEALD, the ninth child of Oliver and Patty Heald, was born Jan. 20, 1835. She married, at Harrisville, Nov. 24, 1859, Alonzo French, born in Orange, Mass., Nov. 14, 1831. One child:

(i) GERTRUDE[8] MIRA FRENCH, born June 2, 1862, at South Royalston, Mass. She died June 23, same year.

10. EDWIN[7] HEALD, born July 4, 1837, died Aug. 17, 1840.

24

vi. HENRY[6] WRIGHT, (*Oliver and Martha[5] D.,*) the sixth child of Oliver and Martha (Dunster) Wright, was born Sept. 17, 1795, in Nelson, N. H.; lived with his father on the "old clearing;" was a farmer and carpenter. He united with the Congregational (Orthodox) Church about 1817. He married Lois Kimball, June 5, 1821, at Nelson. She united with the same church about two years before their marriage. They carried on the farm, living in the same house (the new house), but in separate apartments, until the death of his mother, 1838. His father lived with him until his death, 1846. Henry then removed his family—one half of whom he had buried in Nelson (three of that half died of scarlatina), to Clinton, Mass. They both removed their church membership from Nelson to Clinton when they went there, 1849. He died in Clinton, Aug. 26, 1852, was buried in Clinton Cemetery. His widow, Lois, (1872) lives with her daughter, Lura Ann. She gave the family history. They had eleven children, all born in Nelson, only three of whom are now living. The deceased ones were all, except Ellen and Selena, buried there. Unmarried.

1. EMALINE[7] WRIGHT, born April 6, 1822, died Aug. 6, 1843.

2. SELENA[7] WRIGHT, born May 19, 1823, died Sept. 5, 1859, in Clinton, buried there, unmarried.

3. ANNA[7] WRIGHT, born July 9, 1825, died April 24, 1832, of scarlatina.

4. LOUISA[7] WRIGHT, born June 9, 1827, died March 6, 1833.

5. HENRY[7] DUNSTER WRIGHT, born March 14, 1829, died April 22, 1832, of scarlatina.

6. JANE[7] ELIZABETH WRIGHT, born Feb. 13, 1831, died April 12, 1832, of scarlatina.

7. LURA[7] ANN WRIGHT, born May 28, 1833, when 16 years old united by profession with the Orthodox Church in Nelson, Rev. Gad Newell. She removed her church relations to Clinton at the time of her father's removal there. She taught school in Holden. In 1866 and '67 she was connected with the Freedman's School in Washington, being in charge of the boarding department.

24

8. SAVINA[7] WRIGHT, born June 8, 1835, united with the church in Nelson, with her sister, Lura Ann. She graduated at the Framingham Normal School, and taught at Lancaster and Gloucester (Cape Ann). At the time of the capture of Vicksburg, she went out there and taught in the· Freedmen's schools in Vicksburg, Washington, D. C., Alexandria, and Montgomery, Ala. Returned to Clinton, June, 1872, and in September established with her sister, Lura Ann, a genteel boarding house.

9. ELLEN[7] ALLETTA WRIGHT, born Aug. 6, 1837, united by profession with the Congregational (Orthodox) Church in Clinton, graduated with her sister Savina, and taught in Waltham two or three years; married Aug. 1, ——, Henry Francis Morgan, of Philadelphia, by whom she had one child,[8] who died an infant. She, Ellen, died in Camden, N. J., was brought to Clinton and buried. Her husband married again, in Gloucester, N. J.

10. GEORGE[7] HENRY WRIGHT, born June 25, 1840, died Feb. 21, 1841.

11. EMMA[7] HANNAH WRIGHT, born Sept. 17, 1843, united with the Baptist Church in Clinton by profession of faith, married April 21, 1862, Alonzo Stedman Davidson, of Clinton. He enlisted a private in Co. G, 36th Mass. Regt.; was promoted to captain; was with Gen. Burnside in Ninth Corps; was in many battles, but escaped unhurt. At the close of the war he was mustered out at Readville. His wife visited him when in camp at Annapolis, and staid ten days. He is now a merchant at Clinton. They had four children, all born in Clinton:

(i) HATTIE[8] EMMA DAVIDSON, born April 23, 1863, died Oct. 3, same year, buried at Clinton.

(ii) NELLA[8] LUCRETIA DAVIDSON, born April 4, 1866.

(iii) SUSIE[8] SALINA DAVIDSON, born May 30, 1868.

(iv) CORA[8] LUCILLA DAVIDSON, born Aug. 1, 1871.

vii. ANNA[6] WRIGHT, *Oliver and Martha*[5] *D., Jason,*[4] *Henry,*[3] *Jona.,*[2] *Henry,*[1]) the seventh child of Oliver and Martha (Dunster) Wright, born July 9, 1797, (July 8 in

24

Family Bible at William P. Wright's,) married Nov. 12, 1816, Cyrus Greenwood, of Dublin, N. H., born June 4, 1792. She was a member of the Congregational Church in Nelson. They lived in Nelson about two years, when they removed to Winchester, N. H., where he carried on the wooden ware business. She died Feb. 9, 1826, and was buried at Winchester. Her remains were disinterred and brought to Nashua afterwards. He died at Nashua, N. H., June 23, 1864, was buried there. They had five children:

1. NEWELL[7] GREENWOOD, (*Cyrus,[6] Oliver Wright and Martha[5] D.,*) born Dec. 10, 1817, at Nelson. He was named for Rev. Gad Newell, the pastor of Nelson Church, and is their only son. When about six months old, his father removed to Winchester. He married Sept. 4, 1839, Elvira Scott. She was born in Vernon, Vt., April 19, 1814. In 1845 he went to Lowell, Mass., as an overseer in the weave room of the Middlesex Corporation. He removed to Concord, N. H., 1848, and thence to Nashua, N. H., where he is a pattern maker. They had three children:

(i) AVALINE[8] LUCINDA GREENWOOD, born March 31, 1841, at Winchester, died at Nashua, Jan. 7, 1861, unmarried.

(ii) MARY[8] ELVIRA GREENWOOD, born March 14, 1847, at Lowell, and now (1872) lives at her father's, in Nashua. A letter from her father, Aug. 18, 1875, says:

"In the first place, I must say my daughter, Mary, was married Jan. 30, 1873, to Mr. Charles W. Atwood, of Nashua, born Sept. 7, 1841; occupation a painter; and now, I am happy to state, they have a little daughter, who wishes to be remembered to you as another branch of the Dunster descendants."

We are happy to add:

(1) GRACE[9] EDITH ATWOOD, born May 9, 1875, at Nashua, N. H.

(iii) CYRUS[8] NEWELL GREENWOOD, born Aug. 22, 1850, at Concord, N. H., is their only son, and lives at his father's. Is a machinist. Unmarried.

24

2. MARY[7] ANN GREENWOOD, born Nov. 20, 1819, at Winchester, married March 5, 1846, John B. Knight, at Nashua. He was born at Hancock, N. H., Sept. 5, 1821. She died at Nashua, July 9, 1852. They had:

(i) CHARLES[8] NEWELL KNIGHT, born Dec. 22, 1846, died Aug. 22, 1847, at Nashua.

(ii) CHARLES[8] A. KNIGHT, born June 9, 1852, at Nashua, and died there, July 23, 1854.

3. AVALINE[7] GREENWOOD, born Nov. 9, 1821, at Winchester, married at Nashua, Nov. 17, 1842, Samuel Atherton, born at Richmond, N. H., March 26, 1812. They had:

(i) ALICE[8] L. ATHERTON, born at Winchester, May 17, 1852, died there, Sept. 5, 1869.

4. LUANA[7] GREENWOOD, born Sept. 21, 1823, at Winchester, married Sept. (18?) 25, 1845, Henry T. Chickering, born Jan. 9, 1822, at Concord, N. H. She died at Concord, July 3, 1849. They had:

(i) ADALADE[8] L. CHICKERING, born at Concord, Sept. 22, 1846. She married at Concord, Nov. 2, 1870, Frank W. Greenwood, born at Ludlow, Vt., Aug. 11, 1835.

(ii) ANNA[8] WRIGHT CHICKERING, born at Concord, Feb. 10, 1849. Unmarried.

5. BETSEY[7] GREENWOOD, born at Winchester, July 26, 1825, died at Nelson, Aug. 23, 1826.

viii. LUCY[6] WRIGHT, (*Oliver and Martha[5] D., Jason,[4] Henry,[3] Jona.,[2] Henry,[1]*) born Aug. 28, 1799, was the eighth child of Oliver and Martha (Dunster) Wright. She was the third daughter. She married June 1, 1824, Leonard Butterfield, born at Dunstable, N. H., very near Dunstable, Mass., the adjoining town. (The survey referred to on p. 138, cut Dunstable near the centre.) His ancestors were all named "Leonard;" and three generations of them, by that name, lived on the same farm, and died in the same room. The memoranda of her family were made in the same apartment. Lucy lived at her uncle's, Isaac Wright, where she became acquainted with Mr. Butterfield. Imitating her mother, she

24

went home to Nelson and "fixed her things," to use her own expression, but it took her longer (because, doubtless, she had more of them). After staying a whole year at Nelson, she was married, and immediately went to the old farm in Dunstable. It is a splendid one, lying in the valley of the Merrimac River, and near Salmon Brook, on which are manufactories to some extent. Her husband died Nov. 29, 1857. She carried on the place for eight years afterwards, but "was glad to give it up. It was too much care for a woman of my years." She was then 66 years old. The place is now carried on by her son, Dexter, who is constantly improving it. They have built a new barn, at the cost of near $3000. She is now (1875) living in his family, with much comfort. In the family wanderings, she had become lost to us, when the accidental mention of her name by a gentleman in the cars, revived the remembrance of her, and an answer to a letter gave notice of her welfare and enclosed her photograph. They had five children:

1. LEONARD[7] SYLVESTER BUTTERFIELD, born June 6, 1825. He married Janette Carruth, in Lowell. They live in Westford, Mass., and have one child, a boy, of eighth generation.

2. MARTHA[7] DUNSTER BUTTERFIELD, born Jan. 4, 1832, mar. Aug. 21, 1856, Adonijah Woodbury Howe, born in Jaffrey, N. H., Sept. 25, 1825. He was the only son of Luke Howe, M. D., and Mary (Woodbury), oldest daughter of Peter Woodbury, of Francestown, N. H. He graduated at Dartmouth College, 1850, and located as a physician in Dunstable, 1851. They live in Westford, and have had ten children, all except one, living:

(i) WOODBURY,[8] b. May 12, 1857, at Dunstable, Mass.

(ii) HENRY[8] DUNSTER, born Sept. 6, 1858, died April 6, 1860.

(iii) MARY[8] ELIZABETH, b. Feb. 2, 1860, at Dunstable.

(iv) EDWARD[8] DEXTER, b. Dec. 27, 1861, at Dunstable.

(v) EMMA[8] ISABEL, born June 27, 1863, at Hollis.

(vi) CHARLES[8] LUKE, born Dec. 26, 1865, at Jaffrey.

(vii) HELLEN[8] WRIGHT, b. Jan. 3, 1868, at Dunstable.

24

(viii) FANNIE[8] LOUISA, b. June 11, 1870, at Dunstable.

(ix) FREDERIC[8] WM., b. Sept. 30, 1872, at Westford.

(x) Son,[8] born June 5, 1875, at South Lancaster.

3. HENRY[7] BUTTERFIELD, the third child of Leonard and Lucy (Wright) Butterfield, died in infancy.

4. GEORGE[7] BUTTERFIELD, born March 8, 1839, worked at the Lawrence Mills, Lowell, several years; married Oct., 1844, Mary E. Taylor, born at Dunstable. They live in Westford, and have:

(i) EMMA[8] GRACE BUTTERFIELD, born Feb. 6, 1869.

(ii) LUCY[8] ARDANA BUTTERFIELD, born Feb.13, 1871.

(iii) IDA[8] RACHEL BUTTERFIELD, born April 26, 1875.

5. DEXTER[7] BUTTERFIELD, born March 15, 1842, assisted his mother on the farm after his father died. He enlisted in Co. A, 2d Mass. Regt. Vols., 1860; was in the battle at Gettysburg, and at the taking of Atlanta; was sergeant when mustered out, Oct. 14, 1864. He married Dec. 7, 1865, Georgiana Kenny, of Leominster, Mass. She was on a visit to her grand-parents, in Dunstable, and unexpectedly, a short time after, made that her future home. They live at the old mansion. They have for their first a pair of twins, born Oct. 13, 1870:

(i) ARTHUR[8] DEXTER BUTTERFIELD.

(ii) ALICE[8] LOUISA BUTTERFIELD.

x. MYRA[6] WRIGHT, (written in some records "Mira") was the tenth and youngest child of Oliver and Martha[5] (Dunster) Wright, born Dec. 30, 1802, at Nelson. She married at Nelson, Dec. 31, 1834, Edwin Jewell, born at Winchester, N. H., April 22, 1809. He was second cousin to Gov. Jewell, of Connecticut. He was a wool carder by trade. In April, 1838, he lost his right arm by having it caught in the machinery at the factory at Harrisville, where he was employed at the time. It was amputated just below the elbow. His general health suffered from it, but he was able to follow his trade until a short time before his death. Myra[6] died at Hinsdale, Oct., 1848, (Oct. 7, 1849, *Abiel Wright's Record*). Her husband married a second time, and died Sept. 8, 1856; both buried at Winchester. They had four children:

24

1. GUSTAVUS[7] ELBRIDGE JEWELL, born Dec. 30, 1835, died July 11, 1838, at Winchester, buried there.

2. SARAH[7] ADALINE JEWELL, born Oct. 21, 1836, died at Winchester, April 5, 1837, buried there.

3. ELBRIDGE[7] ELEXES JEWELL, born May 17, 1838.

4. GUSTAVUS[7] DUNSTER JEWELL, born April 27, 1840, died Aug. 9, 1847, buried at Harrisville.

3. ELBRIDGE[7] ELEXES JEWELL, (*Edwin and Myra,[6] Oliver and Martha[5] Dunster, Jason,[4] Henry,[3] Jonathan,[2] Henry,[1]*) was born May 17, 1838, at Harrisville, and is the only one of Myra's children now living. He gave the information of this family. In a letter, March 16, 1872, he says: "My brother, Gustavus Dunster, lived to be about eight years old, and until the receipt of your letter, to-night, I had not the faintest idea where his name came from; and am glad that I can now claim some relationship to some one on mother's side. Mother died in October, 1848. Father married again; and, as is often the case, my step-mother's views did not fully coincide with mine. Father died Sept. 8, 1857. The widow kept most of the property, except a few things I bought at auction. When she died I was in the army, and her effects were sold by her brother, so that I have nothing in the shape of records, not even the Family Bible. That was sold, and I have never been able to get any trace of it.

"As for me, I have taken care of myself most of the time since mother died. [He was then ten years old. S. D.] When the rebellion broke out I was one of the first to volunteer. Enlisted April, 1861, in Co. A, 2d Regt. N. H. Vols. We went to Washington, and before we were half drilled or armed, were 'On to Richmond!' via Bull Run. Of this you have as good a general history as I could give you. I was taken violently ill with congestion of the lungs, and discharged in August, 1861. I went home and after a long illness recovered, and tried to enlist again, but was refused; but in the draft of '63 was accepted, and went in Co. F, 5th N. H. Vols. Saw no action at all this time. We were stationed at Point Lookout, Maryland, for more than a year, guarding rebel

23

24–25

prisoners. While there, was taken ill again with the old lung trouble. After a long siege in hospital, was discharged, and came here on trial for three months. That was nine years ago, 11th Nov., 1872."

The place he referred to was a situation as steward in Dr. Barstow's Private Asylum for the Insane—Sanford Hall—at Flushing, Long Island, where he still remains.

He married Jan. —, 1867, Emma M. Thomas, of West Boylston, Mass. "She is a descendant on the father's side from Robert B. Thomas, of almanac fame." Her father was Aaron M. Thomas, who died the same day she was born, June 28, 1840. Her mother died Dec. 31, 1846.

"I am said to resemble mother more than father. I enclose a photograph of myself and little girl, so that you may judge what manner of man your cousin may be. Will only add that I am six feet three inches in my stockings."

The photographs came safe; also one of his mother subsequently.

They have one child:

(i) SUSIE[8] EMMA JEWELL, born Oct. 29, 1868.

25. vi. ISAIAH[5] DUNSTER, (*Jason,*[4] *Henry,*[3] *Jona.,*[2] *Henry,*[1]) was born in Cambridge Second Precinct (West Cambridge), April 10, baptized April 12, 1761, by Rev. Samuel Cooke. There is no reasonable doubt that he went to Mason at the time his father moved there, 1769. We can find no certain trace of him in the records of that town. In the office of Secretary of State at Concord, N. H., Hon. J. B. Hill, the historian of Mason, finds his name as a soldier in the Revolutionary war. We think that he was that person for whom "Jos. Herrick was paid £56 8s. for two and a half bushels of rye delivered Jason Dunster, for part of his son's hire for six months service in the year 1781." In that year he was 20 years old, and a suitable person to enlist in such service. In 1782 his father was paid £1 15s. 0d. 1qr., L. M., "for his son's hire." We have seen that it was improbable that it was Henry, his brother. Jason, his

25

next younger brother, was at that time in the Regular Continental Army, for whose pay the town of Mason never assumed the responsibility. His youngest brother, Samuel, was but 14 years old, and no evidence or tradition exists of his having been in the service. Isaiah was never taxed in Mason. The presumption is strong that as soon as he was of age (21), he left Mason to find employment, as many did then and have since, in the neighborhood of Boston. It is certain that he lived in Roxbury all his married life.

He owned or built the hotel called the " Punch Bowl," between Dedham and Boston, at the junction of the turnpike with the old road. In addition to the hotel business he cultivated a farm, and did wagon marketing steadily at Boston. He accumulated a good property there. He is remembered as a well-dressed, somewhat portly, and very genial gentleman, who could well enjoy a joke. With his brother, and their wives, neither of whom ever had any children, he used occasionally to visit their relatives in New Hampshire. On one of these happy seasons, his brother gave to one of the little flaxen haired children a half pistereen. Seeing this he took from the loose change in his pocket a whole one, and holding it up, said, " Now, my lad, which of these would you rather have?" The boy had sagacity enough to choose the larger coin. Giving up the other, and not then comprehending the power of plus and minus, and amazed at such generosity, he ran to his mother to show her what a large piece of money " Uncle Isaiah" had given him, while the uncle for whom he was named had only given him a little one.

The records of Roxbury would probably give many items of his history. Want of opportunity, and the fact that he left no posterity to be interested in his life, must be the apology for this limited account of him.

He married, in Roxbury, ——, Mary Davis, born June 23, 1771, daughter of Deacon Noah and Elizabeth (Weld) Davis, who lived about half a mile distant. Her nuptial ring, when new, inlaid with hair work and engraved M. D., was given to his niece, Mary[6] (Dunster) Kimball, and by her to her youngest daughter, Abby[7] (Kimball)

25-26

Lynch. The date of his marriage is not known. He died in 1815, at Roxbury, and was interred there. He left the larger part of his property to his widow, although it is understood that he was very generous to the sons of his sister, Rebecca Swallow, one of whom was employed in marketing for him. His widow died July 4, 1833. They never had any children.

26. vii. JASON⁵ DUNSTER, (*Jason,⁴ Henry,³ Jona.,² Henry,¹*) the seventh child of Jason⁴ and Rebecca (Cutter) Dunster was born at Cambridge (now Arlington), March 27, baptized April 3, 1763, by Rev. Samuel Cooke. It is very probable that his father brought him to Mason in 1769. No evidence is found of his being there until after the Revolutionary war. There is a well founded tradition that he was "bound out" to a man in Lexington, Littleton or Groton. His widow, in 1852, stated this to be so. Her memory was at that time truly wonderful, although she was then 84 years old. It is hardly credible that when he was only six years old such a disposition was made of him. This making a "chattel" of ones own children, though very common in Massachusetts then, did not usually take place till the age of about ten or twelve. Whatever may have been his *legal condition*, it is certain that he lived there, and that the person to whom he was *given* or *bound out* consented to his enlisting in the Continental Army. The papers, executed in 1818, to obtain a Revolutionary pension are official and copied:

"I, Jason Dunster, of the town of Mason, in the county of Hillsboro, N. H., a Resident Citizen of the U. S., Husbandman, now in the fifty-sixth year of my age, do Solemnly Swear that sometime in the month of March, A. D. 1781, I was enlisted a private soldier in the Continental establishment in the Revolutionary war for the term of three years, and joined my company (the 3d), commanded by Capt. John Hastings, in the ninth Regt. of the Massachusetts line, commanded by Col. Henry Jackson, in the month of July of the same year, at a place called White Plains, having previously served better then three months after my enlistment at Boston,

26

under a Capt. of Engineers, whose name I do not recollect; which term of three years I faithfully served until I was discharged after the peace, which discharge is herewith exhibited, and in the words following, viz:

"By the Hon. Major General Knox, commanding the American forces on the Hudson River. Jason Dunster, Soldier in the fourth Massachusetts Reg., being enlisted for three years, is hereby Honorably `Discharged from the service of the United States.

"Given in the State of New York, the 31st of December, 1783. By the Gen'l Command.

J. KNOX, M. Gen'l.

"Registered in the Books of the Regiment.
THOS. H. CONDY, Adj't., P. S."

"I further state that I have never been on the Pension list of Invalids. I have a small farm, but am embarrassed with debts and am reduced in my circumstances, and think I need the assistance of my country for my support. In the year 1780 I served six months in Capt. Manfield's Co., in Col. Bailey's Regt., in the Mass. Line in the Continental establisment at West Point, and in the Jerseys, so called. JASON DUNSTER.

"Sworn to this 15th day of April, A. D. 1818. Before me. J. K. SMITH, Associate Justice of the Court of Common Pleas."

The court omitted from his statement some facts not necessary to procure the pension, but which rightfully belong to his revolutionary history. He enlisted in April, 1780, for six months, was mustered in at Concord, Mass., and did duty in Boston until his enlistment into the three years' service. When dismissed from the six months' service for that purpose, he received no pay or clothing. When the Massachusetts regiments were reduced he was transferred to the regiment commanded by Col. Brooks, Capt. Lincoln and Maj. William Hull. The regiments were again reduced, and he was transferred to the 4th Mass. Regiment, from which he was discharged, as stated above. When Lord Cornwallis surrendered, 1781, he was in the Northern Department

*23

26

of the army, under Gen. Heath.   With the army he had the small-pox, in the winter of their encampment at Valley Forge.

Many are the stories he used to tell about the march through the "Jarseys," and the daring exploits with the marauders about the Hudson, who were designated "Cow Boys."   They were a horde of "Tories," commanded by Col. Delancy, who made their stronghold at Morrisania, and scoured the fertile valleys of the Hudson, sweeping off forage and cattle for the British Army in New York.   He was discharged from the army at "Pickskill Hiths" (Peekskill Heights), New York.

His application for a pension was accompanied by a schedule of his property, appraised by Joseph Sanders and Dr. Willis Johnson, in which is noted a pew in Mason Meeting House, and horse stable standing near by, valued at $33 for both.

This application for pension was unsuccessful.   He was deemed by those who held the purse strings of "Unc'e Sam" at that time, and who were careful of his "change," to have too much property to be in "Indigent circumstances and need the assistance of their country for their support," which the law required. There is abundant evidence, however, that he had "pretty hard scratching," as they say in New Hampshire, to keep along, and certainly could not educate his family so well as he desired.   After about two years the law was altered so as to be less equivocal, and he received a pension for the rest of his life; and his widow, also, by a more generous law, received a like pension during her life, to which in her old age she often referred as a means of comfort.

When he was discharged, his pay was in "Continental money," a specimen bill of which ($30.00) he kept till his death, often dryly remarking that when he came back from the army he could not get a breakfast for it, else he should have spent it.   That bill safely reposes among other ancestral mementos.

"Congress engaged to make good to the Continental and independent troops the difference in the value of their pay caused by this depreciation." (*Irving's Life Washington, Vol. iv., p.* 37.)

It is not amiss here, to inquire how poor a man must have been to get that pension. Happily the means are not wanting. At the time of trying to obtain his own, he also tried to get a pension for Jonathan Foster, who then lived in his house. The inventory of Foster's estate, appraised by the same Joseph Sanders and Willis Johnson, was this:

"He has no real estate, but has been a Town Pauper for a number of years. He is at present Boarding himself, by the consent of the Town, living with Mr. Jason Dunster.

PERSONAL ESTATE.

Farming utensils..........................	$2 00
Hollow ware..............................	1 00
1 pine table.............................	25
4 old chairs.............................	25
Crockery ware...........................	75
	$4 25

Jos. Sanders, } Appraisers."
Willis Johnson, }

Even this did not satisfy some of the quibbling lawyers. They reasoned thus: "Jonathan Foster is a pauper of the town of Mason. The town of Mason is not in 'indigent circumstances;' therefore Jonathan Foster is not in indigent circumstances."

The papers were sent to Washington, and John C. Calhoun, who was then Secretary of War, (whatever may have been his notions of sociology, and who was never suspected of selling offices,) saw at once the fallacy, and immediately sent him the certificate.

"War Department. Revolutionary Claim.

I Certify that, in conformity with the Law of the United States of March 18, 1818, Jonathan Foster, late a private in the Army of the Revolution, is inscribed on the Pension List Roll of the New Hampshire Agency at

26

the rate of eight dollars per month, to commence on the 1st day of May, 1818. Given at the War Office of the United States, this 5th day of October, 1819.

J. C. CALHOUN, Sec. War."

Mr. D. usually collected Foster's pension and kept his papers, which are found among his own.

After the disbanding of the army, Jason Dunster returned to Lexington, Mass. In 1786 he was taxed for the first time in Mason. He was then 23 years old. In that year he bought of Charles Barrett a lot of land in Hancock, N. H., near his brother-in law, Oliver Wright. In 1800 he bought of Joseph Meriam, his wife's father, lot No. 10, in the 18th range of the town of Mason. This lot of land had been bought of Benj. Knowlton, May 1, 1792, by Mr. Meriam, a few months before the marriage of his daughter, Polly, to Jason Dunster, and they lived on it from that marriage till their death. In 1818, the widow of Knowlton, who had not signed the deed through neglect of the purchaser, made a claim for dowry. This gave great annoyance to him and the family whom they had raised on the farm, and cost him almost as much as he paid for the whole. The thirds were set off by metes and bounds, which she did not expect or desire; but it produced a settlement, although at great cost. It is understood, however, that his father-in-law assisted him much in this trouble.

He owned several other tracts of land in the vicinity, most of which was woodland, which he cleared for lumber and cord wood, the best of which then brought $1.50 to $2.00 a cord, and the best of hard wood lumber $4.00 per M. In 1816 he and his son, Jason, bought one undivided third part of the saw and grist mills at the

NOTE.—Jonathan Foster died in Ashby, March 31, 1821, aged more than 100 years. For near forty years he was supported by the town. "He had an inveterate antipathy to work of all kinds, but was fond of hunting. He would imitate on all fours the running and leaping of a bear. Hence his cognomen, 'Old Bear' Foster." (*Mason Cen.*, 1868, *p.* 22.)

He had a son who also lived at Dunster's house. His wife was almost a "giantess," if such a word exists. She could lift a barrel of cider, and, holding it on her knees, drink from the bunghole.

26

Upper Falls on the Souhegan River, a quarter of a mile from his residence. This mill privilege was the first in Mason, and the nucleus around which the village in that town was built. It was at first called Barrett's Mills, then Dakin's Mills, then Mason Harbor. About 1812 the name was formally altered, when a liberty pole was erected on a prominent knoll, to which a signboard was nailed, lettered "Souhegan Village," and a bottle of New England rum thrown at it by Bill Russell, the architect. It missed the mark, but a second attempt was more successful, and the name was instantly changed, amid a volley of small arms, patriotic toasts, and plenty of Medford rum. "Souhegan Village," however, did not last long. There was a village at the mouth of that river by the same name. They objected to the assumption, and the younger sister was quietly named "Mason Village." This name she bore with dignity till 1872, when an "unpleasantness" in town matters occurred, and the village made a successful secession and came out "Greenville." We are sorry to say that the good old town just past her centennial became estranged, and hope yet to see a reunion under the old flag.

This mill privilege commanded the water of the whole river, although the lot was small, and bounded on the east "by the stone wall on the line of Timothy Dakin's hog pasture." It is now occupied by the Columbian Factories, a very large and successful corporation; and we can assure our friends that the recent name of that village, whatever may have been its origin, has no reference to the colloquial use of that word as sometimes applied to people.

Jason[5] Dunster did a great amount of town business; was Selectman for three years in succession, looked after the poor of the town, &c. With his old papers is a bill against the Factory Company in New Ipswich for the labor of Susannah Zwears, one of the poor of the town, for five months in the factory at ten cents a day, which was paid promptly. She was then woman grown, and the town made a profit on her labor. The town also through him as their agent, "bound out" two of widow Fish's daughters till they were eighteen years old. At

26

the time of the small-pox in that town, he had most of the personal superintendence of the disease, for which his army vaccination had prepared him.

In 1821 the village was established as a separate school district, and many plans for building a school house were proposed. Among the rest, he suggested that it be done by subscription. The plan was rather jocularly received, particularly so by Deacon Dakin, between whom and himself an opportunity for banter was never missed. The Deacon, turning to him, said, "Well, Dunster, I will give as much as you will." Dunster instantly replied, "I will give one half of the whole cost. Now, Deacon, don't back out." The Deacon was not the man to do that. The district immediately took measures to legalize the offer, and voted plans to work by, bought the lot, and chose a committee to inspect the work. Deacon Dakin gave a bond to pay his half to Dunster. He gave the district a bond to do the whole. In these bonds they are styled "Benefactors." A splendid (for that day) brick school house was built, and in it was learned the rudiments of science so useful to our after life. The original papers of this "Benefaction" are in good preservation and filed away for his descendants.

His early entry into the army taught him more of the world than literary accomplishments. His handwriting and orthography would almost defy Champolion, but his memory supplied the defect. In his later days his mental powers were somewhat impaired. They were always eccentric. He died March 21, 1828, aged 65, was buried at Mason Centre, in the Dunster group, and a suitable stone placed over his grave by his widow.

He married at Mason, April 18, 1793, Mary (Polly in many records) Meriam. She was daughter of Joseph and Mary (Brooks) Meriam,* and born Oct. 28, 1768, at Concord, Mass. She was an early member of the Mason

---

* Mason was classed with Brookline (then Raby) for representation at the General Court. "At a legal meeting held at the public meeting house in Mason, December ye 11th, 1775,

"Voted, that those men that sent their votes by Joseph Merriam to the Moderator of said meeting have the privilege of putting in their votes for the choice of the above said representative,

26

Congregational Orthodox Church, and at the time of her death the only member (except perhaps one) who belonged to that church when Rev. Mr. Hill was settled, 1790.

Hon. John B. Hill sent us the original certificate of their publishment, which he found among the papers of his father (Rev. E. Hill). It is copied verbatim:

" *This may Certify that Jason Dunster Ju*. *& Polly Meriam both of Mason have been Published for marriage in the Town of Mason aforesaid as the Law Directs*.....
Jan. 28*th* 1793.......*Joseph Barrett Town Clark*."

She was a woman of kind and candid disposition, and it is believed that no one ever saw her out of temper. When over 80 years old she fell and broke her thigh.

namely: Obadiah Parker, Joseph Ball, Jonas Fay, Abel Shed, Thomas Robbins, Nathan Wheeler, Seth Robbins, John Lawrence."

These were among the "first families" in Mason. At the same meeting (perhaps they had heard from Raby),

"Voted, that James Scripture and William and Elias Eliot have the liberty of putting in a vote for their fathers, their fathers being absent, whose votes were wrote after the meeting began."

"Voted, that the aforesaid Obadiah Parker, Joseph Ball, Jonas Fay, Abel Shed, Thomas Robbins, Nathan Wheeler, Seth Robbins, John Lawrence, have their votes thrown out."

A difficulty followed, and March 7, 1776, the town voted "to send Joseph Barrett to present the proceedings of the town meeting, held Dec. ye 11th, 1775, to the General Court, which the town look upon it that it was not conducted according to Liberty and Justice; and that if the Hon'ble Court do not approve of the proceedings of the town meeting, that the above said Joseph Barrett pray the General Court to set them in some way agreeable to their pleasure for to have the privilege of representation." (*His. of Mason.*)

We are not advised of the result of this commission, and are interested only in the question: *Does* history repeat itself? Whatever it may have been, "Grandfather Merriam" did not suffer in reputation, for as soon as Raby was out of the union and Mason got big enough to send a representative of her own, he was the first one chosen, and the historian of that town says of him: "No citizen of Mason was ever more worthy of this mark of the confidence of his townsmen."

26

From this she never recovered so as to walk, but could get about the room in her chair with castors on it till near her death.   Rev. Mr. Austin preached her funeral sermon, from which a few remarks are copied:

"For more than three-score and ten years was the church of Christ on earth blessed with her fellowship and prayers. —— ——

"While this event is her gain it is our loss.   Several years since she received a fall by which she was entirely disabled from walking.   Until that time her place was promptly and punctually filled in the sanctuary.   She loved to meet with the prayerful in social meeting.   Her place was often filled when others nearer the house of God and younger in years would find excuse for absence. When she worshipped at the centre of the town it was her custom to walk [three miles]. —— ——

"She also willed [deeded] to this church and society her pew here, that by it she might contribute to the support of the gospel after her death. —— ——

"In her last days her affections were manifested with the sweetness and simplicity of childhood.   In my last interview she grasped my hand with earnestness, and when told I would call again, she replied, 'Yes, if I should live so that you can see me again.'   The next time I called it was to give the last look to the dead. She departed without a groan or struggle, in the 90th year of her age."

The funeral services were at Mason Village.   From there she was buried at Mason Centre, and placed beside her husband, which she had repeatedly requested, and a stone similar to his, which she also desired, is erected with the inscription:

"Mary Meriam, widow of Jason Dunster, born Oct. 28, 1768, died May 5, 1858, aged 89 years, 6 months, 7 days.   Mother, thou art gone to the grave."

She made no will, but often said that she wished her property divided equally to her living children, and the children of those deceased; and always added, "Don't disagree about it."   We are happy to state that her dying

26-27

request was fully and literally carried out, and a record made of that fact in Hillsboro Probate Records. Her real estate was sold to her eldest daughter's husband, who had lived on the place and owned the other two-thirds, and her personal property is with her heirs exactly as she desired.

They had seven children, all born at Mason:

28 §. i. JASON⁶ DUNSTER, born July 15, 1794.

29 §. ii. MARY⁶ DUNSTER, born Feb. 16, 1796.

30 §. iii. ISAIAH⁶ DUNSTER, born Dec. 10, 1798.

31 §. iv. BETSEY⁶ DUNSTER, born April 20, 1801.

32 §. v. SAMUEL⁶ DUNSTER, born Aug. 1, 1803.

vi. REBECCA⁶ DUNSTER, born Sept. 25, 1805, was baptized June 8, 1806, and died June 25, 1810, of scarlatina, was buried at Mason Centre.

vii. JULIANNA⁶ DUNSTER, born Feb. 21, 1808, was not baptized, although her mother said she was carried to meeting once. She was a remarkably healthy and promising babe. Her mother, as usual, put her into her own bed, near the middle of it, and left her to go to sleep. The babe crept to the side of the bed and fell off, striking on the side of her head. She dislocated her neck, and died almost instantly, uttering only a single cry, July 26 of the same year; six months old, buried at Mason Centre.

27. viii. SAMUEL⁵ CUTTER DUNSTER, born April 20, 1766, was the eighth and youngest child of Jason⁴ and Rebecca (Cutter) Dunster, and was named for his grandfather, Samuel Cutter, whose genealogy may be found in "Cutter Family of New England," by William R. Cutter, page 52. He was baptized April 27, 1766, by Rev. Mr. Cooke, "privately, being sick." He was only three years old when his father removed to Mason. The proprietors of No. 1, afterwards called Mason, made provision for schools as early as the incorporation of the town, 1768. The schools and the church were the objects of solicitude; and in them the children were trained to the best of the means; so that, though brought up

24

27

afar from the privileges at Cambridge, he had an equal education with the rest of the children, and appears to have made good use of that little learning which has been miscalled a "dangerous thing." That he worked in early manhood "down below," as the towns near Boston were then called, may be true, as tradition intimates. If our memoranda be correct, he was not taxed in Mason till 1798, being then 32 years old, while his brother, Henry, was taxed at twenty. His name appears · in the division of school districts in 1791. He bought his father's farm about 1798, which he sold about 1803.

In 1805 he bought of James Cowee, of Gardner, fifty-five acres of land in Ashburnham, Mass., which he divided with Joel Barrett. The next year he bought of Caleb Wilder, for $40, about one acre of land in Ashburnham, "lying near said Dunster's mill."

In 1819 he bought of Joseph Jewett other land and mills, about one mile northeast of the meeting house, and further down the stream which makes the outlet of the large ponds forming the head waters of the Nashua River. On these he established works for spinning cotton yarn, which were among the first of the kind after its introduction by Slater in Pawtucket.

In addition to the cotton spinning he had a saw mill. These he continued to carry on with good success for many years; selling the yarn, done up in five pound bunches, to the storekeepers and other people in the neighborhood. He sold the factory and privilege to Samuel Barrett, and took in exchange Barrett's farm. Barrett enlarged the works, built a large hotel and other houses, and soon failed, involving Dunster to a very large amount.

Afterwards he bought back the old mill, and recommenced the manufacturing of cotton yarn. The machinery had worn itself nearly out. New inventions to facilitate the production and cheapen the expense had been elsewhere made. He had not kept pace with improvements, and consequently found himself unable to compete in what at first had been a lucrative business. He lost again; and finding it useless to go on further, gave up the business to save what he had not already

27

lost.   To one of his nephews he made the sage remark: "Old men must not begin new business."

He was kind and generous, without hope of reward, thoroughly honest, positive in opinion, and eccentric in practice.   He made a will giving the interest of his estate to his wife for her support, and directing the principal to be given one-half to Joel Barrett, one-quarter to Abel Foster, of Brookline, N. H., one-quarter to Lyman Townsend, of ——, Vermont, neither of whom were related to him.   In his will he directed that if his wife married again she should have no income from his estate, but the legatees should come into immediate possession of his property.   She married again, "but was sharp enough to get them to sign a writing to. have her still draw the interest."

In the will he says: "I give to Martha Wright, the wife of Oliver Wright, living in Nelson, N. H., the sum of twenty-five dollars."   And adds: "The reason I have made this disposition of my property is that I have no children, and no brothers or sisters, except the said Martha Wright; and all the relations of myself and wife are so numerous and scattered about that should I have given my property to them all, or made a selection of a portion of them, I fear it would occasion more ill-will and hard feelings than all of it would be worth."

On his death bed he was dissatisfied with the disposition he had made of his property, and sent for the maker of the will, who, after ascertaining that his wife, who supposed he had more property than he really possessed, would be content with the scanty means and unnatural condition the will imposed, declined to alter anything, and let him depart, mind unquiet, will disowned.

He had some crude notions, original with himself, of what has lately been called "development."   He died April 19, 1839, was entombed at Ashburnham Centre, in a tomb he owned.   His remains were removed to a lot in the new cemetery at Ashburnham, at which grave stones were erected and the lot well ornamented by his widow.

He was twice married.   His first wife was Hannah Townsend, the oldest daughter of Samuel and Hannah (Lawrence) Townsend.   She was born in Northborough,

27-28

Mass., Aug. 8, 1770, married by Rev. Mr. Hill, Jan. 12, 1792, at Mason, where her father then lived. She died at Ashburnham, Aug. 8, 1826, was entombed, but removed when her husband was. He married second, Madamoisella Townsend, the youngest daughter of the same parents, and sister to his first wife. She was born in Mason, March 19, 1794. She took care of her sister in her last sickness. They were married in Ashburnham, March 1, 1827. Neither of his wives ever had any children. After his death she married, Sept. 5, 1851, Silas Keyes, of Temple, N. H. He died Nov. 25, 1852. She has since resided with a nephew in Ashby, Mass. Is in good health, although now (1876) 82 years old, and 25 a widow, having, to use her own expression, "hard work to make both ends meet." She contributes to the ancestral relics a "silver brooch worn by your uncle in his young days." It is like a Past Master's jewel, although he was not a Freemason. On it he engraved very roughly "S. D."

28. i. JASON⁶ DUNSTER, (*Jason,*⁵ *Jason,*⁴ *Henry,*³ *Jona.,*² *Henry,*¹) the first child of Jason⁵ and Mary (Polly Meriam) Dunster, was born July 15, 1794, and was baptized by Rev. E. Hill, as his mother stated, but we find no mention of the baptism in Mason Church records. In early boyhood he had all the advantages of the school that the town could afford, being about six weeks in winter and ten in summer, and going nearly two miles for that scanty education; but he made good use of those advantages. At an early age he was qualified to instruct others, and did it with good success, especially in the government of unruly boys. In a district at New Ipswich those boys had turned a former teacher out of doors, and were "masters of the situation." He was solicited to continue the school, to which he consented, after he had closed the one he was then instructing, being about a fortnight. At the time appointed he went to the school house and found all present, to whom he addressed his inaugural. "Boys! I have come to keep this school, and I *shall* keep it. First class, take your places to read in the Bible, beginning where you left off." There was no more rebellion in that school, but a most

Jason Dunster died March 1878 at Needham, Mills, N.Y. and there

28

successful result, especially so in those who had made the disturbance. In the other parts of the year he worked on his father's farm. When about twenty-two years old he bought with his father one-third of the mills at Mason Village, and attended them. Being a central locality, there was a large custom of grinding and bolting grain and sawing lumber, which employed his whole time. He was popular among the people of Mason, and was early *honored*, as it was then called, with military office, rising in grade till he commanded the company in the west part of the town, and is still dubbed "Captain" among his neighbors.*

In the war of 1812 he volunteered as an ensign, and was stationed at Fort Washington, in Portsmouth, N. H. For that service he now receives a pension. When the troops were no longer desired he was entrusted with paying their wages, which was done by Treasury Notes.

He wrote to his father, Nov. 4, 1814: "There are no funds on hand for the payment of the troops, and many think we shall not receive the money; but we are determined not to leave the place till we *are* paid."

* The military etiquette of those days happily belongs to the lost arts. We, too, have a paper bearing the broad seal of the State of New Hampshire, and certifying, nearly after the fashion of that of a house servant from her last place of employment, to our fidelity, *courage*, &c., and promising us "to hold Office during good Behaviour;" signed, David Lawrence Morrill, "Governor of Our State."

The annual training came off, by statute law, on the first Tuesday of May. The enrolled men, living near an officer, made it a point to call on him before daylight to "wake him up." Their arrival was announced by the discharge of a musket. The officer soon made his appearance at the door, pretending surprise when he was saluted by a volley from the whole squad, in rather uncomfortable proximity to his feet. This done, they were invited in, and "Egg-nog," for which the hens and New England rum had been laid under contribution, was furnished, with the request to "drink just as much as you want to."

At one o'clock, as directed by summons, they appeared on the common, when the First Sergeant showed his skill by placing the men in line according to their height, then by manipulation and counter-marching he got the small ones in the centre. This being done, the Captain was informed that the company awaited his orders. He then drew his sword, marched and exercised them

*24

28

At the arrival of the treaty of peace in Mason he was at home; and the people of the village met at the store, which was illuminated at its two front little windows, to hear the treaty read, which duty was assigned to him as being the best reader in the village. He read it. Some of the more discerning ones asked, Is that all? He replied it was; and read it again. They rejoined: There is nothing said about "Free Trade and Sailors' Rights;" and wondered, as many have since, "what they had been fighting about."

He sold his part of the mills about 1818, and engaged with a brother-in-law in manfacturing satinets in Ashburnham. This was done to assist his partner, who had become embarrassed. Like most undertakings of this kind, it was disastrous to him. He went to Westport, in the neighborhood of the Adirondack mountains, in Essex Co., New York, and there purchased wild land, which he has since made into a good farm. But it was by hard labor at chopping, rafting on the lake, attending

awhile, when they were drawn up in line and each soldier inspected. If any were deficient in equipments they were fined according to penal code: For priming wire and brush, six cents; for two spare flints, two cents; all of which was collected by due process of law.

Then followed various evolutions, among which "whipping the snake" was a favorite one. This consisted in following the Captain in single file while he marched in the form of a helix till near the centre, when he faced about and came out from the apparent snarl at the same point he entered. This, if successfully done, usually produced the applause of the bystanders. Sometimes, however, some of the company failed to follow their leader, and the result was a tangle, which again required the manipulation of official skill. The company were then ordered to stand at ease, which simply meant to sit down on the ground, when they were served, at the expense of the commissioned officers, with an abundance of grog made of Medford rum, of which they partook *ad libitum*, being served by the corporals as their part of the expense. After other maneuvers, followed a sham fight, not always true to name, and the company was dismissed with a patriotic speech.

The whole regiment was called out in the fall, when the town furnished the provisions of the day, not omitting a quarter of a pound of powder to a man, plenty of new cider and a bountiful supply of liquor, all of the best quality. After the close of a training, we have seen a single soldier drink, on a wager, a pint

28

saw mills, and teaching in the winter, that he was enabled to lift his embarrassments and build a comfortable house and barns. Now, the West Shore Lake Champlain Railroad runs through that farm. He writes: "After 55 years in this place, we can now get to the rest of the world without crossing the lake." He is now (1876) living on that place, with good health, and able to do considerable work, although in his 82d year. He, with his wife, visited his friends in New Hampshire, Massachusetts and Rhode Island, in the fall of 1875.

He has been twice married; first, to Azubah Felt, Oct. 23, 1816. She was the daughter of Aaron Felt, of Temple, N. H., and born Oct. 31, 1794. They lived at his father's, in Mason Village. She died there, Oct. 23, 1818, of consumption; was sick most of her married life of just two years. She was buried at Mason Centre, and a suitable stone is erected at her grave in the Dunster group. They had one son:

of Medford rum without taking the measure from his lips; and can add, too, that he appeared afterwards "none the worse for liquor" [Please understand this in a colloquial sense.]

This custom of *drinking* was at that day almost universal at trainings, raisings, huskings, and even at funerals, where, after a hopeful consolation to the bereaved, a solemn admonition to the impenitent and a prayer for their conversion, a pail of "toddy" was carried round, first to the minister, then to the chief mourner, and following established precedence, to the children of the neighborhood.

In an old Day Book, 1818, given us by a relative just outside of the Dunster family, whose husband "kept store," which curiosity has gathered among the "relics," are found 18 charges for rum within 25 consecutive entries, which are relieved once by trusting "Joseph *Noble* for ¼ ℔. Tobacco, 10 cents," for which he paid cash 12 days afterwards; and again, "to one hair comb, 10 cents, and ¼ ℔. of Tobacco, 9 cents," charged "Widow Scribner," and posted into ledger. One cent discrimination in favor of the widow.

With such surroundings many fell. An intimate friend caught a glimpse of this gulf when just on its edge, and was startled. Planting himself on "I *will!*" he wrote in cypher, a habit then common with him, a little pledge, the first he ever heard of, and formed a society, "alone, all alone;" and fifty years of faithfulness have secured property, favor, confidence, respect and honor, of which the blindfolded goddess often gets credit which belongs not to her.

"Speak but the commanding word, I will, and it is done."—*Chaucer*.

28

i. HENRY[7] JASON DUNSTER, born at Mason, Sept. 19, 1817. After the death of his mother he lived with his grand-parents (Dunster), at Mason Village, until 1823, when his father had married again, and Henry Jason was carried up by his grandfather when he removed the goods of Jason[6] to Westport. He lived with his father the most of the time until he married, Nov. 7, 1840, Martha Jane Persell, born June 21, 1820, daughter of David and Elizabeth (Williams) Persell, of Georgia, Vermont. Martha's mother died when she was four years old. They lived one year in a house near his father's, after which they lived in a house on another lot bought by his father. He was of a melancholy temperament, but was highly respected. He died June 26, 1857. Buried at Wadham's Mills Cemetery.

His widow lived in Westport, keeping the family together with the assistance of his father. She was married second, Nov. 30, 1867, by Rev. E. Marsh, pastor of the Methodist Episcopal Church at Elizabethtown, N. Y., to Henry Bateman Lewis, of that town; his second wife. She had kept his house before her marriage.

Henry[7] and Martha had seven children, all born at Westport:

1. ELIZA[8] EULACIA DUNSTER, born Dec. 15, 1841, lived at Crown Point, Benson, Vt., and at Westport with Mr. Allen, who had adopted her sister Harriet. On her thirtieth birthday, Dec. 15, 1871, she married Oscar Taylor, of Westport; his second wife. She died, after a very distressing sickness of a week, Sept. 26, 1872, at Elizabethtown, and was buried at Wadham's Mills, beside her husband's first wife. She was a member in full communion of the Methodist Episcopal Church, and "died in happy confidence of blessed immortality," leaving no children.

2. LUCIUS[8] FELT DUNSTER, born Aug. 22, 1843, died Dec. 9, 1848, of scarlatina; buried at Wadham's Mills.

3. WHEATON[8] HENRY DUNSTER, born Nov. 26, 1845, died Dec. 23, 1848, of scarlatina.

4. MYRON[8] NEWELL DUNSTER, born Jan. 9, 1848, died Dec. 17, 1848, of scarlatina.

28

Thus they lost three little children in a fortnight by that mysterious and apparently uncontrollable disease.

5. HARRIET[8] MARIA DUNSTER, born Oct. 23, 1849, was adopted after the death of her father by David Lewis Allen, of Westport Village, with whom she lived until her death, June 10, 1865, by consumption; buried at Wadham's Mills.

6. WHEATON[8] HENRY DUNSTER, born Oct. 11, 1852, lived with his maternal aunt's husband, Deacon Hiram Hale, of Georgia, Vt. He married May 31, 1875, Elizabeth Waller, of Georgia, Vt.

7. ATHELIA[8] SARAH DUNSTER, born Jan. 1, 1855, lived with her mother till about 1865, then with her grandfather. She married Nov. 24, 1875, George B. Mitchel, a sash and blind maker, of Westport, born ——, 1853?

Jason[6] Dunster married second, Hannah Hardy, of Westport. She was born May 12, 1797. The next year after he went to Westport he was taken sick with a fever, and for some days little hopes of his recovery were entertained. During all this sickness she carefully nursed him till he recovered. Soon after, she was taken down with the same typhoid fever, which was then at that place alarmingly prevalent. She was also dangerously sick. This acquaintance, begun in sympathy, ripened into affection, and was consummated by their marriage, Jan. 19, 1823. He had built a house on the clearing he had made, and they commenced housekeeping there. His father removed most of his goods and furniture to the new locality, and with them took the little boy of his former wife, who had in the meantime lived with him. He was kindly received by his new mother, an event not always realized. Her kindness to him never waned. They had eight children, all born at that home in Westport:

ii. AZUBAH[7] FELT DUNSTER, named for his first wife, was the first child of the second marriage. She was born Sept. 14, 1823; lived at her father's till about 20 years old, and then with her uncle, in Providence, R. I.; returned home afterwards in feeble health, and died of

28

consumption, June 2, 1849. "She was an amiable and intelligent young woman; a member of the church, and died in faith;" was buried at Wadham's Mills.

iii. LOUISA[7] PHEBE DUNSTER, born Sept. 6, 1825, united by profession with the Orthodox Congregational Church, of which she is still a member. She was married May 10, 1849, by Rev. Charles Spooner, at Westport, to Morris Sherman, born May 6, 1824, in Essex (town), Essex Co., N. Y. He was son of Humphrey and Anna (Reynolds) Sherman; learned the trade of mason about 1836; worked on the prison at Clinton and other public buildings. Religious opinions Evangelical. They boarded with her father's family about five years, when they bought a house at Wadham's Mills Village, in which they have since lived, except two years when he carried on a farm in Westport. They have had four children:

1. SARAH[8] AZUBAH SHERMAN, born May 1, 1850, educated at the public schools and at Vergennes (Vermont) High School, taught in 1868 and every year since. In 1874 she taught in Camanche, Iowa. In the fall of 1875 she was affianced to Frank Henry Stacy, of Clinton, Iowa. He was born at Westport, N. Y., May 29, 1850. His parents settled in Camanche about 1855, with the colony from Westport, when it was open prairie. He was telegraph operator at Low Moor, but is now a conductor on the Chicago and North Western Railroad. She went home that fall, and returned to Iowa April 26, 1876. They were married on the 30th, at Camanche.

2. ELLERY[8] JAMES SHERMAN, born Nov. 25, 1852, educated at Westport public and High School, and at Elizabethtown High School, where his record stands the highest in the school. He learned the trade of fancy painter in Vergennes, Vt. Has marked original design. Was occupied as accountant and superintending business at Wadham's Mills. In June, 1876, he went to Camanche, Iowa. He graduated at the Business College, Clinton, Iowa, March 1, 1877.

3. CLARA[8] HANNAH SHERMAN, born June 19, 1857, died Dec. 21, 1862, of scarlatina; buried at Wadham's Mills.

28

4. CARROL[8] MORRIS SHERMAN, born April 15, 1864, living with his parents at Wadham's Mills.

iv. SARAH[7] DODGE DUNSTER, fourth child of Jason,[6] named for her Grandmother Hardy, whose surname was Dodge, born Sept. 8, 1827, was married at Westport, by Rev. Mr. Spooner, May 30, 1848, to Wait Powers Bristol, born at Panton, Vt., Oct. 28, 1821, son of Aaron and Irene (Powers) Bristol. She died when Wait was 16 days old. They kept house at Wadham's Mills till June, 1857, when they removed to Camanche, Iowa, where they own a quarter section of good land, about three miles from Camanche Village, and about a mile and a half west of the Mississippi River. Have a good stock of cattle and horses, and are in comfortable circumstances. They have had six children:

1. HARRIET[8] (called HATTIE) MERRICK BRISTOL, born at Westport, Sept. 29, 1850, died of consumption, at Camanche, May 4, 1871; unmarried; buried at cemetery near Camanche Village.

2. JULIA[8] HANNAH BRISTOL, born at Westport, Sept. 19, 1852, died of inflammatory fever, June 9, 1858; buried beside her sister.

3. MARY[8] LOUISA BRISTOL, born at Camanche, Nov. 15, 1858, died there of lung fever, Jan. 7, 1862.

4. FRANK[8] JASON BRISTOL, born July 17, 1861, died of dropsy, at Camanche, Feb. 21, 1866; buried at Camanche.

5. CHARLIE[8] SAMUEL ISAIAH BRISTOL, born Sept. 19, 1868, was named for *all* his uncles.

6. EUGENE[8] ELLERY BRISTOL, born Feb. 15, 1871.

v. CHARLES[7] CARROL DUNSTER, (*Jason,*[6] *Jason,*[5] *Jason,*[4] *Henry,*[3] *Jona.,*[2] *Henry,*[1]) the fifth child of Jason and fourth of Hannah (Hardy) Dunster, was born March 19, 1830. He worked on the farm at home till of age, and remained in the vicinity until 1853, when he was employed by the surveying party of the West Shore Lake Champlain Railroad, from Whitehall to Plattsburg. That survey being done, he went to Illinois and resided a year at Niles, twelve miles north of Chicago; afterward went

28

to Lockport, Ill., and was employed in Norton's ship-yard one season; then was engaged in building bridges and locks on the Illinois and Michigan Canal. In this employ he continued till 1856; then went to Minnesota, where he located in the County of Steel a land warrant for 160 acres, which was granted to his father for services in the war of 1812. He spent that winter in Illinois, but returned to Steel County and staid till 1859. Having sold this land, he went back to Westport and engaged in farming. He now carries on his father's farm besides his own, and is making a successful business, and improving the place by buildings. He is administrator on the estate of Orrin Hardy, in Westport. He married March 19, 1860, when just thirty years old, Rachel Benson, daughter of David Benson, of Elizabeth-town, N. Y. Her father was in the war of 1812, and now receives a pension. Three children:

1. CLARA[8] LYDIA DUNSTER, born Dec. 23, 1867.

2. ELSIE[8] HANNAH DUNSTER, born Oct. 30, 1871.

3. MARY[8] ELIZABETH DUNSTER, born Feb. 11, 1875.

vi. SAMUEL[7] KIMBALL DUNSTER, (*Jason,[6] Jason,[5] Jason,[4] Henry,[3] Jona.,[2] Henry,[1]*) was born Aug. 14, 1832. He lived with his father till of age, having the advantages of the common schools only, although early manifesting an unmistakable desire for a more thorough education which was beyond his reach. On the 11th of April, 1853, he left home for the East. After this time he kept a diary of his experience. A few of the leading events only are copied for want of space. The journal ought to be preserved.

After working at various places he settled down at Andover, Mass., near the Phillips' Academy, and engaged in making shoes for a living, and at the same time attended the Academy as a student, hiring a room and boarding himself, living alone, and working all the time he could spare from his studies. He had worked awhile at Lowell, and while there or at North Tewksbury, became personally interested in religion, and joined the open communion Baptist Church there, although residing at the time at Andover. He was baptized by

28

immersion, June 11, 1854. Leaving Andover with regret, he went to Lynn, where he could obtain a better living at the same business.

At Lynn he became acquainted with Elizabeth Jane Wallace, daughter of Moses and Rachel (Hanson) Wallace, of Cohasset. She was born March 10, 1843, at Sandwich, N. H. They were married Oct. 16, 1860, at her father's, (Beachwood,) Cohasset. They kept house at Lynn until Nov. 26, 1861, when he felt impelled by duty—a point he always regarded—to enlist into Co. K, 24th Regt. Mass. Vols. He finished up what work he had on hand of his employers, J. P. Newhall & Co., who urged him to stay with them, offering better inducements, but he declined. He took his wife and babe to her father's, and then made preparations to join his company at Readville. He writes:

"Dec. 1, 1861—Sunday—Remained with my wife at her father's. Attended meeting with her. Donned my uniform for the first time. It seemed the saddest day of my whole life. Lizzie cannot endure the thought of my leaving.

"Dec. 2—Monday—Was obliged to leave in the morning. If I had fully realized what the separation would have cost me, I fear my patriotism would have been insufficient to have taken me away. Neither of us have been able to rest for several days. It does not seem possible for a person to suffer more than my wife has. But the word had been passed. I could not turn back without feeling disgraced, although I was not legally holden. With earnest prayers for our preservation, I had to leave. I do not wonder that Lizzie fainted."

He staid at Readville a fortnight, then went by Providence to New York, thence by steamer, Eastern Queen, for Annapolis. Near here they encamped, and staid till Jan. 7. Dec. 31st he writes:

"I like as well as I expected, and do not regret enlisting. *But I do want to see Lizzie and the baby.* What wouldn't I give to be at home awhile. The month has seemed almost an age. Well, live and hope."

25

28

Jan. 7, 1862, they went on the steamer Admiral for Roanoke.

"Jan. 19—Chaplain held meeting for officers, but none for us. We had a social meeting on deck.

"26th—Walked on the beach and enjoyed reading testament and *thinking* (underscored in diary).

"Feb. 7—Attempted landing at Roanoke. Steamer aground about six miles from the battle which was then raging. When it commenced I could not keep the tears from starting, but as it progressed I became reconciled to it, and felt disappointed that we could not be there and take our part."

The troops from the abandoned steamer were landed and marched to take part in the battle. He writes:

"We met a stream of wounded men passing to the rear. The first had lost an arm. The stump was bandaged, but the blood covered his clothes and the litter on which he was carried. Then would come one supported by two comrades. Another with one side of his head shot away, and his brains scattered over his clothes. Many followed, some just alive. It was a sad, a sickening sight."

Then follows a most graphic account of the battle, and the occupation of Newbern, N. C. His diary gives each day's experience, and some of it is written in a blank memorandum found at Newbern, a part of which had been used as an "Express Freight" book, and elegantly lettered as such.

While at Newbern he was a constant correspondent of the "Bay State," printed at Lynn, over the signature "D. K. S." His initials reversed. He refers to near a hundred letters he wrote between June and Dec., 1862.

July 21 of that year, "A man killed by lightning in camp." Aug. 13th, Dr. Green gave him the temporary charge of the hospital, and soon after he was appointed Steward, which post he held till the close of the war.

Among his diary items is a chronology of events and battles, sketches of marches, and many very interesting notes of actual observation. In the pocket of a note-

28

book we find a photograph of his child, which appears to have been with him during his whole army life.

At the close of the war, about 1866, he went to Philadelphia, and was engaged with Mr. Turner in making and putting up lightning conductors on buildings, which he carried on till his health failed, in the summer of 1872, when he came to his father's at Westport, and died there of consumption, Nov. 26, 1872.

His wife staid at her father's and at Mr. Cutting's, a neighbor of his, for about three years, then with her Aunt Cutting at Weston, Mass. In January, 1865, she removed to his father's, Jason Dunster, of Westport. Her husband visited her there on furlough about that time, and then returned to the army again. She died at Westport, of consumption, Nov. 16, 1866. They were both buried at Wadham's Mills Cemetery.

We find in the Essex (N. Y.) Republican of Dec. 12, 1872: "Died at Wadham's Mills, Nov. 26, 1872, Mr. Samuel K. Dunster. —— —— He was amiable, candid and conscientious. He died a peaceful death. His submission was genuine. A few days before he died he remarked: 'I desire to be saved; but am willing to be lost should it be God's will.' The last few days were characterized by growing faith. He spoke calmly of his funeral; requesting his pastor to speak to the living, exhorting Christians to be faithful, and sinners not to delay to repent and believe in Christ. His last words were whispered—'I am happy.'   W. H. W."

They had but one child:

1. CHARLES[8] KIMBALL DUNSTER, born at Lynn, March 23, 1861. He lives with his uncle, Charles C. Dunster, to whom his father specially commended his only child. He is being well cared for by his grandfather and uncle both.

vii. ISAIAH[7] HARDY DUNSTER, (*Jason,[6] Jason,[5] Jason,[4] Henry,[3] Jona.,[2] Henry,[1]*) the seventh child of Jason[6] and sixth of Hannah (Hardy) Dunster, was born at Westport, Feb. 28, 1835. He lived at his father's until he went West, in 1859. In the summer of 1857 he united

28

with the Methodist Church at Westport by profession.
Of that church he has been and is still a firm and consistent member.

At the particular request of the writer he put on paper
the subsequent experience of his life, which, in most instances, we have quoted from his manuscript, abridging
in some things, but not altering even his language in
regard to his "war experience." That is given exact.

"Feb. 14, 1859—Left home intending to go to Kansas. Stopped at Camanche, Clinton Co., Iowa, to visit
a sister (Sarah D. Bristol), but have made my home
with her since. Was engaged in farming till I went
into the army. The destructive tornado of June 3,
1860, passed directly over Camanche. Its width was
about half a mile, but its power seemed unlimited.
Quite a number were killed or injured west of us. At
Camanche (a village of perhaps forty houses) there were
thirty-two persons killed and many severely injured.
Buildings were blown like chaff; and the statement is
made, on reliable authority, that a log lying at a saw
mill on the *west* bank of the Mississippi, intended for
sawing, was found on the *east* bank after the tornado
had passed. The river there is not less than half a mile
wide; we think more.

"At the time Fort Sumter's guns echoed through the
land, being busily engaged in farming, but feeling that
my life work was set for me to do, and with a full understanding of a soldier's hardship and requirement, I
enlisted on the 12th of August, 1861, in Co. A, 8th Iowa
Infantry. The company remained the same during the
war, being filled up from time to time with new recruits.
Went into quarters at Davenport, Iowa, and after being
organized and equipped, went to Benton Barracks, St.
Louis. After a stay there, took cars on railroad west
to Sedalia, and then marched to Springfield, Mo., and
thence back again by railroad to Sedalia, where we spent
the winter, in small cloth tents, upon the prairies.

"This trip was a very hard one for us at the time,
being unused to it, and such a short time doing it, and
wholly uncalled for, with insufficient rations. We lost

28

twelve men out of Co. A upon this trip by the effects of
it.   But what was that when the bet was won—for there
was a bet of $200 between Gen. McKinsly and Col.
[Adjt. Gen.] Steel, marching against time.   About first
of March took cars and came to St. Louis again.   Boat
down the river to Cairo.   Up Ohio and Tennessee to
Pittsburgh Landing, and into camp.   Very many sick,
owing to bad water we had and other causes.

"The well remembered Sunday morning of April 6th,
firing commenced between the two armies, and continued to increase till about ten o'clock, when we were
actually engaged at the front.   We had a rise of land
for our position, and held it until four o'clock, after
being charged upon.   At this time our forces had been
driven upon the right and left, and we were surrounded
and made prisoners to the number of about 2500.   [He
gave us *orally* a somewhat amusing account of his capture.   In assisting a wounded comrade he had become
separated from his company.   After the firing ceased
an officer approached him and ordered him to throw
down his gun.   He felt indignant at the order, the
thought of being a prisoner not entering his mind; so
he said, "Who are *you?* to make such a demand."   The
officer said, "They will shoot you if you don't do it."
Not noticing his uniform, and at the moment not able
to recall the word "Confederate," he said, in his blunt
way, "*Are* you Union or rebel?"   To which the officer
replied, "We are none of your —— Lincoln Yankees.
We have beat you; own up and throw down your gun."]
"In the main, at this time, we were well treated.   They
gave us much credit for our fighting.   'Boys, we've got
you, but you fought well.'   They marched us about six
miles that night.   Spent the night in mud and rain.
Next day to Corinth.   Took cars thence to Memphis.
Remained there one day.   Then cars again to Jackson,
Miss., then to Mobile.   Boat on the Alabama, Tombig-
bee and Black Warrior rivers to Tuscaloosa, where four
hundred of us remained one month in two rooms of an
old tobacco warehouse, fitted up for prison use.   Our
situation was not a pleasant one.   The filth of the place
and the small amount of food were just enough to keep

*25

28

soul and body together, if it did not stay too long. To
live in any comfort at all we often had to kill off the lice
known as grey backs, which, by the way, I have no great
love for, especially when I did not get enough to eat and
could not well spare any of myself for them to feed upon.

"After a month's stay we were again on the move
down the river, which we enjoyed much better than at
Tuscaloosa. Up and down in such a climate, and many
things of interest were enjoyed, but the hunger was not
pleasant. Down next to Mobile, and then up to Montgomery, where we met many of our boys who were taken
with us, but sent to a different place. To this time we
had not known what our destiny was to be. Here, we
were rejoiced at a parole. Parole was that ' I promise
upon Honor that I will not again take up Arms in defence of the North, nor aid in any form whatever until
I am regularly exchanged.' This parole we separately
signed. Went to Atlanta, Chattanooga, and Birdsport
[?], on Tennessee River. Waited a day or two, then
down the river a few miles, where we were received by
our men, and took cars for Huntsville. What a privilege this, after 58 days of a prison's fate, to feel again
that I was in a measure a free man. What a pleasure to
see the Stars and Stripes instead of the one we had been
under. There were about 400 of us, and we left about
the same number at Tennessee River who expected soon
to follow us; but our men refusing to receive them, they
went back for four months more to prison life, and
many still remain in a prisoner's grave. I cannot excuse
our government for it, either. Perhaps I never did
relish a meal more than the first one at Huntsville of
coffee and hard-tack.

" During my prison life I received favors for which I
felt grateful. One was a pair of new shoes. Marched
from Huntsville to Columbia, 75 miles. Had it not
been we were going north we could not have done it,
many being weak. Cars to Nashville, where we staid
three weeks; thence to Cairo and St. Louis. Here at
St. Louis, I think, we were worse used than we had been
in all our prison life. By order of Gen. Schofield we
were to be furnished with arms [those detailed] and

28

should be detailed for guard duty. There was a feeling of indignation at thus being called upon to violate and compromise our honor. I was among the first to be detailed. Not going, I was waited upon and marched to guard-house. To this I did not object. I was placed under guard with ball and chain, which I wore one week. During this time I was called before a court martial, and told that if I would go upon duty I would be released. As I did not choose to do so, the trial went on, and being called to speak for myself, I said that I was taken prisoner in the discharge of my duty, and fairly taken. That while a prisoner I was of no use to the government, and that I had given my word upon honor that I would not take up arms nor do soldiers' duty until I was exchanged, and I would not unless the War Department ordered it, and then I would hold them responsible, if such a thing could be, and not till then. Taken back to guard-house. At end of a week we were called to headquarters to see if we wished to be released to do duty; but as we did not, they hand-cuffed two together and sent us back again. Remained under guard 40 days. The sentence, being six months labor on public works, with ball and chain, upon half pay, was then remitted and I was released. In the meantime, the governors of Iowa and Illinois being informed of the facts, wrote to Gen. Schofield that with such a state of affairs and with such indignities heaped upon the soldiers, enlistments had stopped. Some of the paroled prisoners had done duty under protest.

"I was exchanged about the first of January (1862), and the regiment being reorganized, we were again on our way down the Mississippi River, and went into camp at Dicksport, La. We were set to work cutting the levee to let the water into the much talked of Vicksburg Canal. Went on a campaign to Jackson; then to rear of Vicksburg; then took position in front and rear of enemy's fortifications. Upon Grant's charge our brigade was held as a reserve. It being a failure, with great sacrifice of life, it was given up, and a different plan gave us Vicksburg. Went under Gen. Sherman to Jackson; then came back and went into camp near

p. These Hand cuffs are now in my Library — a memento, that a "Dunster" will submit to indignity and insult & tyranny rather than violate his word. — S Dunster

28

Vicksburg to recruit and rest. After spending summer resting, was again up the river to Memphis. On my way, I was presented with a Captain's commission by a schoolmate who was Lieut.-Colonel of a colored regiment then being organized. From Memphis went to Pocahontas, where I was honorably discharged. Proceeded to Little Rock, Ark., the headquarters of the regiment. Remained about three months, and nearly completed the company, when the Lieut.-Colonel, five captains and ten lieutenants were dismissed, without any trial, to give place to others, by order of Gen. Steel. For this outrage and injustice the War Department severely reprimanded Gen. Steel, and offered to reinstate these officers; but we were out of the service, and I, for one, felt too indignant to accept again, and the War Department honorably discharged me."

He returned home again with poor health, but soon improved, and has since made his home at his sister's, in Camanche, employed in farming and teaming. He is still unmarried.

viii. MARY ⁷ MERRIAM DUNSTER, named for her grandmother, was born Nov. 4, 1837. She was well educated, and of an affectionate disposition. To her, her Grandmother Dunster, at her death, gave the gold necklace she had long worn. She lived at her father's, with the exception of a few months, during her whole life. She died of consumption, Dec. 21, 1872, unmarried. From the Essex County Republican we copy:

"This is the third affliction the household has been called to suffer in as many months—the last of three heart wounds of which each succeeding one was deeper. In Elizabethtown, Sept. 26, Mrs. Eliza E. Taylor, a grand-daughter, died suddenly. Mr. Samuel K. Dunster, a son, who had passed most of his time away, returned in October last and died of consumption, Nov. 26. Now we chronicle the death of a daughter, the youngest and tenderest of the household, upon whom its interests and sympathy were centered. For ten years she suffered with poor health. The last two years were characterized by gradual but certain decline. For the

28–29

last few months it has been apparent to all that she must soon bid us adieu. She died rejoicing in hope. During the last few days her mind was calm and peaceful. 'Not my will, but Thine be done' was her prayer. She desired grace to enable her to wait with patience until the summons came. 'Meet me in Heaven' was her last message to absent friends. Her passing away was falling asleep.

> 'Asleep in Jesus! peaceful rest
> Whose waking is supremely blest.'

As shadows, cast by flitting clouds, chase each other across the fields and out of sight, so have they, the dear departed, fled, one after another, to the unseen realm.

W. H. W."

ix. ELLERY⁷ GARFIELD DUNSTER, the ninth child of Jason and eighth of Hannah Dunster, was born Jan. 8, 1844. He died Dec. 11, 1848, of scarlatina.

This was the fourth child who died in that family circle in three weeks of that fatal disease.

29. ii. MARY⁶ DUNSTER, (*Jason,⁵ Jason,⁴ Henry,³ Jona.,² Henry,¹*) the second child of Jason⁵ and Mary (Polly Meriam) Dunster, was born Feb. 16, 1796. She was baptized by Rev. E. Hill, Feb. 25. She had all the advantages of the common school as it was then, but no other. She made good use of that, and for the times was well educated. She lived with her parents, and was of great service in spinning and weaving by hand. In that way all the domestic clothing was made. The ponderous old loom adorned the attic long after its usefulness had departed. At the time of the great September gale (1815) she was engaged in preparing for her marriage outfit. The roof of the then new house, strongly framed with ridge-pole and braces, was lifted so as to show at the top a wide opening, but falling back into place it remained firm, and she received no injury. She married Dec. 28, 1815, Benoni Cutter Kimball, born in Temple, N. H., March 13, 1791. He was the son of Isaac and Sally (Sarah Cutter) Kimball. They lived on the second farm in Temple, on the Mason Vil-

29

lage road. (*History Temple.*) He was named for his mother's brother, Dr. Benoni Cutter. He was a house carpenter; was finishing the inside of Jason Dunster's new house when he became engaged to his daughter.

He built a new house at Mason Village, in which they at first lived, and afterwards built another there, in which they lived until he bought the two-thirds of the Dunster homestead, about 1835, and the other third at the death of Widow Mary Dunster, 1858.

He was an influential member of the Congregational (Orthodox) Church, and took a prominent part in organizing the new church at Mason Village. His wife was a devoted member of the church to which they both united, in 1826, at the same time by profession, and had all their children baptized at Mason Centre. In all the religious enterprises they took an active and leading part. She died very suddenly of heart disease, May 31, 1864, and was buried at Mason Village Cemetery. He died March 29, 1865, of diabetes, which painful sickness he bore with Christian patience. He was buried beside his wife. They had fifteen children, all born at Mason Village. To these parents was granted the blessed privilege of seeing every one of them, except the two who died in infancy, united with a Christian church by profession, and all worthy members of society.

1. BENONI[7] KIMBALL, (*Benoni and Mary[6] Dunster,*) the first child of Benoni and Mary (Dunster) Kimball, was born Dec. 23, 1816. He was a carpenter. Worked in Boston on Shawmut Avenue Church. He united with Mason Centre Church. He had been baptized, Sept. 16. 1826, on profession of parents, but like his ancestor, doubted its validity. He was married by Rev. Mr. French, at Peterboro, N. H., to Jane A. Spring, who was then living at Mason Village. They lived in Boston, where he died of small-pox, July 15, 1840. When his friends told him of his approaching end, after a moment's silent prayer, he said, "The Lord's will be done." He was buried at the strangers' burying ground. They had no children. His wife returned to Mason, and after two or three years, married Rev. Mr. Burn-

29

ham, a Christ-ian minister, and went West. She had two children by him.

2. GEORGE[7] KIMBALL, (*Benoni and Mary[6] Dunster*,) born May 30, 1818. School education at village. Work--ed with his father at carpentry. He married April 6, 1841, Phebe Rideout, daughter of Jacob and Sarah (Simonds) Rideout, of Milford, N. H., and built a house on the Dunster homestead. He had lived at Fitchburg, where she became a member of the Congregational Church. They also lived at Springfield, Mass., where they had a son:

(i) GEORGE[8] BENONI KIMBALL, born July 16, 1842. He died at Springfield, Sept. 20, 1843, and was brought to Mason Village.

On the formation of the village church they both removed their church relations to it. She died Feb. 23, 1861, of cancer in the breast, which was once removed without any benefit. For a large part of her eight or ten years' sickness she was helpless. She died at Fitchburg, but was buried at Mason Village. Her husband staid a short time at Fitchburg, and then went to Springfield Armory, where he was inspector of guns. Here he married 2d, Aug. 5, 1862, Mary Ann Johnson, daughter of William and Eliza (Tweedy) Johnson; married by Rev. Joel Bingham, of Westfield. She was a member of the Episcopal Church in Springfield. With that church both are now connected. About 1871 he bought a farm about four miles north of Lawrence, Kansas. He now lives in Lawrence, and works at Kimball Bros. machine shop. They have had two children:

(ii) HERBERT[8] WILBER KIMBALL, born at Springfield, March 8, 1864, died in Reno Township, Kansas, May 7, 1873, of cerebro-spinal meningitis. He was wonderfully mature in intellect and learning. He suffered that dreadful disease one hundred and two days, when death relieved him. We find an extended notice of that little boy, nine years old, in a Lawrence paper, and think not a word has been over-drawn. We saw him when racked with pain and limbs distorted, still he was calm and patient. "In the school house which had been the

29

scene of his little triumphs, the beautiful burial service
of the Episcopal service was pronounced by Rev. J. K.
Dunn, and the wasted and wearied body of little 'Bertie'
is now at rest in the Oak Hill Cemetery at Lawrence."

(iii) CORA[8] LENA KIMBALL, daughter of George and
Mary Ann (Johnson) Kimball, was born at Lawrence,
Kansas, Jan. 28, 1867. She possesses much of her
brother's intelligence and tact at learning.

3. MARY[7] ANN KIMBALL, born Jan. 19, 1820, died
Sept. 30, 1824, buried at Mason Centre. Removed to
Mason Village Cemetery, 1866, and reinterred there.

4. ELIZA[7] ANN KIMBALL, born Sept. 1, 1821, baptized Sept. 16, 1826, joined the Congregational Church
at Mason Centre. Married at her father's, on the Dunster homestead, Oct. 22, 1843, by Rev. Joseph B. Hill,
to George Gardner Amsden, of Springfield, son of Hollis
Amsden, of Mason. Lived in Amherst, N. H., and
Mason Village. She died Sept. 6, 1846, and was buried
there. They had no children.

5. ADDISON[7] KIMBALL, born Feb. 7, 1823, died
March 5, same year.

6. FRANKLIN[7] KIMBALL, (*Benoni and Mary[6] D.,*)
the sixth child of Benoni and Mary (Dunster) Kimball,
was born Jan. 6, 1824, baptized Sept. 16, 1826, united
with Mason Centre Church by recent experience and
profession. Worked with his father as house carpenter.
Worked at Fitchburg as pattern maker. He married
Sept. 8, 1847, at Stoddard, N. H., Elizabeth Davis, born
Nov. 28, 1822, daughter of Asa and Abigail (Hodge-
man) Davis, married by Rev. Isaac Robinson. She was
a member of the Congregational (Orthodox) Church at
Fitchburg, where they both lived when married.

In 1857, with his brothers, he removed to Lawrence,
Kansas, where he has resided since. He has been a
member of the City Council of Lawrence. He was there
when Quantrell made his murderous raid on that city,
but was not disturbed, being at a little distance from the
scene of destruction. He is a member of the firm of
"Kimball Brothers," machinists and founders. They
have had three children:

Cora Lena graduated at Kansas
the University Lawrence. Time
very full course

29

(i) FRANCES[8] EMOGEN KIMBALL, born at Fitchburg, July 15, 1850, is very well educated, having graduated at the Kansas State University in Lawrence. She lived with her parents till Nov. 18, 1873, when she was married by Rev. Mr. Cordley, at her father's, corner of Pinckney and Tennessee streets, to Arthur Carruth, of Lawrence. They now reside in Topeka, Kansas. He is in the book business. They have one child:

(1) CHARLES[9] ARTHUR CARRUTH, b. Nov. 21, 1875.

(ii) CHARLES[8] FREDERICK KIMBALL, (*Franklin,[7] Benoni and Mary[6] Dunster,*) was born at Fitchburg, Mass., Feb. 2, 1857. Is well educated. Resides at his father's. Is a machinist, employed by Kimball Bros.

(iii) MARY[8] ABBIE KIMBALL, born at Lawrence, Kansas, Dec. 7, 1859, died July 4, 1860, buried at Oak Hill Cemetery, Lawrence.

7. ISAAC[7] NEWTON KIMBALL, born at Mason Village, Dec. 7, 1825, was baptized Sept. 16, 1826. United with Mason Centre Church by profession in 1844. He learned the carpenter's trade of his father; afterwards worked in Fitchburg; was taken sick with typhoid fever there; came home, and died at the Dunster homestead, Sept. 5, 1845; was buried at Mason Village. He had a splendid intellect, and death only conquered his determination to have a collegiate education.

8. SAMUEL[7] DUNSTER KIMBALL, (*Benoni and Mary[6] (Dunster), Jason,[5] Jason,[4] Henry,[3] Jona.,[2] Henry,[1]*) born at Mason Village, Aug. 27, 1827, was named for his uncle. He united with Mason Centre Church by profession in 1844, with his brothers, Isaac Newton and Frederick. He learned the trade of machinist. Worked at Clinton and Fitchburg. At both places he kept house. At the time of the "Kansas-Nebraska" excitement (1854) he was one of the pioneers to make a settlement at Lawrence, which was then open prairie. In this they had a double object,—bettering their condition, and making Kansas a Free State. He, with his brother Frederick, went out in advance of the colony from Worcester County. Their families soon followed. Two of his brothers,

26

29

Franklin and Edward, afterwards joined the colony.
They formed a partnership, "Kimball Brothers," and
did an extensive business as machinists and founders.
He was a member of the City Council six years, three of
which he was President of the Board. He was Mayor
of the city in 1867 and '68. Was a member of the
Board of Education, and Chief Engineer of the Fire
Department. He married at Mason Village, Nov. 15,
1849, Adaline Amelia Livingston, daughter of Benjamin
and Milly (Sanders) Livingston, of Sharon, N. H., then
residing at Mason Village. They were married by Rev.
William Olmstead, the first pastor of Mason Village
Congregational Church, to which she united by profession.

At the time of Quantrell's raid on Lawrence, Aug. 21,
1863, he was taken from his own house, No. 20 Kentucky street, and marched under guard to a sort of
prison, made of the City Hotel, on Massachusetts (?)
street, and there confined. After taking him (it was
early in the morning and he scarce had time to dress)
they set his house on fire, and piled the furniture, bedding, &c., on the flames to make sure of its destruction,
then left the premises. His wife, brave woman! immediately set about extinguishing the flames, and succeeded in saving the house, although much of the furniture was destroyed. The parlor, where the fire was
kindled, was badly burned; and in 1872 a table was
shown us with the leaves badly burned and one leg
nearly burned off. To our mind, it was the most interesting *ornament* of the parlor in which it stood. It will,
we trust, be kept as a memento of that horrid scene at
which fiends might blush. He was liberated when they
left the city. He still resides in that house, and continues the business of machine making. We might add
he was a delegate to the famous Congregational Council
of Plymouth Church. They have had no children.

9. FREDERICK[7] KIMBALL, was born at Mason Village, June 9, 1829. He united with the Congregational
Church at Mason Centre in 1844. He learned the carpenter's trade of his father. Worked at Fitchburg, and
afterwards at St. Johnsbury, Vt., for Fairbanks & Co.,

on scales for weighing. In 1854 he removed to Lawrence, Kansas, and became a partner with his brothers. They built a small steamer for lumbering on the Kansas River. This department of their business was managed by him. He built a residence on Kentucky and Winthrop street, adjoining his brother's.

In Quantrell's raid, Aug. 21, 1863, his house was sacked. He concealed himself, and for a time was safe; but they set the house on fire, when he attempted to escape, but was made a prisoner and shot in his own door-yard. He was unarmed and had made no resistance. *That* wound was not fatal, and he was left for a few moments, when he made his way to a wooded ravine near his house. Here he was discovered, and again shot, this time fatally. He was seen by a colored woman to raise his hands afterwards. That was his only movement. He was not found, although in sight of his house, till the afternoon of that fearful day, when he was numbered with the one hundred and forty-three who were killed outright or died of their wounds. Scarce one of them was armed, and many were shot as if for the *amusement* of the murderers. "It is doubtful if the world has ever seen such a scene of horror; certainly not outside of savage warfare." (*Rev. R. Cordley.*) He was buried at Oak Hill Cemetery. By the exertions of his wife and daughter the flames were put out and the house saved. In that ravaged home they still (1872) live.

Frederick was married by Rev. Mr. Davis, at Fitchburg, Oct. 20, 1852, to Martha Farnsworth, born Oct. 16, 1831, daughter of Levi and Abigail (Matthews) Farnsworth, of Fitchburg. After the death of her husband she united with the Congregational Church at Lawrence. She remained a widow till July 3, 1868, when she married Walter Howell, of Lawrence, by whom she has Clarence Howell, born October, 1871.

They had two children:

(i) ELLA[8] FREDERIKA KIMBALL, born at St. Johnsbury, Vt., April 15, 1854, was a babe when her parents went to Lawrence. She was well educated at the public schools, which were early established there. She after-

29

wards graduated at the Kansas University, and took
high rank.   She united with the Congregational Church
at the time her mother did, and is active in the enterprises of the day.   Her education and tact eminently
qualify her for argument.   Her quiet and easy deportment give her an uncommon influence in the contro-
versies of the day.   She was married at Lawrence, Oct.
6, 1875, to Leland Cooper.   He is an express messenger
on the Lawrence and Galveston Texas Railroad.

We have been lately informed that Ella[8] Frederika, as
well as her cousin Emogen,[8] "were in the State University only about three years; but like most young ladies
they followed their natural inclinations and *graduated*
in the great school of matrimony."

They have one child:

(1) NELLIE[9] FARNSWORTH COOPER, born Aug. 20,
1876,—thus by one month snatching away from her
cousin, Grace Warren Landrum, the honor of being the
youngest named in the "Dunster Descendants."

(ii) LILLIAN[8] MARIA KIMBALL, born at Lawrence,
June 26, 1861, died at Fitchburg, Dec. 1, 1863.

10.   JAMES[7] KIMBALL, (*Benoni and Mary[6] Dunster,
Jason,[5] Jason,[4] Henry,[3] Jona.,[2] Henry,[1]*) the tenth child
of Benoni and Mary (Dunster) Kimball, was born at
Mason Village, April 18, 1831.   United with the Second
Congregational Church at Mason Village, July 1, 1849,
Rev. William Olmstead.   He learned carpentry of his
father, and worked at cabinet making and school furniture at Lebanon, N. H., and also at Weston, Mass.   He
kept a store for a time at Mason Village.   When the
Government put its whole facilities at Springfield to
making guns he went there and was employed in stock-
ing them.   Soon became an inspector of the work.   That
position he held until the Providence Tool Co. obtained
the large contract for guns of the Turkish Government.
These arms were to be examined by U. S. Inspectors,
and he was detailed for that purpose.   He now resides
in Providence, R. I.   He married Sept. 1, 1853, Maria
Corbin, born at New Ipswich, N. H., Nov. 20, 1829,
daughter of Stephen and Mary (Squires) Corbin.   He

29

(Mr. C.) was the first conductor on the Mason Village Railroad; was afterwards conductor on the Ohio Central Railroad. He was killed at Spencer's Station, on that road, April 22, 1862.

They have had but one child:

(i) JAMES[8] NEWTON KIMBALL, (*James,*[7] *Benoni*[6] *and Mary D.,*) was born at Weston, Mass., Feb. 26, 1855. He graduated at the Springfield High School, and has since been engaged in practical engineering. Was long employed on the Springfield Water Works. Since their completion has been surveying on railroads.

11. MARSHALL[7] KIMBALL, (*Benoni and Mary*[6] *D., Jason,*[5] *Jason,*[4] *Henry,*[3] *Jona.,*[2] *Henry,*[1]) born at Mason Village, Oct. 2, 1832, is a farmer, and owns the Dunster homestead Lot No. 10, in 18th Range. He was educated at public schools and Appleton Academy, at New Ipswich; taught school in Mason three terms; united with the Mason Village Congregational (Orthodox) Church, May 6, 1849, by profession; was elected deacon of that church Nov. 5, 1858, which office he still sustains. He enlisted in Co. C, 16th N. H. Regt. Infantry Vols. Oct. 18, 1862; stationed at Louisiana; mustered out at Concord, N. H., Aug. 2, 1863. In 1867 he built himself a large and convenient barn, from the cupola of which he fell, striking on the roof and other portions till he reached the ground, 40 feet in all. He was severely lamed, from which he has not entirely recovered. In 1870 he was one of the Selectmen, and has held other offices in town. He was married May 15, 1859, at the village church, by Rev. George E. Fisher, to Louisa Judith Allen, born Oct. 7, 1832, daughter of Oliver and Harriet (Harding) Allen, of Mason. She graduated at Appleton Academy, and taught school in Mason and other towns constantly for ten years, and until her marriage. She is gifted as a writer. She wrote the "Song of Welcome" for the Mason Centennial Celebration, 1868. They have six children:

(i) ELMER[8] ALLEN KIMBALL, born Jan. 18, 1862. He is now at New Ipswich Academy.

*26

29

(ii) MARY[8] LILLIAN KIMBALL, born June 2, 1864. Her grandmother was buried from the same house on the same day.

(iii) FRED.[8] BENONI KIMBALL, born March 18, 1866.

(iv) LENA[8] HARRIET KIMBALL, born Nov. 22, 1870.

(v) FLORA[8] LOUISA KIMBALL, born Feb. 8, 1872.

(vi) EDWARD[8] MARSHALL KIMBALL, b. Sept. 13, 1873.

12.   MARY[7] KIMBALL, (*Benoni and Mary[6] D.,*) born Feb. 10, 1834, united with the Mason Village Church by profession, July 1, 1849, Rev. William Olmstead. She was a tailoress for ten years. Was on a visit to her brother James, and became affianced to James Madison Post, of Lebanon, N. H. He was the son of Edwin and Mrs. Eunice (Gove) Post, of that town. Her maiden name was Eunice Wells Hall. He is a cabinet and furniture maker. They were married at her father's, on the Dunster homestead, by Rev. E. Davis, of Fitchburg, Dec. 3, 1863. Reside at East Lebanon, N. H. They have four children:

(i) EDWIN[8] DUNSTER POST, born Feb. 3, 1866.

(ii) JENNIE[8] MARIA POST, born April 7, 1868.

(iii) KATE[8] ESTELLE POST, born Oct. 6, 1870.

(iv) ELLA[8] LOUISA POST, born Oct. 20, 1873.

13.   ELLEN[7] MARIA KIMBALL, (*Benoni and Mary[6] D.,*) was born at the Dunster homestead, Mason Village, June 29, 1835. With her brother James and sister Mary she united with Mason Village Church, July 1, 1849. She was a tailoress. Married Sept. 20, 1858, James Henry Ferguson, born at West Boylston, Mass., Jan. 7, 1836, son of James and Sylvia (Stevens, daughter of Hon. John Stevens) Ferguson. He was a machinist. Went to Wisconsin and staid a few months, thence removed to Lawrence, Kansas, where he was in company with Kimball Brothers. In 1862 he came to Springfield, Mass., and was engineer at the U. S. Armory. In 1865 he went into the electrotype business (Lovejoy, Son & Co., Vanderwater street, New York). Owns a residence in Brooklyn. They have had three children:

(i) FRED.[8] IRVING FERGUSON, born at Lawrence, Kansas, July 8, 1859, died July 18, 1860, buried there.

(ii) JAMES[8] WILLIS FERGUSON, born at Brooklyn, N. Y., April 14, 1866. He died of diphtheria, at Brooklyn, Nov. 18, 1874, was buried in the Kimball group at Mason Village Cemetery.

(iii) EVA[8] MAY FERGUSON, born May 14, 1873, at Brooklyn, at their new residence, No. 121 St. Mark's Avenue.

14. EDWARD[8] KIMBALL, born at the Dunster homestead, Dec. 26, 1836, learned the machinist's trade at Putnam's shop, Fitchburg. Went to Kansas with his brother Franklin, and became a member of the firm. He boarded with his brother Samuel at the time of the raid, and with him was taken from the house and confined at the temporary prison. He was a celebrated musician. From his funeral sermon by his pastor, Rev. Richard Cordley, we add a few items of his life—have no room for more.

"The life of our Brother Kimball, and the power we *now* feel he had over us, suggest important thoughts. 1. *It shows the power of a true life.* There was no pretense about Mr. Kimball. There was no attempt at influence—no striving for position. He was merely true. His life made its own mark. He was firm on all moral subjects, never failing to speak or act when the occasion came; but he was never obtrusive, never trying to make himself felt. Meet him where you would he was always the same. On the street, in his foundry amid the blaze, dust and heat, he was the same genial, Christian gentleman as when in the concert room or the church. 2. The example of our brother shows that a man's power is from his life, not his professions. Mr. Kimball made few professions. He never told of himself. People never would have known him from his words. 3. Fidelity will always be appreciated. Our brother was a marked illustration of this law. During the twelve years past he has been a great deal more than a *leader* of the choir. It is this unselfish fidelity that has so won our hearts. It has not been merely in gath-

29

ering and leading the choir that he worked, but in everything that pertained to the music of the church.

"When this church edifice was just above its foundation, and our resources fell far short of its completion, he suggested the idea of an organ, 'to cost at least $3000.' I told him 'it was preposterous to think of it. The society was already burdened to its utmost endurance. They could scarcely finish their church. It would only discourage to add more.' He replied: 'I have a plan to reach the organ and not to interfere with the church. We will form the young people into an Organ Association, and by socials, festivals and concerts, in two years from the dedication of the church, we shall have an organ and no one feel the poorer for it.' He carried out his plan vigorously, and we dedicated the organ *with* the church, instead of two years later.

"I am amazed to see how his quiet influence has permeated every stage of our growth. But we miss him most for the personal ties which had grown so strong. As I look back over the past, a panorama passes before me. As scene after scene goes by, one familiar face appears prominent in all. I see the city in ruins. A worse than savage foe has laid it waste. The bodies of the dead are strewn here and there. The houses of the people are in ashes. The 'mourners go about the streets.' Prominent in that picture is the face of our brother, coming out of peril and threatening and abuse, but coming safe, and helping cheerfully, yet sadly, in the work of restoration.

"I see a procession of our citizen soldiers marching up Massachusetts street on their return from the border. It had been a time of peril and painful anxiety. Price and his army were on the border, and our friends had been ordered out to repel his attack. They had been gone from us several weeks. For two days, battle had been going on almost within hearing. One morning it was announced that our friends were returning and victory was assured. I saw them first as they came up from the bridge, dusty and worn and weary. The first face I recognize is that of our brother before us, as he marched before the rest, with the band playing that

29–30

familiar air, which never sounded so glad before, 'When the boys come marching home again.'

"His place is vacant. His chair and stand are draped in black. In the delirium of his last sickness he would often be talking of music. His last words were, 'Fading, still fading.'"

He died Sept. 23, 1873, of typhoid fever, at his brother Samuel's house, which had long been his home. The funeral services were at the Congregational Church, and were closed by the singing of that hymn which had apparently been the theme of thought as he passed to the harmony of Heaven. He had never been married. Was interred at Oak Hill Cemetery, Lawrence.

15. ABBY[7] JANE KIMBALL, was the youngest of that family of fifteen children, all of whom were singers and musicians of a high order, and attained that position mostly by self-culture around the family board. Their father was never known to even attempt music, and their mother was an indifferent singer, although, like most children, she "went to the singing school."

Abby was born at the Dunster homestead, May 23, 1838. She united with Mason Village Church, May 3, 1857. She was a tailoress, and worked at that place until her marriage, at the residence of her father, by Rev. S. J. Austin, Dec. 28, 1858, to John Robinson Lynch, born July 21, 1828. He was the son of George Henry and Margaret (Curry) Lynch. He united with the Mason Village Church by profession, July 4, 1858. He is a blacksmith, and doing a good business at the shop he has built on a part of the Dunster homestead, near the railroad station, where he has also built a good house by his industry and frugality. They are both interested in the welfare of the church and community. Being without children she takes an active part in Sabbath Schools and other religious objects. She possesses the wedding ring of Mary Davis Dunster, referred to on page 257.

30. iii. ISAIAH[6] DUNSTER, (*Jason,*[5] *Jason,*[4] *Henry,*[3] *Jona.,*[2] *Henry,*[1]) the third child of Jason[5] and Mary (Meriam) Dunster, was born Dec. 10, 1798. He re-

30

ceived the common school education of those days, and
worked on the farm of his father till of age (1819), when
he went to Weston, Mass.   Before leaving Mason he was
affianced to Betsey Warren Russell, daughter of Hubbard and Sarah (Warren) Russell, and sister of Moses
Russell, who married Betsey Dunster, his sister.   She
died Jan. 31, 1820.   While living at Weston, which he
did several seasons, he became acquainted with and married, Feb. 6, 1823, Ruth Sophia Fisk, daughter of Jonas
and Abigail (Pierce) Fisk, of Waltham.   (Mrs. Fisk,
afterwards Mrs. Haywood, died at Weston, Oct. 6, 1875,
aged 94 years.)   She, Ruth Sophia, was born Sept. 27,
1804.   They resided a while at Waltham, then removed
to Mason, N. H., where he bought two-thirds of the
Dunster homestead, and lived on it until about 1830;
thence removed to New Ipswich, N. H., afterwards to
Holliston, Mass.   They also lived at Bustleton, Pa.,
Sanford, Me., and at Providence, R. I.; in these three
places employed in print works.   From Providence he
went to Attleboro, Mass., where he carried on a farm
bought by his son.   He died of liver complaint, at that
farm, Aug. 4, 1857; was interred at Mount Hope Cemetery in that town.   His widow has lived most of the
time since at Attleboro.   They had two children:

1.   ELIZA[7] SOPHIA DUNSTER, born at Waltham, April
5, 1824, lived with her parents in their repeated removals; employed the latter part of these years in the print
works, sewing calico for printing.   At Providence she
married Moses Mason (his second wife), Aug. 29, 1844.
He was the son of John and Hannah (Richardson-
Campbell) Mason, and was born at Attleboro, May 29,
1802.   When married he was engaged in store keeping
at Providence.   In the spring of 1847 they removed to
Attleboro Falls, where he traded seven years.   He now
resides on the old homestead, and is engaged in farming.
She died there, Aug. 7, 1866.   He has a third wife.
They had eight children:

(i)   MOSES[8] HENRY MASON, (*Moses and Eliza[7] Dun-
ster, Isaiah,[6] Jason,[5] Jason,[4] Henry,[3] Jonathan,[2] Henry,[1]*)
born at Providence, R. I., May 27, 1845.   Common

30

school education. When 16 years old, learned the machinist's trade, at which he worked only a year. Was then clerk and paymaster for H. M. Richards and E. I. Richards & Co., jewelers. Afterwards attended Bryant, Stratton & Mason's Commercial College, in Providence. While there, was kept by them writing in the Quartermaster's office, making out the claims of Rhode Island against the United States for service of troops in the rebellion. Afterwards went to New York city, as salesman and clerk for G. W. Shepherdson, and Webster & Gage (a Chicago house). Returned to Attleboro, and was clerk, paymaster, &c., for H. M. Daggett, for three years. Then went into the jewelry business at Attleboro Falls on his own account, (Mason, Draper & Co.) which they are still very successfully carrying on.* He was married at the Second Congregational Church, Rev. H. Peloubet, Nov. 11, 1869, to Emma Maria Staples, born April 30, 1850, daughter of Isaac Braman and Frances Dyer (Penno) Staples, of Attleboro. Have no children.

(ii) CHARLES[8] EDWARD MASON, (*Moses and Eliza[7] Dunster,*) was born in Providence, R. I., Jan. 25, 1847. His parents removed to Attleboro Falls same year, where

---

* At a church fair, held Thanksgiving week, 1876, an easy chair was among the articles to be disposed of by voting to the most popular man in Attleboro. On examining the "votes actually cast," Henry Mason had a plurality of 404, ascertained by an "honest count." At the close of the fair six stalwart men bore the chair on their shoulders to his residence, preceded by the Band, who had in like manner obtained a new flag, followed by a torchlight procession. (The torches had been used a few nights before by the bewildered politicians.) The boys on the road let off fireworks as a side show. Mr. Brady made a set speech, in which he spoke of the veneration with which the chair would be looked upon by the recipient's *posterity*, and made a formal presentation of it. Mr. Mason made an impromptu reply, and invited his guests to a generous entertainment, got up on strict temperance principles. The voters had paid ten cents each as "intimidation." The church made $200.00 by the chair. The Band had a chance to show off their new flag. The audience were well pleased with their hospitality, and retired without saying a word on the "Presidential muddle," which had been the only talk for three weeks; and Henry sits quietly in his beautiful brown silk seat adorned with scarlet puffs, with his unsolicited title of "The most popular man in Attleboro."

30

he attended school, and assisted his father in the store.
When 15 years old, went to learn the trade of machinist,
staid about three years; thence went to H. M. Daggett's
braid factory as engineer of the steam and water power.
In 1865 went to the American Screw Co., Providence,
and worked on machines for making screws, where he
staid about three years; then came to East Attleboro and
worked at making jewelers' tools.   Went into the jewelry business on his own account in 1871.   He married
Oct. 20, 1872, Lydia Carpenter Bliss, born Jan. 4, 1849,
only daughter of Rodolphus and Lydia Short (Carpenter) Bliss.   They reside at her father's, where she super-
intends the housekeeping.

(iii) SAMUEL⁸ DUNSTER MASON, (*Moses and Eliza*⁷
*D., Isaiah,*⁶ *Jason,*⁵ *Jason,*⁴ *Henry,*³ *Jona.,*² *Henry,*¹) born
at Attleboro, Sept. 4, 1848, was named for his great-
uncle.   Went to public school, "Falls" district, and
one year at North Attleboro High School.   In 1865 he
learned the machinist's trade; staid about a year; was
then employed by H. M. Daggett to do repairs and keep
the machines for making braid in order.   When only 18
years old he was sent to Paterson, N. J., to start a braid
establishment there.   In 1869 went to R. Blackinton's
jewelry establishment as a tool maker.   Jan. 1, 1870, he
went into company with his brother Henry and Charles
Draper, (Mason, Draper & Co.) in the jewelry business.
They have been successful.   He is very ingenious at that
business.   Their establishment is at Attleboro Falls.   He
married Dec. 10, 1873, Emma Frances Draper, sister to
their partner, and only daughter of Lorenzo and Harriet
Newell (Shaw) Draper, North Attleboro.   She was born
July 23, 1843.   They reside at the "Falls."

(iv) CARRIE⁸ (CAROLINE) ELIZA MASON, the fourth
child and eldest daughter of Moses and Eliza⁷ Sophia
(Dunster) Mason, was born at Attleboro, Feb. 23, 1859.
After her school education she was employed at Daggett's
braid factory, assorting, counting and packing.   At this
she became very dexterous and perfectly correct.   These
qualifications were fully appreciated and rewarded.   In
1870 she went to Chicago with a friend, just married,
and has resided with her ever since, preferring that

30

locality to her birth-place. They now reside at South Evanston, about ten miles down the lake from Chicago. She is unmarried.

(v) EDWARD[8] S. MASON, (*Moses and Eliza*[7] *Dunster,*) born Dec. 21, 1851, was a member of the High School. Worked at machinery about two years, then went to R. Blackinton & Co.'s, taking the place left by his brother Samuel. In July, 1869, he joined the Baptist Church (Calvinistic) by profession. He married Dec. 7, 1871, Mary Caroline Pierce, daughter of Wightman and Patience Carr (Kingman) Pierce, from Pennsylvania. She is a member of the same church. He built a house on a lot bought of his father, in which they now live. He is now employed by his brother Charles. They have two children:

(1) LILLIAN[9] ELIZA MASON, born Oct. 9, 1872.
(2) EDWARD[9] HENRY MASON, Nov. 1, 1874.

(vi) ADILAID[8] LOUISA MASON, born Jan. 9, 1854, died Feb. 7, same year.

(vii) MARIETTA[8] FRANCES MASON, born Dec. 28, 1854, received a good common school education. For several years has been employed in making jewelry at Freeman & Co.'s.

(viii) FREDERICK[8] MASON, (*Moses and Eliza*[7] *Dunster,*) born at Attleboro, Jan. 22, 1857, had a good education at common and High School. Is learning the jewelry business at his brother's, (Mason, Draper & Co.)

2. HENRY[7] DUNSTER, (*Isaiah,*[6] *Jason,*[5] *Jason,*[4] *Henry,*[3] *Jona.,*[2] *Henry,*[1]) the second child and only son of Isaiah and Ruth Sophia (Fisk) Dunster, was born at New Ipswich, N. H., April 13, 1831. After a common school education he learned the jewelry business at North Attleboro, in which he was engaged a number of years as maker, salesman, and manufacturer on his own account, in Attleboro, Providence and other places. He did a variety of other business, in Chicago, St. Louis and Cincinnati. Was engaged as director of amusements at St. Louis Opera House. Made a voyage to England and France as director of a Panorama of the

27

30

Rebellion, but the scenes being mostly Union victories, it "did not draw," and was a losing concern. On his return he was made Inspector of the Providence Horse Car Railroad. For the last three years he has been a commercial agent for large establishments of ready-made clothing in Providence and Boston. He has resided mostly in Providence. He married at Providence, R. I., Oct. 6, 1851, Jane Mellen, born Feb. 3, 1831. They have two children:

(i)   IDA[6] LOUISA DUNSTER, (*Henry,[7] Isaiah,[6] Jason,[5] Jason,[4] Henry,[3] Jona.,[2] Henry,[1]*) born at Attleboro, Sept. 25, 1852, was educated at Providence. She graduated in June, 1871, with distinguished honor, at the High School, after passing through all the grades in lower schools, and attending the High School the whole four years. She wrote the valedictory poem, which elicited much applause. She united with the Fourth Baptist Church on profession of faith, and was baptized by immersion, May 28, 1871, by Rev. Dr. A. H. Granger. Was dismissed in October, 1874, by letter to the church in Shreveport, Louisiana, of which her husband was then pastor. She was married at her father's, in Providence, by Rev. Dr. Granger, ~~Dec. 10, 1873~~, to William Warren Landrum, eldest son of Rev. Sylvanus and Eliza Jane (Warren) Landrum. He was born at Macon, Georgia, Jan. 18, 1853. Was converted at ten years of age, and united with the First Baptist Church of Savannah, Ga. when thirteen years of age, his father being at that time pastor of the church. He was prepared for college at the Chatham Academy in Savannah, and in his fifteenth year entered the Freshman class of Mercer University, then located at Penfield, Georgia. Here he spent two and a half years.

In February, 1870, he came North, and entered the Sophomore class of Brown University, Providence, R. I. He graduated in 1872, being nineteen years of age, and the youngest member of his class. In September, same year, he entered the Southern Baptist Theological Seminary, Greenville, South Carolina, to prepare for the ministry of his chosen denomination, in which for four generations his ancestors had been preachers of the word.

[handwritten margin notes: "S Apl 28 1874"]

[handwritten at bottom: Ida (Dunster) Landrum died in Richmond Virginia. beloved respected and mourned for. All the ministers Richmond (19) attended her funeral as]

30

His theological course closed April, 1874, and in May, same year, he was ordained at Jefferson, Texas, where the Southern Baptist Convention was then in session. The ordaining Presbytery were:

Rev. Dr. Jno. A. Broadus, Greenville, S. C.
   "   " William Williams,   "   "
   "   " H. A. Tupper, Richmond, Virginia.
   "   " William Carey Crane, Independence, Texas.
   "   " Sylvanus Landrum, Memphis, Tenn.
   "   " G. Daniel, Walthamville, Georgia.

He was installed pastor of the Baptist Church at Shreveport, Louisiana, the same month, May, 1874.

In the spring of 1876 he was called to take the pastoral charge of the First Baptist Church at Augusta, Georgia, where he is now preaching. While at the Theological Seminary he spent all his vacations and spare time in preaching to the colored population at the rice and cotton plantations, much to their benefit, but a serious inroad on his health. His wife is now (June, 1876,) on a visit to her friends in New England. He came North about the middle of July.

Personating the *little one*, he writes: "My father wanted a boy, but since GOD has decided a girl was better, he has not complained. Indeed, he and my mother are just as happy and proud as any two people ever were. I have my father's eyes and hair, but my other features are exactly like my mother. I know my uncle will be proud of the Dunster blood in his little 'great grandchild.'" [Vicariously.]

(1) GRACE[9] WARREN LANDRUM, born at Providence, R. I., 53 Vernon street, July 18, 1876, at 1½ o'clock, P. M.

(2) The story entitled "Grace Warren," published by the Southern Baptist Publication Society, had its scene at the old homestead of Gen. Eli Warren, in Houston Co., Georgia. He was the great grandfather of the "little one." From this she has her name. She is the youngest "descendant" heard from.

(ii) HENRY[8] DUNSTER, (*Henry,[7] Isaiah,[6] Jason,[5] Jason,[4] Henry,[3] Jona.,[2] Henry,[1]*) the only son of Henry and Jane (Mellen) Dunster, was born at Providence, R. I.,

(2) Margaret Lothrop Landrum. both children are in Richmond va with their father who has married.

30-31

May 25, 1857.   Has passed through all the grades of the public schools in Providence, and finished last year at the High School.   He entered Brown University, Sept., 1876.   (Harvard by choice, but Brown by convenience.) He has been much assisted in his education, as was his sister also, by their Aunt Sophronia (Mellen), Mrs. William Batchelder.

We forgot to mention in its proper place the receipt of the photograph of Henry[8] Dunster, who was "buried in his well," taken soon after, with his crutches on his knees, also that of his son Henry,[9] and make acknowledgment under another Henry[8] Dunster, who is drinking at the "Pierian Spring."   By our neglect, he gets an extra notice, free of expense, which really belongs to his "cousin."   Their great grandfathers were brothers.

31.   iv.   BETSEY[6] DUNSTER, (*Jason,*[5]*Jason,*[4]*Henry,*[3] *Jona.,*[2] *Henry,*[1]) the fourth child and second daughter of Jason and Polly (Meriam) Dunster, was born April 20, 1801.   Her mother, whose countenance always brightened at the mention of any incident in her blameless life, related, when she was 80 years old, that "her husband had gone down to the east part of Mason to move his father to Ashburnham, and coming home in the evening, he saw a light in the 'best room,' as he came out of the woods, and knew something was the matter, and Betsey was born before he got home."   There was but one glass window in that end and only five in the whole house, of 12 lights—6 by 8 glass.   It was two stories in front and one in the rear, with a lean-to roof. The other windows were sawed from the "feather edged" boards, and held in place by cleats nailed across them, after the fashion of those days.   It stood end to the road; and the front yard, to which there was no access except over a fence or through the front door, which was seldom opened, had no ornament except the old well, whose "swape" dates back in principle to the days of Pharaoh, when it was called "Shadoof," and in practice, to the forest trees; and the old cider mill, which stood close by.   The sweet juice, pressed out by ponderous wooden screws, was enticing to the children.   The

31

youngest boy, just beginning to run about and imitate the larger children, attempted to "suck cider through a straw." Wanting their dexterity, he lost his balance and was immersed in the foaming liquid which filled the tub. His eldest sister was near, and drew him out, unconcious. He lived to tell the story to his grand-children.

Mason Village at that time had only four houses, three of which had similar roofs, but they were ornamented with additional windows.

The old cider mill long since made room for a larger and more convenient house. Improvement added a wing to either end of that. The old house got out of the way of "progress," its frame enlarged, makes a tenement in the village. The old well is covered up by the culinary department. The centennial year put a French roof in place of the strong one which withstood the "gale of '15," and saved from death the present owner's mother; and memory, shocked with the history of individual impiety, social faithlessness, national wrongs and their removal by a greater crime, baptized in blood, revisiting those early scenes, asks, without hope, for this innocent, happy, natal home.

In that "best room," the only plastered one in the house, with its "nicely sanded floor," that mother, sitting in the "great chair," often gathered her ruddy children in double row about her knee, and with a silent prayer for its fulfilment, taught them that "Man's chief end is to glorify God, and enjoy Him forever."

This contrasts strangely with the fashionable presiding genius of a palatial residence voluntarily turning over her feeble offspring, deprived of air and light, to the paid for sympathy of the wet nurse, who vainly strives to put a bloom on its faded cheek by artificial cosmetics and the "invisible rays" of blue glass. In the end followed, perhaps, to its grave by "cunning women, such as are skillful of lamentation," as the Prophets put it.

Betsey was the pet of her grandfather, who died when she was four years old. She received a common school education only. She married May 27, 1819, Moses Russell, born in Mason, Dec. 2, 1793, son of Hubbard and Sarah (Warren) Russell, born in Cambridge, and a

*27 *Moses* Russell died March 1st 1885 being 91 years 3 months old. Betsey (Dunster) Russell died o[ ] 31 1885 both buried at Gree[ ]

31

nephew or brother of that Jason Russel who was bar-
barously shot in his own house on the return of Percy's
men from Lexington. They were married at her father's,
by Rev. Ebenezer Hill, and immediately commenced
housekeeping at a residence he had just built on his
father's farm. Here they lived until 1842, when he sold
the place, and bought a farm in the westerly part of
Mason (Lot No. 6 in Range 8), which now makes the
southeast corner of Greenville. His farm, by an error
in an ancient survey, was claimed by both towns, and he
was taxed by both, but was finally given up by Mason,
and no longer resided on "disputed territory." He and
his wife both united by profession to Mason Centre
Church, and remained members of that church till the
church was organized at Mason Village, of which they
are now members. They are in tolerable health for so
old people.

They have had four children:

1. ISAIAH⁷ DUNSTER RUSSELL, (*Moses and Betsey⁶ D.,
Jason,⁵ Jason,⁴ Henry,³ Jona.,² Henry,¹*) born at Mason,
Aug. 1, 1820, and named for his uncle, had the scanty
advantages of schools in that part of the town. When
quite a young man, scarce out of boyhood, he was employed by John Boynton, the founder of the common
school fund of ten thousand dollars in Mason, in selling
tinware, of which Mr. B. was a large manufacturer. In
1843 he engaged in the sale of hardware, stoves and
house furnishing materials, carrying on at the same time
a shop for tin, sheet iron and copper work. In business
he has been unusually successful. Has a very pleasant
residence on the hill east side of Worcester, Mass. His
business has all been done in that city. In 1841 he
united with the Mason Centre Congregational Church on
profession. Is now a member of the Union (Orthodox)
Church, Worcester. He married, at Worcester, April 7,
1846, Nancy Maria Wentworth, born at Worcester, Sept.
27, 1825, daughter of Jonathan and Nancy (Fisk) Wentworth. She is a descendant of John Wentworth, Governor of New Hampshire, when the charter of Mason
was obtained (1768). Hon. John Wentworth, of Illinois,
often known by the cognomen of "Long John," was of

31

the same family. She is a member of same church.
They have had three children:

(i) ADDISON[8] CHARLES RUSSELL, born Feb. 7, 1847,
died Aug. 10, 1851; buried at Rural Cemetery in Worcester.

(ii) CHARLES[8] ADDISON RUSSELL, (*Isaiah,*[7] *Moses
and Betsey*[6] *Dunster,*) born at Worcester, March 2, 1852,
was educated at Worcester common and High School,
and also took private lessons with a class of young men,
taught by Mr. Harris R. Green, Principal of the Oread
Seminary. He entered Yale College, and graduated in
class 1873. He was selected as one of the oarsmen in
their boat races, and has several trophies of success, such
as silver oars, &c. He is now (1876) city editor of the
Worcester Press. Is unmarried, April, 1877.

(iii) ANNIE[8] MARIA RUSSELL, the only daughter of
Isaiah and Maria (Wentworth) Russell, born Aug. 10,
1864, is now receiving her education at the Worcester
schools. She is making rapid advances, (too rapid, we
think,) and excels in drawing. A specimen of her's was
selected by a committee in Boston, from the whole State
samples, to be sent to the Centennial at Philadelphia as
one of the seven only sent for that purpose; and a specimen also was selected for the neatness of an arithmetical
problem for the same purpose.

2. JULIA[7] ANN (JULIANA) RUSSELL, (*Moses and
Betsey*[6] *Dunster,*) born at Mason, east side, May 7, 1824,
was named from the infant of her grand-parents, who
died by a fall from the bed. She united with the church
at Mason Centre the first Sabbath in January, 1840, by
profession. She was married at her father's, west side,
by Rev. Joseph B. Hill, Sept. 22, 1842, to Henry Hazard
Sawin, born Sept. 15, 1821, at Shelburne, Mass., and
named in honor of Com. Oliver "Hazard" Perry. He
was son of Bela and Rebecca (Barber) Sawin. In "Notes
of the Sawins," page 34, he is represented as son of Moses
Sawin. This is incorrect. He is brother of Rev. The-
ophilus Parsons Sawin, and descended from John Sawin,
of Watertown. They first lived at Mason Centre, then at
the village. In 1852 they removed to Holden, Mass.,

31

where he carried on the tin plate business, and about 1862 removed to Worcester, where he carries on plumbing and tinware making. He united with the Mason Centre Church in May, 1840, at which time about thirty were added to that church. He and his wife are both members of Plymouth Church in Worcester. They have had eight children:

(i) ABBIE⁸ JANE SAWIN, born at Mason, July 10, 1843, married at Worcester, Sept. 3, 1867, Charles Allen, born in Springfield, Sept. 30, 1843. He is a machinist, and resides in Worcester. "He enlisted for three months in April, 1861, from New York city, in the 'New York Zouave Regiment;' served with his regiment four months, they being kept over time; enlisted for three years from Worcester, Oct. 5, 1861, in the 25th Massachusetts Regiment; was with Burnside at the taking of Roanoke, Newbern, and in other battles in North Carolina; re-enlisted, Dec. 17, 1863, in the same regiment for three years, as a veteran volunteer; was in the different battles in Virginia, under Gen. B. F. Butler; with his regiment joined Grant's army in May, 1864; was shot through the ankle and had his foot smashed by a piece of shell at Cold Harbor, June 3, 1864; did not recover from wounds so as to rejoin the regiment and was discharged. He was but 16 years old when he enlisted in the New York regiment; had been refused acceptance in Massachusetts regiments on account of his minority, and 'scooted' over to New York without his parents' permission and enlisted. When wounded at Cold Harbor he was left nearly a day lying on the battle field, and it was some three days before he was removed from the field hospital to comfortable quarters. He served as private all through his term." (*C. A. Russell.*) They have one child:

(1) MAUD⁹ ADA ALLEN, born Oct. 18, 1868.

(ii) JAMES⁸ ADISON SAWIN, born Feb. 2, 1845, at his grandfather's, died there, Feb. 19, 1845; buried at Mason Centre. After the death of his sister he was re-interred beside her at Mason Village.

(iii) MARY⁸ ELIZA SAWIN, born Jan. 18, 1846, died at her grandfather's, March 22, 1848.

31

(iv) GEORGE[8] HENRY SAWIN, (*Henry,[7] Moses and Betsey[6] D.,*) born at Mason Village, April 6, 1849, is a joiner and house carpenter. He united in 1867 with the Methodist Church, Park street, Worcester. He married Aug. 24, 1868, Amanda Ward Merryfield, born Feb. 3, 1849, daughter of Louis Ward Merryfield, of West Boylston. Mr. M. owned the first cultivated farm in that town, and his descendants hold the place by possession only. No deeds were ever passed. They have had two children, both born at Worcester, where the parents reside.

(1) BERTHA[9] G. SAWIN, born May 10, 1871, died the next day.

(2) WALDO[9] HENRY SAWIN, born Sept. 15, 1872.

(v) WILLIE[8] HERBERT SAWIN, the fifth child of H. H. and Juliana (Russell) Sawin, born at Mason Village, Sept. 4, 1852, united with the Old South Church (Congregational) at Worcester, July, 1871. He withdrew from that church and united with Grace Church (Methodist) in that city. He is a partner with his father,— plumbing, &c. He married June 17, 1875, Jennie Hobbs, adopted daughter of Mrs. William Hobbs, of Worcester.

(vi) ELIZA[8] MARIA SAWIN, born at Holden, May 4, 1855, joined Grace (Methodist) Church in Worcester, June, 1873. She died at Worcester, Dec. 20, 1874, of typhoid fever; was buried at Mason Village.

(vii) FLORA[8] MARCELLA SAWIN, born at Holden, Oct. 4, 1857, with her sister united to Grace Church, June, 1873. She was married at the same time her brother Willie was, June 17, 1875, to Herbert Eugene Noyes, son of Samuel and Lucy (Morse) Noyes, of Worcester. He is a member of Grace Church also. They reside in Worcester. He is a boot maker.

(viii) LELIA[8] GOODHUE SAWIN, born Sept. 4, 1861, at Holden, resides with her parents. Is a member of the High School.

3. ADISON[7] RUSSELL, the third child of Moses and Betsey (Dunster) Russell, born at Mason, June 27, 1831,

31–32

was sorely afflicted with asthma from a child until he removed to his brother's in Worcester, where he was nearly free from it. Whenever he visited his parents at Mason he had a return of the complaint, which again subsided at Worcester. When a boy he did not lie down for weeks, but slept in an upright chair. He united by profession to the Mason Village Congregational Church, July 4, 1852. He was employed by his brother Isaiah D. as salesman. This trust he discharged with care and faithfulness. About 1868 he went into the stove and hardware business on his own account. He married Sept. 14, 1865, Carrie Elizabeth Carey, of Shrewsbury, Mass. He was taken sick with typhoid fever in the fall of 1874, and did not fully recover his health, but lived till July 11, 1875. He was buried at Worcester. His widow, who is a member of the same church, still lives in one of his houses. His brother settled his estate. They had no children.

4. ELIZA[7] JANE RUSSELL (*Jane* not on the town records), the fourth child of Moses and Betsey[6] (Dunster) Russell, born Dec. 16, 1837, was educated at Mason public schools and five terms at Appleton Academy, New Ipswich. She taught school twelve terms in Mason, New Ipswich, Wilton, Holden, and Leominster, each term being the summer of the year, except in her own district, where she taught in winter also. March 1, 1857, she united by profession to the Orthodox Congregational Church at Mason Village, of which she is still a member. She married Sept. 28, 1869, Henry Lyman Newell, born at Pepperhill, Mass., Oct. 31, 1844. His father was of Mason, and brother to Ezra Newell, the early blacksmith and scythe maker at Mason "Harbor." He is a member of the same church. They live on their father's homestead, and take care of the "old folks" with great kindness. They have no children.

32. v. SAMUEL[6] DUNSTER, (*Jason,*[5] *Jason,*[4] *Henry,*[3] *Jona.,*[2] *Henry,*[1]) the fifth child of Jason and Mary (Polly) (Meriam) Dunster, was born Aug. 1, 1803. His early education was limited to the small district school, two miles distant, keeping about eight weeks in winter and ten in summer. At sixteen, he had not begun arithme-

32

tic or geography. He then attended Appleton Academy six weeks, and received the preceptor's certificate of being well qualified (?) to teach a common school, which he did for several winters with success. In the summer of 1821 he worked with his brother-in-law at house carpentry, having until that time worked on his father's farm (what work he did, for that he was not noted). The next season he was engaged, in his native village, to learn the trade of machinist. Here he devoted his spare time to practical self-education; became a surveyor of land, and did engineering in his own and the adjacent towns.

In the spring of 1826 he went to Dover, N. H., and worked as a machinist, most of the time as a pattern maker. The next year, without any solicitation on his part, or even knowledge of their wishes, he was selected by the managers of the Dover (now the Cocheco) Manuf'g Co. as a suitable person to learn the calico printing business, with a view of its future superintendence. Calico printing in this country was then in its infancy, and the operatives were mostly foreigners of not the best habits. He was engaged in order to remedy troubles which were of frequent occurrence. Although he knew nothing of the business he was paid a liberal salary and engaged for five years. Before the expiration of that time the print works changed owners, which involved a change of managers. He recovered, however, the salary for the whole time. Afterward he went to Bustleton, near Philadelphia, in Pennsylvania, and there became a partner in a print works on the Pennypack Creek, and worked at machine printing. In this business he was successful.

In 1834 he sold out, and soon after bought the "Province Mill," on the Mousum River, in the village of Springvale, Sanford, Maine. A stock company was formed under the name of Franklin Manuf'g Co. He fitted up the works, and managed them for three years, when, dissatisfied with the selling agents in Boston, who got control of the stock, he withdrew from the management, but unwisely held his interest in the company, which failed soon after, with a total loss of his stock and nearly all his property.

32

In 1838 he bought a large farm in Durham, N. H., to which he removed and staid a year, then went to Rhode Island, leaving his family in Durham till 1840. He worked as a machine printer with Gov. Allen, in Providence, and at other places, till 1842, when he went to Coventry, R. I., to superintend a print works there, which was removed the next year to Johnston. This he managed till 1848, when he again went to Gov. Allen's as a printer.

In 1852 he was offered the situation of Assistant Manager of the Cocheco Print Works, where he had begun that business. He held that place till 1859, when he again returned to Rhode Island. He there furnished cloth for a print works, but the owner of the works was unable to go on, which left him with a large quantity of cloth in the ·hands of New York merchants, who took another large slice out of his savings. Tired of change, and disposed to save a competence (estimated by Agur's standard) for himself and family, and entertain his friends with "farmers' fare," he bought the Old Parsonage of Rev. Mr. Weld, in West Attleboro, Mass.

Before leaving his native town he was made a Free Mason. This made him a better man, and gave him an introduction to many friends in Dover and elsewhere. He attained a prominent position in that order, and was at one time presiding officer over Lodge, Chapter and Council, member of Encampment, &c.

He hates "humbug," *(that* word expresses it best) whether in religion, politics, or social life. He early wished to know more of his ancestors and kindred. Comparative leisure in later life, with good health, have favored that desire.

In religious views he is not easily described. Educated in childhood and taught the Westminster Catechism by a pious mother, and at her death given a copy of the "New England Primer" as her special bequest, which he preserves with care, as containing the ground-work of his mother's faith, he would endorse that system, divested of some of its rough corners and unfortunate technicalities. In his younger days the wranglings about forms of faith kept him aloof from personal attention to

32

religion. When he bought the Springvale Print Works, various denominations were holding union religious meetings in one of the larger buildings—the first he had ever seen. This gave him interest, which was followed by new views of Divine goodness, human welfare and personal duty. After the meetings closed, as he occupied a prominent position in that village, great efforts were made to gather him into all of the churches. To this he expostulated with a minister, and was answered that "There was no harm in pushing *his* ship by the others." Not choosing to take passage for the sake of coming out a "length ahead," he has remained free from sectarian obligations.

He was married at Rochester, N. H., by Rev. Isaac Willey, Oct. 12, 1828, to Susan Perkins Dow, born July 22, 1806, in Hollis, Maine, and daughter of Jeremiah and Betsey (Perkins) Dow, descended, on the father's side, from Henry Dow, of Watertown, and on the mother's, through Solomon,* from Joshua Perkins, one of the early settlers of Dover. They have had five children:

1. MARY⁷ SUSAN DUNSTER, born at Dover, N. H., Aug. 9, 1830, died at Bustleton (now a part of Philadelphia), Penn., June 27, 1832, of whooping-cough. She was remarkable for early development—more like an adult than a child. She was buried at Pennypack Cemetery, in Bustleton, near the church. Her headstone is inscribed: "The Grave of MARY SUSAN DUNSTER, born Aug. 9, 1830, at Dover, New Hampshire. Died June 27, 1832. Premature in Intellect, she was lovely even in Death. Let the little stranger rest among you."

2. MARY⁷ SUSAN DUNSTER (named for her sister), the second child of Samuel⁶ and Susan (Dow) Dunster, born June 27, 1833, at La Grange Village, Bustleton, Penn., was educated at the schools in Providence. Was in the High School when her father removed from Prov-

* Maj. Sol. Perkins was the first to subscribe for the burying ground at Rochester, N. H., and the first one buried in it. (*John M. Duffee's Oration.*)

28

32

idence to Durham, N. H. She was married at Providence, by Rev. J. Leavett, Dec. 25, 1849, to Joseph E. Smith, then a salesman in William Hale's hardware store, in Dover, N. H. They kept house in Dover. He afterwards went to San Francisco, Cal., where he was in the hardware business. Expecting that to be their permanent home, she went in the summer of 1853 via Cape Horn, in the "Water Witch," Capt. Plumer. The ship sprung a leak off Brazil, and put into Rio Janeiro, where she spent three or four months, most of the time (after going through the acclimating fever) in the mountains, at Bennett's Hotel, Tijuca, amid coffee plantations, tropical fruits, and in a lovely climate. The ship was repaired, and reached San Francisco, but on the next voyage made a total wreck.

Mr. Bennett remembered her, and a few years after sent her a beautiful suit of photographs of his hotel, and other views of magnificent Brazilian scenery.

They resided at San Francisco till the great fire in 1854. Being burnt out, with a loss of everything, she returned to her father's in Dover, by the way of Panama, before the railroad was done, riding across the Isthmus on mule back. She resided with her father most of the time until the death of her sister, Sept. 17, 1873. Since that time she has had the care of her sister's children, in Chicago. She is a member of the Episcopal Church; was confirmed by Rt. Rev. Bishop C. Chase, Oct. 27, 1861, at Dover, N. H. They had two children:

(i) ALICE[8] SMITH, born at Dover, N. H., Dec. 23, 1850, died at Providence, Aug. 15, 1851; carried to Dover for burial at Pine Hill Cemetery.

(ii) HELEN SMITH, born at Dover, April 18, 1855, died at Dover, Sept. 7, same year, was buried beside her sister.

3. EDWARD[7] SWIFT DUNSTER, (*Samuel,*[6] *Jason,*[5] *Jason,*[4] *Henry,*[3] *Jonathan,*[2] *Henry,*[1]) the third child of Samuel and Susan (Dow) Dunster, was born at the village of Springvale, Sanford, Me., Sept. 2, 1834. He was named after Dr. Edward Swift, an eminent physician of

32

Easton, Penn., who was an intimate and respected friend of his father. On the removal of his father's family to Providence, R. I., he was educated at the public schools there, was admitted to the High School at twelve years of age, and was there prepared for College. He entered Harvard University (the collegiate course) in September, 1852, being admitted without conditions. He graduated with high honors in 1856; the subject of the "part" assigned to him in the Commencement exercises being "The first President of Harvard College." A severe illness—typhoid fever—prevented him from appearing at Commencement. On his recovery, in the fall of 1856, he went to Newburgh, N. Y., and became private tutor to a son of Henry W. Sargent, Esq., who lived in Fishkill, just across the Hudson River. At the same time he began the study of medicine with Dr. M. Stephenson, of Newburgh. Young Sargent was admitted to Harvard College in July, 1858. He then went to New York and became a student in medicine with the celebrated Prof. E. R. Peaslee, M. D., with whom, as pupil and assistant, he remained associated for some years, and the intimacy thus begun has continued in other relations ever since. Attended medical lectures at Dartmouth College in the summer of 1858, and in the succeeding winter at the "New York College of Medicine and Surgery," where he was graduated M. D. in March, 1859, having received the highest prize awarded by the Faculty for general proficiency in his studies. Entered St. Luke's Hospital as an interne on the day after his graduation, and remained there until August following, when he resigned to accept the situation of Demonstrator of Anatomy in Dartmouth College, Dr. Peaslee being then the Professor in that department. Lectures concluded, he returned to New York and established himself there as a physician.

When the war broke out in 1861, he tendered his services to the State authorities, and for a few days acted as Surgeon of the "Mozart" regiment of volunteers. This position he threw up to enter the Regular Army, into which he was admitted in June, 1861, after a severe competitive examination, standing second in a class of

32

twenty-eight. His commission as Assistant Surgeon is
dated Aug. 5, 1861. He was ordered to report for duty
with Gen. McClellan, who was then in the field in
Western Virginia, operating against Gen. Lee. He
reached the advancing army on Rich Mountain the day
after the engagement there. This was the first fight of
any magnitude in the rebellion; and here were his first
experiences of the horrors of war; though compared with
the terrible scenes of a few weeks and years later it was
the merest child's play. There were about 30 dead and
150 wounded, most of whom were still lying on the field.
At Beverly, five miles beyond, at the base of the mountain, he established hospitals for the care of the wounded.
This village of thirty or forty houses, which he entered
just at dusk that evening, was absolutely deserted—the
inhabitants having been told that they would all be mur-
dered if the Union Army came into the place.

These scenes were not entirely without the humorous
element. In a letter to a friend he says: "We had a little
war for our own amusement last Friday night. The pick-
ets somehow got frightened, and reported seeing large
bodies of men coming down from the mountains. They
then began to shoot and run. It was really dangerous
to be outside of the house. I slept at the hospital that
night, as the men were badly scared and would not be
assured that I was not going to leave the town." By the
transfer of the Senior Surgeon, Dr. Wirtz, U. S. A., a
few weeks later, the supervision of all the hospitals here
devolved on him.

In the Cincinnati Commercial we find this reference
to these hospitals, where both the Southern and the
Union sick and wounded were cared for alike, though
in separate buildings: "Capt. Zeke Tatem, of Co. D,
is here sick with typhoid fever. He is at the residence
of a Mrs. Arnold*, a lady who has won the confidence,

---

*Mrs. Arnold was a sister of the celebrated "Stonewall" Jack-
son. Dr. D. made his headquarters at her house during the most
of his stay in Beverly. He often spoke in terms of admiration of
her many noble virtues. She made no distinction in caring for
the sick and wounded on either side, but her life was a mission
of mercy to all. Mrs. A. presented to Dr. D. a dirk knife forged
from an old file. The blade is ten inches long, and the scabbard

32

admiration and esteem of the troops for unremitting attention to the sick, night and day. The boys call her the Florence Nightingale of Western Virginia.—— —— Dr. Dunster, U. S. A., an efficient and attentive surgeon, is in charge of five hospitals here." Dr. D. remained three months in Beverly, and was then assigned to the duty of constructing hospitals at Grafton and Parkersburgh, and subsequently he was appointed by Gen. Rosecrans, then commanding the Department, Medical Inspector for the Southern half of the department. His associate in the other half was Dr. William A. Hammond, who afterward became Surgeon-General of the army. In the following summer, 1862, he was ordered East, and again, much to his satisfaction, assigned to duty with his old commander, Gen. McClellan, who was now operating on the "Peninsula" in Eastern Virginia. He was made Medical Director of the hospitals transports, and in this capacity had charge of shipping the sick and wounded of the army. His headquarters were located first at the "White House," on the Pamunkey River, and when this place was abandoned, at Harrison's Landing,* on the James River. In the eight days prior to the evacuation of the last place, he shipped nearly 13,000 sick and wounded soldiers on the transports under his command. Some of these were sent to the hospitals North; others, to the vicinity of Fortress Monroe. Gen. McClellan being at this juncture

---

is of leather fastened with lead rivets. It was left at Mrs. A.'s house by the Rev. Dr. Atkinson, President of the Hampden Sydney College, who commanded a company—mostly enlisted from his own students—in a Virginia Confederate regiment, which was in the fight of Rich Mountain. This weapon is preserved as a memento of the *earnestness* with which even *good* men can engage in deadly conflict.

* He related to a friend afterwards: "When we were going up the James, I was charmed by the view of a beautiful plantation adorned with shrubbery and gardens. When driven from the 'White House' we stopped at the spot I had so much admired when going up. Not a green thing was visible. Contending armies had blotted out every vestige of vegetation."

Through all these times of strife he went unarmed. The sick and wounded gave him unbounded confidence, and named him

*28

32

relieved of the command of the army, Dr. D. found himself, as it were, without an occupation, but the respite was short, for in a few days he was ordered to Philadelphia to assume charge of the Turner's Lane Hospital, and at the same time to act as member of the board for the examination of candidates for the Medical Department of the army. His next army service was in Washington, as an assistant to the Surgeon-General, Dr. Hammond, his old associate in Western Virginia. From thence he was transferred to the U. S. Military Academy at West Point, where he remained until his resignation from the army, Feb. 1, 1866. He was brevetted Captain and Major, U. S. A., and before his resignation, had passed his examination for promotion to the grade of full Surgeon.

On resigning from the army he went to New York and again established himself in the practice of medicine. In July of that year he became editor of the New York Medical Journal, and held this position for five years. At about the same time he was appointed one of the attending physicians to the "Out Door Department" of Bellevue Hospital, in the class of diseases of children. In 1868 he was appointed Professor of Obstetrics and the Diseases of Women and Children in the medical department of the University of Vermont, at Burlington. He gave the lectures here but two years, as his many and exacting duties in New York would not allow him to be absent for the time required. The authorities of the College very generously held the place open for him, and declined his resignation until 1871, having given him the privilege of appointing a substitute in the work. In 1869 he was appointed to the same chair in the

---

the "Little Doctor." One of the wounded whittled from a single pine stick a pair of pliers and pincers, having all the movements and parts in one ornamental combination, which he gave to his surgeon. It was all he had to give. It is preserved as a specimen of West Virginia whittling. A Southern officer, who was taken prisoner at Rich Mountain, gave the Doctor a fine set of surgical instruments, in gratitude for his care and kindness to the Confederate wounded. The ladies of Philadelphia appreciated his attention to the sick at Turner's Lane, and presented him with a silver headed cane, with his monogram beautifully intertwined.

32

flourishing Medical College of Brooklyn, known as the "Long Island College Hospital." He filled this chair for six years, resigning in 1874. In July, 1869, he assumed the charge—as Resident Physician—of the Infants' Hospital on Randall's Island, New York city, and also became Physician in Chief of the other hospitals and institutions on the Island, generally known as the "Nursery." In these institutions there were constantly from 800 to 1000 children, affording an unusually large field for the observation and study of the diseases of children. The mortality in the Infants' Department had been a "scandal and a reproach to the profession," but by the adoption simply of improved hygienic surroundings and securing better nursing and attendance, Dr. D. had the satisfaction of reducing this mortality to a point almost equal to the mortality at large, i. e., of children not living in crowded institutions. For this, frequent acknowledgments were made in the reports of the "Commissioners of Charities and Corrections," who were the officials in charge of all the public institutions.

In 1871 Dr. D. went to Dartmouth College and gave the course of lectures on Obstetrics for his former preceptor, Prof. Peaslee, who now generously divided his chair, retaining the portion devoted to Diseases of Women and assigning to Dr. D. the teaching of Obstetrics. This chair he still holds, and yearly makes a summer visit to New Hampshire for the purpose of delivering his lectures. In 1873 the Professorship of Obstetrics and Diseases of Women and Children in the University of Michigan was tendered to him, and after due deliberation was accepted. This involved the resignation of his positions in the institutions on Randall's Island. He removed to Ann Arbor, Michigan, in October of that year, and now resides there, and is engaged both in teaching and in the practice of his profession. He has contributed many papers to various Medical Journals, a few of which have been published in separate form. They are: "The Relations of the Medical Profession to Modern Education;" "The Logic of Medicine;" "The History of Anæsthesia;" "Notes on Double Monsters;" "The History of Spontaneous Generation." Is a mem-

32

ber of various learned societies, mostly medical. Among them are: The New York Academy of Medicine; The New York Historical Society; The American Geographical and Statistical Association; The Michigan State Medical Society, &c., &c.

He married Nov. 4, 1863, Rebecca Morgan Sprole, born at Philadelphia, Pa., Nov. 6, 1835, daughter of the Rev. Dr. Sprole, of Newburgh, N. Y., formerly Chaplain and Professor of Ethics in the U. S. Military Academy, West Point. They have had four children:

(i) CLARA⁸ BERTRAM DUNSTER, born at West Point, N. Y., Dec. 19, 1865.

(ii) WILLIAM⁸ SPROLE DUNSTER, born in New York city, Nov. 20, 1867, died at Newburgh, N. Y., July 13, 1868, buried there.

(iii) BESSIE⁸ MORGAN DUNSTER, born in New York city, (Randall's Island,) July 25, 1870.

(iv) ANNIE⁸ ELIZA DUNSTER, born in New York city, (Randall's Island,) Sept. 1, 1873, named for her aunt who died in Chicago two weeks after her birth.

4. CALEB⁷ EMERY DUNSTER, the fourth child of Samuel and Susan (Dow) Dunster, was born at the village of Springvale, Sanford, Me., July 27, 1836. He died there Oct. 7, same year, and was buried at the cemetery at Sanford Corner. A suitable stone marks his grave.

5. ELIZA⁷ ANNIE DUNSTER, (*Samuel,*⁶ *Jason,*⁵ *Jason,*⁴ *Henry,*³ *Jona.,*² *Henry,*¹) the youngest child of Samuel and Susan (Dow) Dunster, was born at Durham, N. H., Oct. 24, 1838. Upon the removal of her father's family to Providence, she became a member of the public schools, and passed through all the grades up to the High School, to which she was promoted. Her father, just at this time, removed to Dover, N. H., where she attended Franklin Academy for a short time, and then went to Bradford (Mass.) Academy, from which she graduated, after a full term of four years, with the highest honors, although the youngest in the class of 1856. She was remarkably fond of Latin and Geometry. She

32

could demonstrate from memory every theorem in the
first four books of Euclid and draw the diagram.

At her graduation she wrote the parting hymn, which
was equivalent in that institution to the valedictory of a
college course. After graduation she attended Mrs. Willard's School at Troy, N. Y. Closing her term there she
went to St. Charles, Illinois, as a teacher. While there
she obtained by her own address a situation in the Amite
Female Seminary, at Liberty, Mississippi, as Instructor
in English Literature, and other branches. The troubles of the times broke up that seminary, and she returned and was soon after appointed a teacher in the
public schools at Chicago. In topical subjects, which
are a prominent exercise there, she raised her school to a
higher standard than any other one in the city. She
taught there until her marriage.

Very early in childhood she manifested an aptitude
for rhyme, which she improved or neglected as impulse
prompted. At Bradford she wrote several pieces for the
"Olive Branch." At Chicago she wrote for two years
the New Year's Address for the "Chicago Tribune,"
the leading Republican paper of the West, in one of
which she reviewed the political situation with the tact
of an old campaign leader. At New Year's, 1867, the
submarine cable was a success, and the Lake Tunnel
just completed. These she thus notices:

What has last year left as dowry to the hand-maids, Science, Art?
Ah! how rife with grand achievements is the Scientific part!
Buried in the ocean's bosom, down below the mighty deep,
'Mid the wrecks of myriad vessels, where their human cargoes sleep,
Darts the lightning, chained and tempered, guided by a single thread,
And from Europe to our *own* land, instant weal or woe is read.
Wondrous triumph of a genius! Whispered words are eager caught.
Thro' abyss of depth unfathomed, news and rumors now are brought.
Europe bids the States " Good morning ;" Liverpool doth New York greet!
Fast Chicago joins the refrain, Commerce asks the price of wheat ;
So the " Cable " prates and gossips, spinning out the watery miles,
And the " Mermaids " laugh and listen, laving it with dripping smiles.
Fact! it seems there's nothing left now ; Science may her hands but fold,
Wonder if the future ages can excel our doings bold!
At some distant " Happy New Year " will Orion's glittering belt
Gossiped be in *star-hung* Cables, and his salutations felt?
Shall the growling " Ursa-Major " send dispatches to the earth,
And the " Pleiads " hunt their Sister, telegraphing of her worth?

Nor forget we great Chicago, mighty umpire of the West,
Wreathe for her distinguished honor, for she leadeth all the rest.
Queen she is of all the cities ; Commerce, Art, Religion, too,

32

Here have built their proudest temples; mammoth structures rise to view
As by magic. and, completed. always are the largest, best,
Spite of foreign grunts and envies, spite of Eastern sneers and jest.
Who but she has wrought a "Tunnel" poising lakes upon its back?
Never resting till she brought us crystal waters o'er its track?
Now Farewell! ye slimy waters! fluid of most dubious look!
Henceforth shall our drink be limpid, lucid as the babbling brook.
Here "adieux" we make in parting, to our piscatory friends;
Showers of blessings, not of fishes, haply now the "Tunnel" sends.

She wrote also a reminiscence for the reunion of her class at her old Bradford teacher's, Miss Gilman, in Boston, and many productions for literary societies in Chicago, of which she was a member. Always wrote from the impulse of the moment, and never thought of preserving copies of them.

She was married at Beloit, Wisconsin, by Rev. Dr. H. N. Brinsmade, July 5, 1862, to William Taylor Baker, born at Winfield, Herkermer Co., N. Y., Sept. 11, 1841, son of William and Matilda (Peabody) (Williams) Baker. He is an extensive dealer in grain and general commission.

"Mrs. Eliza Annie Baker was confirmed in Christ's Church [Protestant Episcopal], April 14, 1865, by Rt. Rev. Henry J. Whitehouse, Bishop of the Diocese of Illinois, and has remained a communicant, in full standing, in the same parish to the date of her decease.

CHAS. EDW'D CHENEY, Rector."

The great Chicago fire commenced Oct. 8, 1871, at 10 o'clock P. M. This was subdued, but another broke out before morning on the 9th, which, in twenty-four hours, destroyed almost the whole city.

Mrs. Baker, with two of her children, had returned from her annual visit to New England the day before, leaving her two little boys at her father's to come on with her sister. They returned to Attleboro and spent the winter, although their house at Chicago was not burned. Feb. 26, 1872, their youngest child was born, whom she invited its grandfather to name. He called him HENRY DUNSTER BAKER, and he was baptized by that name, July 7, 1872, at Christ's Church, Chicago, by Charles Edward Cheney.*

* Charles Edward Cheney, born at Canandaigua, N. Y., Feb. 12, 1836, educated at Hobert College, Geneva, N. Y., went to Chicago, in 1860, and commenced preaching in a small edifice in

32

The summer of 1873 was, as usual, spent at the East. During that summer she called on nearly all the associates of her early days, and returned to Chicago about the first of September. A few days after she entered a public carriage for a ride. The driver had left the horses: they became frightened, and ran down Wabash Avenue. She attempted to get out, but was thrown against the curbstone, and taken up insensible. Immediate surgical attention was given. Consciousness returned, and she was thought to be not dangerously injured. After a few days she became delirious, and died Sept. 17, 1873. Her last intelligent request was that her nurse, who used to sing to her daily, should sing, from the German, "When the swallows homeward fly." Her funeral was appointed for the next Saturday, but was postponed to the next day to await the arrival of her friends from the East.

Mr. Cheney, her pastor, made an affectionate address, and nearly his whole congregation attended her funeral at the family residence. The services were closed by singing, "Jesus, lover of my soul" to the tune she had asked her nurse to sing to her.

23d street. His zeal in the service of Christ, and his eminent ability, soon gathered a larger congregation than could be accommodated there. In 1865 a new and larger church was built in Michigan Avenue by his society.

Conscientiously believing that "regeneration" was a Divine gift, not bestowed by formality, he determined, in the fall of 1868, to omit that word from the baptismal service. For this he was soon called to account. He averred that the omission was not sufficient to separate him from his chosen people. A vindictive trial was had and he was adjudged to be unworthy of Christian communion, and was in set form excommunicated "from the church of God." An effort was then made to wrest the church property from the society who had built it, and thereby, as was said of a similar case of conscience in Massachusetts, "punish the heretic and drive him out of the colony." By a sagacious movement of Mr. C.'s friends, made in exact accordance with law and the rules of business, the property was saved to the society, and Christ's Church at Chicago became the united centre of the movement which culminated in the organization of the "Reformed Protestant Episcopal Church," which affiliates cheerfully with all Evangelical denominations; and Mr. Cheney is now the Rt. Rev. Presiding Bishop of that Communion.

32

She was buried at Graceland, a beautiful cemetery about ten miles down the Lake, in a spot selected by her and her husband for "Little Willie." Mr. Cheney read the burial service at her grave.

To a request for a sketch of his remarks, Mr. Cheney replied: "You speak of gratitude for what I said at your daughter's funeral. I assure you it was the sincere utterance of my heart. Mrs. Baker was exceedingly dear to Mrs. Cheney and myself. Our acqaintance began when she was in deep affliction [the death of Willie, her first born], and the ties thus formed grew stronger every year. She was universally beloved by all our church as well as by a large circle of friends outside its limits. Her fondness for literary pursuits and literary society rendered her the centre of attraction for a great many who had similar tastes, while her devotion to her family and children was her chief charm to those who knew her best.

"I deeply regret that I am unable to funish the address which I made at her funeral. It was wholly extemporaneous, and I have no sufficient outline preserved to be a guide in attempting to write it out.

"Besides what I have already alluded to, viz., her literary culture and her love for her children, the most marked characteristics of Mrs. Baker's life here were her cheerfulness under all circumstances, and her unselfish, gentle, Christian spirit. These made her beloved by rich and poor alike; and her memory is cherished by many who will never forget her words and deeds of kindness."

They had six children:

(i) WILLIAM[8] DUNSTER BAKER, born at Attleboro, Mass., Sept. 12, 1863, died at Chicago. Inscription on marble monument: "Willie Dunster, son of William T. and Eliza Annie Baker, died July 27, 1864, aged 10 months, 15 days."

(ii) CHARLES[8] HINCKLY BAKER, named after his father's partner, born at Chicago, Nov. 30, 1864, baptized May 21, 1865.

(iii) HOWARD[8] WINFIELD BAKER, named after his father's native town, born at Chicago, March 19, 1866, baptized Nov. 4, 1866.

(iv) ANNIE[8] MERRIAM BAKER, familiarly called by her mother "Kitty," born at Chicago, March 29, 1868, baptized June 21, 1868. She had the scarlatina when a child, which left her deaf. She has partially regained her hearing, and speaks considerably. She is under tuition to learn to enunciate.

(v) BERTHA[8] COZETTE BAKER, born at Chicago, Nov. 14, 1869, baptized June 12, 1870.

(vi) HENRY[8] DUNSTER BAKER, born at Attleboro, Feb. 26, 1872, baptized at Chicago, July 7, 1872.

All except Willie baptized at Christ's Church, by Rev. Mr. Cheney.

Charles Hinckly Baker and Howard W Baker both graduated (full course) Civil Engineering June 17 1886 with distinguished honors at Cornell University Ithica N.Y. They are both now (1887) at Seattle Washington Territory — on the Seattle Lake shore & Eastern Rail Road Charles — Chief constructor of wharves bridges & terminal facilities and Howard Superintendent of the trestle bridge 3½ miles long. This Salary being $1800.00 ... a year

And now, my kindred, for your sake, mainly, and to preserve our names, have these accumulated scraps been put together. It is a *Family Story*, and therefore not open to professional criticism. To claim that it is without error would be preposterous. We have done what we could; and when " Old Mortality " shall pause before our slumbering dust, scattered broadcast from the icy North to the Golden Gate,—on the pathless wild,—beneath the lovely palm,—or in the vasty deep,—marked, perchance, by a crumbling headstone,—may he rechisel our names and there inscribe:—and in the *unerring* record of the SUPREME ARCHITECT of the universe, whose NAME the ancient Hebrews never pronounced but in a most reverential posture and in a low breath, may we find *our names*, and against them written that significant word—placed by our Ancestor with his own hand on the first SEAL OF HARVARD COLLEGE—

[N O T E.]

In the gale on Friday morning, March 9th, at half-past nine o'clock, one of the large elms [noticed on page 97] standing in front of the house of Samuel Sewell, Esq., was broken and blown down by the high wind. Another elm, nearer to the house, lost two large limbs. It is now impossible to ascertain the exact age of these trees, but they were placed in their present position before 1774, and hence must have been growing there on the memorable morning of the battle of Lexington, April 19th, 1775. Perhaps John Hancock, or Samuel Adams, or the fair Dorothy Quincy, observed the young elms budding in the early spring, or remarked upon their beauty when they found a refuge at the house of Madam Jones, on the eventful morning of the battle. And years after they had slept in their graves, and not one witness of the battle of Lexington survived, these trees, beautiful in their old age, looked upon the citizens of the town, as they rode in procession to celebrate the anniversary at Lexington, in 1875. These trees were planted and tended by a negro named Cuff, a faithful servant of Madam Jones, the widow of Rev. Thomas Jones, the second minister of Woburn Precinct, now Burlington. His grave may yet be found in the ancient burial ground at Burlington, but the trees he planted for the adornment of the home of his mistress and her descendants, have been for years a more fitting memorial of his faithful service than the grey slate stone fast sinking into the earth. These trees were both struck by lightning about fifty-two years ago, and in the same month of last year, one of them was again visited in like manner. The marks of the first stroke were plainly to be seen, on the trunks of both trees. In both instances, being much higher than the house, they probably saved it from much damage, and possibly from destruction. These trees have always been highly prized by the inhabitants and owners of the house they have sheltered, and they will long be remembered and regretted, by the occupants of the dwelling, which they have ornamented and protected for more than a hundred years. (*Woburn Journal, March* 24, 1877.)

We would gladly receive any other facts of family interest, especially Records, Additional History, correction of errors, etc. They will be carefully preserved for future reference,—

"For *thee*, who, mindful of th' unhonor'd dead,
    Dost in these lines their artless tale relate;
If chance, by lonely contemplation led,
    Some kindred spirit shall enquire thy fate—"

INDEX.